RESILIENCE
DYNAMISM
TRUST

50 Landmark Statements by MAS Leaders

Published by
Monetary Authority of Singapore
10 Shenton Way, MAS Building, Singapore 079117
and
World Scientific Publishing Co. Pte. Ltd.
5 Toh Tuck Link, Singapore 596224

USA office: 27 Warren Street, Suite 401-402, Hackensack, NJ 07601
UK office: 57 Shelton Street, Covent Garden, London WC2H 9HE

British Library Cataloguing-in-Publication Data
A catalogue record for this book is available from the British Library.

About MAS' 50th Anniversary Logo and Title Page Design

MAS' 50th Anniversary logo, as shown on the cover, was designed by Star Chen, the winner of an in-house competition. The theme *Serving our Nation, Securing our Future* looks back on MAS' service to our nation for the last 50 years and looks forward to our future with MAS' commitment to ensuring Singapore's economic security. The five overlapping curves in the logo indicate the five decades of MAS' service, ending off at the "5" and is left open to represent a continuing chapter of progress and possibilities heading into the future.

The design on the book's title page showing the iconic MAS building rising above the skyline of the Singapore financial district was adapted from another staff entry for the competition by Amanda Goh, Nada Jumabhoy and Serene Chew.

Editors' Note

Some editing of the original statements or speeches were made for prior errors, consistency and post-delivery updates.

Reproduction of Speeches and Photos

Parliamentary speeches starting on pages 4, 70, 114, 183, and 374 were used with the permission of the Parliament of Singapore.

Some photos on page xi have been reproduced with permission from Ministry of Information and the Arts Collection, courtesy of National Archives of Singapore, as well as Public Utilities Board Collection, courtesy of National Archives of Singapore. The photos have been cropped and converted to black and white from their original copy.

RESILIENCE, DYNAMISM, TRUST:
50 Landmark Statements by MAS Leaders

ISBN 978-981-124-524-4 (hardcover)
ISBN 978-981-125-012-5 (ebook for institutions)
ISBN 978-981-125-013-2 (ebook for individuals)

For any available supplementary material, please visit
https://www.worldscientific.com/worldscibooks/10.1142/12501#t=suppl

Editorial Team

MAS: Tai Boon Leong, Dawn Chew, Bridgitte Lee, Francis Quek,
Luz Foo, Sandy Ho, Liew Yin Sze, Susan Lim, Mok Pei Hong, Abigail Ng, Evelyn Sit,
Lim Tuang Lee (Adviser), Jerome Lee
WSPC: Chua Hong Koon, Nicole Ong, Lai Ann, Jimmy Low, Yolande Koh

Printed in Singapore

RESILIENCE DYNAMISM TRUST

50 Landmark Statements by MAS Leaders

World Scientific

MAS 50
Serving our Nation
Securing our Future
1971 - 2021

MAS
Monetary Authority of Singapore

Foreword

A Perennial Goal: Coupling Prudence with Innovation

The Monetary Authority of Singapore (MAS) is not often in the public eye. It has however played a critical role in Singapore's economic development, keeping inflation low to support sustained economic growth, preserving financial stability and trust, advancing the development of a global financial centre, and judiciously managing a significant component of Singapore's reserves.

This 50th anniversary compilation provides convenient access to the thinking behind MAS' policies and strategies as they have evolved, through 50 landmark statements by its leaders.

The span of MAS' roles has grown over the years, and has made it quite distinct among its international peers. It began with narrow functions: indeed its name as a monetary authority rather than a central bank had its origins in the days of the currency board system, when currency issuance was managed outside of MAS. It has long since become a full-fledged central bank, conducting monetary policy, managing Singapore's official foreign reserves, and ensuring overall financial stability and a reliable payment system.

However, MAS is also one of few central banks that are an integrated financial regulator. It oversees the full span of banking, insurance and capital market activities, fostering the soundness of individual financial institutions and safeguarding the interests of investors and consumers of financial products. Additionally, MAS has taken on the mandate of promoting a vibrant financial hub with a skilled workforce, connected to global and regional markets.

An underlying theme in this compilation is a strategic vision that combines prudence with an appetite for innovation. MAS has a unique dual reputation. It is viewed as stricter than most prudential supervisors, with Singapore's record of financial stability being testimony to this. But it is also, among supervisors, one of the most facilitative of business development and proactive in promoting technological innovation and green finance.

These two bearings at the heart of MAS' strategies have not been incompatible. They will be inseparable in a future where financial stability will itself depend on a progressive response to the challenges of disruptive business models and the climate crisis.

MAS has been willing to depart from convention in crafting policies to fit Singapore's own circumstances. In the early 1980s, MAS chose to use the exchange rate as its instrument of monetary policy, and effectively gave up control of domestic interest rates and money supply. In the midst of the Asian financial crisis, MAS embarked on a bold liberalisation of Singapore's financial sector rather than hunker down.

Unusual too for a central bank, MAS has worked in close coordination with government ministries to implement macroprudential measures, aimed at preserving financial stability, promoting a sustainable property market, and safeguarding financial prudence of households. Be it in the areas of macroprudential stability, jobs and skills, digital technologies, sustainability, or financial literacy, MAS has been able to work collaboratively with other public agencies without loss of autonomy where it counts as a central bank or financial supervisor.

I am privileged to have been closely engaged with MAS over the last four decades, working alongside many dedicated and highly capable officers and my colleagues on its Board. I pay tribute to all those who led and served in MAS over the last 50 years, for their deep professionalism, unstinting drive for excellence, and commitment to public service.

Tharman Shanmugaratnam
Chairman, Monetary Authority of Singapore

Contents

MAS Leaders

Chairmen

Hon Sui Sen
Jan 1971 – Jul 1980

Goh Keng Swee
Aug 1980 – Jan 1985

Richard Hu
Jan 1985 – Dec 1997

Lee Hsien Loong
Jan 1998 – Aug 2004

Goh Chok Tong
Aug 2004 – May 2011

Tharman Shanmugaratnam
May 2011 – Present

Managing Directors

Michael Wong Pakshong
Dec 1970 – Feb 1981

Lim Kim San
Mar 1981 – Sep 1982

Yong Pung How
Oct 1982 – Jun 1983

Richard Hu
Jul 1983 – Dec 1984

Goh Keng Swee
Jan 1985 – Apr 1985

J. Y. Pillay
Apr 1985 – Oct 1989

Lee Ek Tieng
Nov 1989 – Dec 1997

Koh Yong Guan
Jan 1998 – Mar 2001

Tharman Shanmugaratnam
Apr 2001 – Oct 2001

Koh Yong Guan
Oct 2001 – May 2005

Heng Swee Keat
Jun 2005 – Apr 2011

Ravi Menon
Apr 2011 – Present

List of Abbreviations

ABS	The Association of Banks in Singapore
ACU	Asian Currency Unit
ADB	Asian Development Bank
ADM	Asian Dollar Market
AML/CFT	Anti-Money Laundering and Countering the Financing of Terrorism
ASEAN	Association of Southeast Asian Nations
ASEAN+3	ASEAN plus Japan, China and Korea
AUM	Assets Under Management
BCCI	Bank of Credit and Commerce International
BCCS	Board of Commissioners of Currency, Singapore
BIS	Bank for International Settlements
CFTC	Commodity Futures Trading Commission
CPF	Central Provident Fund
D-SIB	Domestic Systemically Important Bank
DPM	Deputy Prime Minister
EC	European Commission
EDB	Economic Development Board
EFTPOS	Electronic Funds Transfer at Point of Sale
ESG	Environmental, Social and Governance
ESM	Emeritus Senior Minister
EU	European Union
FAA	Financial Advisers Act
FAST	Fast and Secure Transfers
FDI	Foreign Direct Investment
FHC	Financial Holding Company
FTA	Free Trade Agreement
FX	Foreign Exchange
G-SIB	Global Systemically Important Bank
G20	Group of Twenty
G3	Group of Three
G7	Group of Seven

GDP	Gross Domestic Product
GIC	Government of Singapore Investment Corporation
GNP	Gross National Product
GST	Goods and Services Tax
IBF	Institute of Banking and Finance
IEA	International Energy Agency
IMAS	Investment Management Association of Singapore
IMF	International Monetary Fund
IRAS	Inland Revenue Authority of Singapore
MAS	Monetary Authority of Singapore
MNC	Multinational Corporation
MOF	Ministry of Finance
NEER	Nominal Effective Exchange Rate
NIC	Newly Industrialised Country
OECD	Organisation for Economic Co-operation and Development
OFR	Official Foreign Reserves
OTC	Over-the-counter
P2P	Peer-to-peer
POSBank	Post Office Savings Bank
QFB	Qualifying Full Bank
REER	Real Effective Exchange Rate
SES	Stock Exchange of Singapore
SFA	Securities and Futures Act
SFEMC	Singapore Foreign Exchange Market Committee
SFF	Singapore FinTech Festival
SGQR	Singapore Quick Response Code
SGS	Singapore Government Securities
SGX	Singapore Exchange
SIBOR	Singapore Interbank Offered Rate
SIMEX	Singapore International Monetary Exchange
SOR	Swap Offer Rate
UPOS	Unified Point of Sale

EVOLUTION OF A CENTRAL BANK

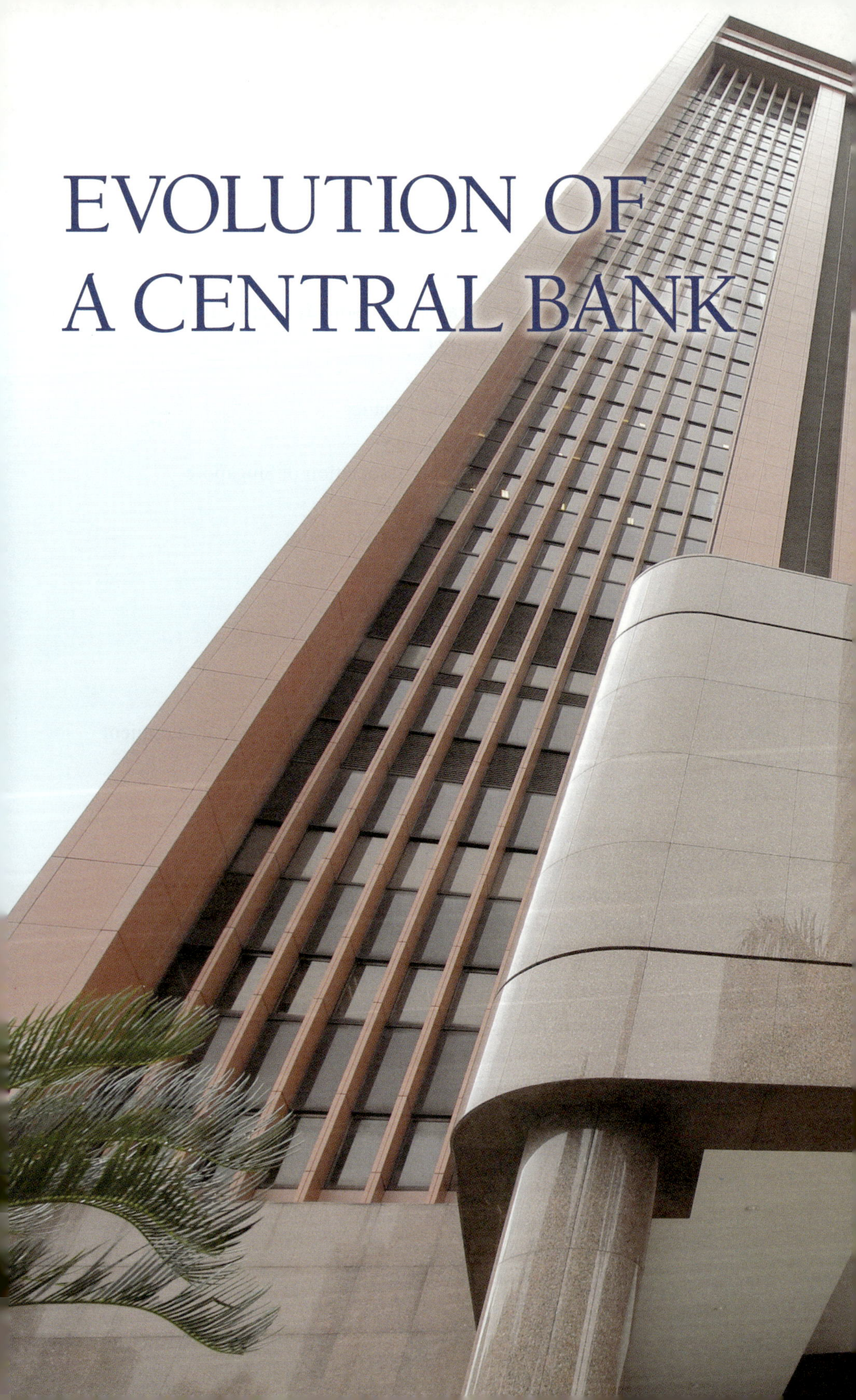

MAS
Monetary Authority
of Singapore

Evolution of a Central Bank

This section presents statements by all six of MAS' Chairmen over the last 50 years, tracing the genesis of MAS as Singapore's central bank and integrated financial regulator, and describing how it has fulfilled its mission of promoting sustained non-inflationary economic growth, and a sound and progressive financial centre.

In September 1970, Minister for Finance Mr Hon Sui Sen tabled in Parliament the Monetary Authority of Singapore Bill to consolidate under MAS the monetary and financial regulatory functions that were at the time spread across different agencies within the Singapore government. Mr Hon explained that "rationalising the structure and organisation of the system, the bringing together, under one single authority, of all these different organisations will enable a coherent and uniform policy to be developed for all monetary matters".

MAS was established in 1971 as Singapore's *de facto* central bank, with Mr Hon as its first Chairman (1971–1980).

Between 1971 and 2002, MAS performed all the functions of a central bank except the issuance of notes and coins, which was under the purview of the Board of Commissioners of Currency Singapore (BCCS). Dr Goh Keng Swee, who was the second MAS Chairman (1980–1985), explained in an article in 1992 that Singapore continued with the currency board system after independence to signal its commitment to maintaining a strong and convertible Singapore dollar and that this was "the best protection against inflation". By 2001, confidence in the Singapore dollar had become sufficiently entrenched that the need to separate monetary policy from the function of issuing money was no longer relevant. In 2002, MAS absorbed BCCS to become a full-fledged central bank.

Taking stock at MAS' landmark anniversaries, Singapore's leaders paid tribute to MAS for carrying out its varied functions with distinction and noted how MAS had done well also because of the conducive Singapore system within which it operated.

Speaking at MAS' 25th anniversary in 1996, Prime Minister Mr Goh Chok Tong, who later became the fifth MAS Chairman (2004–2011), observed that the same principles that guided MAS as a central bank and financial regulator also underpinned policymaking in Singapore — namely, prudence, stability and confidence.

Dr Richard Hu, Minister for Finance and the third MAS Chairman (1985–1997), highlighted in a 1997 speech that monetary policy did not operate in a vacuum and that a healthy fiscal position enabled MAS to focus on its mission of price stability.

Speaking at MAS' 30th Anniversary Conference in 2001, Mr Lee Hsien Loong, Deputy Prime Minister and the fourth MAS Chairman (1998–2004), observed how MAS, having built a reputation for credibility and prudence, was also becoming more dynamic and responsive amid a dynamic financial landscape. At MAS' 40th anniversary in 2011, this time as Prime Minister, Mr Lee noted that MAS had contributed significantly to Singapore's development and in turn benefitted from Singapore's strong political leadership, sound policy fundamentals, and openness to the world.

Mr Tharman Shanmugaratnam, Deputy Prime Minister and the sixth MAS Chairman (2011 to-date), speaking at the opening of the MAS Gallery to commemorate MAS' 45th anniversary in 2016, described how generations of MAS staff had helped to make MAS an organisation of excellence and one of the best-regarded central banks and financial regulators in the world.

Establishing the Monetary Authority of Singapore

Mr Hon Sui Sen
Minister for Finance
Second Reading Speech in Parliament
Monetary Authority of Singapore Bill
2 September 1970

In Singapore, as a result of historical factors, the various monetary functions normally associated with a Central Bank are currently being performed by a number of Government departments and agencies. For instance, the responsibility for the currency issue lies with the Currency Board, which is a statutory authority. Then, the Commissioner of Banking and the Commissioner of Finance Companies is responsible for the regulation and supervision of banks and finance companies, whilst the Exchange Control Department is responsible for all matters concerning foreign exchange. Finally, the Department of Overseas Investment in my Economic Development Division is responsible for the management of the Government's external assets, while the Accountant-General is responsible for the sale of Treasury Bills to banks and other financial institutions, the raising of domestic loans and the management of the clearing house system.

Quite clearly, the task of co-ordinating and directing the policy of these diverse organisations makes for a full-time occupation and while the present system of ad hoc control by committee has worked reasonably well up to now, the increasing complexity of modern banking and monetary management makes it necessary to streamline the system. Apart from rationalising the structure and organisation of the system, the bringing together, under one single authority, of all these different organisations will enable a coherent and uniform policy to be developed for all monetary matters. In addition, it is hoped that with the passage of time will come the development of greater professional expertise. This is vital for the efficient functioning of a modern monetary system.

It is therefore proposed in the Bill now before the House that there should be established a Monetary Authority of Singapore, comprising the departments I have mentioned with the single exception of the Currency Board. It is considered, for the time being, that the currency-issuing functions of the Board should remain with it and that the Board should continue as an independent and separate statutory authority. The automatic mechanism of the Currency Board with its 100% external assets backing has been and will be of great psychological importance in maintaining confidence in the Singapore Dollar. Thus the operations and the assets backing the Currency issue will be unaffected and will continue to be clearly identified. The Monetary Authority will therefore for the time being have no note-issuing functions.

I would now like to discuss in some detail the provisions of the Bill for the establishment of the Monetary Authority of Singapore. Part II of the Bill provides for the establishment, capitalisation and administration of the Authority. Clause 3 sets up the Authority as a body corporate. The authorised capital of the Authority will be $30 million, while the paid-up capital will be such amounts as may be approved by the Government from time to time. This is laid down in clause 5. Clause 8 provides for a Board of seven directors comprising the Minister for Finance, who will be the Chairman, the Permanent Secretary (Economic Development) of the Ministry of Finance, who will be the Deputy Chairman, the Accountant-General and four other members who will be appointed by the President. Of the four members appointed, one will be the Managing Director of the Authority. The Managing Director will be entrusted with the day-to-day administration of the Authority and will be answerable to the Board for his acts and decisions.

It is envisaged that the staff of the departments which I have named earlier will be transferred to the Monetary Authority. Clauses 17 to 20 of the Bill provide for this. It is intended that employees from these Government departments will be transferred to the Monetary Authority on terms no less favourable than those that they are enjoying with the Government. The value of their pension rights will be safeguarded in any Authority pension or provident fund schemes. The Authority shall act on the advice of the Public Service Commission in regard to appointments, promotions and termination of employment, dismissal and disciplinary control of its employees.

Clause 21(1) will enable the Authority to take over the powers of the Government under the Banking, Finance Companies and Exchange Control Ordinances. It is further envisaged that it may be necessary in future for the Authority to administer other functions in any specified law relating to banking, investment or other financial matters, and provision for this is made in clause 21(2).

It will be necessary to transfer to the Authority certain assets and liabilities of the Government arising out of statutory requirements in the banking and finance companies legislation. Banks and finance companies are required to maintain, as part of liquidity requirements, a statutory reserve with the Accountant-General based on 3% of their deposit liabilities. This amounts to approximately $120 million. As the Authority will now be responsible for these matters, clause 21(3) provides for the transfer of liabilities together with their matching assets to the Authority.

Clause 22 outlines in detail the powers of the Authority, e.g., it may accept deposits of money; issue demand drafts; purchase and sell gold and foreign currencies; purchase and sell Treasury Bills and Government securities, etc. Clause 23 lays down the general principles under which the Authority's funds may be invested.

The Authority in its functions as banker and financial agent to the Government will mainly be responsible for the managing of the external assets of the Government, undertaking the issue and management of Government loans and of Treasury Bills. In this capacity, the exercise of powers by the Authority will remain subject to the respective legislation pertaining to these subjects. The Treasury Bills issue will be made under the Treasury Bills Ordinance, the issue of registered stock will be made under the Development Loan Act, while the investment of Government's external assets will be subject to the Financial Procedure Act.

Clauses 26 to 40 contain miscellaneous and transitional provisions which provide for such matters as the financial year of the Authority, submission of annual accounts, powers to make regulations, etc.

Sir, I beg to move.

Singapore Parl Debates; Vol 30; Sitting No 5; Col 211–215; 2 September 1970.

Why a Currency Board?

Dr Goh Keng Swee

Extract from: Prudence at the Helm: Board of Commissioners of Currency Singapore 1967–1992

12 June 1992

Singapore finds herself in the unique position of being the only independent state to issue its currency under the Currency Board System (CBS). The CBS is, in every sense of the word, a colonial relic. When the sun never sets on the British Empire, the currencies of British colonies were issued under the CBS. This provided for 100% backing of the note issue in overseas reserves, namely Sterling deposits in London. This allowed the automatic conversion of the local currency into the British pound.

The CBS served both sides reasonably well. Since the 19th century up to about 1929, the pound Sterling was the pre-eminent world currency. Colonies had stable currencies, meaning that the rampant inflation observed today in many ex-colonies did not occur. The British enjoyed substantial inflows of capital from their Empire and this helped to make London the world's leading financial centre. To be fair to the British, it should be said that the independent Dominions — Australia, Canada, South Africa and New Zealand — also kept their overseas reserves in London at that time when they were free to keep them elsewhere.

In the post-War years, rapid decolonisation took place. In every instance the newly independent state established a Central Bank with note-issuing powers. The requirement of 100% backing in overseas assets was abolished. Singapore stood out as the sole exception. We retained the CBS and when the Monetary Authority of Singapore (MAS) was set up in 1970, it performed all the functions of a Central Bank except for note-issuing powers. How and why did we preserve such a strange anachronism in this age of electronic finance? The decision to proceed along these exceptional lines was a collective decision of the Cabinet. Each member reached this decision in his own way and I will explain mine.

When I was studying economics at Raffles College in pre-War days, the Keynesian revolution broke out with the publication of John Keynes' *The General Theory of Employment, Interest and Money*. Today, critics, including Sir John Hicks, are agreed that it was a badly written work and made for difficult reading. I can attest to the latter. As an undergraduate, I read the book from cover to cover no fewer than three times, some chapters even more. What puzzled me most was that Keynes measured variables and aggregates, such as National Income and Money Supply, in terms of what he called "Wage Units". I asked my professor what this meant and why Keynes did this, but could not get a satisfactory reply. Nor did the literature of the day prove more helpful.

Years later, the truth dawned on me. The Keynesian remedy for curing unemployment — the burning issue of the day left behind by the Great Depression years — involved a serious risk of inflation. Of course, Keynes knew this. The remedy he recommended took the form of expansion of bank credit through central bank policies to finance government expenditure. This extra spending will create additional demand for goods and services, thereby reducing unemployment. But if economic variables are measured in wage units, inflation would be factored out as wages will rise in keeping with price increases. If variables such as the consumer price index or interest rates and aggregates like money supply, were measured in wage units, their increases would be reduced to the extent to which wages rise.

There is a further difficulty to contend with. The Keynesian system is a closed one, that is, it takes no account of foreign trade. This is admissible in theory, but in practice, since all modern states engage in foreign trade, a Keynesian stimulus will lead eventually to balance of payments deficits if governments do not exercise restraint in time. A part of the increased incomes people receive will be spent on imports and when exports do not increase in proportion, a trade deficit will occur. In the immediate post-War years, Keynesian economics won widespread acceptance in both academic and government circles in Britain and the United States. Confidence increased in the ability of governments to maintain full employment and stable economic growth through Central Bank credit policies and government fiscal (budgetary) policies. However, by the mid-1960s, certain stubborn difficulties appeared and refused to go away. In Britain, this took the form of balance of payments troubles which led to the devaluation of the pound in November 1967.

America experienced troubles in a different form. Because all major world currencies fixed their par values in terms of the US dollar and the US dollar was pegged to gold at US$35 per ounce, America could not devalue the dollar except by raising the price of gold. This the government was unwilling to do for political reasons. Eventually, what happened was an increase in inflationary pressure in the US and a decline in confidence over the convertibility of the US dollar into gold at US$35 per ounce because of increasing US dollar balances accumulated overseas as a result of trade deficits. In the end, gold convertibility of the US dollar was suspended in August 1971 and, shortly thereafter, the regime of floating currencies came into being. World currencies continue to float till this day.

My Cabinet colleagues took careful note of these dramatic events as they unfolded on the world's financial scene. None of us believed that Keynesian economic policies could serve as Singapore's guide to economic well-being. Our economy was and is both small and open. Financing budget deficits through Central Bank credit creation appeared to us as an invitation to disaster. There was no effective way of exchange control in an open trading economy like ours to deal with inevitable balance of payments troubles.

Another contributing factor was the world outlook of my colleagues — the old guard as they are now called. We all grew up under difficult conditions and did not believe anybody owed Singapore a living. The way to a better life was through hard work, first in schools, then in universities or polytechnics and then on the job in the workplace. Diligence, education and skills will create wealth, not Central Bank credit.

Hence, we were not impressed by claims — excessive as they turned out to be — that governments could bring about prosperity through spending. It did not surprise us that the Anglo-Saxon countries which adopted such policies got into trouble. We also noted that the Germans and Japanese did not believe they could "spend their way to prosperity", as the phrase went. Like Singaporeans, they set store on diligence, education and skills.

Against this background of leadership thinking, it is hardly surprising that the CBS was preserved with its legal requirement to back the currency note issue with at least 100% of overseas assets. Actually, these assets stand at 110% because it is only after this level has been reached that the earnings of overseas assets can be transferred to the government's Consolidated Account. Cabinet's collective purpose in retaining the CBS was threefold. First, to inform the financial world that our objective was to maintain a strong convertible Singapore Dollar. This remains the best protection against inflation. When nearly two-thirds of our citizens' expenditure is spent on imported goods, a strong Singapore Dollar helps to keep consumer prices down.

The second purpose was to inform our citizens that if they wanted more and better services, they must pay for these through taxes and fees. There is no free lunch here. Third, we wanted to indicate to academics, both local and foreign, that what is fashionable in the West is not necessarily good for Singapore. A perceptive mind is needed to distinguish the peripheral from the fundamental, transient fads from permanent values.

It is also not surprising that when MAS was set up, the Chairman was by law the Finance Minister. World Bank experts advised us against this. Since MAS was effectively a Central Bank, the Chairman should be an independent person with sufficient authority to resist a Finance Minister's request for money to finance a budget deficit. The World Bank believed that putting the Finance Minister in charge would be like asking a cat to look after fish. But Singapore has always worked on the principle that government expenditure on education, defence, social and economic services, etc., must be paid for out of government revenues — taxes and fees. It is the Finance Minister's prime duty to balance the budget and, if possible, accumulate a surplus for the rainy day. Successive Finance Ministers have been doing just this. They do not need an independent Central Bank Governor to persuade them not to run budget deficits. The World Bank's anxieties were misplaced.

What would happen if a future government, returned by a complacent electorate, were to do what the World Bank feared? Democratically elected governments the world over are exposed to the temptation of winning votes through promising better and cheaper services and at the same time lower taxes. This has happened not only in rich countries but also in poor developing countries. Rich countries have the resources to get by for a few years by borrowing on the international markets, but in poor countries, punishment comes quickly in a cruel way — high rates of inflation, economic decline and political instability. These three factors reinforce each other in a way which makes escape from misery difficult.

In Singapore, an irresponsible government does not need a Central Bank to finance lavish spending as a means to win popularity. We have substantial overseas reserves which can serve this purpose. However, the recent constitutional amendment contains a provision for an elected President to block this dangerous method of vote-catching. But if the electorate, misled by soft-headed opinion makers, persists in wanting the good life without working for it, constitutional safeguards cannot stop foolish behaviour for all times. What will happen if the electorate chooses this option is that after a brief period of high living, Singapore will spiral downwards and eventually become another miserable developing country.

In conclusion, I want to correct any impression this article may have given that I think poorly of Keynes as an economist. I do not. He is the greatest economist the world has produced this century. He introduced a new way of looking at an economic system, in a different way from the classical greats such as Adam Smith, David Ricardo and Alfred Marshall. The classicals saw the system as one consisting of producers and consumers, each making his own decision as a producer or a consumer. They studied how a free market harmonises their interests. Keynes looked at how the system functions as a whole. Keynes gave birth to a discipline we now call macroeconomics.

Another Cambridge economist, Richard Stone, worked out a method whereby the macro-system can be divided into sectors and sub-sectors, examined how these sectors were related to each other and explained how their transactions could be measured. His landmark work led to the establishment of the United Nations System of National Accounting. This is the way modern states estimate the level and composition of their annual Gross National Products (GNPs). The combination of Keynesian theory (now better understood after the lessons of the 1960s) and National Accounting gives governments a practical way of evaluating economic performance. In this way, modern states are able to manage their economies much better than they did in the pre-War years.

The Great Depression which started in 1929 was the result of grave mismanagement by governments and Central Banks of Europe and America. It was in response to the wrong policies of that period that Keynes created his new system of economic analysis. If one has to fault Keynes on any point, it would be the title of his book. This should have been *The Special Theory of Employment, Interest and Money*. His prescriptions were intended to address the special circumstances created by the Great Depression. By calling it a General Theory, he led lesser minds than his into believing that his prescriptions could be applied under all circumstances, with unhappy consequences, as we have noted.

Prudence, Stability, Confidence: The Fundamentals of Good Government and Sound Central Banking

Mr Goh Chok Tong
Prime Minister

MAS 25th Anniversary Dinner
10 May 1996

Introduction

During the past 25 years, the Monetary Authority of Singapore (MAS) has made two principal contributions to the Singapore economy. It has promoted macroeconomic stability, and safeguarded the soundness and integrity of our financial system.

On this 25th anniversary of the MAS, I would like to reflect on the fundamental principles that have underpinned these contributions. There are close parallels between the principles of good government and sound central banking. These principles are worth restating and reaffirming.

Fundamentals of Economic and Financial Policies

Prudence, stability and confidence. These are the fundamentals underpinning policy-making in Singapore. The principal role of the government is to improve the quality of life of its people. This it does by providing a stable and secure environment — both political and economic — for its citizens to better themselves. When stability is in place, there will be confidence.

Confidence is the all important intangible factor in a country's development, very much like the reputation of a person. Confidence is achieved through correct policies, efficient implementation, and fair and honest conduct. For a small country with no natural assets, this intangible asset is absolutely critical. This is why we are so concerned with political and economic stability, industrial peace, social cohesion, law and order. They constitute the bedrock of our success, and indeed of our very survival.

Stability and confidence are in turn fostered through long-term policies based on prudence. Prudence has been a key common thread running through the fabric of Singapore's public policies.

The three qualities of prudence, stability, and confidence are also highly prized by central bankers. Central bankers inhabit a world characterised by fast changes and huge movements of funds. Today, capital markets transmit international economic and financial disturbances swiftly and widely, from one epicentre to another. Globalisation, deregulation and financial innovation, while promoting growth and development, have increased risk of instability. More than ever, an emphasis on prudence and the need to maintain stability and instil confidence in a country's financial system are required.

Maintaining Macroeconomic Stability

A stable value of money is a key fundamental for a healthy and growing economy. John Maynard Keynes put it this way: "There is no subtler, no surer means of overturning the existing basis of society than to debauch the currency." For our businessmen, unstable prices create uncertainty, hamper business planning, and inhibit long-term investment. For our workers, high inflation erodes the purchasing power of their salaries, eats into their Central Provident Fund (CPF) balances, and discourages savings. Fortunately for Singapore, our inflation rate has been low and our currency strong.

Singaporeans are rightly concerned about the cost of living, but they give little credit to the Government for successfully maintaining one of the world's lowest average inflation rates. During 1971 to 1995, our inflation rate averaged 4% per annum, compared to 6.3% for the industrial countries, and 33% for developing countries.

We sometimes take price stability for granted. Low inflation has preserved the real value of our CPF savings and protected our purchasing power. Our wages in real terms have grown, on average, by nearly 5% each year since 1971. Today, our purchasing power is about three times higher than it was 25 years ago. If inflation had averaged 6% each year, instead of 4%, our purchasing power would have increased by only two times, instead of three times.

The external value of our currency tells a similar story. In 1971, it took three Singapore Dollars to buy one US Dollar. Today, it takes just one dollar forty cents to exchange for one US Dollar. In 1971, it took seven dollars forty cents to buy one Pound Sterling. Today, just two dollars twenty cents would be enough. In fact since 1971, the Singapore Dollar has appreciated against most of the major currencies.

MAS has been able to contribute to macroeconomic stability because it takes a medium to long-term perspective when making policies. In the 1960s, the view that central banks had to balance two potentially conflicting goals, economic growth and price stability, prevailed. Through expansionary monetary policies, governments and central banks frequently sought to boost short-term economic growth by allowing a temporary increase in inflation.

That view is now widely discredited. There is now a consensus that stimulating economic growth while tolerating higher inflation is ultimately self-defeating. Increasingly, the emphasis of monetary policy is on the long-term, to achieve low inflation as the basis for sustained economic growth. This is what MAS has been doing.

Yet, I frequently hear calls from some of our manufacturers and exporters for an easier exchange rate policy. They want a weaker Singapore Dollar, so as to boost their competitiveness in external markets. While a weaker currency may indeed help achieve higher export and Gross Domestic Product (GDP) growth in the short run, this comes at the cost of higher wage growth and inflation, which will soon undermine our competitiveness. The ultimate consequence of a weaker exchange rate is higher prices, not higher exports.

In Singapore, the Government has always looked beyond the short-term political costs of its policy actions and focused on the long-term good. This often means taking a pre-emptive approach, to anticipate and deal with problems before they arise. In the case of MAS, it means dealing with inflation before it becomes entrenched.

MAS' ability to preserve the purchasing power of our currency is possible only because of the conducive policy environment within which it operates. In many developing countries, the poor state of government finances gives the central bank little latitude to pursue its primary objective of price stability. Monetary policy is subordinated to the role of financing the government's budget deficits. Sometimes, the central bank is effectively nothing more than a printing press churning out currency notes for the Ministry of Finance. This must lead to inflation and hyper-inflation.

How can the central bank be made free to pursue its primary objective of non-inflationary growth? There are two approaches. The first is to have an independent central bank free from political interference. The second is to have a government that shares the central bank's commitment to macroeconomic stability and provides a conducive environment.

Professor Alan Blinder of Princeton University and a former Vice Chairman of the Board of Governors of the United States (US) Federal Reserve System recently wrote: "... the political process in democratic — and even undemocratic — countries is not known for either patience or long-time horizons ... So if politicians made monetary policy on a day-to-day basis, they would be sorely tempted to reach for short-term gains at the expense of the future — that is, to inflate too much. Knowing this, many governments wisely try to de-politicise monetary policy by putting it in the hands of unelected technocrats who are given long terms of office, are well insulated from the hurly-burly of politics, and are instructed to fight inflation."

Prof Blinder's analysis of how the political process in many countries subverts the long-term good for short-term gain is correct. But I wonder if granting statutory independence to the central bank will, in itself, ensure macroeconomic stability. I would argue that having the right people in the government and in the central bank is the more effective answer.

MAS has been able to maintain macroeconomic stability mainly because Singapore's political leadership has set that as its mission. MAS will no doubt agree that Singapore's low inflation and strong currency are not solely due to its efforts. They were made possible because of the ethos of financial prudence within the government itself.

The Singapore Government has run fiscal surpluses virtually every year since the late 1960s. The main reason is that we regard state welfarism as drug addiction. It undermines one's capacity and desire for work. There are no populist handouts and price support schemes here, or subsidies to loss-making state enterprises. Our statutory boards and government-linked companies have followed principles of commercial viability. The healthy state of our public finances has made MAS' task of preserving the value of the currency that much easier.

In Singapore, the government and the central bank have worked in concert to ensure macroeconomic stability. Monetary and fiscal policies have reinforced each other in providing the framework for sustained and non-inflationary economic growth. Singapore is rather unique in that the Minister for Finance is also the chairman of the monetary authority. When we first instituted this arrangement in 1971, the International Monetary Fund (IMF) and the World Bank were alarmed. As Dr Goh Keng Swee, the prime mover behind the setting up of MAS, recalled in 1991: "The World Bank believed that putting the Finance Minister in charge would be like asking a cat to look after fish."

As it turned out, our Finance Ministers are more like bulldogs than cats. The World Bank's anxieties were misplaced. This reinforces my earlier point that people, more than just separation of powers, ultimately determine the performance of a country's central bank or economy. And as long as we continue to have as Finance Ministers people like Dr Goh, Lim Kim San, Hon Sui Sen, Dr Tony Tan and Dr Richard Hu, MAS will be able to maintain macroeconomic stability and confidence in the economy.

Safeguarding the Integrity of the Financial System

Confidence is the key to modern financial systems. The entire financial intermediation process — whether it is through the banking system or the capital markets — rests on confidence: the trust that deposits are safe, bonds are redeemable, contracts are binding. Take this vital pillar away, and the entire structure collapses, with devastating consequences for the economy. Investors, lenders, and depositors will withdraw their funds. The savings-investment process will suffer. Interest rates will rise, to reflect heightened risk. Capital will flee to safer countries.

Confidence is sustained by safeguarding the stability and integrity of the financial system. The primary means for achieving this is prudential regulation and supervision. The most basic reason for prudential oversight is depositor protection. The average person has neither the specialised knowledge nor the detailed information to assess the soundness of a bank. The second objective is to avoid a systemic financial crisis arising from fraud or mismanagement. Insolvency and illiquidity are highly contagious. The third objective is to encourage efficiency and fair competition in the financial services sector.

Laxity in prudential regulation is dangerous. There is a saying in financial markets: "Money has the timidity of a gazelle, the speed of a cheetah, and the memory of an elephant." Like a gazelle, financial markets are sensitive to the slightest signs of trouble in a country. Like a cheetah, capital flees such a country with utmost speed. And like the proverbial elephant, markets have long memories of a country that has been in trouble before. This is why countries with a history of financial instability have such a hard time trying to attract capital even after putting their house in order. Confidence is a precious commodity. Once lost, it is difficult to regain.

Prudential oversight must therefore be proactive and preventive. It must seek to avoid systemic failure, rather than wait for a crisis to happen and then respond. Often, this means having to think ahead, to think laterally, and to think the unthinkable.

The integrity of our financial system has been maintained amidst turbulent external conditions. During periods of increased stress in international financial markets, such as the October 1987 stock market crash, the Gulf crisis in 1990/91, and more recently, the Mexican peso crisis, Singapore emerged unscathed and remained a place where market participants could make transactions and do business with confidence.

Prudential regulation is not a popular thing. It inevitably engenders criticism. When times are good and markets expand, critics will complain of onerous supervisory standards. They will espouse less stringent requirements. But when times are bad and crises erupt, the regulators come under criticism for not being strict enough. MAS must therefore walk a fine line, striking a balance between over-regulation, which tends to inhibit growth, and under-regulation, which tends to erode investor confidence.

Singapore's financial sector has come a long way since 1971. Financial services were then centred on domestic activity and support for entrepot trade. Today, the financial sector is far more extensive and has an international orientation. We now have a vibrant banking industry with a large offshore dimension, the world's fourth largest foreign exchange market, a well-developed stock exchange, a rapidly growing financial futures industry, a regional insurance centre and a promising fund management industry. Our financial sector provides an efficient conduit for recycling part of global surplus funds for lending and investment in the rapidly growing economies of the Asia Pacific region.

MAS' emphasis on liberal and competitive financial markets has been part and parcel of the government's broader philosophy of letting market forces drive the economy. In the mid to late 1960s, we embarked on a strategy of export-oriented industrialisation through foreign direct investment. To attract multinational corporations (MNCs) to invest in Singapore, a major prerequisite was an open financial system to facilitate the free flow of capital and profits. Financial liberalisation was also necessary for developing Singapore as a financial centre.

Our policy of outward orientation has encouraged many reputed financial institutions to locate their operations in Singapore. They have brought with them much needed financial expertise and talent. In the banking sector, foreign institutions have introduced new and wide-ranging instruments. By enhancing market competition, they have helped reduce the cost of financial services to customers. In the securities industry, foreign participation has helped enhance market liquidity, improve the quality of investment research, and increase the sophistication of the market with the listing of derivative products.

Some market participants tend to view liberalisation and regulation as conflicting objectives. This is a mistaken view. Liberalisation is not simply a question of removing regulations. We believe that liberalisation yields its benefits only within a sound regulatory framework. Singapore's development as an international financial centre over the last 25 years has owed as much to its regulatory and supervisory policies as to measures aimed at promoting competition and innovation.

Technological changes and financial innovation will spawn ever newer and more complex instruments and products in the market. The external financial environment will be marked by increased volatility. Regulatory regimes and prudential standards must be constantly reviewed and updated where necessary, to take account of these challenges.

Other financial centres will emerge in the region. They will offer stiff competition. But this need not be to our disadvantage if we position ourselves well, consolidate our strengths, and exploit our comparative advantages. East Asia is experiencing large inflows of foreign capital and expansion in trade and investment. There will be strong demand for services such as fund management, project finance and privatisation advice. All these present exciting growth opportunities for Singapore's financial sector.

On the macroeconomic front, MAS' key challenge will be to maintain price stability in an increasingly labour-short environment. We are a mature economy now. We cannot grow by 8–10% each year without generating inflationary pressures. We cannot keep increasing the size of our foreign workforce indefinitely. MAS must be prepared to act well in advance to moderate the periodic bouts of economic overheating that may be inevitable. But it must do this with a fine touch, without risking a sharp slowdown in economic growth.

Conclusion

I began my speech by noting the congruence between some of the fundamentals of good government and sound central banking. Like Singapore, MAS must continually adapt its strategies to changing circumstances and conditions. But the fundamentals of prudence, stability and confidence do not change. They served us well during the last 25 years. They will remain as relevant and valid for the future. And to ensure that these fundamentals are entrenched, MAS must always have people of prudence, integrity and foresight in charge.

I congratulate MAS on its 25 years of achievement.

Macroeconomic Policies in Singapore: Principles, Milestones and Future Prospects

Dr Richard Hu
Minister for Finance and Chairman, MAS
Economic Society of Singapore Annual Dinner
22 March 1997

Introduction

Sound monetary and fiscal policies are the foundation of a stable economy. Although stability by itself does not lead to development, without it, all other efforts are likely to be in vain.

Just compare the experience of the East Asian economies with that of Latin America. Despite an abundance of natural resources, heavy inflows of foreign capital and a talented and skilled workforce, growth in Latin America averaged 2.3% per annum since 1980. Over the same period, East Asian economies grew three times faster. Monetary stability and fiscal prudence created a hospitable climate for private investment and productivity growth in East Asia. Fiscal profligacy, mounting debt, overvalued exchange rates and high inflation robbed Latin America of at least a decade of growth.

Singapore's own development experience highlights the importance of macroeconomic stability for economic growth. Our commitment to sound monetary and fiscal policies has underpinned investor confidence, encouraging sizable inflows of foreign direct investment.

The aim of both monetary and fiscal policies in Singapore is the same, namely to promote sustained, non-inflationary growth of the economy. Monetary policy has a more macro orientation, focusing on the management of aggregate demand to ensure low inflation. Fiscal policy has a more micro orientation, focusing on supply-side issues like addressing market failures and providing the right incentives for saving, investment and enterprise.

This evening, I would like to reflect on the fundamentals and challenges underlying the making of monetary and fiscal policies in Singapore. First, I will touch on the basic philosophy and premises, setting out our objectives and the strategies to achieve them. Then, I will take stock of the key monetary and fiscal developments since the recession in 1985. Finally, I will share with you what I think are the key monetary and fiscal challenges in the years ahead.

Monetary Policy

Let me begin with monetary policy. A fundamental principle governing monetary policy in Singapore is that low inflation provides the basis for sustained economic growth and long-term competitiveness. The reasons for this are clear. Low and stable inflation reduces uncertainty in business decisions, and encourages investors to take a long-term stake in the country. Stable consumer prices also moderate wage pressures, underpinning the long-term competitiveness of our exports.

The world has come a long way from the old economic orthodoxy that moderate inflation may have to be tolerated to achieve higher growth. This view is now widely discredited. Among developing countries, economies with lower rates of inflation have tended to have higher rates of income growth per capita. Quite clearly, there is no long-term trade-off between the two major economic policy objectives — of growth and price stability. Hence, the appropriate goal for monetary policy is to focus on the long term and keep inflation low. And this has been the operating philosophy of MAS.

How do we achieve the goal of low inflation in Singapore? There are two objectives we need to fulfil: the first is to keep out imported inflation;

the second is to contain domestic cost pressures. And the monetary policy strategy to achieve both objectives is the same: to maintain the strength of the Singapore Dollar. A strong currency acts as a shield against foreign inflationary pressures. This is an important factor in an economy where 60 cents out of every dollar that is spent is on imported goods. A strong currency also helps to moderate external demand when the economy is overheating, thereby helping to relieve labour market pressures.

Yet, in my 12-odd years as Chairman of MAS, I have had no shortage of complaints about the strong Singapore Dollar. I can understand the calls from some of our manufacturers and exporters for an easier exchange rate. It is true that a weaker exchange rate makes our goods cheaper in foreign currencies and thereby helps boost exports and GDP in the short run. But such a policy has adverse macro consequences in the long run.

Ultimately, what is relevant to the ability of our exporters to compete in international markets in the long term is not the nominal exchange rate but the real exchange rate, i.e., the nominal rate adjusted for cost or inflation differentials across countries. A weaker nominal exchange rate translates into higher prices domestically. Then, wages rise to reflect both these higher domestic prices and the tighter labour market arising from the initial increase in export demand. Rising prices and wages feed on each other, and lead to an appreciation of the real exchange rate that offsets the initial gains in competitiveness. Studies by MAS suggest that the bulk of the initial gains in competitiveness arising from a weaker exchange rate are lost within three years through higher inflation. Worse, the higher inflation tends to become entrenched, with adverse consequences.

Some of you may not be entirely convinced. You may look at Singapore's real exchange rate and point out that it has risen despite low inflation. And indeed it has. But the relevant comparison is with what the real exchange rate might have been if we had prevented the nominal exchange rate from appreciating and allowed inflation to creep up. In all likelihood, the real exchange rate would have appreciated just as much, if not more.

A comparison with Hong Kong's experience may be illuminating. Singapore and Hong Kong are city-state economies extremely open to international trade and capital flows. But their monetary policy regimes differ sharply. Hong Kong's maintains a pegged exchange rate, at 7.8 Hong Kong Dollars to one US Dollar. Singapore's monetary policy over the last decade has been characterised by a trend appreciation of the Singapore Dollar against most major currencies.

The divergent movements in the nominal and real exchange rates of Hong Kong and Singapore provide an interesting perspective. In nominal terms, the Hong Kong Dollar has been relatively more stable. Against a trade-weighted basket of currencies, the Hong Kong Dollar has appreciated by a cumulative 19% since 1990. During the same period, the Singapore Dollar has appreciated by 24%. But in real terms, that is taking account of cost differentials, the Hong Kong Dollar has appreciated by 42% while the Singapore Dollar has appreciated by 29%.[1]

During this period, both countries faced conditions of tight labour markets and economic overheating which required a real exchange rate appreciation. Singapore chose to accommodate this through a nominal appreciation while keeping inflation low. Hong Kong, on the other hand, with its nominal exchange rate pegged to the US Dollar, had little choice but to allow inflation to rise. As a result, it experienced a much faster real exchange rate appreciation that posed difficulties for its export sector. Manufacturing exports have stagnated in Hong Kong since 1990, while they have nearly doubled in Singapore during the same period.

It is not my intention to find fault with the Hong Kong economy, which remains one of the most vibrant and resilient in the world. Indeed, a good part of Hong Kong's poor export performance can be explained by the shift of much of its manufacturing base to southern China. Moreover, the importance of the political and economic stability that Hong Kong's currency peg has made possible is not to be underestimated. My point is a more limited one: that the relative stability of Hong Kong's nominal exchange rate has come at the price of higher inflation and has not translated into unproved export competitiveness.

---

[1] Singapore's NEER is from published IMF sources, while Hong Kong's NEER is from the Hong Kong Monthly Digest of Statistics. Both REERs are based on MAS estimates, derived by adjusting the NEERs for relative unit labour costs in the two economies vis-à-vis their top ten export markets.

More broadly speaking, empirical studies have shown that countries experiencing rapid productivity growth, increased savings rates and strong capital inflows tend to have an appreciating real exchange rate. These factors are at play in Singapore as well as in many of the economies in this region, indicating that our real exchange rates will have to appreciate over time. The question really is whether this occurs through a strengthening of the nominal exchange rate, or through a less desirable way via inflation. Singapore's approach of allowing the nominal exchange rate to adjust upwards has helped us to avoid the kind of macroeconomic problems that have plagued some of the East Asian economies, such as excessive monetary growth and destabilising capital flows.

Looking to the future, what are the main challenges for monetary and exchange rate policy in Singapore? On the positive side, the global inflationary environment has become more benign. There are reasons to believe that this is reflective of a structural disinflationary bias rather than just a cyclical phenomenon.

First, the globalisation of economic activity has led to increased productivity and efficiency in the manufacture of a wide range of products. This has exerted downward pressures on prices in general. Second, the supply shocks of the 1970s and 1980s — in the prices of crude oil and primary commodities — are not likely to be repeated, certainly not in the same magnitude. Indeed, the supply shocks of today — whether it is in consumer electronics or memory chips — have tended to be disinflationary. Third, central banks the world over are much more focused on the pursuit of price stability. Monetary policy has become more preemptive, striking at inflation before it has a chance to take root.

What do these trends mean for Singapore? To the extent that foreign inflationary pressures become more muted, our exchange rate does not have to appreciate as much as it did before. Indeed, many of you watching the Singapore Dollar would have already noticed the much more gradual rate of appreciation in recent years. If the global inflationary environment continues to be favourable, it is not unreasonable to expect a continuation of this more modest rate of appreciation.

I must sound a note of caution, however. While central banks seem to have successfully tamed consumer price inflation, the spectre of asset price inflation continues to haunt many countries. Central banks are still grappling with the issue of how to deal with rapidly rising asset prices against a background of relatively stable consumer prices. This could well be the main challenge facing central bankers in coming years. And we, in Singapore, are not immune to this challenge.

Our exchange rate appreciation has successfully dampened inflation in tradeable goods, but has not been as effective against inflation in the non-tradeable sector, particularly in asset markets like property. It appears that the crux of the matter is this: surplus domestic savings and strong inflows of foreign capital, in the context of an appreciating currency, have led to low interest rates. This helped fuel the property market inflation of recent years. Our dilemma is that we cannot raise interest rates in an attempt to dampen asset inflation because our monetary policy is centred on the exchange rate, which remains the key macroeconomic variable. This was why we had to introduce the package of fiscal measures in May last year to curb excessive price inflation in the property market. MAS will continue to monitor both consumer and asset prices as part of its mission to ensure a stable macroeconomic environment in which the country can grow and prosper.

Fiscal Policy

Let me now turn to fiscal policy. A fundamental premise underlying our fiscal policy is that the private sector is the engine of economic growth. Government's role, through tax and expenditure policy, is to provide a stable and conducive environment for the private sector to thrive.

A basic principle of fiscal policy in Singapore is to avoid running persistent deficits. Our aim is to run modest surpluses in good years to augment our foreign reserves. These reserves provide an important buffer, given the small and highly open nature of our economy and virtual lack of natural resources. A healthy reserve position also instils confidence among foreign investors and underpins Singapore's status as a major financial centre.

Unlike many other countries, fiscal policy in Singapore does not play an active role in counter-cyclical demand management. It is true that in times of economic slack, we have accelerated some of our infrastructure spending, as we did to some extent with the MRT and other projects during the 1985/86 recession. But, by and large, we have avoided the kind of Keynesian pump-priming that many countries have resorted to during periods of weak economic growth.

There are two reasons for this. First, as a highly open economy with a large import leakage, an expansionary fiscal policy has limited effects on boosting GDP. Second, and more importantly, our philosophy has always been that tax and expenditure policies be justified on micro economic considerations. If a project is not worth doing on the basis of a social cost-benefit analysis, we will not do it merely to pump prime the economy.

The Singapore government has been running fiscal surpluses in almost every year since the late 1960s.[2] These surpluses are a major component of our national savings. Since 1984, budget surpluses have averaged 4% of GDP. In more recent years, it has risen to 8% of GDP, partly on account of cyclical factors that helped boost revenues. But the main structural factor underlying our healthy budget position has been the relatively low level of operating expenditure. Development expenditure in Singapore has actually been higher than in the G7 economies, reflecting the high priority we place on building a world-class infrastructure. Likewise, differences in revenue intake cannot explain Singapore's more favourable fiscal position. In fact, Singapore's operating revenue as a percentage of GDP has been significantly lower than that in the G7 economies, although comparable to that in Taiwan and Korea, and slightly higher than in Hong Kong.

Quite apart from the macroeconomic implications of the overall fiscal stance, revenue and expenditure policies affect resource allocation at the micro level. I would like to touch on these in somewhat greater detail.

On the revenue side, we have two key objectives. The first is to raise

[2] The budget surplus for Singapore is defined as operating revenue less operating and development expenditure. Unlike the case for the other countries, it does not include investment income, capital receipts and interest payments.

sufficient revenue to finance both operating and development expenditure. The second is to maintain an internationally competitive and socially equitable tax regime. The challenge, of course, is to strike a balance between these objectives.

Our strategy has been to build a broad revenue base. This reduces the vulnerability of revenue intake to adverse changes in economic conditions. We have, over the years, achieved a better balance between tax and non-tax revenues, and within tax revenues, shifted more towards indirect taxation.

Non-tax sources constitute a fifth of the Singapore government's current revenues.[3] By way of comparison, in the G7 economies, they make up less than a tenth of total revenues. Of course, about one-third of our non-tax revenues derives from the sales of Certificates of Entitlement (COEs) for motor vehicles, where revenue generation is not the objective. But a good part of the rest of our non-tax revenues comes from a variety of user charges. User charges reflect an important principle of our fiscal policy, namely that of partial or total cost recovery for goods and services provided by the government. In addition to broadening the revenue base, user charges serve a key economic function: they prevent over-consumption of publicly provided services and minimise distortions to the efficient allocation of resources.

The breadth of our revenue base is even more evident when we look at our tax mix. In 1984, direct taxes accounted for two-thirds of our total tax revenues. Today, they make up just over half. In comparison, direct taxes, including social security taxes, contribute about three-quarters of the total tax revenues of the G7 economies.

The growing importance of indirect taxation reflects our ongoing shift towards taxing consumption rather than income. There are good economic reasons for doing this. Taxing income discourages enterprise and incentive. It also discourages savings. And looking to the future, the twin factors of slower economic growth and an ageing population must mean an erosion of the income tax base. The move towards a more consumption-based tax

[3] This refers to revenues excluding investment income and capital receipts.

system will help make our fiscal position more resilient to demographic change. The Goods and Services Tax (GST) implemented in 1994 was a step in this direction.

A broad base is only one element of a good tax system. To meet the other objective of maintaining an internationally competitive tax regime, we must also keep the rates of taxation low.

A cross-country comparison might shed some light on where we stand in this regard. Singapore's top marginal income tax rate for individuals has come down from 45% in 1984 to 28%. The average for the G7 economies is 51%; even the US, which has the lowest rate among the G7 countries, taxes those in its top income bracket at 40%. The top rates in Taiwan and Korea are also higher, at 40%. Among our major competitors, only Hong Kong has a lower rate than us, at 20%.

Our corporate tax rate has also become very competitive. It has declined from 40% in 1984 to 26%. Our current rate is much lower than the average of 39% levied on corporations in the G7 economies. The effective corporate tax rates in Korea and Taiwan are also much higher as dividends paid by companies are subject to withholding tax. Only Hong Kong is lower at 16.5%.

We are also competitive in terms of non-income-based taxes. Like Hong Kong, Singapore does not tax capital gains. In contrast, both Korea and Taiwan, as well as each of the G7 countries, have capital gains taxes. Our goods and services tax, at 3%, is only about a quarter of the rate of consumption tax in most of the G7 countries. The average import tariff in Singapore is about 0.4%, miniscule compared to the 6.5% average in the G7 economies and the 9% average in Korea and Taiwan.

Perhaps the ultimate test of a country's low tax credentials is to compare its total tax receipts with its national income. In Singapore, the tax-to-GDP ratio during 1990–94 was just under 16.5%. This is less than half the average ratio in the G7 countries. The tax-to-GDP ratio in Korea and Taiwan is also higher, at 20% and 19% respectively. Hong Kong, of course, has the lowest ratio, at 11.5%.

I am making these cross-country comparisons to illustrate two important points. The first is that, Singapore is among the most lightly taxed countries in the world. Second, in an environment where the global competition for capital and technology has become very intense, it is important that we continue to maintain a tax regime that is internationally competitive. And, our healthy fiscal position gives us the latitude to maintain our long-term competitiveness.

Let me now turn to government expenditure policy. Our first objective is to maintain strict control over spending. We aim to keep government expenditure below 20% of GDP. The second objective is to invest in areas which generate returns to the economy. Once again, the challenge is to strike a balance between the two objectives.

Government expenditure is controlled by regulating state welfarism. Our strategy has been to encourage economic self-reliance by promoting social mobility. Instead of providing large unemployment benefits and price support schemes, we prefer job creation and market competition. The provision of subsidies has been selective and confined mainly to education, healthcare and public housing. The avoidance of large-scale public assistance programmes also serves to guard against a culture of dependence.

The ethos of financial rectitude extends throughout the public sector. The government has always insisted that statutory boards and other public enterprises operate commercially. There are no bailouts. This is how we have managed to keep government transfers and subsidies to less than 4% of GDP. In the G7 economies, they account for nearly 16%, four times as much.[4]

Prudence in spending has not been at the expense of our other objective, namely to provide the necessary social and physical infrastructure that the market might not provide efficiently. Our strategy has been to invest in people, and to invest in the future. Education, infrastructure and primary health care have been key priorities. About 30% of government

[4] Transfers and subsidies refer to social assistance grants, unfunded employee pensions and welfare benefits, as well as grants to private industries and public corporations to cover operating losses.

expenditure is devoted to development projects, like building schools, hospitals, roads and parks.

What are the main challenges for fiscal policy in the 21st century? I believe the main challenge will come from the twin effects of slower economic growth and an ageing population. Private savings rates will decline. Government expenditures per capita will increase relative to revenues, as the proportion of taxpayers in the population diminishes. Spending on health care will grow sharply, as it has in nearly all of the advanced economies undergoing demographic change. There would also be substantial increases in expenditure related specifically to the aged, such as homes for the elderly, institutions for the destitute, senior citizens' clubs, etc. It is not inconceivable that in 20–30 years' time, the government's primary operating budget could go into deficit. The only buffer that we have against the overall government budget also going into the red is the stream of investment income that the government will earn on its overseas assets.

This is why it is of paramount importance that we generate surpluses and accumulate reserves while the economy is still growing rapidly and most Singaporeans are still in their working years. Otherwise, a future government would have to raise taxes on younger generations, or borrow from abroad, to meet its financing needs.

It is equally important that we preserve the fundamentals of our fiscal policy, namely to eschew state welfarism and emphasise self-reliance and community help. The experience of the advanced economies suggests that slower economic growth and the increased electoral power of senior citizens could exert pressures on a future government to spend more on social services. It is possible to accommodate a modest increase in welfare expenditures, particularly subsidies for health care for the poorest sections of the aged population. But a generalised increase in government welfare expenditures along the lines of some Western European countries would be disastrous. It would sap our economic vitality. We must be on our guard to avoid such a scenario.

Conclusion

Maintaining consistency in macroeconomic policies is not an easy task. In many countries, macroeconomic management does not exist as a coherent package. Particularly in cases where political leadership is fragmented, government bodies in charge of different policies have different priorities and views on how the economy should be managed. Monetary policy is often a handmaiden of profligate fiscal policies, with the central banks operating as nothing more than printing presses for ministries of finance. This is a sure recipe for macroeconomic instability.

This is perhaps why central bank independence is the current rage in academic and policy circles. The argument is that an independent central bank, insulated from political interference, will be able to focus on the long-term and pursue policies aimed at low inflation. I have some sympathy with this view, especially in countries beset by waves of populist economic policies.

But central bank independence is not a panacea for all macroeconomic problems. Over the last decade or so, many central banks have become more independent and focused on their primary objective of price stability. And indeed, inflation rates have come down the world over. But national governments have continued to run fiscal deficits, driving up interest rates and crowding out private investment. They have also failed to rein in welfare expenditures or institute much-needed structural reforms, especially in labour markets. Against a background of tight monetary policies, the result is slow economic growth and high unemployment.

In Singapore, we have adopted a balanced approach. We have macroeconomic coordination at the highest levels of government, but considerable autonomy and independence at the operational levels of monetary and fiscal policy. More importantly, both sets of policymakers share common ethos of financial prudence and conservatism. A healthy fiscal position has absolved MAS of the need to finance the government budget and given it the freedom to focus on its primary mission of price stability. In the final analysis, fiscal soundness, rather than statutory independence, is the best guarantee of central bank effectiveness.

A consistent macroeconomic package, where monetary and fiscal policies reinforce each other in providing a conducive framework for sustained economic growth, will remain one of our greatest assets as we embark on the 21st century.

Credibility, Confidence, Dynamism: MAS in the New Economic and Financial Landscape

Mr Lee Hsien Loong
Deputy Prime Minister and Chairman, MAS

MAS 30th Anniversary Conference
20 July 2001

Introduction

A new economic and financial landscape is emerging. Financial markets are becoming globalised; cross-border capital flows are larger and faster; financial institutions are consolidating and restructuring on a massive scale; and new and complex financial products are emerging, driven by technology and market pressures. Amidst these upheavals, MAS' goals as a central bank remain unchanged: low inflation for sustained economic growth, and a sound financial sector for markets to grow and thrive.

MAS is a unique organisation; it is the only institution in the world that combines responsibility for monetary policy with supervisory oversight of the entire financial sector — banking, insurance and securities. In addition, it has the task of promoting the development of Singapore as an international financial centre. I shall describe how MAS has met its responsibilities in these three areas over the past 30 years, some of the key events that have shaped our policies, and how we intend to move forward in the new economic and financial landscape.

Building Confidence and Credibility

Monetary Policy

MAS was born in turbulent times. It was 1971. The US dollar was under intense pressure, due to mounting inflation and balance of payments problems brought on by the Vietnam War and Great Society programmes. In August 1971, just months after MAS was formed, the US suspended convertibility of the US dollar into gold, plunging international currency markets into turmoil. In June 1973, the Bretton Woods system of fixed exchange rates finally collapsed, and the Singapore dollar was floated.

Having witnessed these tumultuous events and the instability they caused, the Singapore Government enshrined a strong and credible currency as one of the key pillars of macroeconomic policy, and charged MAS with the responsibility of ensuring it. Tight fiscal discipline, a healthy balance of payments, and a vibrant Singapore economy underpinned the steady strengthening of the Singapore dollar.

A second defining moment in the evolution of MAS' monetary policy came in 1981 when global inflation accelerated in the wake of the second oil shock. Dr Goh Keng Swee, who took over as Chairman of MAS, clarified low inflation as the key policy objective and shifted the focus of monetary policy onto the exchange rate as the principal policy instrument. The high import content of our domestic expenditures meant that domestic inflation in Singapore was largely determined by changes in foreign prices and the exchange rate. Traditional monetary policy instruments such as money supply and interest rates were ineffective in controlling output and prices given the openness of our economy. As Dr Goh explained: "In 1981 there was a clearer recognition that the way to beat inflation is to have a strong Singapore dollar."

Internationally too, a hard currency was an important sign that the Singapore Government pursued a disciplined economic policy, and that Singapore was different from the many developing countries which chronically outspent their revenues and depreciated their currencies.

At the same time, a new international consensus on monetary policy had emerged with a greater awareness of the costs of inflation. The notion that mild inflation might be good for growth had been debunked by the experience of industrial countries in the 1970s. Instead, the industrialised countries with the lowest inflation such as Germany and Switzerland, had experienced the lowest unemployment rates. The simple Phillips Curve, which implied a trade-off between inflation and unemployment, went out of fashion.

In line with our emergence as an international financial centre, we progressively dismantled exchange controls in the 1970s, until the last restriction was removed in 1978. The absence of exchange or capital controls made the conduct of an exchange rate-centred monetary policy that much more difficult. Our small and open economy was especially vulnerable to sharp swings in the exchange rate or speculative attacks. We could not afford to assume that speculation in international financial markets was invariably self-stabilising and that speculators who bet wrongly against the Singapore dollar would automatically be punished.

Therefore, MAS maintained an explicit policy of not encouraging the internationalisation of the Singapore dollar. It limited the extension of bank credit in Singapore dollars to non-residents except for economic activity, and buttressed this with some restrictions on interbank Singapore dollar derivatives, such as currency and interest rate swaps and options, which might have helped financial players to leverage or hedge their positions. This policy made it harder for would be speculators to short the Singapore dollar, and signalled unambiguously our disapproval of such speculation.

This framework served us well. That we encountered very few speculative attacks in practice perhaps showed that the policy was effective. The strength and stability of the Singapore dollar instilled confidence and kept inflation low. Price stability provided the foundation for sustained economic growth, which in turn provided the basis for continued strengthening of the Singapore dollar.

We benefited immensely from this virtuous cycle. Over the past two decades since 1981, the Singapore dollar has risen steadily by more than 70%, on a trade-weighted basis. Domestic inflation has been among the lowest in the world, averaging 2.0% per annum compared to 6.5% for the OECD countries. In real terms, GDP growth averaged 7.6% a year, while GDP per capita in 2000 was two and a half times the level in 1981.

Financial Supervision

MAS' second responsibility is oversight of the financial sector. MAS was an integrated supervisor long before this became internationally fashionable. When it was formed in 1971, MAS was responsible for both monetary policy and the supervision of banks. It took over supervision of the insurance industry in 1977, and the securities industry in 1984.

From the beginning, MAS' approach to supervising the financial sector was centred on a strict admission policy, high prudential requirements and rigorous enforcement. We sought not only to maintain systemic stability, but also to protect individual institutions from failing, and the public and investors from losses. Lacking any track record, this approach was necessary to establish credibility with international financial institutions and their home regulators. When it emerged that Singapore had been spared the fallout from the collapse of BCCI because MAS had steadfastly refused BCCI entry despite persistent lobbying, MAS' reputation as a thorough and uncompromising regulator went up.

But despite our best efforts, we did have one major failure — the Pan-El crisis in 1985. Pan Electric Industries, or Pan-El, was a holding company with interests in hotels, property and marine operations. It went into receivership in November 1985, threatening the solvency of many stockbroking firms with whom it had forward contracts. MAS closed the stock exchange for 3 days while a lifeboat fund was organised. The four major local banks agreed to provide a standby line of credit, to aid the affected stockbrokers and restore market confidence.

Pan-El showed up certain weaknesses in our regulatory framework. Following Pan-El, MAS revamped the Securities Industry Act, raising standards and putting in place mechanisms for the proper regulation of the market. MAS considerably tightened its supervision of the stock exchange and the securities industry. To some extent this tighter approach permeated beyond the securities industry to other parts of the financial sector, and continued right up to 1997, when we shifted course.

Development of the Financial Industry

MAS' third responsibility was to promote the development of the financial industry. Singapore did not become a financial centre by accident or luck. The Government saw an opportunity to develop Singapore as a regional financial centre. We had a time zone advantage, bridging the gap between the close of markets in the US and the reopening of business the next day in Europe. We were also well-placed, with our good infrastructure and political stability, to serve as a point of intermediation for fund flows in an industrialising Asia.

We started by permitting banks to establish Asian Currency Units (ACUs) to accept non-Singapore dollar deposits. This paved the way for the creation of the Asian Dollar Market, the counterpart of the Eurodollar Market in London. We attracted international banks to set up ACUs here, and abolished withholding tax on interest income earned by non-resident depositors. We introduced a lower tax rate of 10% for offshore income.[1] From these modest beginnings, the Asian Dollar Market expanded, to reach total assets of US$500 billion today.

Another major initiative was the creation of SIMEX. In 1984, the Gold Exchange of Singapore expanded beyond trading of gold futures to include financial futures and renamed itself the Singapore International Monetary Exchange (SIMEX). SIMEX was the first financial futures exchange in Asia. Well before exchange linkages became the norm, SIMEX co-pioneered the world's first mutual offset trading link with the Chicago Mercantile Exchange, facilitating round-the-clock trading. Renamed SGX-DT, the derivatives exchange today trades a broad range of interest rate, fixed income, equity and energy derivatives.

A later initiative was the programme launched in 1994 to develop the fund management industry in Singapore. Our fund management industry

[1] In 1973, we reduced the corporate tax for ACU interest earnings from overseas loans from 40% to 10%. We extended this to fees and commissions received by ACUs in 1976.

was small compared with other financial centres. The Central Provident Fund (CPF) system was absorbing the bulk of the population's long-term savings, and starving the private fund management industry of local funds. The Government liberalised the rules to allow CPF savings to be invested in approved unit trusts and fund management accounts. MAS and GIC went on to give modest mandates to external fund managers, although these could only be the seed money to grow the industry. At the end of 2000, the total assets managed by Singapore-based financial institutions was $276 billion, four times the $66 billion in 1994 when we embarked on the programme.

New Directions

The approaches that we took in monetary policy, financial supervision and development have served Singapore well. We maintained low inflation and a macroeconomic environment favourable to growth. Our capital markets have grown rapidly over the past few years, while our forex market is one of the largest in the world. With over 200 banks and merchant banks, 150 insurance companies and 160 investment advisors in Singapore, we have become a major financial centre.

But past achievements will not extrapolate into future successes, unless we update our policies to meet changing conditions. Policies that worked in the 1970s and 1980s needed rethinking by the 1990s. In 1997, we began a comprehensive review of MAS' policy framework and approach, which has led to fundamental changes. Our work is far from done, and we anticipate many challenges ahead.

Credibility and Dynamism — MAS' Approach to Future Challenges

Monetary Policy

In monetary policy, certain verities are not likely to change. We will continue to manage the exchange rate as our principal policy variable. The primary objective will still be to maintain price stability and the purchasing power of the Singapore dollar, over the medium term. We will continue to guard against destabilising speculation in the Singapore dollar.

However, the international environment has changed. We are witnessing larger capital flows and more volatile financial markets. G3 currencies have tended to undergo prolonged periods of misalignment, followed by sharp corrections. For a while after the Asian crisis, when currencies that were quasi-pegged to the US dollar collapsed in a disastrous contagion, a consensus was growing that the only sustainable exchange rate regimes for emerging markets are either a hard currency peg or a totally free float.

These corner solutions are not suitable for Singapore. A free floating exchange rate would mean relinquishing our most effective inflation-fighting instrument. On the other hand a fixed exchange rate, pegged say to the US dollar, would lock our economic fortunes to US monetary policy, with no assurance that it would be appropriate to the state of our economy. The intermediate option of a managed float remains the best approach for us.

In our experience, a managed float helps to buffer the adverse effects on the economy of short-term financial volatility, and to avoid sustained currency misalignments that can be damaging to our export sector. Managing the float requires us to lean against the wind at times, but provided our exchange rate policy is aligned with economic fundamentals, and our ability and determination to counter destabilising speculation is not in doubt, we need to intervene less than might be expected.

Until recently, MAS did not reveal its view of the exchange rate, what it had done, or what it intended to do. But going forward, MAS recognises the need to be more communicative and less opaque about its exchange rate policy. Hence we have been making half-yearly monetary policy statements announcing our prevailing policy stance. We have also published the movements of the trade-weighted Singapore dollar, hitherto a closely guarded secret. We envisage that if market participants and the public understand our policy stance better, there will be less uncertainty, and policy implementation will be more effective.

We have also reviewed and refined our policy on the internationalisation of the Singapore dollar. The balance of risks between not relaxing the non-internationalisation policy on the one hand, and lifting some specific restrictions in a progressive manner on the other, has shifted. With a more mature financial industry and a more internationalised economy, corporate players and financial institutions have a greater need for Singapore dollars and its derivatives for commercial transactions. At the same time, the economy and financial system have grown and become more resilient and our ability to manage the exchange rate has strengthened.

This is why MAS has liberalised the non-internationalisation policy, leaving only the most essential restrictions in place. This has enabled the bond market to take off, with foreign players raising Singapore dollar bonds, but swapping the proceeds into a foreign currency before taking them out of the country. We will continue to fine-tune the non-internationalisation policy from time to time, but the policy is no longer a significant constraint on the development of our capital markets or financial sector.

Financial Supervision

MAS has also, since 1998, been reviewing and updating its approach to regulating and supervising the financial sector. First, we have instituted a fundamental shift in emphasis away from "one-size-fits-all" regulation of institutions to risk-focused supervision, and from merit-based regulation of products to a disclosure-based regime. Second, we have embarked on a programme to liberalise access to all parts of the financial industry to stimulate greater competition and dynamism. These reforms are aimed at providing a more conducive environment for innovation and enterprise while promoting high standards of risk management, so as to help make Singapore a premier financial centre in Asia.

But these changes are just the beginning. MAS must continue to review and update its regulatory and supervisory framework, to appropriately address the risks and exploit the opportunities presented by the changing financial landscape. Let me outline three major challenges, and their implications for our regulatory and supervisory framework.

Future Challenges

The first challenge is that institutions will be larger and more complex. Singapore banks are merging, in search of greater scale and efficiency. They are following a worldwide trend. Bigger banks are better placed to attract high-calibre talent, invest in cutting-edge technology, and diversify their risks. But they will also require tighter management and closer supervision, and the systemic consequences of difficulties in a large bank are more severe.

Secondly, the soundness of Singapore's financial system will increasingly depend on factors outside MAS' control. As our institutions expand their presence in the region, their financial strength will be tested by their exposure to regional markets. At the same time, we are opening our markets further to foreign players. This will also increase the risk of contagion as the soundness of foreign institutions is dependent on their home market and global operations.

Thirdly, we have to cope with new business models and financial products that are emerging faster than ever. Technology and competition are transforming the way in which financial services are produced and distributed, and driving the convergence of financial products and service providers. The traditional divides between banks, securities firms, and insurers are blurring. Securities firms are offering deposit-like products; banks are selling insurance under the rubric of "bancassurance"; and insurance companies are offering investment-linked products as substitutes for unit trusts. As Mr Andrew Crockett, General Manager of the BIS, said recently, the challenge for regulators will be to "create rules of the game that are robust to fad, fashions and arbitrage".[2]

How should MAS respond?

How should MAS respond to these challenges? Our objective remains to promote a sound and progressive financial sector. Our approach to rule-setting must adapt to new developments, be sensitive to the effects of regulation on industry and be focussed in identifying and addressing risks.

---

2 "Issues in Global Financial Supervision", Remarks at the 36th SEACEN Governors' Conference in Singapore, 1 June 2001.

We have already broadened the limits within which institutions have free play. We must now aim to develop a pro-enterprise supervisory framework that will encourage innovation and dynamism without compromising the safety and soundness of the financial system. Such a framework will comprise the following elements:

- risk-focussed, consolidated supervision;
- harmonised regulation;
- sound corporate governance; and
- effective market discipline.

Let me elaborate on these elements of the new framework.

Risk-focussed, Consolidated Supervision

We are adopting a risk-focussed, consolidated approach to the supervision of financial institutions. We will place more emphasis on understanding and evaluating an institution's risk management systems and internal controls. And we will apply this approach on a consolidated group-wide basis across all constituent institutions, local or overseas.

At the micro-level, MAS is improving the processes and techniques it uses to systematically evaluate a bank's operations and risk profile to determine the key areas that require attention. At the macro-level, MAS is enhancing its financial surveillance capabilities, to help identify emerging vulnerabilities, and assess how they will affect individual institutions or business activities, so that we can devote adequate supervisory resources to these areas.

Harmonised Regulation

MAS will also develop a more harmonised and integrated approach to regulation. Consistency in regulation across similar financial activities and products will help level the playing field, lower compliance costs, and reduce the scope for regulatory arbitrage. In this regard, MAS has begun to streamline the licensing regime and put in place a risk-based capital framework across the financial sector.

The new Securities and Futures Act will introduce a single, modular licensing regime for securities and futures intermediaries. The Financial Advisers Act will provide a single licensing regime and a more flexible and integrated regulatory framework, with consistent standards of business conduct for entities engaging in financial advisory activities for all investment products. But this is not a one-off process. As the industries and products continue to evolve, our laws and regulations will have to evolve with them.

We are making progress in applying the concept of risk-based capital. In banking, where risk-based capital standards already exist, MAS is working with the local banks to implement the proposed New Basel Capital Accord. In insurance, securities and futures trading, we are revising the existing disparate capital frameworks, to replace them with a consistent risk-based approach based on common principles and objectives.

Effective Corporate Governance

Over time, we should rely more on corporate governance and market discipline to complement prudential regulation and supervision. Good corporate governance is critical to fostering a strong risk management culture and effective internal controls. Going forward, MAS will further raise corporate governance standards, particularly with regards to enhancing the independence of boards and institutionalising professional management. But this must be phased in judiciously. We cannot impose these standards in a vacuum without regard to the institutional and cultural realities in our corporate sector.

Effective Market Discipline

Market discipline imposes external incentives on financial institutions to conduct their business in a sound and efficient manner. For market discipline to work, there must be timely and accurate disclosure of relevant information. Investors must be sophisticated enough to make good use of disclosed information, and make considered investment decisions appropriate to their needs and risk appetites. MAS will progressively raise disclosure standards in the financial sector to meet international best practice.

Development of the Financial Industry

MAS continues to be charged with the development of Singapore's financial sector. In 1998, we established a new department to focus our efforts on actively promoting the industry, identifying areas of opportunity, and profiling Singapore as an international financial centre.

The task ahead is daunting. External conditions are presently not favourable. The global economy is slowing down. Southeast Asia is taking longer than we had hoped to implement structural reforms that are essential for sustained growth. Investors are waiting to see how events unfold. There are fewer opportunities for institutions to service our immediate region, whether in offshore lending, mergers and acquisitions, or treasury operations.

We can and must look beyond immediate problems, and press on to upgrade our infrastructure and capabilities, so that institutions and investors will have stronger reasons to site activities in Singapore and use our financial markets. Then as Southeast Asia recovers, which in time it will, we will be ready to play our part in its pick up.

We have come a long way since 1968 when we started promoting the Asian Dollar Market. As we evolve into a full-service financial centre, it will become more difficult to identify individual projects or areas to pursue. Our approach is therefore to establish a conducive overall environment, within which market forces can operate and private sector innovation can thrive. We have to:

- develop efficient, comprehensive and world-class infrastructure;
- put in place a sound but pro-enterprise regulatory framework; and
- attract, nurture and retain top talent, both local and foreign.

Such a competitive and pro-enterprise environment will bring out the areas in which we have a competitive advantage. We cannot predict in advance which activities will take off. But when some activities succeed we can promote and encourage their development, always pushing in the direction of market forces, and not against them.

Conclusion

MAS has built a reputation for credibility, prudence and competence over the last 30 years. But major challenges lie ahead. We have to manage exchange rate policy in an increasingly volatile market, build a sound and responsive regulatory environment that allows the financial industry to thrive and promote Singapore as a financial centre even in the midst of adverse external conditions.

It is always easy to shelter from change, to reject anything new and to adopt a risk-adverse approach. But if the sole objective of a captain is to protect his ship, then his vessel would never leave port. Over the last few years, we have altered our course — opening up to, rather than sheltering from, the winds of change.

To navigate in this dynamic environment, MAS will have to continue to strengthen its own capabilities. The pace of change is intense, and the demands on MAS' resources, expertise and judgement will only grow. We must broaden our contacts and consultation with market participants and fellow central bankers and regulators. This is the way to keep abreast of the latest developments in the financial industry, and evolving best practices in central banking and financial supervision.

We must groom a corps of competent and committed economists, supervisors and investment managers within MAS. But this will not be sufficient. We also have to reinforce our team with talent from industry and abroad. We already have foreign and mid-career professionals among our ranks, but we must attract more such persons. Only by building a truly world-class MAS team, will we succeed in our mission — to promote macro-economic stability, and a sound and progressive financial centre.

MAS at Forty: Past Contributions, Future Challenges

Mr Lee Hsien Loong
Prime Minister

MAS 40th Anniversary Dinner

28 November 2011

I am happy to join MAS and our distinguished central bank governors, regulators and CEOs to celebrate MAS' 40th anniversary. This is a significant milestone for MAS.

Central banks and regulators play important roles in modern economies. Their policies have profound impact on the economic and financial stability of their countries and, ultimately, the lives of their citizens. Throughout history, many countries have suffered when the central bank or financial regulator failed in their functions. For instance, hyperinflation, balance of payments crises and financial system crises can often be traced to monetary instability or weaknesses in financial regulation. Conversely, central banks can improve the well-being of countries through sound monetary policies and effective regulation. I am glad that over the past four decades, MAS has fulfilled its mission well and contributed significantly to Singapore's development.

MAS' Contributions to Singapore

First, MAS has ensured price stability. A low inflation environment supports long-term planning and economic growth, and preserves real incomes and wealth. Key to this is a strong Singapore Dollar, which MAS manages through its exchange rate-centred monetary policy. Over the last 40 years, excluding the oil crisis years of 1973–74, consumer price inflation in Singapore averaged about 2% per year, one of the lowest in the world. Although inflation has increased in recent years due to external factors such as the prices of energy and commodities, over the past 10 years the average inflation rate has only been about 1.6%.

Second, MAS has grown the real value of our official foreign reserves (OFR). We are a small nation with few natural resources. Our reserves, of which the OFR are an important part, provide us the means to ride out economic and financial storms. The OFR in particular helps to maintain confidence in the Singapore Dollar in times of crisis, and defend the currency against speculative attacks. Under MAS' prudent management, our OFR have grown from about US$1.4 billion (in 1971) to more than US$200 billion today (about 50× in real terms).

Third, MAS has ensured the safety and stability of our financial sector. As a small economy that is plugged into the international system, Singapore has always been vulnerable to external events and contagion. Yet despite the turmoil in the global economy these past few years, our financial system has not only remained stable, but has been viewed as a safe harbour in a turbulent sea. Credit must go to MAS for its sound regulation and rigorous supervision.

Fourth, MAS has developed Singapore as an international financial centre. The financial sector is now 12% of Singapore's GDP, more than double its contribution 40 years ago. Singapore is one of the leading centres in Asia for foreign exchange and derivatives trading; asset management and private banking; and insurance and reinsurance. More than 150 foreign banks are located here, including several regional headquarters. This has created many good jobs for Singaporeans and contributed to our dynamism and prosperity.

Credit must go to MAS' leaders and staff for their professionalism, hard work and commitment to Singapore. For example, former Chairman Dr Goh Keng Swee restructured MAS' key functions and introduced important policies such as our exchange rate-centred monetary policy. MAS has also had a succession of capable Managing Directors, including Mr Michael Wong who laid a firm foundation as MAS' first Managing Director, and Mr J. Y. Pillay who oversaw organisational changes to strengthen MAS for the challenges of its time. All MAS officers have contributed to MAS' success, and should be proud of what MAS has achieved.

Benefitting from the Singapore System

MAS has not done this alone. It has worked closely with industry to develop the financial sector in a stable and sustainable manner. It has also forged good relations with its international counterparts, whose experiences and cooperation are valuable in our inter-connected world.

Above all, MAS has done well because of the larger Singapore system within which it operates. Singapore's strong political leadership and sound policy fundamentals provide a conducive environment for MAS to pursue its mission independently and effectively.

For many years, the government has maintained an unwavering commitment to fiscal prudence and macroeconomic stability. Given a sound fiscal policy, MAS could concentrate on keeping prices stable, free from the pressure to finance government deficits. Singapore's flexible economic structure, particularly our flexible labour markets, enabled the economy to adjust more quickly to shocks. This reduced the burden on monetary policy to effect adjustments in the real economy and allowed MAS to focus on long-term price stability.

Our legal system is underpinned by a firm adherence to the rule of law and an effective, incorrupt judiciary. This has fostered a regulatory environment that is transparent, predictable and consistent, and promoted trust among the industry and consumers. These are important attributes in the financial sector. MAS benefits from this wider context.

Finally, MAS has benefitted from Singapore's openness to the world and Singaporeans' willingness to work hard and upgrade themselves. On these foundations we have built a vibrant, dynamic and cosmopolitan economy that attracts a wide range of investments. In turn, this economy has facilitated the growth of the financial sector.

How the World and Singapore are Changing

Nevertheless, as our distinguished guests from the financial industry know too well, past performance is no guarantee of future success. We cannot take the future for granted. Our environment is changing and so must we.

This is a critical period for the global economy and financial system. The effects of the 2008 crisis are still being felt. The underlying problems facing the global economy — indebtedness and imbalances — remain unresolved, in particular in Europe. We are experiencing a fundamental reshaping of the economic and financial landscape. Singapore must adjust to this new environment.

Globally, the economic centre of gravity is shifting to Asia. Although the advanced economies remain big markets and world leaders in technology and innovation, their economic growth will likely slow amidst fiscal consolidation and deleveraging. Emerging economies, especially in Asia, are doing well although they are not immune from the troubles in the West. Asian financial markets will continue to deepen and grow in sophistication but volatility will increase as shocks are transmitted more quickly around the world.

Domestically, our economy and society are maturing. We need to keep moving up the value chain to thrive in this more competitive world. Productivity and innovation will be even more important drivers of growth as we run against the constraints of our small size.

Future Challenges for MAS

These developments have deep implications for MAS. I highlight four challenges for MAS.

First, maintaining price stability amidst a more volatile global environment. Because of the economic and political uncertainties in the EU and US, and the worries over global deleveraging and rebalancing, financial markets and capital flows will continue to be volatile, and asset price inflation will remain a risk. At the same time, energy and commodities prices continue to fluctuate around elevated levels. MAS must address these issues to keep prices stable and maintain the pre-conditions for economic growth.

Second, safeguarding the real value of our OFR in a more challenging and risky investment climate. In an environment of lower returns and higher risk, it is all the more important for MAS to preserve the real value of our OFR, to maintain confidence and deter speculation in the Singapore Dollar.

Third, ensuring the safety, soundness and efficiency of the financial system in an increasingly interconnected world. It is neither realistic nor practicable for MAS to aim for zero failures in our financial system. But MAS' regulatory and supervisory regime should be regularly updated and risk-stratified to mitigate downside risks, especially to the public. MAS must remain alert to new developments in the financial sector. Regulation has to keep pace with new products and processes, and larger and more diverse institutions. MAS must take a system-wide perspective, factor in the risks of contagion and prevent the build-up of systemic risks in asset markets or stresses in the banking system so as to preserve financial stability.

Fourth, strengthening our competitiveness as a financial centre. In a highly competitive global environment, MAS must constantly review Singapore's value proposition and growth strategy. Competition from emerging financial centres in the region is intensifying, but the opportunities in Asia, such as infrastructure development and wealth management, are growing rapidly too. MAS needs to continue leveraging on Singapore's system-wide capabilities to strengthen our position as an international financial centre.

Conclusion

MAS has done well over the last 40 years. From its humble beginnings, it is now a key institution of governance in Singapore, an enlightened regulator of our financial industry and a respected partner in the international community. The journey ahead will be every bit as challenging. If MAS remains focused on its mission and displays the same spirit of innovation as in the past, I am confident that MAS will have a bright future.

I congratulate MAS again on its 40th anniversary. Thank you.

Building Credibility

Mr Tharman Shanmugaratnam
Deputy Prime Minister and Chairman, MAS

Opening of the MAS Gallery

16 February 2016

ESM Goh Chok Tong
Family members of Former Chairmen Mr Hon Sui Sen and Dr Goh Keng Swee, and of Former Managing Director Mr Lim Kim San
Former Managing Directors, Mr Michael Wong Pakshong, Mr J. Y. Pillay and Mr Lee Ek Tieng
Current Board Members
Members of the MAS Management and Staff
MAS Pioneers

Thank you to everyone for coming to the opening of our MAS Gallery.

The Gallery is aimed at helping the public understand the mission of the MAS, and its role in promoting both growth and stability of the Singapore economy and financial system.

The Gallery aims to help the public understand:

- how we keep inflation low over the long term through MAS' policies in managing the exchange rate of the Singapore dollar;
- how we supervise the financial sector — the banking, insurance and securities industries — to ensure confidence in our financial system;

- how we promote the development of a vibrant financial centre that serves a good part of Asia and in some respects the rest of the world; and
- how we also seek to ensure that the financial system serves the interests of consumers, and how we try to help Singaporeans manage their finances well.

The MAS staff responsible for the Gallery have put a lot of thought into its design and content. But the Gallery will keep evolving, and we will want it to stay relevant to Singaporeans young and old.

It is significant too that we are opening the Gallery in 2016, when we commemorate the 45th anniversary of the MAS. If we think about what we have achieved in these 45 years, what's most precious is credibility. Credibility is the most precious asset that a central bank and a financial regulator can have.

The MAS' credibility was founded in its early years. I want to mention the leaders and staff who put in place these foundations of today's credibility. Mr Hon Sui Sen in particular, our first Chairman (1971–1980), Mr Michael Wong Pakshong, who was the Managing Director, and the staff at that time, including Mr Ng Kok Song, Mrs Ong-Ang Ai Boon, Mrs Elizabeth Sam. Together they built an organisation, bringing together no fewer than nine different offices and functions in Government at the time, melding them together in one organisation.

They also set the foundations for an international financial centre. Singapore was not a serious financial centre until then. Mr Hon Sui Sen and his team built the foundation for a financial centre that went beyond Singapore. In Mr Hon's words, said back in 1972:

> In Asia, Singapore now offers the best prospects for developing into a financial centre, if not for the whole of Asia, at least beyond the Southeast Asian or ASEAN region.

So it started then, and continued through the years when Dr Goh Keng Swee became Chairman (1980–85). But the most important development in this second phase, starting when Dr Goh led the MAS, was the re-orienting of our monetary policy to one centred on the S$ exchange rate. It was a novel policy at the time. We were one of the few central banks that managed monetary policy by focusing exclusively on the exchange rate. It was not conventional, but it has worked.

Through that second phase in MAS' evolution, with Dr Goh as Chairman and subsequently under Dr Richard Hu's chairmanship (1985–1997), we built credibility in our exchange rate-centred monetary policy. We also built credibility as a no-nonsense financial regulator. That was a very important second phase, in the 1980s and 1990s.

The third phase began when PM Lee Hsien Loong, then DPM, took over as Chairman of MAS (1998–2004). It involved liberalising and opening up our financial sector to greater competition, and at the same time developing further resilience in the system. This third phase continued through the years when ESM Goh was Chairman (2004–2011).

This seemed a contradiction in terms to many countries — liberalising and opening up but at the same time developing resilience in the financial centre. But we have achieved both. We have managed the tension between liberalisation and developing resilience. I think we have managed it rather well. If you look at what happened during the Asian Financial Crisis and subsequently, the Global Financial Crisis, we have come out as one of the safest financial systems in the world.

So that was an important third phase — liberalising and opening the financial centre but also developing further resilience.

Our credibility today rests on each of these three major phases in MAS' development and policies — from the foundational years, to the period when we reoriented monetary policy and then in the last phase, liberalising and developing further resilience of the financial centre. The credibility has added up over the years.

I also want to say that MAS has become an organisation of excellence. This has particularly been due, in my opinion, to the organisational development efforts that began especially in the mid-1980s, when Mr J. Y. Pillay came in as the Managing Director, followed in subsequent years by Mr Lee Ek Tieng.

There was a great focus on organisational development from the mid-80s. It happened that both Mr Pillay and Mr Lee were amongst the most senior leaders in the public sector. They led the transformation of the MAS as an organisation of people. We developed an organisation that provided strong careers for individuals and ensured they worked as teams. It has been a very important effort, this organisational development.

And the third thing I want to mention that is very important to the MAS is its growth of professional expertise. A central bank and financial regulator requires depth of expertise, more so than the general arms of government typically do. We need serious specialists — people who spend years developing expertise in particular fields of MAS' responsibilities. That too is behind our credibility, because you need expertise to have credibility.

Through the years we have developed outstanding professionals, held in high esteem by their peers internationally — Ng Kok Song, Koh Beng Seng, Mrs Foo-Yap Siew Hong who served us for 39 years, Ms Teo Swee Lian, Ong Chong Tee and many others. Our present Managing Director, Mr Ravi Menon, is another example, someone who grew up as a professional within the organisation. We have to keep building deep professional expertise in each of the areas that we engage in.

When you add it all up, MAS is now one of the best-regarded central banks and financial regulators in the world. And it is because of our people. Our people are very well regarded internationally and as an organisation we punch above our weight. That comes from years building up our organisation and building up our people.

Finally I want to thank all the staff — our pioneers as well as current staff, in all the roles that you perform in, in various areas in MAS. Some of you have been through a few or even several departments in your career. I want to thank all of you for making MAS what it is today.

I hope this Gallery is a testament to your work in building up an MAS that has credibility, at home in Singapore and all over the world.

MONETARY POLICY AND RESERVE MANAGEMENT

Monetary Policy and Reserve Management

The speeches and articles in this section explain the philosophy and conduct of MAS' unique exchange rate-centred monetary policy; MAS' emergence as a full-fledged central bank following the merger with BCCS; the evolution of MAS' macroprudential policies as a complement to monetary policy; MAS' approach to managing the external reserves accumulated through its monetary policy actions; and the scope for monetary integration in Asia.

An Exchange Rate-Centred Monetary Policy

A 1980 speech by Mr Michael Wong Pakshong provides a vivid picture of how central banks in the 1970s had been struggling to tame the scourge of high inflation. During that time, MAS used a variety of monetary instruments to contain inflation, with mixed results.

The quest for price stability eventually led to the adoption of an exchange rate-centred monetary policy framework in 1981. Addressing Parliament in 1984, Dr Goh Keng Swee explained why MAS had to operate monetary policy differently from other central banks. Dr Goh articulated the rationale for MAS' exchange rate-centred monetary policy framework and explained why regulating the supply of money — a common instrument of monetary policy in many central banks at the time — was not pertinent to Singapore.

In 1985, when Singapore went into recession, the Singapore dollar came under strong speculative attack. In two consecutive short statements to the media, Dr Goh sought to dispel the misguided belief that the Singapore government had wanted a cheaper Singapore dollar on the premise that it would benefit the export industries. Dr Goh clarified that a weaker currency would do little to boost exports given the high import content of Singapore's exports. At the same time, the ensuing increase in inflation unleashed by the depreciation would lead to a rise in wages, negating any initial competitive benefits from the depreciation. On Dr Goh's instructions, MAS intervened in the foreign exchange and money markets to counter the speculation. Within days, the exchange rate recovered, cementing MAS' resolve and ability to defend the Singapore dollar.

In a seminal article in 1992, Dr Teh Kok Peng and Mr Tharman Shanmugaratnam formally expounded the rationale for the choice of the exchange rate as the instrument of monetary policy. Being a small open economy with very high dependence on imports, the exchange rate rather than the interest rate had a direct influence on inflation. Further, with virtually no controls on capital flows, it would be difficult for MAS to target the domestic interest rate. The article also explained the way monetary policy was conducted in Singapore, with MAS intervening in the foreign exchange market to manage the float of a trade-weighted exchange rate of the Singapore dollar within a policy band.

A Full-Fledged Central Bank

In 2002, MAS merged with the Board of Commissioners of Currency Singapore (BCCS) to become a full-fledged central bank. Speaking in Parliament, Mr Lim Hng Kiang noted that the merger allowed for the rationalisation of common functions without compromising the overriding objective of managing the currency and maintaining confidence in the Singapore dollar.

Evolution of Macroprudential Policies

At the inaugural Asian Monetary Policy Forum in 2014, Mr Ravi Menon noted that while the global financial crisis of 2008–09 demonstrated that macroeconomic stability did not guarantee financial stability, there was no consensus on how to secure financial stability and whether monetary policy had a role to play. Mr Menon said expansionary monetary policies globally posed risks to financial stability, household leverage, and asset price inflation in many emerging market economies. He laid out Singapore's approach of focusing monetary policy on price stability and employing macroprudential policies to promote financial stability, household prudence, and a sustainable property market.

Managing Singapore's External Reserves

In a 2019 speech in London, Mr Menon gave an account of how Singapore's external reserves were managed. For a city-state with no natural resources, Singapore's reserves provided an important buffer during crises, served as an endowment from which income was drawn to help finance government expenditures, and helped to undergird confidence in the Singapore dollar. MAS was one of three entities managing Singapore's financial assets, alongside the Government of Singapore Investment Corporation and Temasek Holdings. Given its monetary policy function, MAS' tranche of reserves was the most conservatively managed among the three, with an emphasis on liquidity.

Scope for Asian Monetary Integration

In his Per Jacobsson Lecture in 2006, Mr Shanmugaratnam observed that, as Asia recovered strongly from the 1997–98 financial crisis, the debate on Asian monetary integration had evolved. The conventional wisdom regarding the merits of optimal currency areas and intermediate exchange rate regimes had also shifted, with the emergence of a more nuanced view in favour of reducing excessive exchange rate volatility through the use of various policy instruments. Mr Shanmugaratnam argued that these shifts, and the greater heterogeneity of starting conditions in Asia, suggested that the euro experience might not be entirely relevant for the region, as the costs of losing monetary and exchange rate independence would outweigh the benefits from having a single currency. He suggested that the prevailing path towards *de facto* monetary coordination in Asia — characterised by managed float regimes and commitment to low and stable inflation — would be superior to any attempt aimed at formal currency coordination.

How to Cope with Inflation with Particular Reference to Singapore

Mr Michael Wong Pakshong
Managing Director, MAS
Hong Kong Management Association Conference
19 September 1980

The theme 'Living with Inflation', which your Association has chosen for this year's Conference, is indeed apt as it is of interest to all of us, whether as consumers or as policy-makers. I do not have the answer to inflation but nevertheless, I am pleased to be here this morning to share some thoughts on the subject with you based on the Singapore experiences.

The last time I had the pleasure of attending your annual Conference and addressing you was in 1975. Most of the world's economies were then recovering from one of the worst post-war recessions. It was a unique experience as recession with widespread unemployment occurred simultaneously with severe inflationary pressures. Today, five years later, the panacea for inflation has still not been found and in fact, there are indications that the problem is more deeply entrenched in most of the world's economies. Inflationary forces are still raging in the major industrial nations.

Developing and less developed countries have also not been spared from the menace of inflation. Its effects have been pervasive not only in countries which practice free enterprise but also apparently in the socialist states. This, therefore, raises the question of whether inflation is here to stay and that perhaps, at best, the economists and policy-makers can only control this economic disease but are powerless in eradicating it.

Inflation has been described by Mr Arthur Burns, former Chairman of the Federal Reserve Board in the United States "as the economic equivalent of high blood pressure". I fully concur with Mr Burns when he likens the damage which inflation can do to the economy to that which high blood pressure does to the human body. Just as high blood pressure threatens the lives of those who suffer from it, persistent inflation, if left unchecked, would similarly weaken the economic health of a nation.

Your Association too realises that there is no solution yet for the problem of inflation. Hence, I have not been asked to speak on 'How to Solve the Problem of Inflation' but on 'How to Cope with It'. I believe this is what has happened in the world's economies. Countries have merely been or are coping with the problem of inflation rather than solving it. Perhaps, some countries have been more successful than others in handling the problem. Singapore has not been spared the ravages of inflation. But fortunately, except for the period 1973/74, price increases have not reached a level where it has become a problem requiring top priority attention in our economic management. Nevertheless, we monitor our rate of inflation closely and use all instruments and measures available to prevent the rise from getting out of hand.

In the 1960s, our general price level was relatively stable with the consumer price index averaging increases of no more than 1 to 2% a year. As inflationary pressures built up in some of the major world economies in the early 1970s, precipitated by the quadrupling of oil prices, the general price level in Singapore also started to rise. This increase reached an unprecedented level of more than 22% in 1973 and 1974. The acceleration in consumer prices was, however, successfully brought down to 2.6% in 1975 when Singapore also experienced its lowest rate of real GDP growth of 4%. In 1976, consumer prices even showed a decline of 1.9%. However, since then, prices have been on the rise again. In the first half of this year, the consumer price index registered an average growth of 9.7%. In comparison with the experience in 1973 and 1974, this increase is not high but it is nevertheless higher than the range of price increases of 3 to 5% each year in the last quarter of the 1970 decade. It has become evident that inflationary pressures are accumulating in the Singapore economy. But so far, there is no cause for alarm. We do not expect a repetition of the 1973 and 1974 price escalation.

In outlining Singapore's experience in coping with inflation, it is also necessary to identify the sources of inflationary pressures. Being a small and open economy, Singapore is essentially a price-taker in the world markets for both its exports and imports. This characteristic works to the disadvantage as well as the advantage of Singapore or more generally, for a small open economy which is also totally free from exchange control. This means that the world's inflationary pressures are more easily transmitted into the country. Singapore cannot avoid the rise in international prices of crude oil, raw materials, food and manufactured goods.

Being the third largest oil refining centre in the world has helped Singapore in ensuring an adequate supply of oil for a longer period when oil shortages occurred in the world. This has, however, not insulated Singapore from the effects of the world's oil price increases. The 1973 and the current oil price escalation have contributed directly to the rising energy costs in Singapore. Utilities and transport costs have increased sharply in 1974 after the 1973 oil price hike and again in 1979 and the first half of this year. In these instances, prices in Singapore have been allowed to rise as part of the aim is to encourage energy conservation.

As Singapore is a resource-scarce economy, almost all its requirements of consumer, intermediate and capital goods are imported. Apart from oil, Singapore has a high degree of dependence on foreign supply of food. The food item carries a weightage of close to 50% in the consumer price index. The changes in food prices, particularly rice and other cereals, have been the single most important factor contributing to the movements in the consumer price index. This was seen in 1974 when the pressure from rising food prices, compounded by increasing energy costs, resulted in one of the highest rates of increase in consumer prices on record. In 1979 and for the first half of this year, despite increasing energy costs, pressures on price increases have not been as strong as in 1974, as the rise in international prices of rice, wheat and other food products has not been as high.

The advantage of being a small economy is that the possibility of diversifying and switching to more competitive import sources is there. We have indeed diversified our sources of imports during the 1970s, particularly for intermediate and manufactured goods. This has contributed towards keeping our inflationary pressures reduced. Apart from the diversification of sources of supply, the Government has also been gradually dismantling tariff protection for local industries. While these measures are aimed largely at encouraging the upgrading and improving the competitiveness of such industries, they have also helped to bring down imported inflation.

Another factor which has helped to moderate imported price inflation is the appreciation of the Singapore dollar. The decision to float the Singapore dollar in mid-1973 was partly to alleviate the problem of sharp price increases, by having a more realistic rate for our currency. Over the years, the continued favourable economic performance of the Singapore economy has permitted a strong Singapore dollar to be maintained. This policy is also made possible by the continued foreign capital inflows into Singapore. Despite the persistent trade and current account deficits, the overall balance of payments has consistently been in surplus. This has exceeded S$1 billion each year in the past two years. With the strength of the Singapore dollar being maintained, Singapore's import prices have not risen as rapidly as the increase in the world's export prices. Between 1973 and 1979, Singapore's unit value index for imports rose by about 80% compared with the rise of over 100% in the world's export prices.

From the demand side, the pressures from domestic sources have also been contained to some extent. Government fiscal policy has always been one of financial prudence. Throughout the 1970 decade, the Government has always had an overall operating budget surplus each year. For the public sector as a whole, a surplus had also been achieved except for the 1975 financial year when prospects of slower economic growth necessitated increased public sector development expenditure as a means of pump-priming the economy. The public sector has, therefore, generally been a deflationary factor in Singapore.

Financial operations of the Government have also been a restraining factor on inflation. This is essentially in the large mobilisation of domestic savings through the Central Provident Fund scheme. The Central Provident Fund is a compulsory savings scheme for all employees in Singapore. When the scheme was introduced in the 1950s, the contribution rate was only 10% of the employees' total wages. Today, the rate has risen to 38.5%. Employers are required to contribute 20.5% of the employees' wages into the Fund while the employees contribute 18% from their wages. In 1979, the gross contributions to the Fund totalled S$1.9 billion. This is approximately 10% of our gross domestic product at current prices. These large contributions to the Central Provident Fund have, therefore, helped to sterilise a significant amount of potential purchasing power or potential demand for goods and services. It has, therefore, helped to dampen the strong consumer demand arising from an expanding economy. In any case, the rise in consumer demand following increases in disposal income is reflected in import leakages because of the openness of the Singapore economy.

Since 1975, monetary policy has been largely accommodative and has not aggravated price increases. The main objective of monetary policy has been to provide adequate liquidity to facilitate economic growth and to maintain price stability. During the 1970s, Singapore's gross domestic product at current prices grew at an average rate of 14.8% while money supply (Ml) expanded by 15.6% per annum. This close and parallel development in economic growth and monetary expansion during the past ten years has been achieved amidst turbulence in the international monetary system. Monetary policy has, therefore, not exacerbated inflationary pressures in Singapore.

Public authorities and consumer bodies have also been effective in checking profiteering and ensuring adequate supplies of essential commodities as well as providing the benefits of co-operatives. In addition, consumer education and imposition of price restraints to change consumption patterns are among the more direct measures taken to help moderate price increases. Inflation in the housing market for a large sector of the population has also been minimised through the Government's extensive public housing programme. In Singapore, about 65% of the population live in flats built by the Housing and Development Board, a Government agency, entrusted with the provision of housing for the lower income groups. About 58% of these Housing and Development Board flats are owner-occupied. Another Government-related organisation, the Housing and Urban Development Corporation, has also been recently increasing its development programme to improve the housing needs of the middle income groups.

In conclusion, it can be said that the mix of fiscal and monetary policies as well as Government regulations and positive actions have resulted in low inflationary expectations in Singapore. This has contributed significantly towards containing any excessive price increases. This is evident from the experience in 1973 and 1974 when the rise in the general price level was brought down sharply to less than 3% in 1975 after increases of more than 22% in these two preceding years. Although inflationary pressures have been brought down to a more manageable level, we may have to recognise the fact that our economy is developing an inflationary bias due to our continued emphasis on economic growth. Hence, we will have to continue to monitor closely price movements and their sources of growth and to take the necessary actions to keep the rate of inflation down to a tolerable level. We have not been able to eradicate the problem of inflation but we have been able, so far, to cope with it.

Which of the Monetary Aggregates Does MAS Watch?

Dr Goh Keng Swee
First Deputy Prime Minister and Minister for Education, and Chairman, MAS
Second Reading Speech in Parliament
Monetary Authority of Singapore (Amendment) Bill
24 August 1984

I wish to take this opportunity to explain to Members some aspects of the arcane art of Central Banking as practised in industrial countries and in Singapore. The classical model of a Central Bank is the Bank of England in Victorian England. Today it is the Federal Reserve System of the United States which carries most weight in the world's financial system, far in excess of the proportion of the world's GNP generated in the US.

Central Banks, whether of the classical mould or in its modern variety, perform two essential functions:

(i) They regulate the supply of money;
(ii) They regulate banks.

A third function has been added since the collapse in 1971 of the Bretton Woods system of fixed exchange rate parities. Central Banks look after the external value of their nations' money by active intervention or benign neglect or, in some unhappy instances, by desperate improvisation.

The Monetary Authority of Singapore (MAS) is Singapore's Central Bank. However, because of the unique feature of Singapore's economy, the way it works is quite different from the practices of the Bank of England or the Federal Reserve System. This is not because we are perverse by nature. It is because the structure of our economy and the manner Government manages the public sector introduces a novel situation probably without parallel elsewhere.

Let me explain this by reference to the three Central Banking functions. Every economics freshman knows that Central Banks of industrial countries keep a close watch on money supply in an effort to counter inflation which got out of hand in the late 1970s and early 1980s. The Federal Reserve System tracks three measures of money supply called Ml, M2 and M3. I will not explain what these Ms mean except to say that their definitions vary from time to time, as they must when major financial innovations take place.

What is important to note is that the Federal Reserve System aims to keep the growth of these monetary aggregates within publicly stated limits; in the case of Ml, the current limits are between 4% and 8% annual rates of growth. The Federal Reserve System is not alone among Western Central Banks in having to check the growth of money supply. There are two reasons why Central Banks have to control the money supply. First, people are fed up with inflation. Second, people also do not want to pay the price of fighting inflation in the only sensible way, that is, for the Government to balance the budget and for the country to live within its means.

Under the system of one-man-one-vote, governments are elected to deliver the good things of life. However, the voters are not easily persuaded that these must be paid for by taxes. Taxes are unpopular everywhere, with or without representation.

The result is predictable — huge budget deficits which have to be financed by government borrowing. Where savings are high, as in Japan, budget deficits can be easily absorbed; where savings are low, as in the United States, these deficits have to be financed in three ways: savings of Americans, savings of foreigners and credit creation by the Central Bank. Since the last option is closed by anti-inflation policy, the US budget deficit, now running at record highs, is financed by the first two means, i.e., savings of Americans and savings of foreigners. The Federal Reserve, by keeping money supply under control in the face of large budget deficits, has caused US real rates of interest to rise to unprecedented heights, thereby drawing in large amounts of foreign capital. In effect, a good part of the US government budget deficit is financed by foreign loans. Only a rich and powerful country like America can conduct this kind of fiscal policy without attracting the stern gaze of the International Monetary Fund.

In Singapore, which of the monetary aggregates does the MAS watch, Ml, M2 or M3? The answer is none. This does not prevent the Government from regularly publishing data on our Ml, M2 and M3. From time to time, academics perform clever statistical exercises to trace the relationship of these numbers with others, the Consumer Price Index, for instance.

Why do we ignore our Ms? For the very reason Western Central Banks have to watch theirs. Their public sector accounts are in a state of chronic deficit; ours are in a state of chronic surplus. We are in a state of chronic surplus because employees have 50% of their pay packets sequestered into the Central Provident Fund. Further, the Finance Ministry does not pan easily with the revenues harvested by its assiduous tax collectors.

So the MAS is probably the only Central Bank that does not have to watch the Ms. What then does it watch? It watches the foreign exchange rates. The collapse of the Bretton Woods system was due to the improvident nature of elected governments, under constant pressure from voters to live beyond their means. This event, i.e., the collapse of the Bretton Woods system, is much to be regretted for, in a world of gyrating foreign exchange rates, it is not a comfortable one for Central Banks of small countries.

Let me explain how the MAS works the system of floating rates. We create what is called a basket of currencies. Anybody can create his own basket. Ours is based on the value of trade with major trading partners. We — that is the Ministry of Finance, the Ministry of Trade and Industry in consultation with the MAS — decide the future worth of this basket. In other words, the value of the Singapore dollar in terms of the US dollar, the Japanese yen, the Deutschmark, Pound Sterling, etc. Upper and lower limits are then set and the MAS is given authority to manage the float within these limits. This is done by buying or selling foreign currencies against the Singapore dollar or by swap operations. The intervention currency is usually the US dollar, as is the practice with nearly all Central Banks. That is why Mr Paul Volcker is such an important person.

Because the public sector is in a state of chronic surplus, funds regularly flow from the banks into the MAS because Government accounts, other than for petty cash, are kept with the MAS. If these funds are not re-circulated back to the banks, the system will soon seize up. Funds are returned to banks when the MAS buys foreign currencies. Such purchases also serve the purpose of keeping the Singapore dollar from appreciating too much.

It works beautifully guided by Adam Smith's gentle, invisible hand. So long as we continue to work diligently and skilfully, so long as we spend carefully, and so long as we do not lend Singapore dollars to foreigners, it will continue to work beautifully — unless some calamity overtakes the world banking system. Do not bother about the horrendous deficit in our balance of trade. That will look after itself. The free enterprise system rewards those great Victorian virtues of industry and thrift. But alas these human traits are unfashionable in the contemporary world. As a result, the services of economists are in great demand everywhere to find out what has gone wrong and how to put it right. Unfortunately, the profession gives conflicting advice on both diagnosis and prescription.

Let me now turn to the other function of a Central Bank, the regulation of banks. Banks in Singapore conduct business in our currency as well as in foreign currencies. The latter business is conducted mostly by large international banks who have established branches here.

Off-shore banking business in Singapore is an off-shoot of the Euro-currency market. One feature of the Euro-market is relative freedom from regulation by the Central Bank of the host country. Indeed it is freedom from regulation that is the *raison d'être* of off-shore banking. No Central Bank wants to be too fussy about off-shore banking for fear that the banks will move elsewhere.

However, the banking failures in 1974 of the Herstatt Bank and the Franklin National Bank forcefully reminded members of the rich countries'

Central Banks club, the Bank for International Settlements at Basel, how vulnerable a totally unregulated market could be. This led to the formation in 1975 of the Basel Committee, also known as the Cooke Committee, which laid down guidelines on Central Banks' supervisory roles. These guidelines became grandly known as the Basel Concordat.

The 1975 Concordat was revised in 1983 in the light of developments in banking practices, banking supervisory techniques and experience in applying the Concordat. The 1983 Concordat clarifies that it does not address itself to lender of last resort aspects of the role of central banks. The 1975 Concordat was misunderstood by the media to include this aspect, i.e., lender of last resort, when Banco Ambrosiano of Luxembourg collapsed in 1982 under scandalous circumstances. In addition, the 1983 Concordat incorporates the principle of consolidated supervision to enable parent authorities to monitor the overall risk exposures and capital adequacy of banking groups. Under the principles of supervision laid down in the 1983 Concordat, the supervision of solvency of foreign banking branches is defined as the primary responsibility of parent authorities while that of subsidiaries as the joint responsibility of the parent and host authorities. The supervision of liquidity for both foreign banking branches and subsidiaries is stated as the primary responsibility of the host authorities.

These matters are of importance to Singapore as an international financial centre. We are members of an entity called "The Off-shore Supervisors Group" formed in 1980 representing 14 countries which offer host facilities to off-shore financial institutions. The group conducts periodic discussions with the Cooke Committee. In one of these discussions, members of the Group and the Cooke Committee agreed that they would discourage their banks from establishing in financial centres where there are no proper and adequate systems of supervision.

I draw attention to these matters, even though they do not directly concern the Bill, to show that the supervision of banks in their international activities is a complex and delicate business and that comprehensive, binding and clearly defined principles have yet to be established. It could well be that central banking can never be reduced to vigorously defined rules and we must learn to live with uncertainty. The subject is of concern to Singapore and the well-informed Singaporean should keep abreast of events.

A revision of the MAS Act is now timely. The Act was introduced in 1970 and amended once in 1972. Since 1972, however, there have been substantial changes in the structure of the financial market, together with a proliferation of different types of financial institutions. Over this period, the number of commercial banks has increased from 44 in 1972 to 125. Also, the number of merchant banks has increased, from five to 51. In addition, there are currently four discount houses, eight international money brokers and five credit card companies.

Furthermore, in recent years there have been structural changes in the financial operations of the Government and an increasingly significant portion of the Government's activities are being carried out through statutory boards and government-related companies. Since one of the objects of the Authority is to act as banker and financial agent to the Government, the Authority's powers in this regard should be extended so as to take into account these changes.

With these introductory comments, I will now deal with the main provisions in the Bill. The proposals in the Bill, in general terms, will:

(a) provide greater autonomy upon the Authority in relation to employment of its staff and make changes to the organisational structure of the Authority; and
(b) widen the scope of the Authority's functions and duties to enable it better to perform its role as regulator of the financial system as well as banker and advisor to the Government, having regard to the changes that have occurred in the financial environment.

The principal amendment affecting the structure of the Authority appears in clause 3. These amendments would enable the President to have greater flexibility than at present in the appointment of directors to the board of directors of the Authority as well as the deputy chairman of the board.

With reference to the amendments dealing with the Authority in relation to employment of its staff, it should be mentioned that since October 1981 the Public Service Commission has granted autonomy on personnel matters to all statutory boards. Moreover, consequent to its reorganisation, a personnel policy was adopted to attract and retain able staff, bearing in mind the competition from the well-paid banking sector is quite severe. To reflect this policy, section 17 of the Act has been repealed and re-enacted in clause 6 to confer upon the Authority powers to appoint employees, determine their remuneration and terms and conditions of their employment, to appoint advisors and to make rules for these purposes.

In addition, opportunity has been taken to revise certain other provisions of the Act which affect existing, future and former employees of the Authority. As regards former employees of the Authority, the obligation to preserve secrecy in relation to the affairs of the Authority has been extended to them (clause 5). In relation to existing and future employees, protection is conferred upon them in clause 8 from personal liability in relation to acts done in good faith in the course of the discharge of their duties under the Act. Further, since the Authority can only grant housing and vehicle loans to employees, there is a need to extend this power to grant loans for other purposes approved by the Authority, for example, the purchase of micro-computers for personal use. Clause 16 confers such a power upon the Authority.

The next group of amendments seek to widen the scope of the Authority's functions to embrace changes that have occurred in the financial operations of the Government. They would empower the Authority amongst other things:

(a) to pay at its discretion interest on deposits;
(b) to accept deposits from companies in which the Government has substantial interests; and
(c) to act as agent in respect of companies in which the Government has a substantial interest.

Clauses 9 and 14 so provide. The aim of the amendment so described is to furnish such Government companies in which the Government has a substantial interest an alternative avenue to place surplus funds at their discretion, as the funds of these companies are essentially public funds.

Also, it will be noted that the Authority will assume additional responsibilities in respect of the Insurance Act and the Securities Industry Act (clause 7).

Moving on to another matter which also concerns the powers of the Authority, I draw attention to clause 13. The purpose of clause 13 is to provide a regulatory framework for the increasing number of other financial institutions that do not fall entirely within either the Banking or the Finance Companies Acts. These institutions such as merchant banks, discount houses and credit card companies have come to exert a significant impact on monetary and credit conditions in the country in recent years. A new section 24C is accordingly inserted which empowers the Authority to require financial institutions whose operations are considered to affect:

(a) monetary stability and credit and exchange conditions in Singapore; or
(b) the development of Singapore as a financial centre; or
(c) the financial situation in Singapore generally, to be approved by the Authority for the purpose of carrying on business in Singapore. Approval may be withdrawn in certain circumstances by the Authority, though an aggrieved financial institution has a right to appeal against a withdrawal to the Minister.

Additionally, the Authority will be empowered to issue directions, guidelines and conditions of operations to approved financial institutions in relation to such matters as the activities they may engage in or the range of service that they may provide. An additional new section 24D allows the Authority to levy fees on such financial institutions. The only other clause in the Bill that is worthy of special mention is clause 17. This clause would confer a qualified immunity upon the Authority from defamation actions. Such an immunity is considered necessary if the Authority is to properly discharge its supervisory functions over financial institutions. This kind of provision is not new in our law for a similar immunity has been conferred on the Securities Industry Council in recent amendments made to the Companies Act.

Sir, I beg to move.

Singapore Parl Debates; Vol 44; Sitting No 7; Col 1982–1999; 24 August 1984.

Why a Strong Singapore Dollar?

Dr Goh Keng Swee
Deputy Chairman, MAS

Press statements issued when the Singapore Dollar came under speculative attack

Following the onset of recession in Singapore in mid-1985, the Singapore Dollar came under speculative attack. MAS, under the direction of its then Deputy Chairman, Dr Goh Keng Swee, issued a public statement on 16 September 1985 to explain the government's reasons for a strong currency. At the same time, MAS also intervened in the foreign exchange markets to support the Singapore Dollar and simultaneously withdrew market liquidity — thereby causing overnight interest rates to soar above 100% in order to punish short-sellers.

These actions inflicted heavy losses on the speculators and convinced financial markets that MAS was serious in not allowing the currency to weaken. In all, MAS only used about US$100 million (or less than 1%) of its foreign exchange reserves but the Singapore dollar quickly recovered. On 18 September 1985, MAS issued a second statement to signal that its intervention had "achieved its purpose" and conveyed why. Speculators were also well advised "to leave the Singapore dollar alone" and warned "this exercise will be repeated if speculation on the Singapore dollar re-emerges".

MAS' decisive actions and well-communicated steely resolve in September 1985, underpinned by strong economic fundamentals, left little doubt that the central bank was serious in maintaining a strong Singapore dollar and the episode established MAS' market intervention credentials.

Statement by Dr Goh Keng Swee, 16 September 1985

There is a widespread belief in the financial markets that the Singapore Government wants a cheaper Singapore dollar. This belief springs from the argument that a cheaper dollar will benefit our export industries. Both the belief and the argument are wrong.

So far as the manufacturing industries are concerned, the "local content" of our exports averages around 20%. This consists of wages, rents, cost of utilities and purchase of locally-made components.

The last item is small in most cases and most of the components are imported. A depreciation of the Singapore dollar increases the cost of imported components, by far the largest cost item.

To be of value to the export industries, countries in balance of payments difficulty devalue their currencies usually by 20%, a small devaluation, to 50% or more, a major devaluation.

A 20% devaluation of the Singapore dollar will reduce manufacturing costs in foreign currency only by 4%; it will increase the cost of imports in Singapore dollars by 20%.

Since most of our consumer goods, including food, are imported, the cost of living will eventually rise by between 12% and 15%. This will lead to an increase in wages and most of the small initial benefit of devaluation will be lost.

Currency depreciation therefore does not help our export industries. It is different in countries where local content of manufactures is large.

Recently, there has been a sustained speculative attack on the Singapore dollar. The Monetary Authority of Singapore is taking action to repel that attack.

Statement by Dr Goh Keng Swee, 18 September 1985

The MAS intervention operation has achieved its purpose and liquidity is being injected into the market. What conclusions can be drawn from this exercise?

First, the MAS can influence exchange rates of the Singapore dollar more effectively than other central banks manage theirs. This is not because we are cleverer than other people.

The reason is the prudent fiscal policy of the Singapore Government which stands in marked contrast to fiscal policies of several developed countries who finance chronic budget deficits by borrowing domestically or internationally.

This prudent fiscal policy and the structure of our banking system in which some banks are heavily dependent on inter-bank funding give strong leverage to MAS' open market operations.

Second, speculators have suffered heavy losses. Those who must speculate on currencies are well advised to leave the Singapore dollar alone. They should choose softer targets as this exercise will be repeated if speculation on the Singapore dollar re-emerges.

Some speculators have borrowed from banks to finance speculation. Banks are advised to recall such loans or not renew them on maturity when the purpose of the loan is known to be currency speculation.

Some corporations with bank credit lines have drawn upon these credit lines at prime lending rates to re-lend to the inter-bank overnight market at a profit. Business corporations should stick to their chosen fields and not act as financial intermediaries.

There is much concern over what the US-Singapore dollar rate will be. The short answer is that if the US dollar strengthens against other major currencies — the deutschemark, the yen and the pound — it could also strengthen against the Singapore dollar. Conversely, if it weakens against them, it could weaken against the Singapore dollar. In the past, the Singapore dollar has generally fluctuated less than the major currencies against the US dollar.

Exchange Rate Policy: Philosophy and Conduct Over the Past Decade

Dr Teh Kok Peng
Deputy Managing Director (Economics)
Mr Tharman Shanmugaratnam
Director (Economics)

Chapter 16, Public Policies in Singapore: Changes in the 1980s and Future Signposts
1992

Introduction

The value of the Singapore dollar rarely escapes public comment. In an economy which is among the most open in the world to international transactions of one kind or another, the exchange rate touches on virtually every facet of economic life. Yet the philosophy and conduct of policy on the exchange rate are not widely understood. The purpose of this chapter is to clarify these issues, drawing on policy developments over the past decade[1].

The thinking that has guided Singapore's monetary policy has been based on both local and international experience. The first section of the chapter outlines the consensus which emerged among central banks around the world in the 1980s. Monetary policy in Singapore has nevertheless been influenced by the distinctive features of the economy, and the circumstances under which the MAS has operated. These features are set out in the next section. They provide the rationale for the shift to an exchange rate-oriented monetary policy in Singapore since the start of the 1980s.

The operation of exchange rate policy is then discussed and specific policy responses to changing economic conditions in the last decade are examined. The main strands of the discussion are pulled together in the conclusion.

Goals of Monetary Policy: The New International Consensus

Central banks in most developed economies have usually described their aims in terms of the pursuit of "non-inflationary growth". Until the late 1970s, this often implied several objectives such as economic growth, full employment, price stability and a satisfactory balance of payments. Not all these objectives were consistent in the short run. With few exceptions, central banks would seek to balance these objectives by switching from one priority to another in a series of seemingly short-term trade-offs.

The results were manifestly poor. Economic growth in the industrial countries declined to a post-war low in the 1970s, while inflation reached a post-war high. Part of the explanation for this no doubt lay in the 1973 oil shock. Increased prices of oil and raw materials led to sharply higher inflation in the industrial economies while the adverse shift in their terms of trade had a recessionary impact on domestic demand. Yet it was also evident that countries which concentrated on offsetting the loss of demand by adopting stimulative domestic policy suffered a persistence of inflation in doing so, while failing to achieve any sustained increase in growth.

Often enough, loose monetary policy aimed at avoiding an economic slowdown resulted in lower growth and higher unemployment in the long run as inflation increased. A consensus began to emerge out of this experience. The earlier post-war belief that some increase in inflation had to be tolerated in order to achieve higher growth and higher employment lost ground to the view that lower growth and higher unemployment were the most likely outcome of higher inflation.

The industrial economies with the lowest inflation records in the 1970s — Germany and Switzerland — were recognised as having had among the lowest rates of unemployment (see Chart 1). Japan also had low unemployment in the 1970s despite high inflation. However, inflation in Japan was due to its heavy reliance on imported fuels and raw materials which made it especially vulnerable to the 1973 oil shock rather than the absence of policies to control inflation following the shock.[2] By the 1980s, it had the lowest rate of inflation among the industrial economies, and the lowest unemployment rate besides Switzerland (see Chart 2). Although German unemployment increased with the rest of Europe in the 1980s, it remained below the levels in its inflation-prone neighbours.

Central banks began to return to the classical objective of monetary policy, that is, of safeguarding the value of the currency with respect to its purchasing power. The tendency in the 1980s was therefore to direct monetary policy primarily towards achieving low and stable inflation. There has been renewed recognition of the view that price stability provides the basis for sustained economic growth.

Central bankers were not alone in the new consensus. If the 1970s were the decade when politicians rediscovered the costs of inflation, the 1980s were the decade when they sought the attractions of price stability. As Paul A Volcker, former Chairman of the Board of Governors of the US Federal Reserve System, put it:

> What we think of as central bankerly qualities, an emphasis on restraint and continuity and prudence, seem to have come more in style. In a turbulent world, the importance of restoring a sense of stability is more clearly recognised; that recognition in itself turns attention to central banks and monetary policy. Indeed, some now argue forcibly that price stability should be the principal goal — perhaps the only goal — of monetary policy. That thought was quite foreign to the earlier post-war generation, at least in the United States and many other countries.[3]

The consensus has extended beyond the developed economies to the developing economies, which have always been more inflation prone. Many of the latter experienced severe economic costs as a result of high inflation in the 1980s, reinforcing their difficulties in servicing their debts.

Spiralling prices and a continuous loss in the value of their currencies contributed to a collapse of investor and creditor confidence, and substantial capital flight. Consequently, as Chart 3 illustrates, developing economies with higher inflation have tended to have lower rates of income growth per capita over the last decade.

Even the newly emerging, market reforming socialist economies are part of the new consensus. The absence of a reliable price mechanism and a monetary policy which could ensure the smooth functioning of that mechanism is recognised as being a chief failure of these socialist economies, and offers lessons for many others.

Why Is Inflation Costly?

Most serious observers would agree that inflation is both socially divisive and leads to a less efficient economy.[4] It redistributes income and wealth in an arbitrary fashion. The most obvious example of this inequity is the hurt inflicted on those living on fixed income, such as pensioners. Inflation erodes their purchasing power. Even with moderate inflation of 5%, pensions will lose half their value in less than 15 years. Again, low income earners are generally hit hardest, since consumption takes up a larger share of their incomes. People whose savings are not large enough to be shifted into assets that are protected against inflation will also be unfairly hurt.[5] Debtors will generally gain at the expense of creditors, since inflation reduces the real value of future obligations.[6]

Besides being socially divisive, inflation undermines the efficient functioning of any market economy. It distorts the price mechanism which provides the information that everyone requires to make sensible economic choices. Price movements are easily misread in an inflationary environment, since the relative prices of goods and services are made less transparent by large increases in the general level of prices. If prices in general are going up by 10%, the fact that the price of a particular product rises by 7% goes largely unnoticed.

Once inflation gains momentum, employers and employees have to negotiate more frequent agreements to adjust wages and salaries. Businesses have to adjust frequently their cost and price calculations, and find it more difficult to make investment decisions. Some of these costs can be avoided if people have perfect foresight, and are able to modify their behaviour to adapt to future increases in prices. This may be possible in theory, but is scarcely relevant in practice. Experience shows that the higher the rate of inflation, the less stable it is, and the greater the uncertainty about future costs and prices.

The uncertainty generated by inflation creates additional costs. Workers attempt to bid up wages, not only because prices are rising but because they lack confidence in the future rate of inflation. Countries with persistent inflation have also had to suffer higher interest rates, to compensate not only for expected inflation[7] but also the risk of an unexpected acceleration in inflation. Uncertainty over inflation thereby leads to an increase in real interest rates.

The incentive for long-term investment is reduced. Businesses may be able to hedge against some uncertainties, but can usually do so only in the short term. Moreover, businesses turn their attention away from new, income-generating investments towards assets which yield gains in an inflationary environment. By encouraging exaggerated expectations of capital gains in assets such as real estate, inflation often contributes to cycles of over-investment in such markets. Equally, inflation tends to encourage borrowing to finance investments in such assets, which in turn can lead to instability in the financial system.

The Importance of Credibility

The social and economic costs of inflation, despite being widespread and pervasive, are often overlooked until inflation reaches high levels. By then, the task of reducing inflation will itself inflict costs on the population. A sustained reduction in demand is required to wring inflationary expectations into the system. This is more so in countries where governments have been unwilling to pursue firm, anti-inflationary policies in the past, and the population attaches little credibility to its ability to do so.

The Latin American economies were perhaps the best examples of stubborn inflationary expectations in the 1980s, although several developed economies like the UK have had difficulties in reducing inflation for the same reason. The basic lesson that arises from these experiences is that low inflation is almost always easier to achieve where inflation has been kept under tight control in the past. Credibility in anti-inflationary policies is self-fulfilling.

Singapore's Economic Circumstances: Implications for Monetary Policy

The structure and circumstances of the Singapore economy have had important consequences for macroeconomic policy. In particular, the choice and effectiveness of monetary policy instruments in Singapore have been substantially shaped by these circumstances — especially the high degree of openness to trade and capital flows.

Openness to Trade

Singapore's small land area and population have limited the range of production possibilities and the size of the domestic market. Therefore it needs to import even the most basic requirements, and to export to pay for these requirements and beyond. This has necessitated an open trade policy, with very few import restrictions.[8]

Singapore's openness to trade is virtually without parallel (see Chart 4). As Chart 5 shows, both its imports and exports are very large in relation to the GDP, even if we exclude the entrepot trade and exports of refined oil. They have also increased in importance since the 1970s. Singapore's openness can also be seen in the high import content of its expenditure and output. From the 1983 input–output table (the latest published), it is estimated that imported raw materials, equipment and components constituted about 60% of total expenditure and 70% of exports.

Why Monetary Policy Is Centred on the Exchange Rate

Singapore's small size and openness have important consequences. First, because it is too small to influence world prices, Singapore is a price-taker.

Producers in Singapore have to accept prices dictated by global supply and demand.

Second, the high import content means that changes in world prices or in the exchange rate have a powerful influence on domestic prices, either directly or indirectly. Estimates show that for every 1% increase in import prices, consumer prices will increase by about 0.7%. In other words, a 5% rate of import price inflation will mean a 3.5% rate of CPI inflation, even in the absence of any independent domestic sources of inflation. Changes in the exchange rate to offset changes in foreign price levels would clearly have a significant effect on inflation.

There is another channel by which the exchange rate influences domestic inflation. Because exports play the central role, the exchange rate has an influence on total demand in the economy — at least in the short term. It thereby influences the demand for domestic resources, especially the demand for labour. A weak exchange rate can lead to overheating of the economy, a tighter labour market and a consequent higher growth of domestic wages and other costs.

Managing the exchange rate is thus the most effective way of maintaining price stability in a small, open economy like Singapore. The openness of the economy also means that domestic monetary instruments, such as money supply or interest rates, do not have as direct an influence on domestic inflation as the exchange rate does. They also do not have a significant influence on the overall level of economic activity — given the predominant role of external rather than domestic demand. Unlike the larger industrial economies, where investment is often significantly influenced by interest rates, the predominance of foreign investment in Singapore limits the importance of the cost of domestic borrowing.

At the same time, the exchange rate is not a useful instrument for achieving sustained, as distinct from temporary, improvements in export competitiveness. While it is true that a lower value of the currency reduces unit labour costs relative to those of competitor countries, the high import content of Singapore's exports means that the effective export subsidy of a given exchange rate depreciation is low, compared to most other countries.

Over the medium term, such a subsidy would also be whittled away as wages increase in response to consumer price increases and the tightening of the labour market following the weakening of the currency. This distinction between the short-term and long-term implications of exchange rate changes is discussed later.

Openness to Capital Flows: Implications for Domestic Monetary Policies

Singapore has virtually no controls on inflows and outflows of foreign currency funds by residents and foreigners, whether in amount or destination. Besides the absence of exchange controls, Singapore also has a very liberal policy towards foreign direct investment, with no limitation on the extent of foreign ownership (except in the onshore banking sector).[9]

Singapore's role as an international financial centre has also led to a large offshore banking sector called the Asian Dollar Market (ADM). Its assets, denominated in foreign currencies (mostly US dollars) totalled US$390 billion at the end of 1990, dwarfing the assets of the onshore domestic banking system of $134 billion (US$77 billion). There are no controls on capital flows between the ADM and the domestic banking system, enabling holders of Singapore dollars to easily convert into foreign currency deposits and vice versa.

The lack of control on capital outflows, the small economic base and a high savings rate have all provided an incentive for Singapore's government and private sector to diversify their asset holdings across countries and currencies to spread risk. On the other hand, the openness to capital inflows, financial and direct, has resulted in a high percentage of foreign liabilities and assets in the domestic banking system (see Chart 6).

The very large stock of private international cross-country asset holdings results in large and quick movements of capital whenever there are small changes in the differential between domestic and foreign (especially US) interest rates. This makes it difficult to target either money supply or interest rates in Singapore. Net flows of funds from abroad account for the bulk of changes in domestic money supply (see Chart 7).

Domestic interest rates are, likewise, largely determined by foreign rates and market expectations on the future strength of the Singapore dollar. (Chart 8 displays the relationship between Singapore and US interest rates since the 1970s, before adjusting for exchange rate expectations.)

An attempt by the MAS to raise or lower domestic interest rates on any sustained basis, with foreign rates unchanged, would be thwarted by a shift of funds into or out of Singapore. Put another way, high capital mobility implies that the MAS can seek to influence either the exchange rate or domestic variables like interest rates, but not both. The choice of the exchange rate as the focus of monetary policy must imply a loss of control over domestic interest rates.

Hong Kong offers an interesting example. The futile attempt by the colony's authorities in May 1991 to unilaterally raise domestic interest rates vis-à-vis US rates vividly illustrates the difficulty of operating an independent domestic monetary policy while maintaining the HK dollar at a fixed peg to the US dollar. Investors shifted a massive volume of funds into Hong Kong in the weeks following the decision, taking advantage of the higher return on Hong Kong dollars. With the currency's value being fixed, excess liquidity persisted until interest rates were eventually adjusted back to their initial levels in June 1991.

Unlike Hong Kong, Singapore does not maintain a fixed exchange rate peg. An attempt to manage domestic interest rates independent of foreign rates (especially US dollar interest rates) would therefore lead to a high degree of volatility in the exchange rate. Monetary policy aimed at holding domestic interest rates fixed while US interest rates rise (or fall), for example, could lead to a substantial weakening (or strengthening) of the Singapore dollar. The increased volatility of the exchange rate would have potentially damaging consequences for inflation or economic growth. Moreover, persistent volatility in the Singapore dollar would remove the confidence in the currency which has contributed to persistently lower domestic interest rates than offshore US dollar interest rates since the 1970s (see Chart 8).

Fiscal Surpluses and the Institutional Context for Monetary Policy

The freedom which monetary or exchange rate policy has in pursuing its objective of price stability can be heavily constrained by the conduct of the government's fiscal policies. In many developing countries, the poor state of government finances — due to either weak tax collections or excessive spending — gives the central bank little latitude to pursue its proper objectives. Monetary policy is subordinated to the rote of financing the government's deficit, either by extending credit to the government or, in the extreme, simply printing more currency. The ex-socialist economies were extreme examples, where monetary policy proper was virtually non-existent; the central bank merely served as a cashier for financing public sector deficits.

Even among the developed economies, where governments are usually able to borrow in private capital markets, monetary policy can be circumscribed by the existence of high fiscal deficits. As large government borrowings in the domestic capital market lead to higher interest rates and "crowd out" private investors, the scope for tight monetary policy aimed at controlling inflation tends to be constrained.

Whether a central bank is able to maintain an anti-inflationary stance under these circumstances depends partly, but not solely, on its institutional autonomy and corresponding ability to "ride out" short-term political pressures. The German Bundesbank is perhaps the best example of central bank independence in the post-war era.[10] More recently, the Reserve Bank of New Zealand and the Bank of Canada have been charged with the statutory duty of securing price stability, shielded from political interference.

Where formal legislation does not preserve the autonomy of the central bank, its ability to pursue a consistent anti-inflationary policy often rests on the degree of consensus within government on the desirability of low inflation. Where the government shares this belief, even central banks with little formal autonomy from government, for example, the Bank of Japan, are given the latitude to pursue their objective of price stability.

Singapore has been fortunate in that the Government has run fiscal surpluses rather than deficits in virtually every year since the late 1960s (see Chart 9).[11] Even the small deficits in the 1960s were financed by contributions to the Central Provident Fund (CPF).[12] The absence of deficits has given the MAS the freedom to concentrate on its primary objective of maintaining price stability. Indeed, rather than having to extend credit to the Government, the MAS is perpetually in receipt of deposits from the Government and CPF. These deposits have to be continually ploughed back into the domestic banking system to prevent a sharp contraction in liquidity and an excessive appreciation of the Singapore dollar. This is quite unlike many other central banks, which often have to find ways of reining in an expansion of domestic liquidity and preventing a depreciation of their currencies.

The domestic demand management role of fiscal policy in Singapore is limited, given the high import content of domestic expenditures. Within these limits, government development spending has occasionally been used for counter-cyclical purposes. However, the more important role of fiscal policy in the management of aggregate activity has been its effect on supply-side costs. The employers' contribution to the CPF is a wage cost, and government taxes are part of business operating cost. The government has been prepared to change these two costs when necessary. For example, the 15 percentage point cut in the employers' contribution rate and wide range of reductions in government taxes and charges in 1985–86 played a critical role in effecting a recovery from the recession.

The government's willingness to engage in counter-cyclical policies of this nature has reduced the burden that would otherwise fall on monetary policy, and enabled the MAS to concentrate on its primary responsibility of maintaining price stability.

Perhaps the most important advantage faced by the MAS, however, has been the desire of Singapore's political leadership itself to ensure price stability and avoid the social conflicts that are engendered by high inflation. A general ethos of financial prudence has pervaded economic policies since the 1960s, and indeed explains the persistence of fiscal surpluses. With the build-up in CPF contribution rates in the 1970s and 1980s, the government has had an added political commitment to maintaining low inflation, as the basis for preserving the future value of members' balances.

The Implications of Price and Wage Flexibility

Prices and wages in Singapore have been fairly, though not perfectly, flexible. In the absence of import barriers, domestic prices have responded flexibly to changes in foreign prices or demand. There is also a good degree of wage flexibility, at least relative to other countries. While the National Wages Council (NWC) has set broad guidelines for annual wage increases, these guidelines are not enforceable and are, in any case, set with reference to prevailing economic conditions.[13] Since the 1985 recession, there has been an attempt to increase wage flexibility by reducing the size of the fixed wage increment and making bonuses a more important part of annual wages. The NWC has also abandoned all quantitative recommendations on wage increases, with wage-setting occurring instead at a decentralised, enterprise level.

The relative flexibility of prices and wages in Singapore gives monetary policy less scope to contribute to sustained changes in real economic growth than to price stability. In theory, highly flexible prices and wages would take the economy into a so-called 'monetarist' world in which the exchange rate or any other monetary instrument has no impact on real level of output, after a brief adjustment. The only sustained impact is on prices and nominal values. Put another way, changes in the nominal value of the exchange rate are quickly offset by changes in prices and wages. There is therefore no change in real wages and the real exchange rate, which is what matters for real output.

The result is different in a 'Keynesian' world of inflexible nominal wages, and other price rigidities. Since wage growth responds only sluggishly to changes in inflation, the exchange rate has a sustained effect on real wages and competitiveness and can be used to secure real economic adjustments.

The evidence for Singapore is somewhat closer to the description of a "monetarist" than a 'Keynesian' world.[14] In the short run, there are no doubt lags in the pass-through from a stronger exchange rate into lower prices, and some rigidity in nominal wages — if only because wage contracts are rarely revised more than once a year. A nominal appreciation of the exchange rate will not be immediately offset by lower wage growth, and would imply an appreciation of the exchange rate in real terms. Exchange rate policy may then face a short-term trade-off between inflation and competitiveness.

The longer-term trade-off between inflation and competitiveness is essentially non-existent. As shown later, empirical simulations indicate that a weaker exchange rate, aimed at gaining export competitiveness, feeds through fully into higher domestic wages, eliminating the initial gains in competitiveness. For this reason, there is little ground for giving priority to considerations of export competitiveness in the setting of medium- and long-term exchange rate policies.

The Operation of Exchange Rate Policy

Two critical groups of factors, therefore, quite clearly determine the monetary policy strategy to be followed.

The first is the small and open nature of the Singapore economy, real and financial. This means that managing the exchange rate is the easiest and surest way of maintaining domestic price stability. The second is the policy framework in Singapore, and the role of fiscal policy in particular. This has given MAS a large degree of freedom to concentrate on its primary responsibility of maintaining price stability.

Unlike the large industrial economies, which seek to manage domestic monetary conditions while generally allowing the exchange rate to be freely determined, Singapore seeks to manage the path of its exchange rate without maintaining independent targets for either domestic money supply or interest rates. The objective of controlling inflation is similar, but the circumstances and hence strategy differs. Singapore's strategy is similar to the practice of small, open industrial economies such as Austria, Belgium and the Netherlands. Even Switzerland, which was one of the first industrial economies to adopt strict targets for domestic money supply in the 1970s, is viewed by some observers as placing increased importance on managing the exchange rate in recent years.[15]

Developing economies, almost without exception, maintain exchange rate policies of one form or another. However, the Singapore case differs in two important regards. First, many developing countries exercise direct control of their exchange rates by maintaining an official peg of some sort. The scope for unrealistic exchange rates is thereby greater. Second, in many cases, controls are maintained on domestic monetary variables in addition to the exchange rate. This is made possible by the imposition of capital and exchange controls, and is not possible in an economy with modern and open financial markets.

How Is the Exchange Rate Managed?

The MAS manages the exchange rate of the Singapore dollar against a trade-weighted basket of currencies of our major trading partners and competitors — to use the jargon, the nominal effective exchange rate (NEER). Changes in the US/S$ exchange rate alone do not determine either the rate of imported inflation, or our competitiveness as exporters. The basket of exchange rates that we monitor reflects the range of sources of imported CPI inflation and of competitors in export markets.

The Singapore dollar has been a floating currency since 1973. There is no official peg for the value of the currency, against either the US dollar or any basket of currencies. The MAS can, therefore, only influence the value of the Singapore dollar by intervening in the market itself. The intervention operations of the MAS essentially serve to alter the supply of Singapore dollar liquidity in the banking system, thereby influencing the movement of the exchange rate.[16]

The actual operation of monetary policy has been influenced by the institutional arrangement of the CPF and government surpluses being deposited with MAS, as discussed earlier. This has the effect of reducing liquidity in the banking system, and unless offset, would cause the Singapore dollar to appreciate. MAS' actions to restore this liquidity are necessary to neutralise its effects on the Singapore dollar. These actions largely take the form of foreign exchange market intervention operations, in which US dollars are purchased by MAS through the creation of bank reserves. The extent of this intervention is determined by what is needed to keep the exchange rate broadly within the target band.[17]

The trade-weighted Singapore dollar is allowed to float within an undisclosed target band. Generally, the aim is to reduce imported inflation in domestic prices by appreciating the trade-weighted currency. The extent to which the trade-weighted Singapore dollar is allowed to appreciate depends, among other things, on prevailing and projected levels of world inflation and domestic sources of inflation. The objective is to achieve a low and stable rate of CPI inflation.

It is recognised that it would be difficult to totally insulate the economy from a sharp increase in world inflation by an offsetting sharp appreciation of the exchange rate without causing short-run competitive and adjustment problems. Under such circumstances, higher world inflation may be partially transmitted through imports to domestic prices. Nevertheless, an attempt is made to "lean against the wind" to keep domestic inflation below world levels.

Exchange Rate Policy Responses in the 1980s

The decade of the 1980s provides an interesting case study of exchange rate policy responses to changing economic conditions, and the effectiveness of these policies. Three broad phases can be identified, corresponding to the inflationary pressures of the early 1980s, deflationary conditions in the mid-1980s and the renewed build-up in inflation since the late 1980s.

The Early 1980s: From the Second Oil Shock to the 1985 Recession

The shift in conduct of monetary policy in Singapore towards exchange rate targeting, the rationale for which was discussed earlier, occurred in 1981. A forthright description of the new policy regime was given in the *MAS Annual Report of 1981–82:*

> Monetary policy ... differed somewhat in 1981 in that the policy direction was aimed largely at maintaining a strong exchange rate for the Singapore dollar, while ensuring sufficient liquidity to accommodate real economic growth. Underlying this shift in emphasis away from targets for interest rates and money supply growth in the conduct of monetary policy is the view that the exchange rate is a relatively more important anti-inflation instrument in the context of the small and open Singapore economy. Price stability, then, continues to be the prime objective. The emphasis given to a strong exchange rate policy also facilitates the policy of upgrading and restructuring the domestic economy.

The move to a strong exchange rate policy in 1981 took place in an inflationary external environment. The second oil shock in 1979 led to high world inflation, and was the principal reason for Singapore's high inflation of over 8% in 1980–81. Another important reason was the high rate of nominal wage increases that began in 1979. The government's 'high wage policy' of 1979–81 was aimed at shifting the economy towards more capital- and skill-intensive activities. Productivity growth did improve compared to the second half of the 1970s, but failed to match wage cost increases. Substantial growth in unit labour costs resulted (see Table 1). Despite a strong appreciation of the NEER in 1981 then, high inflation occurred.

The move to a strong exchange rate policy in 1981 could also be seen as an attempt to prevent the same degree of import price pass-through as during the first oil shock of 1973–74, when inflation in Singapore reached levels considerably higher than in the OECD countries. In this regard, Singapore was successful. Inflation rates in 1981 and 1982 were below those in the OECD countries (see Table 1).

The gradual decline in world inflation and a strong NEER led to negative import inflation by 1982. However, wage costs continued to escalate after 1981, owing to increased rates of CPF contribution, keen competition for workers in a tight labour market caused in part by a construction boom, and favourable growth expectations on the part of both management and labour. Unit labour cost increases led to significant cost pressures, exacerbated by the boom in domestic demand — particularly stemming from the construction sector.

Inflation in Singapore after 1981 was therefore entirely caused by domestic factors. Indeed, if the exchange rate had not been allowed to appreciate during the period, inflation would have been considerably higher. The decline in import prices kept inflation moderate by offsetting the domestic sources of inflation.

The combination of unit labour costs that were increasing more rapidly than that of competitor countries and, to a lesser extent, the appreciation of the NEER, led to a sharp rise in the real effective exchange rate (REER) in the first half of the 1980s (see Chart 11). The implied loss of international competitiveness was among the main factors which set the stage for the 1985 recession, when GDP growth fell by 1.6%. A convincing explanation of the timing and sharpness of the 1985 recession, however, must turn to the role of demand.

Cyclical downturns in both domestic and external demand played a major role in the recession. The most important was the collapse of the construction boom, with the completion of major projects and the emergence of gross oversupply in all categories of property. As Table 2 shows, this was inevitable after five years of growth averaging 22% per annum.

The decline in external demand in 1985 is less widely recognised. The fact that average GDP growth in the OECD countries remained healthy at 4% in 1985 obscures the sharp contractions in demand that occurred in the industries that mattered to Singapore — especially electronics, ship-repairing, petroleum refining and regional tourism and entrepot trade. As Chart 10 shows, the decline in Singapore's electronics exports in 1985 was indeed more moderate than the decline in new orders of electronic components in its major market, the US.[18]

Singapore was not alone in suffering a decline in export performance in 1985. Korea and Hong Kong also experienced negative growth in exports (see Table 3). This was despite the fact that, unlike Singapore, they had experienced a depreciation in their real effective exchange rates in the first half of the 1980s.[19] Malaysia and Taiwan also had much weaker growth rates in 1985 than 1984. The evidence clearly points to a decline in demand, as a primary source of decline in exports of all these economies. It is nevertheless true that Singapore's export decline could have been less severe if it had been in a more competitive position.

1985–88: Response to Deflationary Pressures

The effects of the economic recession, together with the series of cost and tax cutting measures which the government introduced from mid-1985, effectively eliminated domestic inflationary pressures. In particular, the 15 percentage point reduction on the employers' contribution rate to the CPF in 1986, and the wage restraint practised during the period, caused a sharp reduction in unit labour costs (see Table 1).

From late 1985 onward, the worldwide decline in oil and commodity prices also reduced global inflation. The MAS, which had begun to allow some easing in its exchange policy in 1985 with the onset of the recession, was able to continue such easing in 1986–87 without concern about inflation. Inflation was negative at –1.4% in 1986 and remained low at 0.5% in 1987. The substantial decline in unit labour costs and the NEER also laid the foundation for the economic turnaround in 1986 and the strong recovery in 1987, in the midst of a sharp pick-up in external demand.

1988–91: The Emergence of an Overheated Economy

The third phase of exchange rate policy began in mid-1988, when the NEER began to appreciate in earnest again. The appreciation reflected concerns over the renewed built-up in both domestic and foreign inflationary pressures.

Faced with strong external demand, partly arising from the sharp improvements in Singapore's competitiveness in 1986–87, the economy began exceeding its sustainable rate of growth by the end of the decade. Unemployment fell below 2.5% by 1989, a historically unprecedented level and well below that regarded as full employment in any other economy. The very low level of unemployment had the inevitable result of jacking up wage growth, to well above the rate of productivity growth. Unit labour costs consequently increased by about 6% per annum towards the end of the decade, imparting significant upward pressure on inflation.

Foreign inflationary pressures also increased in the late 1980s. However, the appreciation of the exchange rate since 1988 served to offset these pressures. By 1991, import prices had had a significant dampening effect on CPI inflation (see Chart 12). The stronger exchange rate also exercised a cooling effect on the labour market and the economy, without which domestic inflationary pressures would have been higher.

The merits of the policy of exchange rate appreciation since 1988 are best assessed by considering the outcome if there had been no appreciation of the currency. Simulations using the MAS econometric model suggest that inflation would have averaged about 6% per annum during 1989–91 if the exchange rate had not appreciated since 1988, instead of the 3% average inflation rate actually seen. A weak exchange rate since 1988 would also have had effects beyond 1991. By the time the effects of higher imported inflation worked their way fully into higher domestic costs and prices by the mid-1990s, it is estimated that the increase in the CPI index would have been more than 25 percentage points higher than otherwise projected (see Chart 13).

These estimates of the long-term effects of exchange rate changes lend support to the arguments made earlier. A weaker exchange rate buys an initial improvement in competitiveness, but this is eventually undermined by its inflationary consequences. This is especially so when the economy is already operating at levels of full employment and limited spare capacity. Wages and other domestic costs then react quickly to excess demand. After a few years, the level of competitiveness and output would be back to where they would have been without a weaker exchange rate. Indeed, our simulations show that the initial increase in output growth in 1989–91 would have been offset by lower growth beyond 1992 — averaging only 3% per annum over 1993–95.

Another way of looking at this is that the erosion of cost competitiveness in an overheated labour market cannot be avoided by weakening the exchange rate. An appreciation of the real effective exchange rate is inevitable under such circumstances; the alternative to a nominal appreciation of the currency is merely a greater increase in unit labour costs.

With the continued slowdown in Singapore's labour force growth, its economic growth potential is likely to fall between 5% and 6% over the next decade.[20] As the scope for supply-side growth becomes more limited, however, the economy will be increasingly susceptible to the kind of periodic demand-induced overheating and inflationary pressures which characterise many of the developed economies. A moderation in GDP growth, when it persistently exceeds its potential, would serve to subdue inflationary pressures, thereby ensuring more sustainable growth. This would be at no cost to long-term productivity growth, which is the only basis for a sustained increase in Singapore's standard of living.

The lesson then for monetary policy in the 1990s lies in the necessity of holding to a medium-term, production potential-oriented policy as the basis for ensuring control over inflation. If price stability is traded off for the purpose of sustaining short-term economic growth above the economy's potential, growth itself will ultimately be lowered.

Concluding Remarks

The 1980s were marked by the renewed discovery of the merits of price stability. Central banks began to return to the classical objective of monetary policy — of safeguarding the value of the currency with respect to its purchasing power. There was greater awareness of the pervasive social and economic costs of inflation, and the difficulties of restoring price stability once expectations of inflation are entrenched.

In Singapore, the early 1980s marked the shift towards an exchange rate-oriented monetary policy. The small and highly open nature of the economy, both to trade and capital flows, meant that the exchange rate was the easiest and surest way of maintaining domestic price stability. Unlike the large industrial economies which target domestic monetary variables, Singapore has switched to targeting the path of its exchange rate while eschewing targets for either domestic money supply or interest rates.

The government's avoidance of fiscal deficits, and the commitment of Singapore's political leadership to preserving low inflation, has enabled the MAS to concentrate on its primary responsibility of seeking price stability. The futility of using the exchange rate as a tool to enhance export competitiveness has also been recognised. The initial improvement in competitiveness resulting from a weaker exchange rate is eventually unravelled by a build-up in inflationary pressures. The ultimate consequence of a weaker exchange rate is higher prices, not output.

The lessons of the late 1980s are perhaps most relevant for the next decade. As the economy is increasingly faced with supply-side constraints, the need to avoid an overheating of demand will be essential if price stability is to be maintained. Exchange rate policy would do well to remain focused on medium-term objectives, reacting well in advance to moderate the periodic overheating of the economy that may be inevitable. Credibility in maintaining low inflation is an asset which should be maintained. Exchange rate policies aimed at short-term growth objectives would quickly erode this credibility, and make the task of eventually reducing inflation more costly in terms of economic growth.

Notes

1. The views expressed in this chapter are those of the authors, and are not attributable to the Monetary Authority of Singapore. Comments from Mr Jared Enzler and statistical assistance from colleagues in the Economics Department of MAS are gratefully acknowledged.
2. Japan avoided high inflation during the second oil shock in 1979 through the quick imposition of a stringent monetary policy and restraint in wage growth. The GNP deflator increased by a mere 4% over 1979–80 compared to over 30% in 1974–75, despite an increase in import unit values of roughly similar magnitude in both cases. The prolonged tight monetary policy in the mid-1970s had also reduced inflationary expectations sharply in Japan by the late 1970s whereas the first oil shock had been preceded by a period of stimulative monetary policy and increased inflationary pressures.
3. Extract from the 1990 Per Jacobsson Lecture, Washington, September 1990.

4. This section provides a brief summary of recent academic and central bank literature on the costs of inflation. See, for example, the Annual Report of the Bank of Canada, 1990.
5. Holders of bank deposits (especially savings deposits) tend to be at a disadvantage to owners of equity and other assets which record capital gains under inflationary conditions. Even where interest rates on bank deposits are regularly adjusted for inflation, depositors face a higher tax burden since tax is levied on total interest income — including that portion which compensates for inflation.
6. This only occurs when the debt is at a fixed interest rate, or a rate that lags behind inflation.
7. With the removal of capital controls in most industrial economies in the 1980s, higher expected inflation may also be seen as necessitating higher interest rates in order to compensate investors for the likelihood of currency depreciation.
8. It has some tariffs, but these are imposed to discourage consumption of selected items — chiefly tobacco, liquor and automobiles — rather than to protect domestic production.
9. Government approval, however, is required since there is a policy on the type of industries to be encouraged, with preference being given to more skill-intensive and capital-intensive industries. There are no controls on direct investment overseas by residents.
10. The German Central Bank Act is single-minded in requiring the Bundesbank to carry out its function of regulating the volume of money and credit, with the aim of safeguarding the value of the currency. There is no mention of economic growth, full employment or any other economic objectives.
11. The only deficit since the late 1960s was recorded in 1987. This was due to heavy investment outlays on the Mass Rapid Transit system, and to payments of interest arrears on advance deposits from the CPF when the revamped government securities market was opened. The primary balance (excluding interest payments) remained in surplus.
12. The CPF is a fully funded compulsory old-age pension scheme, with contributions from employers and employees.
13. The econometric evidence indeed suggests that wage growth since the early 1980s has been largely explicable in terms of the level of unemployment, inflation and productivity growth. (Source: MAS Econometric Model).
14. The weight of previous studies on very small, open economies suggests that nominal wages tend to adjust fairly readily to changes in prices. Ross Garnaut (1991), 'Exchange Rate Regimes in the Asian-Pacific Region', *Asian-Pacific Economic Literature,* Vol. 5, No. 1.
15. See, for example, 'Exchange Rate Policy Dominates Money Supply Policy', in *Economic and Financial Prospects,* Swiss Bank Corporation, October/November 1991.
16. It is generally recognised in the literature on exchange rates that 'unsterilised' intervention, which results in a net change in the volume of bank reserves with the central bank, is necessary for changes in the exchange rate to be effected. 'Sterilised intervention', where foreign exchange intervention is neutralised by the central banks' operations in the domestic money or capital markets, usually has little sustained

impact on exchange rates. However, sterilised intervention can sometimes play a role in signalling the central banks' desire to see a change in the exchange rate, thereby altering market expectations.

17. Certain tactical operations in the domestic money market are also undertaken to complement exchange rate policy. They seek to reduce temporary liquidity imbalances arising from seasonal or technical factors, or to smooth out short-term interest rate movements with a minimum of impact on the exchange rate.
18. The US constituted 60% of Singapore's markets for electronic goods in 1985.
19. Hong Kong and Korea are estimated to have had a depreciation of 1.3% p.a. and 2.6% p.a. in their exchange rates over 1980–85. Comparable figures for Malaysia and Taiwan are a depreciation of 0.8% p.a. and appreciation of 4.2% p.a. over the period.
20. See *Annual Report, 1990–91,* Monetary Authority of Singapore, for a more detailed discussion.

Chapter reproduced by courtesy of Times Publishing Limited.

Chart 1 Inflation versus Unemployment in Selected Industrial Economies: 1970–1980

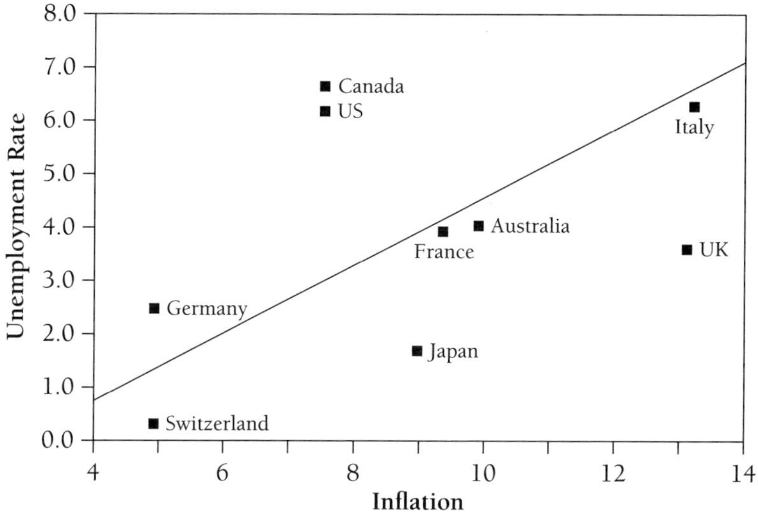

Sources: *IMF, International Financial Statistics and OECD, Labour Force Statistics.*

Chart 2 Inflation versus Unemployment in Selected Industrial Economies: 1980–1990

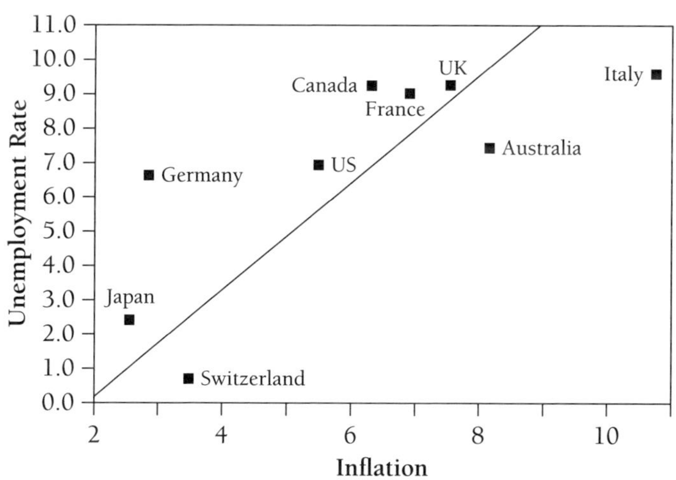

Sources: *IMF, International Financial Statistics and OECD, Labour Force Statistics.*

Chart 3 Real Per Capita Growth & Inflation: Developing Countries (Average 1981–1990)

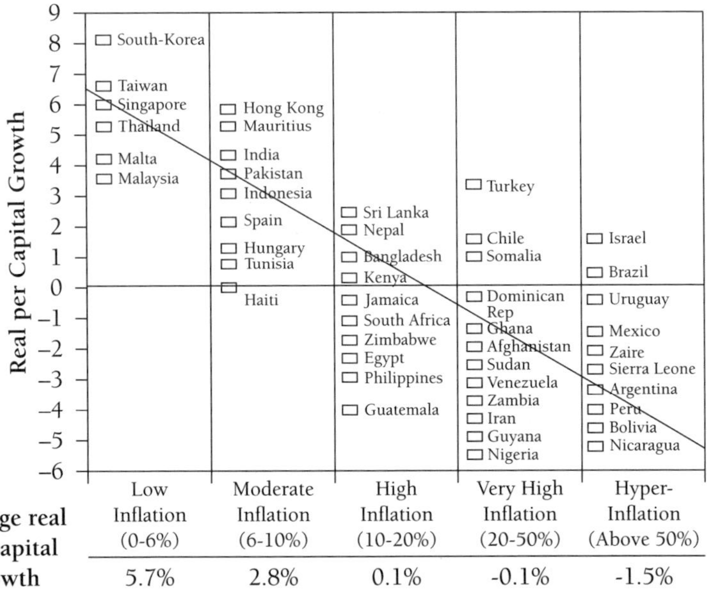

Sources: *IMF, International Financial Statistics and Penn World Table.*

Chart 4 Total Merchandise Trade as % of GDP, 1990

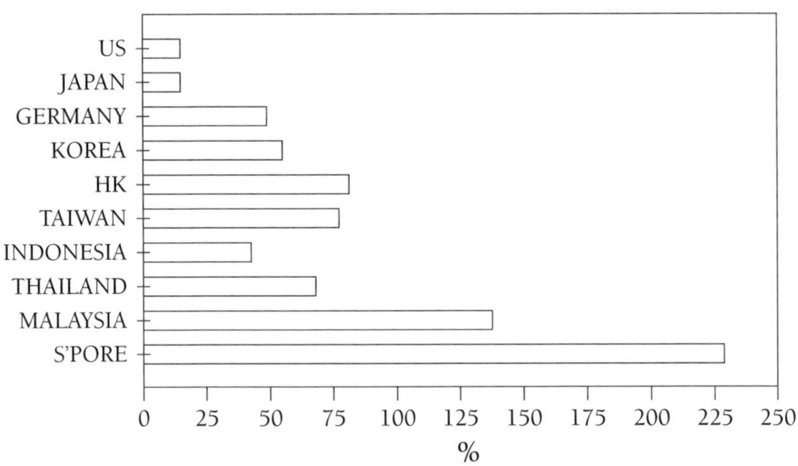

* **excluding entrepot trade**

Sources: *IMF, International Financial Statistics; The Central Bank of China, Financial Statistics, Taiwan District, ROC and Department of Statistics, HK Digest of Statistics.*

Chart 5 Non-oil Domestic Exports as % of GDP

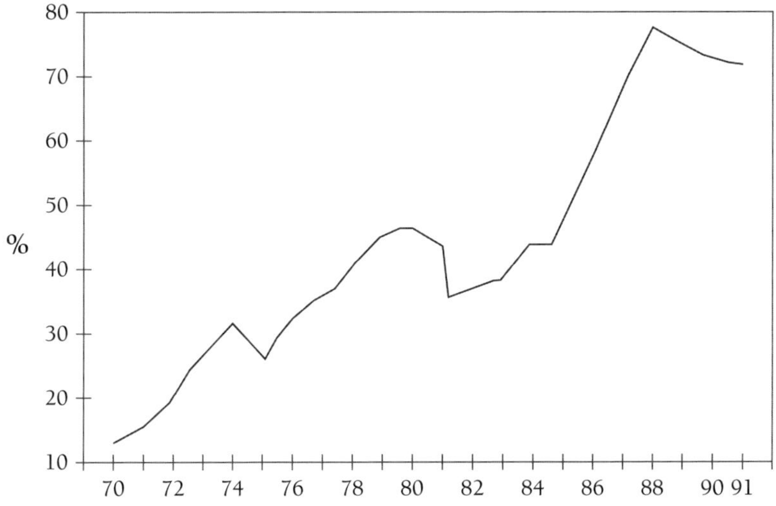

Source: *Trade Development Board and Department of Statistics (DOS), Singapore.*

Chart 6 Gross Foreign Assets and Liabilities of the Domestic Banking System

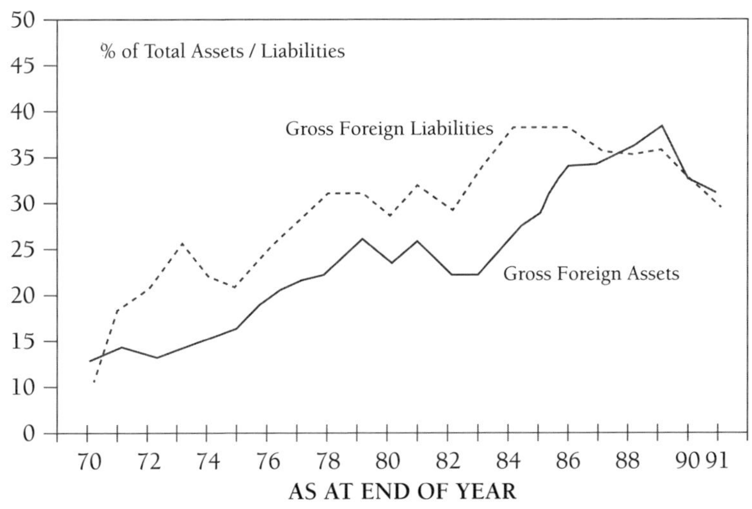

Sources: *MAS, Monthly Statistical Bulletin, various issues.*

Chart 7 Openness to Cross Border Fund Flows

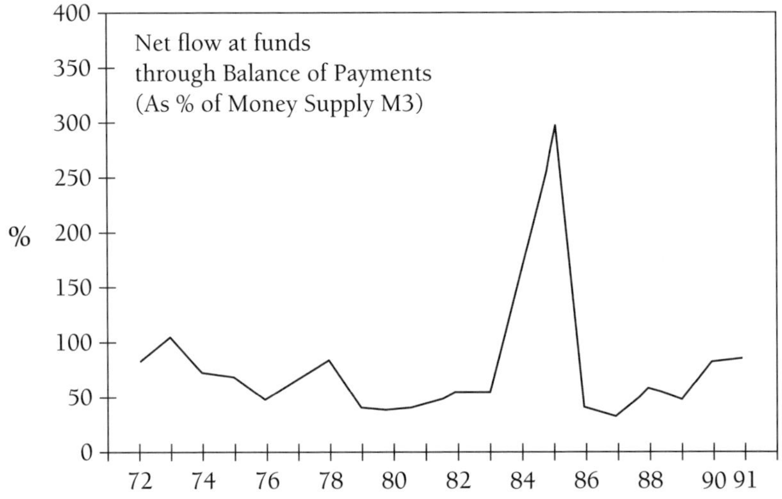

Source: *MAS, Annual Report, various issues.*

Chart 8 Three-month Interbank Interest Rates: S'pore and US 1/

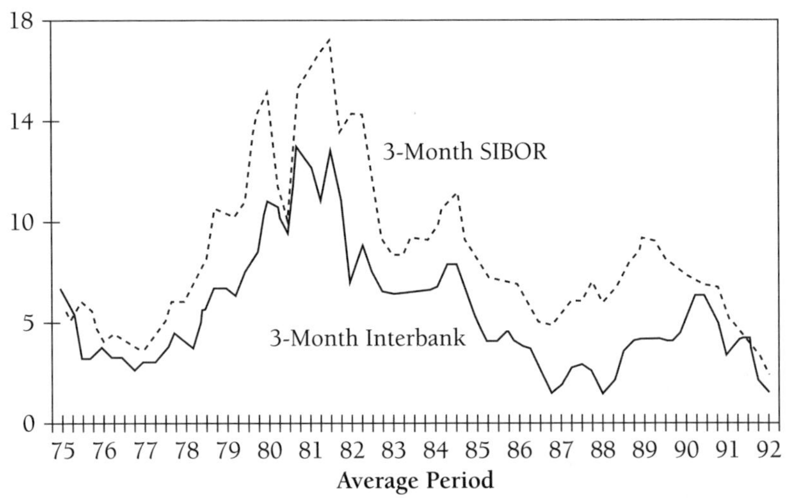

1/ SIBOR rates on US dollar deposits in the offshore ACU market are adjusted here to reflect the cost of reserve requirements on domestic interbank deposit rates.

Sources: *MAS, Monthly Statistical Bulletin and Business Times, Singapore.*

Chart 9 Government and CPF Surpluses

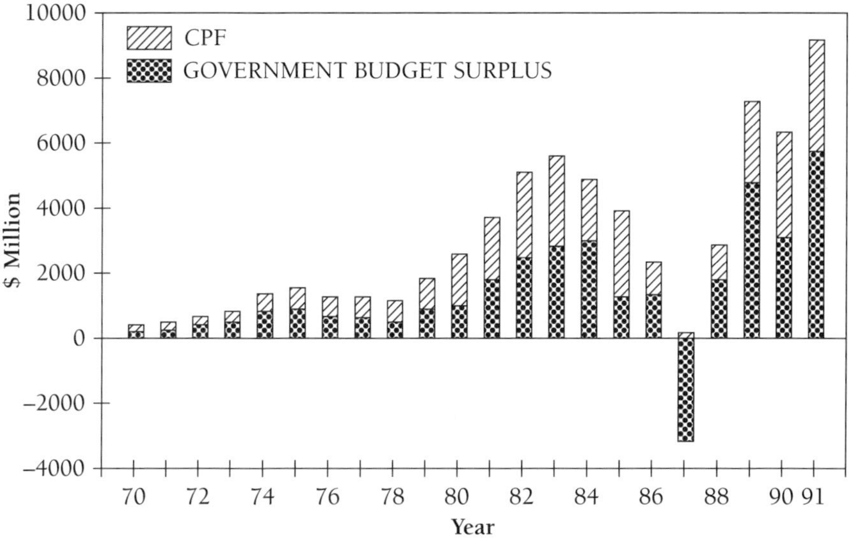

Sources: *Department of Statistics, Singapore, Annual Economic Survey and Yearbook of Statistics.*

Chart 10 Singapore's Domestic Exports of Electronics

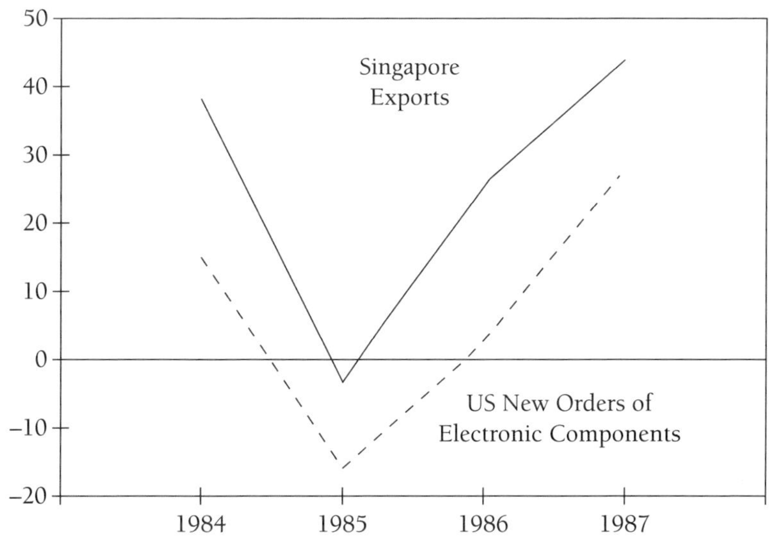

Sources: *Data from official Singapore and US sources.*

Chart 11 Nominal and Real Effective Exchange Rate of S$

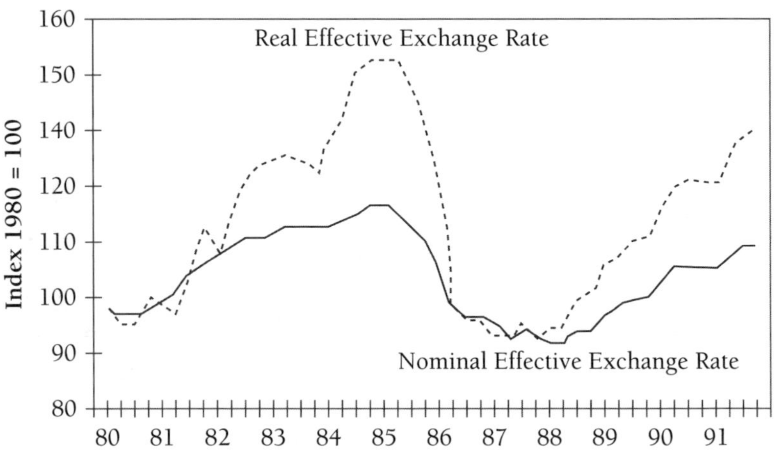

* Note: The NEER is defined in Table 1; it is not official index monitored by the MAS. The real effective exchange rate (REER) is the combination of NEER and unit labour cost of Singapore relative to countries in the same basket.

Sources: *Same as Table 1, plus official data sources for foreign economies.*

Chart 12 Sources of Inflation

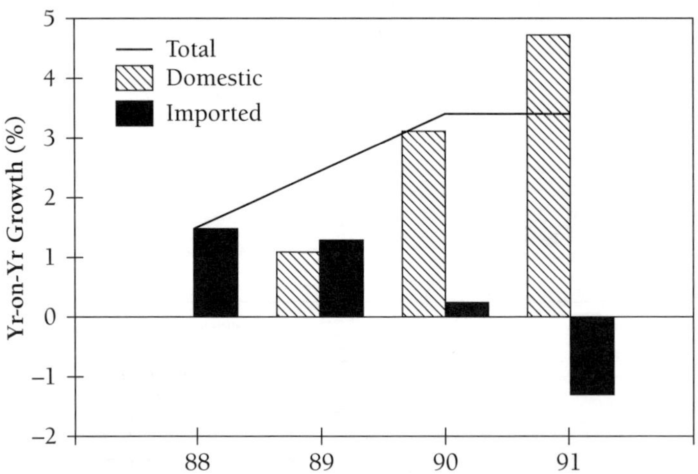

Source: *MAS Econometric Model of the Singapore Economy.*

Chart 13 CPI Level if Exchange Rate Had Not Appreciated from Mid-1988 to End-1991

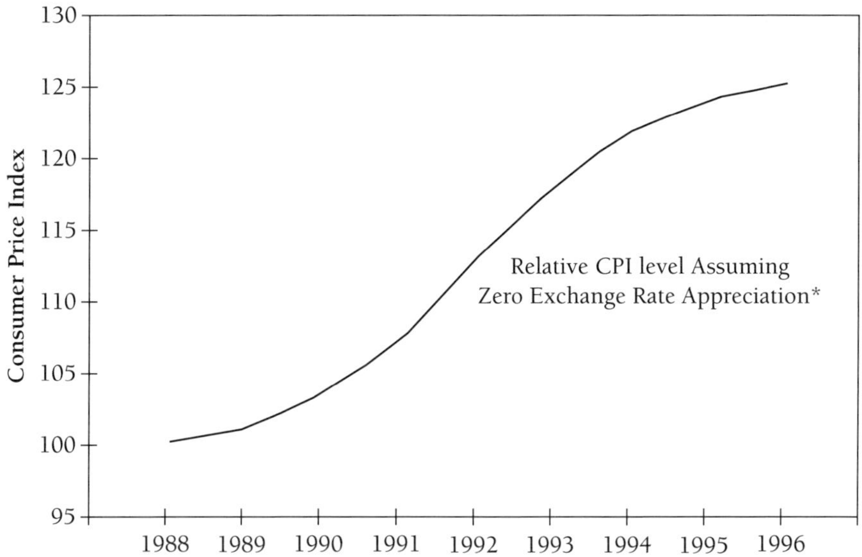

* The graph depicts the simulated path of the CPI if there was zero exchange rate appreciation over the period from mid-1988 to end-1991, relative to the path resulting from the actual appreciation over the period. (Index value of 100 refers to the CPI level resulting from the actual exchange rate appreciation over the period.)

Source: *MAS Econometric Model of the Singapore Economy.*

Table 1 Inflation in Singapore and Abroad, 1979–1991
% change per annum

Year	OECD Consumer Prices	Singapore			
		Imported Consumer prices 1/	Nominal Effective Exchange Rate (NEER) 2/	Unit Labour Costs (ULC)	Consumer Price Index (CPI)
1979	10.4	6.0	4.0	13.6	4.0
1980	13.5	8.8	2.8	8.8	8.5
1981	10.8	4.5	6.5	10.8	8.2
1982	8.0	–1.7	6.6	15.1	3.9
1983	5.6	–4.0	3.0	7.6	1.2
1984	5.6	1.0	2.2	3.9	2.6
1985	4.9	–2.3	–1.6	1.0	0.5
1986	3.0	0.4	–14.1	–11.2	–1.4
1987	3.6	3.8	–5.7	–4.2	0.5
1988	4.3	3.4	–0.7	3.5	1.5
1989	5.4	1.2	6.9	8.5	2.4
1990	5.8	–3.0	6.7	6.1	3.4
1991	5.2	–1.1	3.2	5.9	3.4

1/ This is not an official index. It is computed as a weighted average of disaggregated price indices for imported consumer goods.

2/ Value of the S$ against a weighted average of currencies. The weights used here are computed by the IMF. They differ from those used by the MAS for the purpose of exchange rate policy, although the general direction of the index shown is not dissimilar.

Sources: *OECD Main Economic Indicators; figures computed from Department of Statistics (DOS) Singapore, Monthly Digest of Statistics.*

Table 2 GDP Growth in Singapore and Abroad 1980–1991 (% change per annum)

Year	OECD Real GDP Growth	Singapore			
		Real GDP Growth			Unemployment Rate 1/(%)
		Overall	Construction	Manufacturing	
1980	1.5	9.7	11.0	10.0	3.5
1981	1.6	9.6	17.6	9.3	2.9
1982	–0.6	6.9	36.4	–3.5	2.6
1983	2.9	8.2	29.3	2.8	3.2
1984	5.2	8.3	15.5	7.5	2.7
1985	3.8	–1.6	–15.4	–7.3	4.1
1986	2.9	1.8	–22.4	8.4	6.5
1987	3.4	9.4	–9.8	17.3	4.7
1988	4.5	11.1	–3.9	18.0	3.3
1989	3.2	9.2	1.5	9.8	2.2
1990	2.3	8.3	7.2	9.5	2.0
1991	0.8	6.7	21.0	5.3	1.9

1/ As at June.

Sources: *OECD National Accounts; DOS, Singapore, Annual Economic Survey and Year-book of Statistics.*

Table 3 Export Growth — Selected Countries (% p.a., at 1985 prices)

	S'pore	M'sia	HK	Korea	Taiwan
1980	19.8	7.4	10.4	–11.5	11.3
1981	3.0	–5.9	8.4	5.1	5.4
1982	–5.2	6.7	–2.9	–0.5	–0.7
1983	16.9	22.9	15.1	8.5	15.6
1984	25.9	15.8	16.7	13.1	18.2
1985	–4.1	3.9	–5.6	–1.7	5.4
1986	23.2	25.2	16.5	13.6	32.4
1987	35.4	31.3	21.2	34.7	38.3
1988	40.7	27.8	8.9	27.1	13.1
1989	11.6	29.1	0.1	4.7	12.0
1990	12.5	28.5	–0.5	–2.0	1.2

Note: S'pore — Non-oil domestic exports
M'sia — Manufactured goods HK — Domestic exports

Sources: *Various official sources.*

MAS Merges with Board of Commissioners of Currency, Singapore

Mr Lim Hng Kiang
Minister for Health and Second Minister for Finance, and Deputy Chairman, MAS

Second Reading Speech in Parliament
Currency (Amendment) Bill 2002
23 July 2002

In January this year, the government announced its plans to merge the Board of Commissioners of Currency, Singapore (BCCS) with the Monetary Authority of Singapore (MAS). The merged entity would still be called MAS. This is an organisational change to streamline our institutional structure. There will be no change in the way currency is managed. The Singapore dollar notes and coins that are currently in circulation will continue to be fully backed by the Currency Fund.

Background

BCCS was set up in 1967 to implement the currency board system, which Singapore then practised. The features of the currency board system were: First, the exchange rate was fixed between the domestic currency and a specified foreign currency; second, domestic notes and coins were fully convertible at the fixed exchange rate; and third, the domestic currency was fully backed by foreign assets or gold.

Singapore has progressively evolved away from the system of a fixed exchange rate since the Singapore dollar was floated in 1973. In 1982, convertibility of domestic currency notes and coins into gold and other foreign currencies on demand was repealed. Today, the exchange rate of the Singapore dollar is managed by MAS, against a basket of currencies of our main trading partners, with the objective of keeping inflation low and maintaining the purchasing power of the Singapore dollar.

The only feature of the currency board system that we have retained is the full backing of currency-in-circulation by external assets. Hence, Singapore no longer operates a currency board system except for the full backing of currency-in-circulation. This is required under the Currency Act, and has contributed to confidence in the Singapore dollar. This feature will not change after the merger. Currency-in-circulation will continue to be fully backed by external assets at all times.

From a broader perspective, confidence in the Singapore dollar exchange rate derives from the consistency and soundness of our monetary and fiscal policies, as well as our foreign reserves. The merger of MAS and BCCS will enable us to rationalise common functions and realise efficiency gains, without compromising the overriding objective of managing the currency and maintaining confidence in the Singapore dollar. MAS will become a full-fledged central bank.

This Bill seeks legislative amendments to the Currency Act to effect the merger of MAS and BCCS. This Bill also contains other amendments which are intended to update and streamline certain procedures and provisions in the Currency Act.

I shall now highlight the main amendments proposed in the Bill.

BCCS Funds

Currently, the Currency Act requires that the face value of the currency issued by BCCS must be at least 100% backed by external assets in the Currency Fund. A separate fund — the Currency Reserve Fund — serves as a buffer for the Currency Fund, as the value of the external assets that make up the Currency Fund may fluctuate. All dividends, interest or other revenue from the Currency Fund and the Currency Reserve Fund are paid into a Currency Fund Income Account. All expenses incurred by BCCS are charged to this Currency Fund Income Account.

With the merger, the Currency Fund and the Currency Reserve Fund would be combined as one fund, which would still be called the Currency Fund. The new Currency Fund would continue to provide at least 100% backing for the currency-in-circulation at all times. Clause 6 amends Section 21 to provide that assets in the Currency Fund in excess of 100% of the face value of currency in circulation could be transferred to MAS' other funds at any time. Section 21 is also amended to provide that any deficiencies in the Currency Fund will be made up from MAS' funds. If MAS' funds are insufficient, the balance of the deficiency will be paid out of the Consolidated Fund.

Clause 7 repeals Sections 22A and 23 pertaining to the Currency Reserve Fund and the Currency Fund Income Account. Under the new arrangement, income from the Currency Fund will be ploughed back to the Currency Fund itself, and expenses arising from currency issue and investments will be charged against the Currency Fund.

Definition of Legal Tender

Currently, Section 13 provides the legal tender limits for the various denominations of the currency. The notes and coins issued by BCCS are legal tender up to the value specified in Section 13 for the purpose of discharging any debt or paying for goods and services.

Over the years, BCCS has regularly received queries from the public regarding the definition of "legal tender". Some members of the public were unclear whether merchants could refuse to accept certain coins of small denomination.

The payment for goods and services is essentially a contractual agreement between a willing buyer and a willing seller. Neither party can be forced to enter into the transaction unless he willingly does so. In order to clarify the intent and purpose of the law, Clause 5 will amend Section 13 to allow a merchant to specify that he will not accept one or more denominations of notes or coins as payment for his goods or services. If the merchant does not specify any conditions on how he would like to be paid, then he must accept legal tender for the settlement of the debt, or else the debt may be forgiven.

Conclusion

The proposed amendments in this Bill are part of the legislative amendments required to implement the merger of BCCS with MAS. The proposed transfer of past reserves from BCCS to MAS as past reserves would require amendments to the Constitution. This will be covered separately in the Constitution (Amendment) Bill, which would be presented for Second Reading at the next available sitting. The Constitution (Amendment) Bill will also propose the deletion of BCCS from the Fifth Schedule of the Constitution.

Mdm Deputy Speaker, I beg to move.

Singapore Parl Debates; Vol 75; Sitting No 5; Col 700 –704; 23 July 2002.

Asian Monetary Integration: Will It Ever Happen?

Mr Tharman Shanmugaratnam
Minister for Education and Second Minister for Finance, and Board Member, MAS

The Per Jacobsson Lecture
17 September 2006

Introduction: The Changing Premises of the Debate

The last Per Jacobsson Lecture in Asia was in 1997. Mr. Joseph Yam, Chief Executive of the Hong Kong Monetary Authority, spoke on a topic broadly similar to what I am speaking on today, which is Asian monetary integration or, as he put it at the time, Asian monetary cooperation. September 1997 was at the onset of the Asian crisis. Since then, there have been major changes and considerable evolution in the debate on Asian monetary integration.

The Asian crisis proved deeper than anyone could have foreseen in September 1997. It has left a scar on the minds of Asian policymakers. But the recovery from the Asian crisis has also been robust, a recovery that is founded on structural reforms that were put in train as a result of the Asian crisis. Exchange rate regimes have evolved. They are by and large more flexible. Capital controls and restrictions — some had been in place for a long time, some were put in place during the crisis — have been eased. And trade and investment are proceeding apace. The region is increasingly integrated in trade and investment and, to a lesser extent, in financial flows.

So Asia today is a very different place from 10 years ago.

The original motivation for proposals for Asian monetary integration — which started off as proposals for an Asian monetary fund and a parallel set of proposals for an Asian currency, that is, a common currency or monetary union — had to do with a desire to reduce Asia's susceptibility to shocks, particularly financial shocks. There was also a broader sense that Asia had to be more self-reliant and gain fuller control over its destiny. And this broader sense reflected, in part, a discomfort at the time with what was known as the Washington Consensus, and a particular discomfort over the role of the IMF in the Asian crisis. Monetary union was in some ways a metaphor for Asia wanting to manage its own affairs.

But Asia has evolved. Asia has recovered. While the crisis remains in our minds, we are no longer in crisis. The Washington Consensus, although of course never a fixed or clearly identified set of views, has also been refined over the years. The conventional wisdom, whether at the IMF or in academia or in policymaking circles in the West, has evolved. There is greater circumspection with regard to optimal exchange rate regimes, greater recognition of the merits of intermediate solutions — as distinct from corner solutions — in exchange rate policy. There is a more nuanced view on the merits of capital controls and restrictions in specific circumstances. And there is a much sharper recognition of the need for financial market stability during periods of structural reform and, in particular, of the need to avoid precipitating financial panic.

Not surprisingly, the objectives and motivations behind the continuing debate for Asian monetary integration have also evolved. The objectives are no longer defensive, no longer preoccupied with crisis prevention or resolution. They are now more forward looking. The objectives are about growth, about greater trade integration, about spurring greater cross-border flows of investment within Asia, and about promoting the integration and deepening of financial markets.

It will be useful, before I address directly the issues involved in Asian monetary integration, for us to take stock of how we are faring in trade integration and financial integration, respectively, because these are the ultimate objectives of the proposals that we have before us on monetary integration. Whether what is proposed is a common currency or a parallel currency or managing Asian currencies against a common basket of currencies, the objective is to promote trade and financial integration so as to enhance economic welfare.

Asian Trade Integration Is Driven by Asia's Integration with the World

First, let us take a look at trade. Intraregional trade in Asia is already rather high. No one expected it to get to this point so quickly. In 1980, intraregional exports were about 34% of total Asian exports. That proportion is now 50% — not so different from among the member countries of the North America Free Trade Agreement (NAFTA), although still below Europe, where it is about 61% or so, and certainly below Europe at the time of formation of the European Union (EU), when intraregional trade was about 65% of total trade.

At 50%, a big chunk of Asia's trade is now already intraregional. But it is fundamentally different in nature from Europe in a number of respects. Intraregional trade in Asia has been driven from bottom-up, by the activities of firms involved in cross-border production processes. It is basically a supply-driven process.

One indication of this is in the composition of intra-Asian trade, which is quite different from that of intra-European trade. Intra-Asian trade consists principally of intermediate goods — raw material inputs and components of one form or another — rather than final goods, which is what has characterised much of intraregional trade in Europe both before the formation of the EU and after.

It has been about vertical integration, with China playing a key part in this. The surge in intraregional trade in Asia has in fact been shaped by China's integration into the world economy. Around China has been built a whole set of supply chains in different industries that extend across Asia, including Japan, Korea and Southeast Asia.

This means also that rising intraregional trade in Asia has not been a process of Asia increasingly looking inward. It has been part and parcel of

Asia's integration with the rest of the world economy. If you look at the last 10 years, 1995–2005, intraregional trade within Asia doubled in volume, which is a very substantial expansion by any standard. But, at the same time, there was no change in the share of Asia's intraregional trade to its total trade, because trade with the rest of the world expanded equally rapidly. So, over the past 10 years, the share has remained at 50% — despite the doubling in the volume of intraregional trade.

So it has been a bottom-up, supply-driven process, linked to the manufacturing supply chain, which is increasingly centred on China.

What next? How will this evolve?

I think we are about to enter a whole new phase of growth of intraregional trade in Asia, and, 20 years from now, it is a fair guess that we will have reached a position not very different from Europe today. There are three reasons why I say this.

Three Factors Driving a New Phase of Trade Integration in Asia

First, we are seeing now the start of a new phase of foreign direct investment (FDI) inflows within Asia. There are several factors behind this.

I start with Japan, which is still the largest Asian economy: at market exchange rates, which is what matters for international trade and investment, Japan has the largest GDP in Asia by far, twice as large as that of China. Japan has seen a recovery of corporate profitability and a recovery in the financial position of its banks. It is a healthier economy. And the fundamental transformation in Japan that took place in the 1990s, which was halted for some years, is now likely to pick up pace: the shift from manufacturing to research, and design-driven production, and to services. This will mean a decanting of manufacturing operations, particularly many forms of mass manufacturing that are still located within Japan, out of the country, with major implications for Asia. Take Japan today and compare it with the United States. 24% of Japan's GDP is still in manufacturing, whereas for the United States, the proportion has fallen to 14%. Japan has 18% of employment in manufacturing, compared with 10% for the United States. In both countries, these shares have declined over time, with Japan typically about 15 years behind the United States. And I think Japan is going to continue to move in that direction. It may not reach US levels, but it is going to continue to decant manufacturing offshore. The numbers that we are talking about are very large.

The Economist Intelligence Unit (EIU) estimates that the stock of Japanese FDI abroad will increase by 65% in the next five years. Historically, about one-third of Japanese investment abroad has gone to other countries in Asia. We can expect at least one-third of the increase in the stock of Japanese investment in the next five years and beyond going to the rest of Asia. But it will not be only a China story. Japanese firms have already significantly stocked up on their investments in China. They had been underinvested in China. Their subsequent investments in China have corrected for this, and they are now no longer underinvested in China. So, going forward, for fresh flows of Japanese FDI, we can expect to see a more diversified set of locations — not just China, but Southeast Asia and India as well, that is, a more diversified approach covering the whole of Asia. And with that will emerge new supply chains like what we have seen in the motor industry in Southeast Asia, but extending to a whole set of other industries.

Next, besides Japan, we are now seeing the start of a wave of outbound FDI from other Asian countries that we have not seen before: in particular, from China and India, which will be the major new players in the next 20 years. Chinese and Indian firms are substantial players that are now looking across Asia for new markets as well as new sites for production, much as the Western and Japanese multinationals did in an earlier era. And this, too — whether it is Tata Steel or Huawei, or a whole new set of firms coming out of these two large megaplayers — this too is going to lead to increased intraregional trade.

The second factor that is propitious to the growth of intraregional trade is the fact that the middle class is now coming into its own in Asia. It is already large, but it is now growing much faster than GDP. By some estimates, by 2010, we will have a middle class of about 650 million people in China, India and Southeast Asia. That is about 75% growth in five years, which will mean a tremendous escalation of demand for things that you cannot obtain at home. They will want imported products, which differentiate themselves from the others. This is going to spur a whole new growth of imports, not just from within Asia. There will be an expansion of Asia's demand for the world's exports. The Asian supply chain will increasingly be oriented not just to the United States and Europe but also to Asian final demand as well. This is a new phase in intraregional trade.

The third factor is the broadening of free trade agreements (FTAs). The momentum of FTAs in Asia is growing. The Association of Southeast Asian Nations (ASEAN) was a leader, and ASEAN has now set itself a more ambitious target of achieving an ASEAN Economic Community by 2015 — with a free flow of goods, services, investments and skilled people within the Community. ASEAN is also negotiating with China and India to have FTAs with those two megaeconomies.

What started as bilateral deals have cascaded into regional FTAs and can eventually support multilateral trade liberalisation. It is a cascading process which tends to be a little messy and some say carries the risk of having a "spaghetti bowl" or "noodle bowl" effect. But I would say, better a bowl full of noodles than an empty bowl. Better that we create the momentum and the political economy that favour reform in each of these economies through bilateral and regional FTAs. That can only be propitious to multilateral trade liberalisation.

So this process of FTAs, starting with bilaterals, moving on to regionals and then cross-regional FTAs, is itself going to spur intraregional trade in Asia. This is another reason why I say we are very likely to get to at least 60% of Asian trade being intraregional within 10 years.

A resurgence of intraregional investment and the growing domestic demand spurred by a rapidly expanding middle class will lead to an expansion of intraregional trade, aided and abetted by FTAs that reduce barriers to trade within the region. It is essentially a bottom-up process, aided top-down. With or without monetary union, we are likely to get heightened intraregional trade.

Urgency of Asian Financial Integration

Next, I shall talk about financial market integration — because this too is an important reason behind proposals for a common currency. This is where Asia has lagged, as we all know. Financial market integration has lagged substantially behind trade integration, and this is why Asian saving surpluses are intermediated largely through financial markets outside Asia.

The reasons are also well known. Asian financial markets outside Tokyo are mostly small and illiquid. Bond markets are especially underdeveloped, although government bond markets across the region are now in better shape than they were five or six years ago. However, by and large, the secondary markets for government bonds with maturities beyond five years are not liquid, so there is a lot more work to be done. The corporate bond market is at a fledgling stage. It is more developed in countries like Malaysia and Singapore, where it represents about 40% of GDP but, otherwise, in Asia at large, this is the big opportunity for reform and development in financial markets. My colleagues and I have been speaking about this at other fora, so I will not elaborate here.

Equity markets are more developed but they also are fragmented and less liquid than those in the industrial countries. Market turnover or velocity ratios are generally lower than in the United States or Europe. As a result, Asian equity investors, by and large, have looked elsewhere. They have looked outside Asia to invest surplus funds and to diversify their portfolios. In fact, only 12% of the foreign portfolios of Asian investors are invested within Asia itself. Compare that with the European Union, where about two-thirds of the foreign portfolios of European investors are invested within the EU.

The situation will evolve. It will evolve especially as exchange rates become more flexible so that surplus savings in Asia are not principally held in the form of official foreign reserves but, increasingly, in the form of private holdings of foreign assets.

It will also evolve through collaborative efforts to develop the capital markets in Asia. This is something that cannot be left to the markets alone, because capital markets development requires public goods to be in place.

It requires governments to act, first, to adopt international standards of disclosure and international accounting standards, and, second, to provide harmonised rules and regulations across Asia to increase access and reduce costs for investors. We are working on these issues in several fora, including the Executives' Meeting of East Asia-Pacific Central Banks (EMEAP), ASEAN and ASEAN+3 (ASEAN plus Japan, China and Korea). There is clearly a lot more work to be done.

We also have to set in place the infrastructure that is required for capital markets to be integrated. There is presently no working cross-border clearing or settlement system in Asia for either the fixed-income or equity markets. It is virtually non-existent. This is again something which all of us are working on — the Asian Development Bank and various regional fora. We need some urgency in this process of putting in place the infrastructure as well as the rules and regulations to encourage greater cross-border flow of funds.

Easing Capital Restrictions

It will also require an easing of capital controls and restrictions in Asia. We know that sequencing is important. We know that the pace at which you ease capital controls and lift them has to be shaped by prudential considerations and linked to financial stability, particularly of the banking system. But the direction has to be clear and we cannot afford to be too slow in this process.

Asian policymakers have to address the trade-off that we have always faced: the trade-off between wanting to avoid the volatility that comes with freer capital mobility, on the one hand, and wanting and needing greater liquidity in our markets, on the other. We will not have more liquid markets without a freer flow of capital, both from within the region and from global markets. And everyone wants liquidity — not just short-term investors or alternative fund managers but also long-term investors, who prefer more liquid markets so that they can exit without paying a high price. So what is in the interests of short-term investors is also by and large in the interests of long-term investors.

We have to pay careful attention to sequencing. But we cannot be too slow in lifting capital controls and restrictions in the region if we want to develop healthier and deeper financial markets.

We should aim for a seamless flow of trading, clearing and settlement across the debt and equity markets in Asia. But the outcome of this will not, I think, be what you see happening in Europe, where you have an extremely heavy concentration of financial activity in one financial centre, that is, London, with a number of smaller, satellite financial centres outside London. In Asia, I can see, for a long time to come, vibrancy in several centres: Tokyo, by virtue of the enormous hinterland around it provided by the Japanese economy; Shanghai too, increasingly servicing a large domestic hinterland; Mumbai coming up and eventually occupying the same place; the international financial centres, namely, Hong Kong and Singapore, each having distinct niches, competing with each other, but also complementing each other; and other domestic financial centres — Kuala Lumpur, Bangkok, Jakarta — some of which will also have international niches, like Kuala Lumpur in Islamic finance.

Therefore, I see competition and complementarity in this emerging set of financial centres across Asia — not the London effect.

Asian Monetary Integration: A Way Forward

What do these developments mean for Asian monetary integration?

The debate over Asian monetary integration is now about whether a common currency or some system of coordination of exchange rate policy across Asia can foster enhanced intraregional trade, investment and financial flows. There is a decent economic case for expecting that it would. Most of the economic studies of such currency unions provide evidence that either a common currency or some formal arrangement to link currencies with each other will be advantageous to intraregional trade and financial flows. In the European case especially, it is clear that the development of financial markets and cross-Europe financial flows have been spurred by the introduction of the euro.

Put simply, the European experience involved a schema where

economic integration started principally with trade, then moved on to monetary integration. A single currency, in turn, spurred greater financial integration and reinforced trade integration. The question is whether this European schema is relevant or appropriate for Asia. I would argue that it is not.

Why the European Schema Is Not Appropriate for Asia

The fundamental issue for policymakers concerns the trade-off between the benefits of having a common currency, which arise principally from enhanced trade and financial integration, and the costs of losing autonomy over domestic monetary policy — that is, losing the ability to adjust either your exchange rate or domestic interest rates in response to your own economic cycle. This is the basic trade-off that Asian policymakers inevitably face when they ask themselves if a single currency, or any other form of monetary integration, will enhance economic growth and the welfare of their citizens.

Are Asian countries prepared to lose their ability to use the exchange rate as a shock absorber in certain circumstances? Are they willing to lose the ability to adjust interest rates to respond to economic cycles? And is nominal convergence a necessary prerequisite in Asia for real economic convergence — for achieving a greater commonality of economic cycles in countries across the region and achieving over time a convergence in real incomes?

Even in Europe, this question is still being played out. These are still early days in the experience of the euro zone, but the evidence so far is that nominal convergence has not led to a narrowing of real economic differences. Some argue that nominal convergence has accentuated real economic divergences because of the loss of flexibility on the part of national policymakers to use monetary policy as a buffer or mechanism for adjustment in response to economic shocks.

Asia will face a more challenging task than Europe in ensuring that the costs of monetary integration do not outweigh its benefits. First, because economic disparities in Asia are wider than in Europe — far wider. In Europe, disparities in per capita income across countries are something in the order of 3 or 4 to 1; meaning that the richest economy, in terms of per capita income, is about three to four times richer than the poorest within the group. In Asia, the ratio is about 50–100 to 1.

What this also means is that we are likely to see, for a very long time to come, a large difference in growth rates between Asian economies with low per capita GDPs that are catching up and transforming themselves, like China and some of the ASEAN economies, and the more mature, higher-income, slower-growing Asian economies. This will likely mean different paths for their real effective exchange rates as well.

Second, economic structures in Asia are very different. We have economies that are governed by advanced technology and services, economies that are largely agrarian, and economies where mass manufacturing is the driver of growth. So these are very different economic structures, even with a high overall degree of intraregional trade. The shocks that Asian economies face and their response to shocks will therefore often be asymmetric. This makes exchange rate coordination a tricky task, even under the favourable conditions.

Third, there is a lack of a suitable anchor player. In the 40 years of transition to a common currency in the euro zone, the first 15 years involved pegging to the US dollar while the last 25 years really involved de facto pegging to the deutsche mark. How this became possible can only be explained by events and experiences specific to European history — a history that brought a Germany that had gone through hyperinflation to be totally committed to low and stable inflation, and whose post-war social compact gave the Bundesbank the independence to pursue monetary policy with that singular objective. Further, because Germany was by far the largest economy in the Europe of the last quarter century and the divergences between Germany's circumstances and the rest were not so wide, most European countries were willing to commit themselves to following the Bundesbank. That is how they made this transition to a single currency, over 25 years — and even then with considerable stresses and strains in the union along the way.

Asia does not have the equivalent of a Germany to anchor the transition. Japan, currently the largest economy, has the low inflation preferences required of an anchor country. But Japan is very different from the other economies for reasons I have mentioned — different growth profile, different economic structure, different shocks affecting it, different responses to shocks. And Asia lacks, very obviously, the political history that brought the leading European countries together to decide that as a matter of political imperative, a union was preferable to any other outcome. Asia lacks that.

Will China — which will eventually be the largest Asian economy — play the role of a Germany? This is hard to envisage. China, for the next 20 or 30 years, will be an economy going through major transformation. It is still a principally agrarian society. No one can predict exactly how China will unfold. But an economy going through major structural transformations cannot play the role of anchor. Further, it will take some time before China itself can have an efficient monetary policy transmission mechanism.

So we do not have the advantage that Europe had in making the difficult transition from having different national currencies to a common currency by following a de facto leader in the deutsche mark.

Asia's strength lies in its diversity. This diversity is what makes intraregional trade an attractive and compelling economic proposition. This diversity can also help in the diversification of financial portfolios across Asia. But, it is this same diversity that militates against monetary integration, because it raises its costs, including the risks of destabilisation arising from monetary union.

Intermediate Proposals for Asian Monetary Integration

If a common currency or monetary union is therefore not viable, are there alternative intermediate proposals that are worth considering? Several proposals have been made. Broadly speaking, they fall into two sets.

The first is the idea of a currency basket — for Asian countries to manage their own currencies against a common basket through some form of a coordinated, managed float system. This common currency basket system would serve to constrain monetary policy and exchange rate policy independence among the member countries. Each of us would use the same currency basket as the benchmark, and adopt some form of a peg or managed float against this basket: possibly a band with a centre point, with some flexibility in terms of the crawl of this band, but essentially de facto fixing against a common currency basket.

This is an appealing idea, but it would face great challenges of transition. With freer capital movements — which are essential if we want trade and financial integration — and our divergent economic circumstances in Asia, it would be especially challenging to sustain a system equivalent to the exchange rate mechanism (ERM) or the snake in Europe for a period of years. Even the ERM faced tremendous stresses along the way, requiring great political commitment to the eventual goal of achieving monetary union, to see them through. Asia does not have the same political imperative. So the strains and stresses arising from a coordinated system of pegs or managed floats against a common currency basket will not only risk destabilising monetary integration but could also erode confidence in the larger game of Asian integration in trade and finance.

The second set of proposals involves establishing a parallel currency — an ACU or Asian Currency Unit, just like the former European Currency Unit (ECU). Some of the proponents of an ACU will make it very clear that this is not a transition to a common currency: the proposal is merely for the setting up of a parallel currency, that is, a unit of account that could be used in the settlement of cross-border trade, or by financial institutions as a currency of denomination for bonds and other financial instruments. It will be a market-driven process with no obligation on the part of the national monetary authorities to peg their currencies to the ACU. It is a parallel benchmark of sorts.

I think this is worth considering, particularly if it can promote the debt market in Asia and help develop the regional capital market. It is not in any sense a scheme for monetary integration: there would remain national currencies with national monetary policies. I see it as a scheme for financial integration. It would be useful to have a currency of denomination that is widely accepted across Asia for bonds and other instruments: this is something we can explore.

But most proponents, like Barry Eichengreen, also agree that it will be a very slow process for an ACU, or any parallel currency, to be accepted by the market. Even in Europe, before the advent of the euro, the ECU never really took off as a currency of denomination, whether for financial assets and instruments or for trade. It never really displaced national currencies before the euro actually came into being.

If that was the case in Europe, it is all the more likely to be true in Asia. I would say that we can explore this idea, particularly if we can use a parallel currency to spur the development of financial markets, but it is not a scheme that takes us in the direction of monetary integration as such. And, as some have pointed out, too, prudential supervisors will also want to make sure that financial institutions, particularly banks, when using an ACU as a currency of denomination for loans or other assets, will not face currency mismatches vis-à-vis their national currencies, which have typically been the currencies of denomination of banks' liabilities. So prudential supervision is also likely to hinder the advancement of an ACU.

So an ACU is not a bad idea, but it is not intrinsic to the larger argument of whether we need Asian monetary integration or some form of coordination of national currency movements.

Toward *De Facto* Monetary Policy Coordination

What, then, is the alternative? I think the alternative is what we are already seeing unfold before us. First, Asian exchange rates have now become a lot more flexible, compared with the period before the Asian crisis. To be sure, we are not all rushing toward freely floating exchange rates; in fact, apart from the yen, I do not think there is any other truly freely floating exchange rate in Asia today. But the majority of Asian currencies are now in some form of a managed float, with varying degrees of fixity or flexibility. We are all mostly operating a managed float system, that is, an intermediate solution. That is the first development.

Second, there has been increasing adherence to inflation targeting, or commitments to low and stable inflation as the objective of monetary policy. We see this across the region. Although the inflation thresholds may differ, the thresholds are all coming down. There is increasing clarity and conviction that the objective of monetary policy is to maintain low and stable inflation.

The combination of these two developments — the shift toward managed floats and the shift in the objective of monetary policy toward low and stable inflation — has brought about, de facto, a certain degree of coordination in monetary policy across Asia. Indeed, if you look at the correlation of Asian exchange rates over the past six years, that is, 2000–2006, compared to the years before the crisis, 1990–1996, the correlation for the recent period has been much higher despite the move toward greater currency flexibility.

I think this de facto monetary policy coordination — not top-down, but obtained because national authorities find it in their own interests to move in this direction — is not a bad way to go. It preserves flexibility when required. It allows secular trends in effective exchange rates to diverge over time to reflect the very different rates of productivity growth and the different transformations we are going to see among economies in Asia.

And it retains the agenda for change as a national agenda. Any top-down process, any process that is overly coordinated in Asia — by a committee or body outside of the national authorities — will not incentivise politicians to take ownership of change. The future of Asia is about change and reform in almost every sphere, requiring great political effort to convince populations, convince banks, convince firms, to move, to open up, to shake out the inertia. And unless national politicians and authorities feel that they own the agenda, change is going to be difficult.

This process that we are seeing — market-driven, national authorities responding to their own economic circumstances — leading, de facto, to increased monetary coordination is, I think, the best way to go.

Conclusion: Keeping the Geometry Open

Let me conclude.

Intra-Asian trade has come a long way and has more potential yet. The FTAs that we are working on now across the region will foster its growth, but it is essentially a market-driven process. Market forces are going to take it further. Financial market integration has been progressing more slowly, and there is a lot more work to be done — it deserves greater urgency.

These are the big projects, the welfare-enhancing projects — trade integration and financial integration. These are the projects that will deepen liquidity and lower the cost of capital, spur investment, raise growth and lower unemployment, which are the objectives of Asian policymakers. And they are founded, ultimately, on the diversity that we see in Asia. This same diversity is what will constrain monetary integration, and even the transition to any form of monetary integration.

The present path toward de facto monetary coordination is therefore, in my opinion, superior to any scheme of formal coordination.

Will it be necessary to have a scheme of formal coordination at some point in the future? I don't know. We need not rule it out, but the case is not compelling as it stands. The case is not compelling to move from de facto coordination toward a more formalised arrangement of exchange rate coordination.

We will only know in 20 years' time what the new Asia will look like. We will only know what happens to China, India, Japan and Southeast Asia, and what the interactions will be between them, as we go along. This is a continent in transformation, and that means that we should not fix the geometry too early, whether in trade or in finance or in monetary integration. And monetary integration sends very strong signals on what the geometry is. We should keep the geometry fluid, keep it open, keep it looking outward. That is what has gotten us to where we are today, and remains crucially relevant for tomorrow.

Japanese economists such as Kojima used the metaphor of "flying wild geese" ("*ganko keitai*") to describe the phenomenon of Asian industrial development through regional economic integration. Japan, at that time a leader, passed down technology and know-how to the NIEs (newly industrialised economies), which in turn passed it on to the Southeast Asian countries in a process of collective catch-up. It was a scheme that described the links and interdependencies between the Asian countries and how we ride on each other's strengths. It was a good description of Asia in the 1970s and 1980s. It may be too structured, too hierarchical to describe the Asia that is now evolving. But it is not a bad way to look at Asia going forward, if we see flexibility in the arrangement and constant leap-frogging, yet all countries moving up in tandem.

Asia need not be defensive about not following the European path of top-down integration. We should celebrate the fact that Asia has got where it is through bottom-up, market-driven efforts. Keep it open, keep it fluid and avoid doing anything that leads to a tripolar world.

Getting in All the Cracks or Targeting the Cracks? Securing Financial Stability in the Post-Crisis Era

Mr Ravi Menon
Managing Director, MAS
First Asian Monetary Policy Forum
24 May 2014

Monetary Policy at the Crossroads

I would like to particularly thank Steve Davis of Chicago Booth and Bernie Yeung of NUS Business School. It was your vision and tireless effort that made this Forum possible. You have assembled here a dazzling array of eminent economists and respected practitioners to discuss and debate the most pressing questions in monetary policy today.

One of these questions must be: what role should monetary policy play to help secure financial stability? For two decades before the Global Financial Crisis, central bankers thought they had found the secret sauce of monetary policy. The recipe was simple — an independent central bank, a single target (price stability) and a single instrument (the interest rate). Monetary policy was directed at achieving price and output stability, with the central bank's reaction function well-characterised by the Taylor rule on an ex-post basis.

The recipe worked brilliantly. Sustained price stability and steady economic growth were the order of the day. The result was the Great Moderation. Indeed, monetary policy was getting boring.

Monetary policy was unencumbered by financial stability considerations. To be fair, central bankers were not unconcerned about financial stability. But financial stability was seen as the preserve of prudential regulation and supervision. Academic thinking reinforced policy practice: the macroeconomic models central banks relied on did not map clear linkages between financial and real variables.

Economists warned that it was difficult to identify a financial bubble. How does one tell if the value of an asset reflected economic fundamentals or speculative fever? So, when faced with potential financial vulnerabilities, it was deemed better to clean up after a bubble had actually burst than to try to lean against suspected bubbles.

But beneath the still waters of macroeconomic stability, deadly financial whirlpools were forming. Financial imbalances built up steadily in the advanced economies from the mid-1990s to mid-2000s and culminated in the Global Financial Crisis of 2008/2009. The Crisis sent financial systems into a tailspin and plunged economies into recession. The cost of cleaning up after the bubble had burst proved extremely high. The "clean versus lean" debate has been re-ignited, and within the "lean" camp there are differences over how to lean. Monetary policy has become interesting again.

Financial Stability: What We Know and What We Don't Know

Following the Crisis, there has been growing consensus that it is important for central banks to pay more attention to financial stability. We know now that macroeconomic stability does not guarantee financial stability. Nor does prudential supervision of individual institutions guarantee financial stability at the systemic level.

We also have a much better appreciation of how credit cycles have strong implications for financial stability.

- Moritz Schularick and Alan Taylor describe financial crises as "credit booms gone wrong".[1] Risks to financial stability stem from both the pace of credit creation as well as the level of credit.

[1] The phrase is taken from Eichengreen and Mitchener's 2003 BIS working paper on "The Great Depression as a Credit Boom Gone Wrong".

- Claudio Borio and Piti Disyatat argue that the amplitude of financial cycles, such as for credit, exceeds that of business cycles due to what he calls "excess elasticity" of the financial system. Cross-border financial flows amplify domestic credit booms and domestic monetary policy fails to constrain the credit creation process adequately.
- Frederic Mishkin warns how the bursting of credit-fuelled asset price bubbles can lead to episodes of financial instability that are particularly damaging for the economy.

These findings help us better understand the conditions that led to the Global Financial Crisis. And the concerns remain valid in the post-Crisis environment. Central banks have kept policy rates low for long, and purchased assets in large quantities further out along the yield curve.

Even though the United States is already "tapering" its asset purchases, global financial conditions remain extremely loose. There are signs of growing risk-taking: in the form of leveraged loans, covenant-lite corporate bonds and narrowing spreads on sub-investment grade paper. The risks to financial stability are nowhere near pre-Crisis levels, but they bear close watching. We must not repeat the mistakes of the past.

But there is as yet no consensus on how to secure financial stability and, in particular, what role, if any should be played by monetary policy.

There are three broad approaches to these questions.

- The first is to stick to the status quo. Monetary policy remains focused on price stability and no recourse is made to macroprudential policy beyond the use of capital buffers to pre-empt insolvencies.
- In the second approach, monetary policy explicitly takes account of financial stability in addition to price stability.
- Under the third approach, monetary policy remains focused on price stability, while financial stability is secured with the help of macroprudential policy.

I will keep my remarks on the first approach brief as it is well-known and is still the dominant practice in most central banks today, especially in the advanced economies. Under this inflation targeting approach, monetary policy will not try to respond to credit cycles or asset bubbles unless they have a demonstrable impact on inflation outcomes.

- As Lars Svensson puts it, flexible inflation targeting "remains the best-practice monetary policy before, during, and after the financial crisis."
- John Taylor, who will address us this evening, provides a more rule-based characterisation of this approach through the Taylor rule.
- He finds that if monetary policy in the US had been appropriately configured to macroeconomic outcomes in the 2000s, the housing boom would have ended in 2003 instead of 2006 and that mortgage debt levels would not have risen so high.

Let me now take up the second and third approaches in more detail.

Monetary Policy: Getting in All the Cracks

The intellectual underpinning for the second approach is based on the insight that monetary policy has the potential to affect financial stability through the "risk-taking channel".[2]

- Jeremy Stein puts it succinctly — "Monetary policy is fundamentally in the business of altering risk premiums."

Loose monetary policy can heighten vulnerabilities in the financial system by altering both the perception of risk and the tolerance for risk.

In conventional monetary policy, lower policy rates boost incomes and profits, and enhance asset and collateral values. This reduces banks' estimated probability of defaults and losses, leading to greater leverage and risk-taking.

---

2 Borio and Zhu (2012) coined the term 'risk-taking' channel of monetary policy to refer to the transmission of monetary policy through its impact on asset and collateral values, which would consequently influence agents' willingness to take on risk.

In unconventional monetary policy, large scale asset purchases by central banks depress returns along the entire yield curve. This provides asset managers the incentive to take on more risk, often in a herd-like fashion.

When interest rates are below the natural rate at which desired investment and savings equilibrate, banks will continue to expand credit. When economic agents are determined to take risks, they will find ways to circumvent measures that central banks and regulators have put in place. Non-monetary tools like macroprudential policy will therefore not adequately address the root problem caused by interest rates that are too low.

Under these circumstances, only monetary policy can "get in all of the cracks" to plug the vulnerabilities. An increase in short-term interest rates will trigger a more realistic evaluation of asset and collateral values, income flows and thus risks. This will curtail the extent of leverage created by banks and capital markets and keep asset managers from crowding into risky assets. The effects of monetary policy are all-pervasive, and cannot be easily circumvented.

This approach, if formalised, amounts to augmenting the Taylor rule with an additional term to capture deviations in financial variables from their equilibrium levels.[3] If financial market imbalances are growing, *ceteris paribus*, monetary policy should be tightened, even if it causes further deviations in output from potential in the short term. This approach does not preclude the need for robust financial regulation and supervision. But the key is to get the price of money right, to encourage a more realistic perception and tolerance of risks.

While no central bank currently implements monetary policy in this way, the concept behind the approach may not be as abstract as it seems. I know from my conversations with central bankers that they do not ignore financial stability considerations when setting monetary policy.

[3] The augmented Taylor Rule equation is: $i_t = \pi_t + r_t^* + \alpha_\pi(\pi_t - \pi_t^*) + \alpha_y(y_t - y_t^*) + \alpha_f(f_t - f_t^*)$, where f is a variable that measures financial market vulnerability, and f* is the equilibrium level of that variable.

Why "Getting in All of the Cracks" May Not Always Work

Relying solely on monetary policy to secure financial stability may not always be sufficient. Let me offer three reasons why.

- First, monetary policy could be constrained by its traditional mandate: price and output stability.
- Second, monetary policy could be constrained by global financial factors.
- Third, monetary policy may get in all the cracks, but it may not be able to fill some of them.

I will touch on each of these considerations in turn, drawing from the Asian experience in recent years.

First, it is possible that there is a conflict between the objectives of price stability and financial stability in the short term. Financial cycles have longer frequencies than business cycles, and the two cycles tend to diverge. The interest rate appropriate for price and output stability may therefore not be consistent with financial stability. This has been the case in Asia in recent years.

When Asian economies recovered fairly quickly from the Global Financial Crisis, their central banks raised interest rates. This was, by a happy coincidence, congruent with the need to stem rapid credit growth that was being fuelled by improved economic prospects domestically and easy monetary conditions globally.

But subsequently, economic activity in Asia started slowing down, following the Eurozone debt crisis and other domestic shocks. It became untenable for Asian central banks to raise interest rates further. However, risk-seeking capital flows continued washing into the region, inducing further increases in credit and asset prices. The business cycle and financial cycle began to diverge.

A second constraint on the effectiveness of monetary policy to deal with domestic financial stresses is the prominent role played by international liquidity in fuelling these stresses.

- Philip Lane has detailed the strong inter-linkages between global liquidity conditions, international debt flows and domestic credit conditions.
- Hélène Rey has observed that global liquidity conditions determined by advanced economies' monetary policies, can, at times, override domestic monetary policy even with exchange rate flexibility.
- Maurice Obstfeld, who will speak on this subject in a few minutes, takes a less extreme view. He argues that monetary independence is still possible, but because of the impact of financial globalisation, monetary policy carries a much bigger burden in trying to achieve both financial stability and purely macro objectives.

Recent Asian experience is illustrative. The exuberance in Asian asset markets and consequent build-up of financial risk in recent years has been exacerbated by the global search for yield in a zero interest rate environment. Raising policy rates may not sufficiently alter the level of risk-taking in these economies.

In fact, paradoxically, a central bank that tightens monetary policy to stem financial vulnerabilities could perversely attract more capital flows into the economy, resulting in stronger credit growth and rising asset prices.

Third, it is not clear that monetary policy can fill all the cracks. Monetary policy flows into all the cracks no doubt, but some cracks are just too big to fill.

Financial vulnerabilities are not evenly spread across the economy. They tend to be concentrated in specific sectors and segments, such as in real estate. So, even when monetary policy has configured overall liquidity and risk-taking settings appropriately, specific pockets of financial market vulnerabilities, e.g., a property bubble, could remain.

Monetary policy is too blunt an instrument for addressing such specific risks to financial stability, and it can cause significant collateral damage on the rest of the economy if it tries to do so.

- During a property boom, compared to interest rates, expectations of price appreciation may have a greater influence on current prices.

- Kenneth Kuttner and Illhyock Shim estimate that a 100 basis point increase in the short-term interest rate would lower real annualised credit growth by less than 1 percentage point in the following quarter. Such a rate hike will also reduce real housing price growth by only 1 percentage point.
- Using monetary policy to prick a property bubble may therefore require very sharp increases in interest rates to be effective. But this may have unintended spillovers on other parts of the economy.

Macroprudential Policy: Targeting the Cracks

This brings us to the third approach to securing financial stability: using macroprudential policy, while monetary policy continues to focus on price and output stability. Macroprudential policies can be more effective for "targeting the cracks" where specific vulnerabilities are concentrated.

But what exactly are macroprudential policies? Given its recent rise to prominence, it is still a nebulous concept with differing definitions. Let me offer my thoughts on what macroprudential policy is and what it is not, from the perspective of Singapore, which has been an early experimenter and practitioner in this area.

First, it is closely related to yet distinct from microprudential policy. Some have called macroprudential policy "old wine in new bottles". Yes and no. Many of the tools are indeed the same as the microprudential limits familiar to regulators: loan-to-value ratios, debt-to-income ratios, debt service ratios and so on.

But there are some key differences. When these prudential limits are used for macroprudential purposes, the scope and impact are much larger. Let me give an example.

A loan-to-value ratio of 80% for property loans, applied through the cycles, as we have had in Singapore for many years, is a microprudential tool. But when we limit the loan-to-value ratio to 20% for a third property loan, as we have done in Singapore recently, it becomes a macroprudential measure.

Macroprudential policy may well be old wine, but it is in much bigger bottles!

Second, unlike monetary policy which has a single instrument, macroprudential policy requires a multi-dimensional approach. There is no single instrument that has a stable and reliable relationship with financial stability or asset price stability.

Macroprudential policies encompass more than just counter-cyclical capital buffers. Adjusting capital requirements in a counter-cyclical fashion or increasing the risk weights for loans to vulnerable sectors cannot fill the cracks completely. In a boom market characterised by keen competition among banks, higher capital charges do not translate into sufficiently higher lending rates that can restrain demand.

A cross-country study by the Basel Committee on Banking Supervision shows that a 1 percentage point increase in capital ratios results in a median rise in lending spreads of only 13 basis points.

Dealing with the magnitude of financial cycles or bubble dynamics that economies typically face from time to time requires some absolute prudential limits. In Singapore, we have employed the following limits on property loans:

- Loan tenure cap of 35 years.
- Loan-to-value ratios of 80%, 50% and 40% for the first, second and third property loans respectively, for tenures less than 30 years; for loan tenures more than 30 years, the loan-to-value ratios are 60%, 30% and 20%.
- Total debt-service ratio of 60%, taking into account all debt obligations and using a medium-term interest rate of 3.5% for residential properties. (Current mortgage rates are generally below 2%.)
- Cap on banks' property-related exposures at 35% of their total exposures.

In fact, macroprudential policies need not even be limited to prudential tools at the disposal of central banks or financial regulators. In the face of abundant global liquidity, credit-based prudential measures may not constrain loan growth or asset price increases sufficiently. Singapore has therefore also adopted fiscal measures such as stamp duties on buyers and sellers of properties as part of the macroprudential toolkit.

The seller's stamp duty ranges from 4% to 16%, while the buyer's stamp duty ranges from 3% to 18%. These are essentially transactions taxes that aim to curb the speculative flipping of properties.

Third, it is important to draw a distinction between macroprudential policies and capital flow management measures. Capital flow measures are applied "at the gate" seeking to regulate flows into and out of the economy; macroprudential measures are applied "inside the house" targeted at sectors where financial vulnerabilities are building up.

Capital flow measures are highly distortionary and pose long-term costs to the economy. Clearly, such measures should not take the place of needed macroeconomic adjustments. Capital flow measures may be warranted under extreme circum-stances to safeguard financial stability. But as the IMF puts it, their implementation should be "targeted, transparent and generally temporary".

Asian economies have deployed macroprudential policies to deal with financial imbalances, to a greater extent than other economies. So far, the results have not been bad. They have largely tempered the credit cycle and the pace of asset price increases, while generally maintaining price and output stability.

A Synthesis?

Let me bring together the main strands of my remarks. The view that central banks ought to pay due consideration to financial stability is gathering momentum. I have described two alternative approaches to the status quo to achieving this:

- The second approach incorporates financial stability considerations in the setting of monetary policy; and
- The third actively uses macroprudential policy to help secure financial stability.

Perhaps the differences between the two approaches are exaggerated. Both approaches require the central bank to integrate monetary policy functions effectively with prudential policies.

- In the second approach, strong supervisory and regulatory policies have to be in place even as monetary policy adjusts the level of risk-taking in the economy.
- In the third approach, monetary policy must be appropriately calibrated to the economy for macroprudential measures to effectively target specific areas of imbalances.

In practice, the difference between the two approaches is likely to be one of degree and emphasis rather than of fundamental principle. Central banks will choose the most appropriate combination of the two approaches, taking into account the structure of their economies and the nature of the threats to financial stability existing at any point in time.

And let us not forget the continued relevance of the traditional approach. Just because central bankers had previously ignored financial stability considerations with costly consequences, we must not overcompensate now by placing such an undue burden on monetary policy to secure financial stability, that it becomes detrimental to price and output stability.

We do not need to reinvent macroeconomics. Nor do we need to discard most of what we know about monetary policy, built from decades of rigorous research and painful experience. Much of that knowledge remains relevant. In thinking about the so-called new normal, we should pay equal heed to what is new and what remains normal. No doubt, we need to update our paradigms to meet new realities. But we do not need to overhaul them.

We should also bear in mind that the current situation is highly unusual. We must not fall into the trap of believing that the innovative policy measures being taken now in response to these unusual conditions represent the basis for a new paradigm in the future.

I suspect that when the dust has settled and more normal conditions return, monetary policy regimes will not look drastically different from pre-Crisis days.

I think more central banks will have an eye to financial stability considerations — at least informally — when setting monetary policy. More central banks are also likely to have macroprudential policy toolkits at their disposal, which they will use from time to time but perhaps not on the scale that has been used in Asia in recent years. But in essence, monetary policy will remain largely focused on price and output stability — as it should be.

Perhaps as T. S. Eliot puts it, the end of all our exploring is to arrive where we started and know the place for the first time.

References

Bank for International Settlements (2010), "An Assessment of the Long-Term Economic Impact of Stronger Capital and Liquidity Requirements", Basel Committee of Banking Supervision.

Borio, C and Disyatat, P (2011), "Global Imbalances and the Financial Crisis: Link or No Link?" BIS Working Papers No. 346.

Borio, C and Zhu, H (2012), "Capital Regulation, Risk-Taking and Monetary Policy: A Missing Link in the Transmission Mechanism?" Journal of Financial Stability, Vol. 8(4), pp. 236–251.

Eichengreen, B J and Mitchener, K J (2003), "The Great Depression as a Credit Boom Gone Wrong", BIS Working Papers No. 137.

IMF (2012), "The Liberalization and Management of Capital Flows: An Institutional View", Staff Paper.

Kuttner, K and Shim, I (2013), "Can Non-Interest Rate Policies Stabilise Housing Markets? Evidence from a Panel of 57 Economies", BIS Working Papers No. 433.

Lane, P R (2014), "International Capital Flows and Domestic Credit Conditions", Macroeconomic Review Vol. XIII(1), Monetary Authority of Singapore, Economic Policy Group.

Mishkin, F S (2008), "How Should We Respond to Asset Bubbles?" speech at the Wharton Financial Institutions Center and Oliver Wyman Institute's Annual Financial Risk Roundtable, Philadelphia, Pennsylvania, 15 May 2008.

Obstfeld, M (2014), "Trilemmas and Tradeoffs: Living with Globalization", paper commissioned for the Asian Monetary Policy Forum (draft).

Rey, H (2013), "Dilemma not Trilemma: The Global Financial Cycle and Monetary Policy Independence", Proceedings, Economic Policy Symposium, Jackson Hole, Federal Reserve Bank of Kansas City.

Schularick, M and Taylor, A M (2009), "Credit Booms Gone Bust: Monetary Policy, Leverage Cycles and Financial Crises, 1870–2008", NBER Working Paper No. 15512.

Stein, J C (2014), "Comments on "Market Tantrums and Monetary Policy", speech at the 2014 U.S. Monetary Policy Forum, New York, 28 February 2014.

Svensson, L E O (2009), "Flexible Inflation Targeting — Lessons from the Financial Crisis", Speech at the Workshop "Towards a New Framework for Monetary Policy? Lessons from the Crisis", organised by the Netherlands Bank, Amsterdam, 21 September 2009.

Taylor, J B (2007), "Housing and Monetary Policy", NBER Working Paper No. 13682.

How Singapore Manages Its Reserves

Mr Ravi Menon
Managing Director, MAS
National Asset-Liability Management Europe Conference
13 March 2019

Singapore has official foreign reserves (OFR) of almost US$300 billion. In absolute terms, this is the eleventh highest stock of OFR in the world. As a percentage of GDP and on a per capita basis, it is the third highest in the world.

Singapore's OFR sit on the balance sheet of the Monetary Authority of Singapore (MAS), the central bank and integrated financial regulator. Besides the OFR, there are two other pots of national reserves in Singapore:

- The Government of Singapore Investment Corporation (GIC), a fund management company, manages on behalf of the Singapore Government a diverse portfolio of foreign assets — well in excess of US$100 billion.
- Temasek Holdings, an investment company wholly owned by the Singapore Government, holds equity stakes in a variety of domestic and foreign corporates, amounting to more than US$200 billion.

This morning, let me try to answer three questions:

- What role do the reserves play?
- How are the reserves accumulated and managed?
- How are the OFR managed?

Why Does Singapore Hold Reserves?

Singapore's reserves serve three objectives:

- one, to serve as a buffer against crisis;
- two, to provide a stream of investment income to help finance part of the annual government budget; and
- three, to maintain confidence in Singapore's exchange rate-centred monetary policy. The reserves are thus a rainy day fund, an endowment fund and a stability fund.

The imperative to hold a buffer against crisis is rooted in Singapore's geography and history. Singapore is a city-state smaller than Greater London. It has no natural resources and imports most of its food, including water.

When it became independent in 1965, it had no hinterland and meagre financial reserves. It depended mostly on entrepot trade and hardly had an industrial base. It was not expected to survive, let alone succeed.

An acute sense of vulnerability has been part of Singapore's DNA since its birth. This sense of vulnerability, in turn, underpinned two convictions:

- first, that the only way to survive and make a living is to make ourselves relevant to the world; and
- second, we must build up strong buffers so that we can withstand the shocks that come with being so small and open to the world.

As Singapore grew and prospered as a business and financial centre, its vulnerabilities to the vagaries of global trade and financial cycles also grew. The need to build up a sufficient rainy day fund to tide us through shocks and crises has remained as relevant as ever. Total trade is three times the size of the Singapore economy. Gross capital flows into and out of Singapore are 77% of GDP.

The role of the reserves as a rainy day fund is not theoretical. The reserves have indeed served us well in past crises. They helped underpin confidence in Singapore in the throes of the Asian Financial Crisis. And during the Global Financial Crisis, the reserves were drawn down to finance a package of measures, to preserve jobs by subsidising employers' wage bills and to help viable companies stay afloat by sharing the risk of bank lending.

A second purpose of the reserves is to serve as an endowment. This purpose has grown in importance — and salience — in recent years. The income from investing the reserves provides an increasingly important source of revenue to fund government expenditure. The size of government in Singapore is small. Government spending — comprising both operating and development expenditure — is just about 16% of GDP. But tax and non-tax revenues are even lower, at 15% of GDP. In other words, Singapore runs a structural deficit on its primary fiscal balance.

This is where the investment income from the reserves comes in. The Constitution of Singapore bars the government from borrowing to spend or to spend surpluses accumulated from previous terms of government. Instead, it allows the government to spend up to half of the expected long-term real returns from the net assets invested by MAS, GIC and Temasek. This is known as the Net Investment Returns Contribution (NIRC). The NIRC is already the largest single contributor to revenues in the government budget, accounting for about one-fifth of revenues.

The role of the reserves as an endowment from which to draw a steady stream of income to finance the government budget will become even more important in the years ahead. An ageing population will mean higher expenditures, especially for healthcare, and slower economic growth will mean lower tax revenues.

The third purpose of the reserves is to serve as a stability fund. More specifically, the reserves help to maintain confidence in Singapore's exchange rate-centred monetary policy framework.

As Singapore is a small and highly open economy, inflation and aggregate demand are more significantly influenced by the exchange rate rather than interest rates. Singapore's monetary policy is therefore centred on managing the exchange rate of the Singapore Dollar against a basket of currencies within a policy band. The reserves play an important role in enabling MAS to conduct monetary policy and to secure macroeconomic stability.

How Are the Reserves Accumulated and Managed?

So, how are the reserves accumulated and managed? As I mentioned earlier, Singapore's reserves are held and managed in three distinct pots: MAS, GIC and Temasek.

The government sets the overall investment objectives for the three entities and monitors the risk and return profile of the total reserves. But it plays no role in the investment decisions by the three entities, which are made on purely professional grounds.

MAS, as Singapore's central bank, manages the OFR. The process of accumulating or using OFR is intricately tied to MAS' conduct of monetary policy. MAS may accumulate or sell foreign assets, principally through its intervention operations in the foreign exchange market, to manage the float of the Singapore Dollar. Given Singapore's positive net savings and persistent capital inflows, the nominal exchange rate often tends to appreciate more than what is required to keep inflation low and stable. MAS accumulates foreign assets on average in the process of managing the Singapore Dollar within its policy band even as it sells foreign assets during times of stress on the Singapore Dollar.

As the central bank, MAS is the most conservative of the three investment entities, with the OFR invested mainly in safe and liquid assets. The OFR is sized to take into account its role as a buffer against a large and sudden outflow of capital that would undermine confidence in the exchange rate and Singapore's macroeconomic stability. Traditional measures of reserve adequacy such as the number of months of imports the OFR could finance if all other sources of foreign financing dried up are less relevant for Singapore. A sizable and liquid OFR sends a clear signal that MAS has the wherewithal to resolutely defend the Singapore Dollar against speculative attacks.

The GIC is a professional fund management company that manages the government's foreign assets. These assets are separate from the OFR.

The history of GIC begins with MAS. Through the 1970s, Singapore ran persistent fiscal surpluses, received sizeable capital inflows and had an elevated private savings rate. This led to a substantial accumulation of OFR, well in excess of what was required for MAS' central banking operations.

So, in 1981, the GIC was set up — in today's parlance, as a sovereign wealth fund — to manage part of the reserves for higher returns without the central bank constraints of liquidity. Part of the OFR was transferred from MAS to GIC, which was tasked to invest the reserves in a globally diversified portfolio of asset classes with a higher risk profile to deliver good long-term returns.

The third pot of reserves is managed by Temasek Holdings, an investment company wholly owned by the government. Temasek's history also dates back to the early years of Singapore's development. There was little private capital in those days but a rapidly industrialising economy needed key infrastructure — in aviation, in shipping, in telecommunications, in banking and so on. The government therefore set up enterprises in these areas.

Temasek was formed as a holding company in 1974 for these enterprises so that the government could focus on its roles of policy making and regulation without conflict, while Temasek would own and manage these investments on a commercial basis.

Today, Temasek is an active, equity investor that aims to deliver sustainable long-term shareholder value. More than a quarter of Temasek's portfolio is invested in Singapore, with the rest invested in Asia and global markets. The initial portfolio was provided by the government, but since then, Temasek's funds have come mainly from the investment growth of its own portfolio. Compared to MAS and GIC, Temasek is further out on the risk-return spectrum.

How Are the OFR Managed?

Let me now move to the third question: how are the OFR managed? This is the portion of the reserves that MAS is responsible for.

There are three prongs to MAS' approach to managing the OFR:

- robust risk management;
- balanced asset allocation; and
- efficient investment process.

Robust risk management

The starting point to MAS' approach to managing the OFR is its risk management framework, which sets out the liquidity and risk tolerance levels of the OFR. These relate to:

- the ability of the portfolio to meet liquidity needs under stress conditions; and
- the maximum loss of the portfolio under tail risk scenarios.

These liquidity and risk tolerance levels are determined on the basis of what is minimally required to meet the objectives of the OFR in supporting MAS' conduct of monetary policy. They are factored in the construction of the MAS portfolio and closely monitored on an ongoing basis.

MAS employs a comprehensive range of stress tests to assess the risks to the portfolio on an ongoing basis and establish whether the portfolio remains resilient to potential tail risk events over the medium term.

Three types of stress tests are conducted:

- Historical: Shocks are applied to the portfolio using asset price movements seen in historical stressed episodes, such as the Global Financial Crisis, 2000 dot-com bust, 1994 bond market selloff, etc.

- Vulnerability-based: The portfolio is subject to hypothetical scenarios which stress in turn each of the portfolio's risk factors such as equity, interest rate, credit, inflation and foreign exchange.
- Thematic: These are forward-looking stress tests and are designed by taking into account prevailing market conditions and potential risk events on the horizon.

Depending on the stress test results, MAS will consider appropriate responses and portfolio adjustments when needed. The risk management framework is reviewed on a regular basis to ensure it remains fit-for-purpose.

Balanced asset allocation

Subject to the liquidity and risk tolerance thresholds, MAS seeks to achieve good long-term returns on the OFR through a balanced asset allocation.

MAS invests the OFR in a well-diversified portfolio, probably more diversified than is the case for most central banks. The portfolio is geographically diversified across advanced and emerging market economies, with investment-grade bonds in advanced economies making up the largest share. The portfolio is diversified across asset classes — in cash, bonds and equities. The portfolio has a diversified currency mix, with about three-quarters of the OFR denominated in US Dollars, Euros, Japanese Yen and Pound Sterling, with the US Dollar forming the bulk.

Each asset class in the portfolio serves a function. Cash and nominal government bonds facilitate regular operational needs and can be quickly deployed to fulfil urgent liquidity needs under stressed conditions. Advanced economy inflation-linked bonds are less liquid than nominal bonds but provide inflation protection. Equities provide exposure to long-term growth assets with higher return potential but also with higher risk. MAS' investment horizon is longer than that of many central banks. This has given MAS the flexibility to invest in more volatile (and longer 'duration') asset classes beyond fixed income, including equities.

Both the risk management framework and strategic asset allocation are approved by the MAS Board of Directors and reviewed regularly.

Efficient investment process

MAS strives to achieve an efficient investment process, underpinned by two elements:

- one, judicious benchmark selection and customisation; and
- two, tapping on specialised external investment expertise.

First, benchmark selection. MAS uses asset class benchmarks to represent the investment universe and risk profile of each asset class that can be easily replicated, to evaluate its investment performance.

These benchmarks could be market-capitalisation weighted or customised. For some asset classes, we have chosen to apply certain customisations to market-capitalisation weighted benchmarks, guided by considerations of liquidity, stability and concentration risk.

One area we have applied customisation is in the fixed income asset class, where it is relatively more important to guard against concentration risk. This is because the response to credit risk is more asymmetric for fixed income than for equities. There is limited upside for credit improvement but large downside from the threat of default. We have therefore limited our exposure to some large government bond markets, taking into account the default risk of these bonds.

Another area where we have customised our benchmark is with respect to Renminbi (RMB) assets, in particular Chinese government bonds. Here, the consideration was not to limit exposure but to gain exposure ahead of market benchmark inclusion as markets develop. MAS started investing in RMB assets in 2012, fully expecting market indices to catch up at some point. Indeed, recent announcements by major index providers to include or accelerate the schedule of inclusion for RMB assets in their indices reflect this trend.

Next, tapping on relevant investment expertise. Part of the MAS portfolio is managed by reputable external fund managers. These investment managers are hired for their deep investment expertise and specialised knowledge in particular investment fields.

For instance, factor-based investing is an area that we are watching closely. Institutional investors are starting to look beyond asset classes to view returns via a "factor lens". There are two applications of this approach, return enhancement and portfolio analysis. Looking through asset class labels to underlying risk factor exposures can enhance understanding of return sources. Flipping them around, they also help to enhance understanding of risk drivers.

In fact, the vulnerability-based stress tests that I described earlier are an application of this factor approach. This can help investors to create more efficient and diversified portfolios, compared to a traditional asset class-driven approach. But we are also mindful not to fall into the trap of data-mined quantitative strategies that rely on factors that may not be robust through time.

Conclusion

In Singapore, reserve management is a multi-objective, multi-agency and most importantly, a multi-generational effort.

The reserves serve as a buffer against bad times, as an endowment to finance current needs, and as a foundation for macroeconomic stability.

As custodians of the national reserves, MAS, GIC and Temasek owe a duty of care and responsibility to the ultimate beneficiaries of the reserves — current and future generations of Singaporeans. It is a duty that motivates our investment and risk managers as they go about their work each day, trying to extract value while staying clear of pitfalls, amidst the turbulence, tides and ebbs of financial markets.

FINANCIAL REGULATION AND SUPERVISION

oneRaffles
UOB
ASCOTT

Financial Regulation and Supervision

The speeches in this section trace the continuous improvements in MAS' regulatory and supervisory approach over the years to ensure financial stability and strengthen risk management. The first half of MAS' journey as a regulator till 1997 was one of building strong foundations for a sound regulatory and supervisory framework. This was followed by a period of regulatory reforms, from 1997 to 2008, centred on taking a more risk-focused and disclosure-based approach and liberalising the financial industry to inject greater competition. The period from 2009 to 2016 was marked by alignment with international regulatory reforms following the global financial crisis and an increased focus on market conduct, financial crime, and enforcement. The period since 2016 has been dominated by continuous adaptation of regulation amid rapid advances in technology changing the financial landscape.

Foundations for a Sound Regulatory Framework

A strict admission framework and close supervision in the early years laid a strong foundation for MAS' financial regulatory framework. In July 1979, Mr Michael Wong Pakshong articulated the importance of MAS' gatekeeping role of *ex-ante* screening and licensing of financial institutions, supplemented by close *ex-post* supervision of their activities.

As Singapore's financial sector grew, MAS continued to strengthen its regulatory functions.

In 1980, Mr Law Song Keng described how MAS' approach to insurance regulation helped to protect the interests of policyholders as well as to provide the foundation for the healthy development of the insurance industry. Major changes were made to the Insurance Act in 1986 to improve the supervision of insurers, strengthen their financial positions, and protect policyholders in the event of insolvency of an insurer.

Speaking in 1984 on the first major amendments to banking legislation, Dr Goh Keng Swee explained how enhancements to MAS' supervisory powers facilitated prudential oversight of the banking system and strengthened corporate governance and accountability. Measures were also introduced to ensure that major shareholders of the local banks were fit and proper.

In the aftermath of the Pan-Electric crisis in 1985 that shook the stockbroking industry, Singapore's securities regulation was revamped to promote sound and orderly functioning of the securities markets. In 1986, Mr J. Y. Pillay highlighted measures to strengthen the regulation of stock broking firms. The Securities Industry Act was revised to impose capital requirements on brokers, restrict margin lending, toughen insider trading rules, and strengthen MAS' powers to supervise the industry.

As futures trading developed in Singapore, the Futures Trading Act was introduced in 1986 to require futures markets to operate in a fair and orderly manner. Speaking at the third anniversary of the Singapore International Monetary Exchange in 1987, Mr Pillay explained the role that futures markets played in helping market participants manage their risks.

In 1995, Mr Lee Ek Tieng outlined measures to enhance the regulation of futures traders and to strengthen risk management in financial institutions, following the collapse of Barings Bank arising from unauthorised trading that took place in Barings Futures (Singapore).

In a 1991 speech, Dr Richard Hu provided an overview of MAS' philosophy that the development of financial markets had to take place within the framework of an effective regulatory system. The credibility, soundness, and stability of Singapore's financial sector was a source of strength to long-term financial centre development. Dr Hu explained that MAS had to subject financial institutions to high standards of regulation and supervision given their access to savings from the public, their role in mobilising capital to finance economic growth, and their operation of the payments system.

Risk-Focused Supervision and a Disclosure-Based Regime

Against the backdrop of the Asian financial crisis in 1997 and increased globalisation and competition, MAS undertook a fundamental review of its regulatory approach and launched a series of reforms.

In a seminal speech in 1997, Mr Lee Hsien Loong articulated the shift in MAS' emphasis from a one-size-fits-all regulatory approach towards risk-based supervision. Financial institutions which managed their risks well would be given greater flexibility, while those less well-managed would be subjected to closer scrutiny. Alongside this shift was a move towards greater reliance on market discipline and information disclosure so that consumers of financial products could make better informed decisions.

Mr Lee announced in 2000 the introduction of regulatory measures to separate financial and non-financial businesses within Singapore's locally incorporated banking groups, so as to reduce contagion risks from non-financial activities and to focus management attention on the core banking business.

That same year, Mr Koh Yong Guan described MAS' move towards greater harmonisation of rules across financial activities, as the lines between various financial activities became more blurred.

The enhanced regulatory approach enabled a progressive liberalisation of Singapore's banking industry. In 2001, Mr Lee took stock of MAS' first round of liberalisation in 1999 which opened up foreign banks' access to the retail market and helped precipitate consolidation among the local banks. He also outlined a second round of liberalisation measures.

With a more competitive banking landscape, it was felt necessary to strengthen protection for depositors. In 2002, Mr Lim Hng Kiang announced MAS' decision to introduce a deposit insurance scheme. The commencement of deposit insurance in 2006 was followed by a protection scheme for insurance policy owners in 2011.

In 2000, Mr Lee explained the context for MAS' announcement earlier that year of its intention to regulate securities and futures trading activities under a single licence, and the provision of personal investment and financial planning advice, also under a single licence. The Securities and Futures Act and the Financial Advisers Act were introduced in 2002.

In 2001, Mr Tharman Shanmugaratnam provided an overview of MAS' new approach to the regulation of capital markets, with a strong reliance on disclosure and market discipline, together with raising business conduct standards. He also laid out the new division of regulatory responsibilities between MAS and the Singapore Exchange following the latter's demutualisation and listing.

Supervision of the insurance industry was also updated, alongside a full liberalisation of market access in both the life and general insurance business. In 2002, Mr Lee outlined MAS' move towards risk-based supervision of insurers and risk-based capital requirements for the insurance industry.

Post-Crisis Regulatory Reforms

The strengthening of risk-based regulation and supervision in the late 1990s and early 2000s served Singapore well when the global financial crisis erupted in 2008. Singapore's financial system remained resilient and stable amidst the turmoil experienced by many developed countries and markets.

In 2010, Mr Heng Swee Keat outlined MAS' approach in light of post-crisis international regulatory reforms and the emerging financial landscape. This comprised sensible regulations of high standards; effective supervision; and partnership with the industry to forge a shared responsibility for sound prudential outcomes.

Drawing on experience from the global financial crisis, Mr Shanmugaratnam observed in 2012 that financial systems that had held up well, such as in Canada, Australia, Hong Kong, and Singapore, were anchored by banks with a significant share of the domestic market and that these "anchor" banks were closely supervised and regulated.

Mr Shanmugaratnam announced MAS' new framework to encourage foreign banks in Singapore to deepen their roots in the country.

In 2011, Mr Ravi Menon articulated MAS' approach to the regulation of capital markets post-crisis, aimed at fostering adequate disclosure by issuers; safeguarding the interests of investors; promoting proper market conduct by intermediaries; and ensuring the stability of market infrastructure, including the regulation of over-the-counter trading of derivatives.

Noting that the global financial industry continued to be dogged by repeated cases of financial malfeasance and mis-selling, Mr Menon emphasised in a 2015 speech the need to instil a culture of trust, values, and ethics in the financial industry.

In 2016, Mr Menon provided an overview of MAS' approach to ensuring resilience, dynamism, and trust in Singapore's financial sector. Resilience was achieved through ensuring strong capital and liquidity buffers and proactive risk management in financial institutions. To maintain Singapore's reputation as a trusted financial centre, MAS intensified its supervision of risk governance and culture in financial institutions; stepped up enforcement actions against misconduct; and strengthened its anti-money laundering regime.

Regulation in the Digital Age

From about 2015, rapid advances in digital technologies were beginning to have a significant impact on the financial sector. MAS was one of the early regulators to recognise the rise of FinTech. In a 2016 speech, Mr Menon described MAS' evolving regulatory approach to FinTech, harnessing its benefits while managing its risks.

Against the backdrop of innovative payment services increasingly offered by non-financial players, MAS revamped its regulatory approach to strengthen consumer protection and promote confidence in the use of digital payments. Mr Ong Ye Kung introduced the Payment Services Bill in Parliament in 2019, explaining how the enhanced legislative framework adopted an activity-based approach, tailoring regulatory requirements to the scope of payment services offered.

In 2019, Mr Shanmugaratnam unveiled MAS' new framework for digital banks. Recalling the successful banking liberalisation programme in the late 1990s and early 2000s, and noting the transformative potential of digital technology, Mr Shanmugaratnam articulated MAS' vision to add diversity to the banking system with the entry of new high quality digital banks, while ensuring continued resilience in the new era of digital finance.

Supervision of a Regional Financial Centre

Mr Michael Wong Pakshong
Managing Director, MAS
International Conference of Banking Supervisors, London
5 July 1979

I welcome the opportunity to share the Monetary Authority of Singapore's experience in supervising a regional financial centre. If any of my observations should stimulate a fruitful exchange of ideas about some of the complexities facing banking supervisors and regulators, not only in the much more publicised field of international banking — but also in the more routine — but no less important realm of domestic banking, I would have gone some way towards fulfilling my brief.

At the outset, I should explain that the Monetary Authority of Singapore does not only supervise banks. Our area of responsibility includes:

- Finance Companies (where the regulations are spelt out in the Finance Companies Act).
- Merchant Banks.
- Foreign Exchange and Money Brokers.
- The Gold Exchange of Singapore.
- Insurance Companies and Insurance Brokers.
- Moneychangers (They perform the same function as the BUREAU D'EXCHANGE or CAMBIOS which you have in Europe, but as far as I can see our moneychangers give the tourists a much better deal).

It is not my intention to comment on the Gold Exchange, the insurance industry or moneychangers. In the context of our Conference, they are subjects which fall outside our terms of reference.

In one sense, the fundamentals of supervision are unlikely to be so very different. Insofar as we have adopted a specific way of tackling our task, it may illustrate a response to a particular problem in discharging our responsibilities as supervisors in our environment.

Licensing of Banks

A question which must be faced in the evolution of any country's financial system is establishing the criteria to be applied whereby banks are formally and legally permitted to conduct business as banks. There are a number of issues which must be faced, and the response may be different for domestic banks as compared with foreign banks.

Domestic Banks

There are broadly three factors we take into account in licensing new domestic banks:

- Financial Criteria
  In Singapore, we are not likely to license any locally incorporated bank if its capital is not at least S$50 million (US$25 million).
- Shareholding
  The shareholding must be such that citizens or residents of Singapore own 80% of the paid-up capital. If there is a controlling block of shares, we subject the holders to a searching examination.
- Reputation and Standing of Management
  The proposed management personnel are assessed as regards expertise, integrity and other qualitative factors. We have only issued a limited number of licences. One reason for our present conservative licensing policy is that there are a number of family controlled banks which by and large have remained small and in some cases have attracted a disproportionate amount of supervisory effort. It may be that our existing policy reflects our efforts to avoid increasing the number of

family run banks and bring into existence future problems for ourselves. It would interest me to hear any views whether our policy ought to be modified.

Foreign Banks

- By contrast, ever since the Monetary Authority came into being in 1971, we have issued 73 licences to branches of foreign banks. There are:

1	Offshore Branches	36
2	Restricted Branches	13
3	Fully Licensed Branches	24
		73

- The criteria we have applied in admitting foreign branches have evolved over the years. Initially, the main emphasis was put on the size and ranking in world banking coupled with an assessment of reputation, standing and evaluation by peers and competitors. Almost without exception, we have discouraged incorporation of subsidiary banks controlled by foreign banks and have only permitted branches to be opened. This policy was adopted because of our belief that any bank of repute would be morally, if not legally, committed to give full support to its branch operations.
- We give preference to banks which are adequately supervised in their country of origin as well as requiring evidence that the applicant has been given clearance to branch in Singapore by its supervisory authority.
- But where a bank's headquarters is based in a place where there is little or no supervision, it will be appreciated that regional or local supervisory authorities may be faced with sensitive problems of extreme delicacy.
- Letters of Comfort
  When the Asian Dollar Market was inaugurated, all banks which participated were required to give letters from their head offices

undertaking to make good any foreign exchange shortfall in their operations. Some banks objected and some resistance built up. The Bank of England's request for "comfort letters" broke the logjam for us. Once banks agreed to furnish comfort letters to the Bank of England, there was no valid reason for them not to let us have a similar undertaking.

Consortium Banks

While consortium banks operate in Singapore, there are some signs that the enthusiasm of some of their "parent shareholders" may be flagging. The most obvious sign of this is the appearance of branches of the shareholder banks. Is it possible that consortium banks are going to be neglected and become a potential area for concern? Will the management of consortium banks fall into less capable hands?

Other Deposit Taking Organisations

Should institutions other than banks accept deposits from the public without regulation or supervision?

The Singapore approach is to ensure that any institution that gathers deposits denominated in Singapore dollars from the public must be supervised by the Monetary Authority, with the exception of the Post Office Savings Bank (which is guaranteed by government). All finance companies are licensed by us. No new licences have been issued since the inauguration of the Monetary Authority of Singapore.

Merchant Banks

The first merchant bank was admitted in 1970. Although we do not license merchant banks formally, they have grown in number and we supervise them by requiring them to submit regular returns and lay down guidelines for their operations. Through administrative measures, we decide which merchant banks may operate in Singapore. They are not allowed to accept deposits from the public but may do so from associated companies. Nevertheless, based on our assessment of their expertise and capability, we have also permitted most of them to operate in the Asian Dollar Market.

Where they have Asian Dollar capability, we ask for comfort letters.

There is continuing dialogue with the merchant banks who would like to collect Singapore dollar deposits but are not willing to observe liquidity or reserve requirements. There would be a howl of protest from banks and finance companies if we were to oblige the merchant banks. Nevertheless, I believe further evolution will occur to improve their efficiency.

Again, we have tried to ensure that finance companies and merchant banks are owned and managed by responsible institutions and shareholders. Also, we tended to be nationalistic in the early days by insisting on the majority of the equity of merchant banks being owned by Singapore institutions or nationals. However, we rapidly reached a stage where we ran out of local names and institutions which we could recommend as partners with sufficient confidence. Nowadays, we are prepared to accept merchant banks which are fully owned by overseas shareholders.

Bank Examination and Supervision

Even before Singapore embarked on a policy of admitting banks freely, banks were not subjected to annual on-site inspections. If the truth were told, we carried on with inspections to let new recruits — who were taken on when the Monetary Authority came into being — to gain experience as much as to fulfil our supervisory function.

However, even if we wanted to, I doubt if we can achieve a situation where annual inspections can be performed. Increasingly, we are trying to improve regular and timely returns which are reviewed not only to assess operations, quality of assets, maturity patterns and other indicators to enable us to build a better statistical base to form opinion about the banks in our jurisdiction. An increasing emphasis is being placed on this subject. The third approach is to try and hold frequent meetings not only with top management but also bank staff at various levels in order to evolve a better early warning system.

Apart from the statutory audit required by the Companies Act, banks have internal audits. Some foreign banks also send in their auditors from head office as well and to top it all, there are the inspectors from the

Authority. We believe it is worthwhile to examine how the work done by the various sets of auditors can be used to reinforce our supervisory effort. Furthermore, we are exploring ways to see how the external auditor's report to the banks can be made to mesh in with our work as supervisors. This seems to be an area which has some potential for further improvement and benefit not only for us, but for the auditors also.

Concentration of Credit

Important though the risks of international banking may be, it will be agreed that much of the time and effort of any banking supervisor will still be spent trying to see if there is excessive concentration of credit in domestic operations. The dangers of lending for property development do not need elaboration, nor the risk of lending against stocks and shares in a booming stockmarket, especially against inadequate margin.

It is not unusual for government policies to pose problems for banks, especially policies which endeavour to allocate credit on the basis of non-economic criteria. In Singapore, there is presently some concern that the small entrepreneur is getting a raw deal from the banks. The government wants more investment in industry — preferably in the field of high technology. In any such move, banks sail into uncharted areas and if they comply, some losses are inevitable.

How does a supervisory authority fulfil its obligations as a regulator and supervisor and yet at the same time see to it that any bank losses from following national policies are not excessive? In its zeal to supervise, a central bank if it is not careful may even prevent the achievement of the government's objectives.

The international activities of Singapore banks although expanding are not as important to their domestic business. The examination of domestic operations continues to be an important part of the work of the Banking Supervision Department.

One of the problems faced by banks in developing countries is the varying quality of business accounts. In many cases, accounts are not available at all! In this sort of situation, the bank examiners' task is made much more difficult. If accounts are not available, the obvious question to ask the bank is: "Why did you make the loan?" Invariably, the answer has been: "If I don't make the loan, the bank across the road will." We have made progress by letting all banks know that we are not prepared to excuse the non-availability of accounts. The immediate response open to a supervisory authority is to classify all loans unsupported by accounts.

Foreign Exchange Transactions

I do not wish to anticipate the session dealing with the regulation of a bank's foreign exchange business. I would, however, say that apart from requiring regular returns of spot and open positions, and to assess the degree of maturity transformation, the Authority also keeps an eye on the foreign exchange and deposit brokers. While there is no formal licensing system, no brokers can operate unless we approve. Although we have abolished exchange control, our interest in the market has, if anything, increased.

A representative of the Monetary Authority sits as Chairman of the "Foreign Exchange and Money Market Practices Committee" established upon our initiative. This Committee has published a "Guide to Conduct and Market Practice in Foreign Exchange and Currency Deposit Transactions".

Apart from dealing with the technicalities of market practice, we have through this Committee, given a very clear message that the highest standards of behaviour are expected and that "kickbacks" and other abuses will not be tolerated.

International Banking

To get to the heart of the problem of supervising international banking activity in a regional centre, I would like to relate an incident regarding the branch of an international bank. A certain loan of an international bank was classified by my staff after on-site examination. The local management of this bank did not agree with us. After failing to bring us round to his point of view, the local manager asked whether he would be required to make a provision should the loan be repaid. Obviously we could not insist. About a week later, he informed us that the loan was repaid in full. This naturally surprised us. As a matter of curiosity, we asked him how this was done as we were certain that the loan was doubtful. He replied that he had convinced his head office to transfer the loan to a branch in another centre!

The Singapore operations of an international bank are but a fraction of their worldwide operations and there are real difficulties in trying to understand how they fit in. I have no doubt that we also have to examine and try to understand the large volume of interbank lending. Almost 30% of Asian Dollar loans are made to banks.

Banking Secrecy

While we have laws relating to banking secrecy, the law cannot be used to withhold information from us. To that extent, we are satisfied that the operations of banks in our jurisdiction have not been abused or to provide a channel for criminal activity.

Overbanking

To conclude, I am going to ask a question, "what constitutes overbanking?" No matter how I attempt to define it, any definition that I attempt will not be satisfactory. However, as a supervisory and licensing authority, this question cannot be sidestepped. This question is faced every time a new bank application is received.

In the Singapore context, some of the factors we look at include:

- Is the application for a presence in Singapore motivated by a desire to do domestic or international business?
- Will the admission of the applicant add anything which is not already available from existing banks?

All central banks which also have supervisory responsibilities will be faced with a dilemma in discharging their responsibilities to promote a free competitive and efficient banking system and yet at the same time fulfil their role as supervisors by imposing regulations and restrictions from time to time.

This is a dilemma that will ever be with us.

Regulation and Development of the General Insurance Industry

Mr Law Song Keng
Insurance Commissioner and Actuary, MAS
General Insurance Association of Singapore's Quarterly Lunch
18 September 1980

Introduction

I will like to mention that whatever I am going to say to you is intended only to reflect my personal views and not that of the Monetary Authority.

My talk today is on regulation and development of the insurance industry. This subject is chosen for two main reasons. Firstly, as Insurance Commissioner I am supposed to know the subject. Secondly, it is a subject the insurance industry should be interested in since the insurance industry must operate and develop within the legal framework provided by the government.

Insurance Regulation

Need for Insurance Regulation

Insurance regulation exists in most countries. Although regulation of insurance business was said to have existed in Singapore as early as the 19th century under the Straits Settlement Companies Ordinance of 1889, it was not until 1963 that insurance regulation and supervision was put on a more systematic basis and carried out with a greater degree of earnestness under the Malaysian Insurance Act of 1963. Singapore effected its own Insurance Act in 1967.

I do not for a moment expect any one of you here to question the need for insurance regulation. Nevertheless, I believe it will be educational for us to stop for a moment and ask ourselves this fundamental question: "Why insurance business needs to be regulated or regulated with such peculiar intensity?" I suggest that insurance regulation is justified by a combination of reasons:

i) Insurance is affected with a public interest. So pervasive and essential is the role it is playing in the nation's socio-economic life that the failure of the insurance sector will adversely affect the well-being of the economy and the welfare of the public.
ii) Premiums are paid in advance in return for the insurer's promise to perform its contractual obligations sometime in the future. Will the policyholder's expectations be met by his insurer?
iii) The insurance product is highly technical and in some ways mysterious to the layman. The contract is drafted by the insurer who has superior knowledge over the buyer.
iv) A certain amount of regulation is necessary to ensure a sound and healthy growth of the industry.

Objectives of Insurance Regulation

Granted that insurance business needs to be regulated, the next logical question to ask is what are the objectives of insurance regulation. Only when we are clear of the objectives we are trying to achieve, do we have a yardstick to assess the results of our performance against. To me, the basic objective of insurance regulation is to protect the interests of the policyholder and ensure he gets the most insurance for his money. To achieve this, insurance regulation is aimed at:

i) preserving the financial solvency of insurers;
ii) ensuring fairness, equity and reasonableness in the market place;
iii) ensuring the availability of insurance to meet the needs of society; and

iv) ensuring the quality and standard of insurance services provided by insurers, brokers and agents.

All these goals relate directly to the successful operation of an insurance enterprise. However, the regulator is usually subject to external social political objectives such as the freedom of competition in a free enterprise system or the need for capital resources for economic development.

Conflict of Objectives

One immediately recognises a certain amount of conflict among the goals of insurance regulation I have just described. There is therefore a real need to balance them in practice. How far should we press this one and how far to relax that one. A simple example of a conflict is that existing between the freedom of access to the market in a free enterprise economy and the need for financial strength of the insurers making up the market. Freedom of access to the insurance market would allow new insurers to enter the market freely whereas minimum capital requirements need to be imposed to ensure security to the policyholder.

Philosophy of Regulation

Although you might have agreed with me on what the objectives of insurance regulation should be, this still does not tell you very much on how you would be affected in your operating environment. So I am going to tell you something about my philosophy of insurance regulation. This is perhaps best described by the following beliefs:

i) Regulation exists to serve the public. Like any institution which serves the public, insurance regulation should not be a mere ritual. Instead it must recognise the realities of the market place and society at large. It must be flexible enough to adapt to changes in its environment in order to remain relevant to its purpose. The alternative to intelligent change is not permanence; it is extinction. To the regulated industry, the alternative to regulation is not freedom; it is replacement.

ii) Insurance regulation should involve as much self-regulation as possible. Certain things are best left to the insurers themselves or their trade associations. Free market forces should be allowed to operate to the fullest extent possible. The insurance department should not be doing things which need not be done at all, by the department or anyone else. This is to recognise the department's limited capacity to regulate.

iii) The need for the insurance department to work closely with the insurance industry. There must be mutual trust and confidence on both sides. The department should keep its mind open to ideas and suggestions from the industry, and not operate as a closed system.

Insurance Legislation

The Insurance Act provides the broad legal framework for carrying on insurance business in Singapore. A good piece of insurance legislation should reflect the objectives and philosophy of regulation. As you are already aware, we are replacing our Insurance Act with a new one. In fact, your industry has been consulted on the major proposals. I hope we would be able to get a Bill passed before the end of next year. The new Act would not only strengthen the security of the insurance industry to the benefit of policyholders and the industry itself, it will also, if approved, provide for a large degree of flexibility to my office in the implementation of the Act. By strengthening the financial position of the industry by way of increased financial requirements and proper reserving, the industry could expect to enjoy a larger degree of freedom in the actual day-to-day management of the business. In this way, well-managed insurance companies could be allowed to exercise their entrepreneurial skills to the fullest extent without sacrificing the interests of their policyholders. Flexibility will be needed in adapting our insurance regulations to the changing environment and in our efforts to develop the insurance industry.

Insurance Development

The Past

I will now switch my subject to insurance development. Insurance development is not exactly new to us, having been activated in the early 1970s. By then, the government had already announced its intention to develop Singapore as an international financial centre. It seems only logical that the insurance industry should also be developed to play a more significant role in the economy of Singapore.

Looking back, I must say that the general insurance industry, with the encouragement of the government, has responded quite well to the challenge. Total gross premiums increased from $88 million in 1970 to $380 million in 1979, representing an annual compound growth rate of about 18%. This is higher than the average growth rate of 15% in Singapore Gross Domestic Product at current prices. This shows that the insurance industry has more than kept pace with the economic development of the country. Measured in another way, namely, the ratio of gross premiums to gross domestic product at current prices, the level of insurance industry development has also increased over the past decade. This ratio has exhibited an upward trend, increasing from 1.52% in 1970 to 1.94% in 1979. The second half of the 1970s saw the emergence of professional reinsurers in Singapore. There are now nine of them. Total premiums written by these professional reinsurers totalled $45 million in 1979 which was 200% more than the 1978 figure, and represented about 12% of the industry's domestic premium income. This reflects a new area of future expansion for the insurance industry.

However, insurance development in the 1970s does not only mean an increase in premium volume in line with economic growth. We also saw the establishment of the Singapore Insurance Training Centre (SITC) in 1974 with the important objective of providing education and training of insurance personnel. Together with the staff training programmes of the insurers, the SITC has helped to meet the demand for and upgrade the level of insurance expertise, so very necessary for insurance development. In the 1970s, the smaller and weaker companies were also encouraged to increase their financial resources and improve their management in order to become active participants in the process of development. A 10% concessionary tax rate on income derived from offshore business was introduced to encourage the writing of offshore business especially by the professional reinsurers.

The Future Development

What Is Insurance Development?

For the 1980s and beyond, we must continue with our efforts to develop the insurance industry and make Singapore an important insurance centre. Many a time I have been asked what is meant by insurance development and developing Singapore as an important insurance centre. I would therefore like to define what these terms mean to me. In my view, insurance development should be viewed not merely in terms of the premium volume generated but much more broadly in terms of all the aspects of insurance operations. The following questions are relevant. How well has the insurance industry been able to meet the needs of the insurance-buying public? Has the industry kept pace with economic development? Is the industry providing quality and reliable services? Is the industry well-managed? Is insurance business being conducted with a high degree of technical expertise? Is it being conducted with honesty and integrity? Does the industry have the underwriting expertise to underwrite large and specialised risks and the capacity to retain a significant portion of the domestic risks it accepts? Does it enjoy a high level of public confidence? Is it operating efficiently and providing insurance at reasonable cost? Are the brokers and agents ethical and professional in their conduct of business? I am sure you can find some other factors for judging the level of development of the insurance industry.

What Is Insurance Centre Development?

However, insurance centre development must mean playing more than just a supportive role in the domestic economy. It means developing a volume of offshore business which is not only significant but also profitable.

The extent to which the insurance industry is developed in the way I have defined it will be a key factor of success or failure in our attempt to make Singapore an insurance centre. Can the Singapore market compete in terms of price, service, reliability and expertise?

Rationale for Insurance Centre Development

What Is the Rationale for Insurance Centre Development?

The insurance industry is to be developed alongside the banking sector as part of our aim to develop Singapore as an international financial centre. We wish to develop a more diversified economy to better withstand adverse world economic fluctuations. There is a strong unmistakable correlation between insurance growth and economic development of a country. The highly developed countries are the ones with a high ratio of insurance premiums to gross national product. This should not come as a surprise if one recognises the essential socio-economic role insurance is playing. Insurance development benefits from as well as contributes to economic growth.

Much Remains to Be Done

I believe much remains to be done in insurance development and even much more in insurance centre development. There is no doubt that development is a long-term process, but what is more important perhaps is that a start has been made. We should stay determined to succeed. The industry should continue to strengthen its financial resources, upgrade its management skills and underwriting expertise, and venture overseas, if necessary, when it is ready. It should modernise and improve its management organisation and increase its efficiency and productivity not only to maximise the use of scarce human resources but also to remain competitive. It must adapt to the changing environment and changing needs of the insurance-buying public.

I urge the industry to plan ahead, strive hard and rise to the challenge. My office will try its best to help the industry in meeting this challenge by providing a legal framework that is conducive for growth and development, a flexible approach to insurance regulation that recognises the practical realities of the market place without, of course, sacrificing the security of the policyholder. I will welcome any constructive proposals any one of you can work out. My talk today will be more than worthwhile if you will do your part in our efforts in insurance development for the good of the industry as well as Singapore.

Strengthening the Framework for Banking Supervision

Dr Goh Keng Swee
First Deputy Prime Minister and Minister for Education, and Chairman, MAS
Second Reading Speech in Parliament
Banking (Amendment) Bill
17 January 1984

Since the introduction of the Banking Act in 1971, Singapore has developed into a financial centre of international importance. This is demonstrated by the presence here of a large number of financial institutions of international standing and reputation, the advent of new financial instruments, the rapid development of the Asian Dollar Market, the extensive nature of the financial transactions that are entered into and the numerous financial services that are now being provided. The liberalisation of exchange controls and the development of the capital market have also played their part in making the banking scene in Singapore vastly different from what it was at the time of the passing of the Banking Act.

In the last three years, 1981 to 1983, the contribution of the financial sector to our GNP was large, $1.6 billion, $1.8 billion and $2.1 billion respectively. Growth rates registered were 25.0%, 16.7% and 14.3%. These growth rates were exceeded only by construction. As of June 1983, the industry employed 38,268 persons, mostly in well-paid occupations.

It is, then, hardly surprising that these developments have had a considerable impact on the effectiveness of the existing Act to deal with the many changes that have occurred since 1971. Some of the concepts in the existing Act have to some extent become outdated, other concepts are in need of refinement to meet rapidly changing financial conditions. Thus the decision was taken to conduct a comprehensive review of the provisions of the existing Act to make it a more efficient and flexible instrument for regulating the industry in the long-term interests of both the banks and their depositors and other creditors. It is against this background that the proposals in the Bill now before honourable Members should be viewed.

The Banking Act provides for the organisation, structuring, control and supervision of banks in general. The control and supervision of banks is, as Members know, the responsibility of the Monetary Authority of Singapore. It is well recognised that the supervision of banks is a difficult and often complex operation. Too lax a supervision can lead to abuse and fraud; too strict will stifle growth and enterprise.

Since there is no perfect form of supervision, there must be a constant striving to make this form of control as effective as possible, without overdoing it. A wise Mandarin of the ancient Chinese Imperial Civil Service said that governing a country is like frying small fish. It must not be overdone. This dictum applies to bank supervision, for there are limits to what it can achieve. It cannot, of course, ensure that banks will not make loans or investments that turn out to be bad. The responsibility for making loans and investments must rest squarely on the heads of the directors of banks and that is why it is so important that directors should be persons of integrity and competence who exercise great care and skill in controlling their loans and investment business. A mere examination of returns of banks by the Authority can be no substitute for proper internal control by bank managements.

With these introductory comments, I will now deal with the main provisions in the Bill.

The proposals in the Bill, in general terms, will:

i) improve supervisory powers of MAS over banks;
ii) ensure that control of domestic banks would not pass into undesirable hands;

iii) set limits of credit facilities that a bank may grant to its customers;
iv) enable the Authority to have stricter control over the audit of banks;
v) rectify the anomaly in the provision for priority of deposit liabilities by giving deposit liabilities that have been subject to prudential requirements prior claim; and
vi) replace the existing administrative control over the operation of an Asian Currency Unit by statutory provision.

The first major group of amendments that are proposed in this Bill is concerned with the passing of control of domestic banks to other persons. These appear in clause 5 of the Bill which introduces new sections 14A, B, C and D. These amendments would enable the Authority in relation to a bank that is incorporated in Singapore to control:

a) a take-over of such a bank by the intended acquisition of not less than 20% of its shares;
b) arrangements by which outside persons would be able to determine the policy of such a bank; and
c) the acquisition of substantial holdings, that is, interests in 5% of the voting shares of such a bank.

The purpose of these amendments is to ensure that domestic banks, which form a key sector in the economy, should not pass into undesirable hands. The proposals do not prevent, it will be noted, a take-over by acquisition of shares or the acquisition of substantial holdings in domestic banks but they do seek to ensure that the Authority will be in a position to decide whether the potential new controller or substantive shareholder, as the case may be, is a suitable person to be exercising control or to be having a substantial shareholding in a domestic bank. The proposals will only apply to persons seeking to obtain control of or have substantial holdings in a domestic bank after the coming into force of this proposed legislation. They do not affect past changes of control or past acquisitions of substantial shareholdings. The provisions in new sections 14A and 14B that deal with potential changes of control of domestic banks are, it will be noted, widely drafted so as to embrace not only situations where a person is acting alone to obtain control but also where he is acting in concert with associates.

The amendment proposed by the new section 14D would enable the Authority to obtain from a bank that is incorporated in Singapore information as to the beneficial ownership of shares in that bank. This proposal is closely linked to the function of the Authority in exercising control over take-overs and substantial shareholders for it will enable the Authority to ascertain the ownership of shares held, for example, in nominee names and thus make it more difficult for persons to place themselves in a position so as to obtain control of a domestic bank through such nominees.

The second group of amendments is concerned with the need to ensure that banks in their lending or investment activities conduct their business in a prudential manner and thus avoid over-committing their financial resources. Accordingly, the amendment proposed to section 25 would have the following effect of:

a) changing the existing limit in which a bank may grant credit facilities to a single customer or group of connected customers by lowering the aggregate percentage from an amount in excess of 60% of the capital funds of the bank to 30% of those funds; and
b) limiting substantial loans to an aggregate amount which does not exceed 50% of its total credit facilities.

A substantial loan means, in general terms, a credit facility granted to a single customer or group of connected customers which in the aggregate exceeds 15% of the bank's capital funds.

These amendments are designed to promote prudential banking and at the same time take into account that the capital bases of all the domestic banks have grown very substantially since the original 60% limit was fixed in 1971. The total capital funds of domestic banks have increased more than 11 times, from S$325 million to S$3,849 million during the period 1971 to 1982. The lower limit of 30% should therefore not interfere with participation by banks in major loan projects or interfere with their competitiveness in their domestic and international business. The limitation on the granting of substantial loans is to ensure that banks do not concentrate their commitments too much by lending only to a few big customers and thus increasing their risk exposure. In other words, it discourages them from putting too many of their eggs in one basket.

Clause 8 which introduces a new section 27A has much the same objective in mind. This provision, however, is designed to exercise a measure of control over banks which seek to diversify, for example, into commercial or industrial undertakings to an undesirable extent. Accordingly, it provides that banks shall not enter into agreements to acquire interests of 20% or more in any company, whether incorporated in Singapore or not, without the approval of the Authority. This provision would not apply, however, to a bank's acquisition of such assets in satisfaction of debts due to it so long as, upon making the acquisition, the bank obtains the approval of the Authority to retain these assets as an investment.

To ensure that the prudential limits of section 25 and other sections of the Act dealing, in particular, with the lending and investment activities of banks are not circumvented by the use of subsidiaries or related companies, the Authority may require a bank to aggregate its assets, liabilities or profits, as the case may be, with those of any of such subsidiaries or other related companies. This will enable the Authority to exercise prudential supervision on a group basis. This provision is in line with the practice in Switzerland, and the German bank regulators are contemplating a similar policy.

I now move on to the amendments that are proposed to section 42 which provides for banking secrecy. These proposed amendments have been found by experience in administering the Act to be necessary to relieve the existing rigidity in section 42(3) which deals with the requirement of maintaining banking secrecy. In the main, they are intended to extend the existing exceptions to banking secrecy to cover civil proceedings arising between a bank and the guarantor of a customer or where the bank has been served with a garnishee order attaching monies in the account of a customer or where the information to be disclosed relates to credit facilities granted by a bank incorporated outside Singapore and the information is required by its head office for supervisory purposes. However, other amendments are intended to tighten up the existing exceptions to banking secrecy. The exception that enables a bank to give information about the credit worthiness of a customer has been restricted to the giving of information which is of a general character and not related to details of a customer's account. Again, the exception in section 42(4)(a) providing for a customer of a bank to give permission for disclosure of his bank affairs may be interpreted as meaning that the customer's oral permission is sufficient. The amendment will now make clear that he has to give his written permission.

The Bill proposes new provisions in clause 11 in relation to audits of banks. The new provision will enable the Authority to, in addition to the duties at present imposed on an auditor and largely dictated only by the Companies Act (Cap. 185), call upon the auditor to extend the scope of his audit to give additional information, to carry out other examinations, and to submit a report to the Authority on the results of his work. In addition, the Authority must also be immediately informed if the auditor in the course of his audit discovers serious offences or major losses or serious irregularities that jeopardise the security of creditors or that claims of creditors are not covered by the bank's assets.

Equally important, the conditions that the Authority will lay down for an audit will ensure that the auditor is entirely independent of the bank which he is going to audit. Furthermore, the Authority can insist that a much more rigorous and searching audit is conducted. These amendments, when implemented, should result in external auditors of banks playing a greater role than hitherto in supporting the Authority in the discharge of its supervisory functions over banks. They are clearly designed to give greater protection to depositors and creditors of banks and minimise the likelihood of fraud and other crimes of dishonesty being perpetrated or going undetected. These provisions are based on existing practices of bank regulatory authorities in Germany and Switzerland.

The next major amendments to which I would like to draw the attention of Members appear in clauses 13 and 14 of the Bill. These amendments are concerned with the priority of deposit liabilities in the event of a winding up of a bank that is insolvent or is unable to meet its obligations. Clause 13, which amends section 56, provides that the deposit liabilities of a bank shall have priority over all other unsecured liabilities other than those specified in section 292(1) of the Companies Act. The existing section 56 is far too wide-ranging for it could be construed as giving priority over secured debts and over the preferential unsecured debts that are spelt out in section 292(1). The effect of the amendment is, therefore, that in a winding up, though the claims of the depositors of a bank will rank after the claims of, for example, the liquidator for his costs in the winding up, employees of a bank for their wages and the tax authorities for taxes owed by a bank, their claims will rank above those of the ordinary creditors of a bank. This question of priority of debts, it should be stressed, is only of importance if the assets of a bank are not sufficient to meet the claims of the creditors of a bank.

Clause 14 inserts a new section 56A which provides that amongst the depositors themselves some depositors will have a higher priority ranking in a winding up than other depositors. Thus first preference will be given to non-bank customers of a bank if the deposit liabilities of the bank are included in the computation of the reserve and liquidity requirements in sections 34 and 35.

The second preference will be given to interbank deposit liabilities if they are included in the abovementioned reserve and liquidity requirements. The third preference will be given to deposit liabilities with non-bank customers where the deposit liabilities are not included in the reserve and liquidity requirements. This, as I have explained earlier, will ensure that deposits that have been subjected to stricter prudential requirements be given priority of claim accordingly.

The new section 56B is designed to facilitate the winding up of a bank caused by the liquidator by notice to require every debtor of a bank to redeem any securities he has deposited with a bank within three months of the date of the notice.

Finally, as Members may know, foreign and domestic financial institutions have been operating the Asian Currency Units for many years. The operators of these Asian Currency Units know that though they are subject to the provisions of the Act but, depending on their status as companies incorporated in Singapore or outside Singapore, they have been, under administrative arrangements with the Authority, exempted from certain provisions of the Act. These exemptions have been an integral part of our efforts in developing our offshore market. The purpose of clause 15 is to put these administrative arrangements on a statutory basis. Subsection (4) of new section 69A now expressly lays down the sections of the Act from which persons operating the Asian Currency Unit will be exempted. Such exemptions from regulatory and other requirements are a general practice in the offshore banking business.

The other amendments made by the Bill do not warrant any special mention in addition to what has been stated in reference to them in the Explanatory Statement. While many of the new provisions merely give the force of law to administrative procedures, several are important innovations. It is my intention to keep the situation under observation for about a year during which time we can assess their impact on the banking industry and, if need be, return to the House for another revision.

Mr Speaker, Sir, I beg to move.

Singapore Parl Debates; Vol 43; Sitting No 4; Col 327–343; 17 January 1984.

Recent Turbulence in the Stockbroking Industry and Lessons for Supervision

Mr J. Y. Pillay
Managing Director, MAS
13th Association of Banks in Singapore Annual Dinner
18 June 1986

Introduction

I asked your good chairman to suggest topics that I may safely discuss tonight. After consulting his colleagues, your chairman came back with three suggestions: first, developments in the stockbroking industry; second, progress and plans in the financial sector and third, a generous sentiment this, what the commercial banks could do in these difficult times to strengthen the financial sector and the economy.

Stockbroking Industry

The traumatic events in the stockbroking industry since November last year have taken a heavy toll, among banks no less than brokers. Your interest in a review of that turbulent period is understandable. We shall be condemned to repeat the mistakes of the past if we do not draw the appropriate lessons from that unhappy interlude and do not assess the efforts made to emerge from the maelstrom.

In the confusion that preceded and accompanied the closure of trading on the stock exchange in early December, MAS strove for a way to reconvene trading through preserving the integrity of the stockbroking system. That was done, and could only have been done, with the cooperation and forbearance of the banking community. We express our appreciation that by and large, you showed restraint and wisdom through cooperative efforts to prevent the possible destruction of the stockbroking industry. Self-centred action would surely have resulted in all parties being worse off. I would like to acknowledge as well the herculean efforts of my colleagues in the banking department of MAS in preventing a disaster, as well as the noble contributions by the Big Four banks that launched the lifeboat fund.

As we began to pick up the pieces, we became aware of the poor financial condition of several firms. It appeared impossible to enable all stockbroking firms to survive. To prevent another suspension of trading, which would have dealt a fatal blow to confidence in the stock market and caused much greater losses to the banking system, it was necessary to strengthen the industry through the admission of new, strong members. Thus, the Big Four banks were allowed to set up broking subsidiaries, since they had the financial resources, personnel and knowledge of local trading conditions to enable them to play a key role in reviving confidence.

In February, we went a step further. Chronically sick firms had to be isolated if the public was to regain confidence in the trading system. MAS, in collaboration with the Stock Exchange of Singapore (SES), identified seven stockbroking firms that we felt required independent management, if they were not already in the hands of liquidators or receivers and managers. The SES, subsequently in March, issued a guarantee for transactions through the remaining firms. The deterioration in the stockbroking industry has since been arrested, and trading has been conducted normally.

What do the figures show? In the last six months, the problematical forward contracts have been almost halved, from $617 million in November 1985 to $321 million on 14 June 1986. It is noteworthy that, excluding the seven stricken firms, the stockbroking houses have just $29 million of forward contracts that are outstanding or unsettled. We shall have a clearer picture of the situation when the remaining forward contracts mature at the end of this month.

Equally striking is the substantial decline in loans by financial institutions to the stockbroking industry. Loans to the stockbroking industry have fallen 28%, from $1.06 billion in November 1985 to $760 million on 14 June 1986. An amount of $760 million is still large in relation to the capital invested in the stockbroking industry, but again the seven stricken firms are the weak link, accounting for more than half of outstanding bank borrowings. The remaining 18 stockbroking firms, excluding the Big Four, have meanwhile increased their capital by about $38 million, or 14.3%, since last November.

The strengthening of the stockbroking industry has been accompanied by improvements in the stock market. The Straits Times share index has been hovering around 700 in the last two weeks, compared to its pre-suspension level of 691.8, and its nadir of 563.3 on 28 April. The average daily volume of shares transacted so far this month is some 25 million units, compared to the daily average of 14 million units in November last year. Perhaps the only group of people unhappy with the recovery in the industry and the market are those financial commentators who were quick to pronounce, in the early days of the crisis, that the cancer in the stockbroking industry was malignant.

Nonetheless there have been casualties in the industry and outside it, perhaps inevitably. Of the seven stockbroking firms subject to special control, five were so heavily involved in imprudent forward contracts or trading that they are no longer in business. The remaining two do so only because of your forbearance.

Quite a few banks have not been able to escape unscathed. Some stockbrokers have said that banks led them along with an abundance of credit lines when the stock market was buoyant. Perhaps they were trying to exonerate themselves. Nonetheless, with the inestimable luxury of hindsight and a plethora of cold, hard facts, it is evident that many banks jumped on the bandwagon, intoxicated by attractive spreads and lent heavily to highly-geared firms.

I do not wish to belabour that point considering the pain inflicted on so many banks. But it would not be worth the suffering if we do not draw the appropriate lesson. This is essentially that the virtues of avoiding high concentration in lending, of setting clear credit guidelines and of maintaining tight internal controls, are paramount. These virtues can often be ignored in the headlong pursuit of profit. With the recovery in the stock market, it befalls bankers to be more temperate in making credit decisions.

I am glad to note, as no doubt you all are, that this turbulent episode is drawing to a close. Indeed, from a positive angle, this episode has been a catalyst for reform towards a healthier stockbroking industry, and we should be able to look forward to better days.

The Securities Industry (SI) Act 1986 was passed at the end of March and is expected to be brought into force before long, once the regulations are drawn up. The SI Act 1986 seeks to ensure that broking firms operate more prudently and that they are supervised more closely by the SES. The regulations will impose minimum capital requirements and maximum gearing limits on brokers, as well as restrict the amount of margin trading. The Exchange will be revamping its rules and byelaws as well as its trading system. Proposed changes to the trading and delivery system should drastically reduce the need, or scope, for stockbrokers to provide financing to clients.

The stock exchange has agreed, in the wake of the stockbroking crisis, to corporatisation of stockbroking firms, and it has abandoned its closed-shop attitude. It is also prepared to countenance foreign equity participation in member-firms. MAS is no less tolerant towards foreign equity participation. We would even be prepared to let foreigners hold an equity share of more than 50% in stockbroking houses, so long as they demonstrate technical and marketing ability and are committed to introducing new foreign business. Corporatisation is expected to pick up once the dust has settled and trading regains momentum.

MAS' Role in the Supervision of Banks

May I now turn to certain misconceptions of the role of MAS in the matter of provision of credit by banks. Comments have been passed that MAS should have stopped banks from lending to certain sectors or borrowers. At other times, we were advised to force banks to continue lending to other borrowers.

May I clarify that it is not MAS' role to review every credit transaction that a bank makes. Indeed we are in no position to take such action, which is best left to the acumen and judgment of the management of banks.

MAS is responsible for ensuring that banks conduct their business in a safe and sound manner and for enforcing their compliance with banking laws and regulations. In carrying out this responsibility, we have set out boundaries and prudential regulations within which banks must operate. These regulations require banks to avoid undue concentration of exposure to any group of related borrowers, to undertake thorough credit analysis and to maintain proper monitoring and control systems. Those regulations were tightened in the last amendment of the Banking Act and the promulgation of the set of Notices to Banks. They were not enthusiastically welcomed by the banking community.

Apparently, it is only in a crisis that the need for prudence is accepted. MAS is not omnipotent; once a loan turns bad, no miracle cures can be prescribed.

Banks Should Avoid Diversification into Non-Financial Areas

In view of the increasing trend towards expansion by banks into other areas of activity, coupled with the blurring of lines among the types of financial-services business, I wish to share with you some views on the desirable scope of bank activities.

Banking law in Singapore allows banks to engage in universal banking, whereas the US and Japan have only recently started to deregulate their financial industry and to permit banks to expand into specified areas of financial services. Banks here have enjoyed the advantage of being able to provide a wide variety of financial services, and it is reasonable to expect that more banks will seek to supplement their interest income with non-interest income that other forms of financial activity may generate. A growing number of banks earn a significant portion of their income from fee-based activities, such as foreign exchange, capital-market and fund-management activities. A trend has been established to provide round-the-clock trading activities by a number of forward-looking institutions in order to improve service to global clients. MAS fully supports expansion by banks into those areas of financial services, which add both depth and breadth to our financial markets.

In non-financial areas, banks are well-advised to draw in their horns. Our banking law requires a bank to obtain the MAS' approval should it wish to acquire more than 20% of the share capital of any company. It is also enshrined in the law that banks are prohibited from engaging in wholesale or retail trade. The underlying principle of those provisions is that banks should in general stick to banking and related financial activities, and not wander off indiscriminately into unfamiliar or unrelated areas of business. That sort of expansion could place an unnecessary strain on the management and capital resources of banks. Moreover, the increased risk associated with expansion into non-financial areas may well conflict with the fiduciary duties of bankers, and could lead to weakening of depositors' confidence. Such diversification may also conflict with the primary role of banks of financing their customers.

MAS believes that banks should stick to what they do best, which is financial services. We would therefore want to be thoroughly convinced of the merits of any bank's expansion into non-financial activities before giving our assent. The odds on approval are slim.

Developments in the Financial Sector

May I now turn to the more pleasant subject of developments in the financial sector. Three of them spring to mind, namely, the government securities market, the unlisted securities market (USM) and fund management.

The response from banks to the consultative paper on the development of the government securities market is gratifying. I hope your participation in the market will be equally enthusiastic. We shall be selecting from your midst representatives for a steering committee to evaluate your comments and to implement final developments before launching the market.

The reform of the stockbroking industry has given us the confidence to embark on the development of the USM, which will be launched before the end of the year. A new class of membership, approved associate member, will be created by the SES to enable banks, merchant banks and foreign stockbrokers to deal in USM stocks. Those associate members, besides local stockbroking firms, will be permitted to deal directly with the investing public in USM stocks. Tax incentives in the form of an investment allowance will be considered for market-makers.

To develop the fund management industry, MAS took cognisance of the need to allow investment in the domestic equity market so as to provide fund managers with a business base. In addition, fund managers who do not operate Asian Currency Units may be given special approval by MAS to undertake fund management activities. You are urged to take advantage of the opportunities offered, and to promote strongly these new activities.

May I conclude with a reminder of the important role of financial intermediaries in this difficult economic environment. Funds from banks are the plasma for economic activity. An injudicious curtailment of credit is likely to result in serious contraction of activity. MAS recognises the natural desire of banks to avoid bad debts and losses. Nonetheless, in their own interest, and for the well-being of the economy, banks are advised to refrain from undue credit shrinkage just as much as they eschew unbridled lending.

The Role of a Financial Futures Exchange

Mr J. Y. Pillay
Managing Director, MAS
3rd Singapore International Monetary Exchange Annual Dinner
3 September 1987

MAS has been closely associated with the Singapore International Monetary Exchange (SIMEX) from the outset. Uniquely, notwithstanding our role as regulator, we deployed two of our senior officers, Mr Ng Kok Song and Mr Koh Beng Seng, to serve on the board of SIMEX. Both of them, especially Mr Ng, worked strenuously to widen the range of contracts offered; strengthen links with exchanges overseas, particularly the Chicago Mercantile Exchange, or CME; expand membership and boost the level of activity. I am grateful to those two officers for their contributions. The fact that they have now withdrawn from active management of SIMEX is a sign that MAS believes that the exchange now rests on strong foundations and that the private sector is fully competent to run the show. May I congratulate Mrs Elizabeth Sam on her election as chairlady, and wish her, her board and members good fortune, prudence and stability.

I should not omit to mention the help we have received from the Commodity Futures Trading Commission, or CFTC, of the US, which expeditiously approved the link between the CME and SIMEX. No doubt, the fact that our Futures Trading Act was patterned after the legislation applicable in the US, and that the rules in SIMEX were modelled on CME's regulations, contributed to the early approval.

Growth of SIMEX

SIMEX was launched in 1984 with great fanfare and some trepidation. Thanks to the hard work put in by the board and management of SIMEX, as well as by all the members and locals of the exchange, SIMEX has indubitably come to stay.

Within a relatively short period of three years, SIMEX's daily volume has grown from a mere 1579 lots, in its first year, 1984, to 10,000 lots for the month of June 1987. Bearing in mind that SIMEX has no large domestic base on which to take out a franchise, that rate of progress is quite satisfactory. Like many other components of our financial sector, SIMEX has had to strike out into the wider world to attract business. Hence the word "international" in SIMEX's name. SIMEX, I believe, has earned its spurs by offering an attractive array of international contracts, by successfully reaching out for international business, and by effectively competing with the established futures exchanges around the world.

SIMEX, fortunately, had an important ally in the CME, chiefly through the mutual-offset system. The four mutual-offset contracts listed on SIMEX, namely, three month eurodollar, sterling, yen and deutschemark, have all performed well in comparison with contracts on other international exchanges at a comparable stage of evolution.

Economic Function of SIMEX

The question has sometimes been posed: why do the Singapore authorities support a futures market in Singapore. Is not futures trading just another form of gambling? How does it differ from a casino or horse-racing?

Far be it from me to delve into the merits or demerits of hallowed institutions like turf clubs, or even of casinos. I can only speak for SIMEX. SIMEX, like any other financial institution, serves basically two functions. First, it is an economic activity in its own right, contributing employment, value-added and some foreign exchange receipts, to our economy. Second, like other financial activities, SIMEX provides a service to investors and traders.

The first function, economic contribution, should be placed in its context. The financial and business services sector accounts for 26% of our GDP. If the business services side is stripped off, financial services on their own contribute 14%. Not only is the sector growing, but its share of GDP is rising. MAS has every intention of encouraging the prudent growth of the financial sector and of its share in the total economy.

It is the second function of SIMEX, the service it provides, that principally concerns me today. No service, or no product, can exist just for itself. It has to satisfy a need. Institutions like SIMEX have a crucial role in today's volatile financial markets. The surge in public sector and private sector debt around the world; colossal trade imbalances; the evolution of financial instruments to cope with those developments; the breaking down of barriers among financial institutions; the process of globalisation of institutions and markets; and the impact of the mighty electron on communications and data processing; all have contributed in their own way, and in resonance with each other, to enhancing volatility in financial markets.

Fluctuating prices of financial assets impact in myriad ways on enterprises in commerce, finance and industry. Exporters and importers fret over exchange rate movements as they await receipt or payment of foreign currencies. Fund managers and other investors brood over the value of their investments as stock prices, or interest rates, or exchange rates, oscillate. Pension funds mull over the adequacy of assets to meet future liabilities to pensioners. Multinational corporations meditate on how movements in exchange rates will affect their direct investments.

There are reports that seven Japanese life insurance companies, in their last fiscal year, suffered an aggregate loss of US$10 billion from foreign exchange and market reversals. In April of this year, several leading investment banks in the US incurred losses amounting, in all, to some US$1 billion, in the wake of a sharp spike in interest rates.

Risk, we all know, like taxes and death, cannot be eliminated. It can only be re-packaged, and spread, so that no one individual, or firm, or sector, or region, faces catastrophic loss in the event that markets turn against it. One avenue for hedging is the futures market. That, in a nutshell, is the *raison d'être* for SIMEX, which is fast becoming a key institution in the evolution of Singapore as a risk management centre, that is, as a base for market participants to manage their foreign exchange, interest rate and portfolio, risks. SIMEX, of course, is not the sole medium for risk management. It is but one of an array of vehicles available in Singapore to provide risk takers with risk management facilities.

The Role of the Professional Risk-Taker

To fulfil its economic function, SIMEX must serve the needs of investors, commerce and industry. Yet, it is unrealistic to expect the market to be promoted and developed by corporations. That is why SIMEX has financial institutions serving as brokers and traders; SIMEX also allows individuals to be members, or locals, who are variously labelled as speculators, hedgers or arbitrageurs. All those professional participants are essentially risk takers, who serve to leaven the market and provide the base on which trading, industrial, commercial and investment, corporations may lay off their risk.

It is natural that the bulk of the contracts should be held by the professional players on SIMEX. Thus, about 70% of open-interest contracts in the 3-month eurodollar instrument, on a typical day, are held by banks. The proportion is about the same in the currency-futures contracts. The Nikkei-225 contract, on the other hand, chiefly attracts interest from investment companies and fund managers from financial centres around the world, principally Japan. Three quarters of the open-interest positions in that contract are held by foreign institutions.

The Potential for SIMEX

SIMEX has benefited by being one of the first futures exchanges to be sited in the Asia-Pacific region, still the fastest growing area of the world.

Nonetheless, there are other futures exchanges in this region that also have powerful ambitions. Fortunately, there is no natural law that says that only one exchange can flourish in a time-zone or region. There are several thriving exchanges in Europe as well as in the United States. Indeed, some cities in the United States boast more than one futures exchange.

There is no reason, therefore, for undue anxiety about the potential for SIMEX. Competition should be regarded as a spur. It could be argued that the presence of several futures exchanges in this region enhances the attractiveness of the region to global investors, traders and risk takers, particularly since each of the other exchanges tends to specialise in its own spectrum of mainly domestic contracts. SIMEX, as you know, thrives on international contracts, now exclusively financial, including gold. A study is now under way of the possibility of offering an oil futures contract, which should go down well in what is, after all, one of the leading oil refining and trading centres of the world.

Tokyo and other cities in Japan will, no doubt, want to develop their own futures exchanges. But the head-start SIMEX enjoys confers certain advantages. SIMEX should continue to encourage more institutions in Japan to cover part of their risk on SIMEX, just as foreign-exchange traders in Japan use the Singapore spot market to lay off some of their positions. I am glad to note the heightened pace of your overseas promotion, particularly in Japan, where recently you mounted a successful marketing drive. Our lower cost environment compared to Japanese cities is a strong marketing point.

The more liberal attitude adopted by the Japanese financial authorities has helped SIMEX, for which I thank them. Japanese financial institutions are now able to trade, for their own account, on futures exchanges overseas. The next stage of liberalisation will come when Japanese authorities allow their institutions to trade on foreign futures exchanges on behalf of their clients. We hope that will happen without too much delay.

The Need for Prudence

No discourse from a regulator is complete without the customary word of caution. In your commendable enthusiasm to develop the futures market, attract international business, offer new products, widen membership and raise the temp of business, let it not be forgotten that there should be the tempering influence of prudence and restraint, which like charity, begin at home.

The Futures Trading Act provides MAS with wide powers to intervene in the activities of SIMEX or of its participants. In keeping with our tradition, we would prefer to exercise those powers with restraint, and preferably, at second remove. SIMEX has been established on a sound footing, with a strong board and management. The task of preventing abuse and mischief in the exchange lies, primarily, with the members of the exchange and the board. The watch-word should be self-discipline, which imposes on every member the obligation to behave in a professional and unimpeachable manner, as well as to report to the board instances of misbehaviour that arise anywhere on the exchange. SIMEX cannot afford the taint of scandal, either now or at any time.

I would also like to sound a note of caution to the general public, to think hard before dealing with those firms that are not members of SIMEX but offer futures contracts. There are some such firms, dealing in commodity futures, that have aggressively sought business and engaged in alleged unethical practices. While MAS has no supervisory powers over those firms, complaints that we receive will be referred to the appropriate investigatory authorities.

The Regulation and Development of Financial Markets

Dr Richard Hu
Minister for Finance and Chairman, MAS
Foreign Correspondents Association of Singapore Luncheon
18 June 1991

Introduction

The past two decades have seen changes which have transformed the financial systems of the world. The forces driving these changes were the rapid growth in international trade, the cumulative effects of the 1973 and 1979 oil shocks, the technical revolution in telecommunication and electronic data transmission systems and, more recently, the accelerating trend towards the opening up and deregulation of financial markets worldwide.

The pace of these changes has posed significant challenges to regulators' ability to maintain sound financial systems. We have seen a series of financial upheavals reverberating around the world, starting with the Mexican debt crisis in 1982, the stock market crash in 1987 and more recently, the real estate slump in several major economies. All this has led to increased concern among central bankers for the health of international financial markets, and recent moves by the Bank for International Settlements (BIS) to lay down new prudential rules for banks.

This afternoon I will only touch on some aspects of these problems in the context of Singapore's drive towards the creation of a regional financial centre and how we have coped with them.

In 1968, a decision was taken to develop Singapore into a regional financial centre. Financial services was seen as an ideal growth area, given Singapore's land constraints and scarcity of natural resources. It was also felt that the parallel development of a financial centre would support and complement the growth of Singapore's export-oriented manufacturing industry. Events have proved that the decision was a correct one, as Singapore's financial sector grew at an average annual rate of 19% over the past decade, from 5% of GDP in 1979 to 17% of GDP last year.

This rapid growth has not been without problems but we can fairly claim that it has been achieved without financial disasters. It was recognised from the outset that banks and financial institutions could not be treated like ordinary businesses. Financial markets could not be left to operate unfettered and unsupervised on the basis of "survival of the fittest" as there is simply too much public interest at stake. Besides forming the fulcrum of a country's payments mechanism, financial institutions are depositories of the public's savings, and play a vital role in mobilising savings to finance growth — fuelling investments through the credit allocation process.

MAS was given responsibility to both regulate and develop the financial services sector in Singapore, in the belief that the development of financial markets had to take place within the framework of an effective regulatory system. A balance had to be struck between the opposing needs of giving markets maximum freedom to grow, and the fiduciary responsibility for protecting the interests of depositors and investors.

The task faced by MAS was twofold:

(a) how to attract and hold a sufficiently large number of financial institutions to form the critical mass needed for the development of a financial centre; and

(b) how to set up a regulatory framework which will ensure the maintenance of prudential standards without inhibiting the growth of the markets.

Attraction of Financial Institutions

In the early years, the need to attract a critical mass of banks was crucial. A series of fiscal incentives were introduced to attract reputable international financial institutions to set up operations in Singapore.

Incentives alone would not have been sufficient to attract international financial institutions to conduct their regional activities from Singapore. It was also necessary to provide supporting infrastructure such as efficient air travel and telecommunication facilities, and a pool of skilled manpower.

The Dilemma of Regulation and Development

Alongside the provision of fiscal incentives and infrastructure facilities, I cannot over-emphasise the importance of establishing an effective supervision system to oversee the development of the financial sector. Given that the long-term viability of a financial centre hinges crucially upon investor confidence, regulators must uphold stringent prudential standards and exercise vigorous supervision in order to maintain the stability and soundness of the financial system. We believe that the regulatory burden in Singapore is not too heavy. Our financial legislation focusses primarily on the setting of prudential standards, leaving financial institutions a great deal of freedom in carrying out a wide range of activities. However, MAS has not hesitated to enforce the prudential rules and regulations set. This policy has paid off as there has not been a single bank failure in Singapore since independence. We strongly believe that prevention is far better than cure, particularly for financial markets. The experience in other countries has shown that any failure to apply regulatory standards consistently could be extremely costly.

In the US, a combination of adverse economic developments, the moral hazard incentives of the deposit insurance system and inadequate enforcement of regulatory standards, have contributed to extremely expensive bailouts, which will eventually be borne by the taxpayer. For example, paying off depositors of failed savings and loan (S&Ls) institutions has been estimated to cost taxpayers US$500 billion over the next 40 years. Besides the S&L crisis, US supervisory authorities have also had to inject about US$12 billion in recent years to bailout four large banks. Over the last two years, an average of 470 banks and S&Ls have failed each year in the US.

With our scarce resources, Singapore cannot afford to run the risk of such failures. Hence, when some may legitimately complain that Singapore is over-zealous in enforcement of rules, it is only because of MAS' insistence on adherence to strict prudential standards. We believe that this is a small price to pay to protect the financial system.

The stringent regulatory approach of MAS has been viewed by some as over-regulation, particularly given the current trend towards de-regulation in several industrialised countries such as the US and Japan. Among the deregulatory measures sought as a solution for the troubled US banking system are the lowering of barriers that prohibit commercial banks from conducting securities underwriting and trading activities. There are also proposals to allow interstate banking. In Japan, the aim of liberalisation is to modernise and raise the efficiency of the financial system, and measures include interest rate deregulation, and the loosening of controls over broad areas of financial activities. Like the US, there are also proposals to lower the barriers between commercial and investment banking.

What lessons do such deregulation trends hold for Singapore? I shall suggest that there is little of significance. In Singapore, banks have always practised universal banking. In the US, banks are not allowed to own stockbroking subsidiaries. Here, a major US bank holds a substantial stake in a member of the Stock Exchange of Singapore (SES). In addition, banks and financial institutions in Singapore are not subject to any form of foreign exchange or interest rate controls. Such controls were abolished since the 1970s to promote competition and raise the efficiency of the banking system. In comparison, domestic interest rates in Hong Kong continue to be established by a cartel of banks.

I believe that Singapore already has a relatively free, open and competitive financial system, compared to many other financial centres of the world, and this is readily supported by statistics. There are currently more than 200 banks and merchant banks from 32 countries operating here. The share of foreign banks in lending to residents is 57%. The share of non-bank deposits from residents is 45%. In addition, foreign banks account for 73% of domestic trade financing business. Such high levels of foreign participation is probably unmatched anywhere else in the world.

Global Tightening of Supervision

The upheavals in international financial markets in the 1980s served to highlight the need for vigorous regulation of financial institutions. OECD countries have all moved to tighten supervisory oversight, primarily in capital adequacy, and applying consolidated supervision of financial conglomerates.

The introduction of the BIS, 8% minimum capital assets ratio in 1988 was an important step to boost the soundness of banks. Capital, in the form of shareholders' funds, acts as a buffer for financial institutions in difficult times. The greater the capital, the greater the cushion, and the greater the restraint on management's risk-taking activities as more shareholders' funds are at stake. Under the BIS capital guidelines, banks have until the end of 1992 to raise their total equity to at least 8% of risk-weighted balance sheet items. When the ratio has been fully implemented, the soundness of the international banking system would have been substantially strengthened, as well as creating a more level playing field for international banks. Beyond these, the BIS has also announced that it is considering additional capital adequacy rules to account for banks' exposures in foreign currency, share and money markets. The additional capital requirements could mean a few percentage points further increase in the minimum capital adequacy rule.

We have always recognised the need for our banks to be well-capitalised, and have therefore applied capital standards even higher than the BIS standards. The 8% capital adequacy rule is the minimum recommended. Singapore banks generally have core capital ratios of over 12%. Like the Swiss banks, the strong capital ratios of local banks have been very helpful in retaining the confidence and loyalty of domestic and international customers during periods of instability in international financial markets. Confidence is a key requirement for a financial centre.

There are some who say that high capital ratios mean lower profits. Such fears are not well-founded. Over the longer term, well capitalised institutions are more than compensated because they pay a lower premium on deposits than a less capitalised institution. In the US, a well-capitalised bank such as JP Morgan pays lower interest rates to obtain funds.

In addition to strong capital ratios, another key plank in Singapore's regulatory approach has been its policy to admit only internationally reputable foreign banks. This policy, plus rigorous regulation, has allowed our financial sector to weather even the most severe volatility in international financial markets, thereby maintaining foreign investor confidence in the integrity of our financial system.

Another issue confronting regulators is the need for greater consolidated supervision of financial conglomerates. As financial institutions diversify into a greater variety of activities, and grow and expand internationally, it is increasingly important that regulators should have an overall picture of the risk exposures of the parent company and its subsidiaries on a consolidated basis. Consolidated supervision is also necessary to prevent circumvention of minimum prudential standards through the use of subsidiaries or related entities not under the supervisory authority's purview.

In supervising financial conglomerates, parent and host supervisors must have a clear understanding on their respective roles to ensure that supervision is effective and without gaps or overlaps. Close cooperation is particularly important to Singapore, as the banking sector is dominated by foreign banks operating here as branches, and we need to know that their parent institutions are well-supervised and are in good financial standing.

I should add that Singapore already practises consolidated supervision of local banks. In supervising local banks, MAS not only oversees the international operations of the local banks. It also recognises that a number of local banks belong to groups which have substantial non-banking activities. We have regulations that restrict banks' investments in non-banking activities in order to provide adequate firewalls between the bank and non-bank entities of the group.

Vigorous supervision is also extended to other segments of the financial sector, including the securities and financial futures markets. When the securities industry legislation was amended in August 1986, there was concern that the tightening of regulations could stifle the development of the market. Events have proved otherwise since 1987. Turnover on the SES has expanded at an annual average rate of 18%. Since 1987, an additional 46 Singapore incorporated companies have been listed on SES, with market capitalisation increasing from $36 billion to $81 billion. More importantly, the SES may not have weathered the 1987 stock market crash as well as it did, if the securities industry had not been recapitalised and revamped.

I have so far stressed the importance of financial market supervision and highlighted the international moves to tighten prudential oversight in capital adequacy and consolidated supervision. However, we need to recognise what supervision alone can or cannot be expected to achieve. Supervision, of course, cannot prevent fraud entirely, nor ensure that financial institutions will not make loans and investments which later turn sour. The responsibility for making the loans and investments must rest squarely on the shoulders of the Chief Executives and Directors. Management is also responsible for ensuring that effective internal control systems are in place to prevent fraud or theft. Management must devote sufficient resources to internal control functions.

The Singapore Financial Sector

Singapore's successful development as a financial centre has relied heavily on the maintenance of sound prudential standards linked to strict enforcement of these standards. If we had not had such a system, empirical evidence from other countries suggests that bank failures would have been unavoidable. Without an effective regulatory system, it is questionable whether Singapore would have been able to achieve the development of a financial sector that has consistently grown at twice the overall rate of growth for the economy, and that currently accounts for 17% of Gross Domestic Product.

At this point, I would like to digress to say a few words on the development of the Singapore financial sector. The Asian Dollar Market was started in 1968. It now has an asset size of US$390 billion, with 200 participants. Out of the top 300 banks in the world, 116 have established a presence here. The market plays an important role in the recycling of surplus funds in the region. Countries as far as Europe, Japan and Australia are served by this market.

However, in order to become a regional financial centre, having an international money market is not enough. A broad range of financial services must be available. After international banks established their offices here, there was market demand in the 1980s for trading activities, fund management and other fee-based activities. With the critical mass of foreign financial institutions here already, these new activities also took off.

In the early 1980s, increased demand for foreign exchange transactions could be traced to several factors. Increased international trade, financial deregulation in major industrialised countries and a mismatch in fiscal and monetary policies resulting in higher volatility in exchange rates made greater demands for foreign exchange transactions. Foreign exchange dealers in Singapore seized on these market opportunities. As a result, the average daily turnover in foreign exchange is now US$80 billion, making Singapore the fifth largest international foreign exchange trading centre, after London, New York, Tokyo and Zurich.

Stock, futures markets and fund management activity reflect the recent trend towards risk and fund management. The SES ranks third in trading volume among the Asian bourses. Turnover was $37 billion in 1990. Foreign stocks and shares are also actively traded in Singapore. The total turnover in foreign stocks and shares was $20 billion.

The Singapore International Monetary Exchange (SIMEX) was set up in 1984 to meet demand from regional investors for a market to hedge interest and exchange risks. SIMEX is the only exchange to have a mutual offset system with the Chicago Mercantile Exchange, which enables trading to be conducted almost round-the-clock on the two exchanges.

Fund management was another activity that took off in the 1980s as investors sought to maximise their returns after learning from the experience of the early 1980s that rates of return could be negative. Global investing became popular. The emerging markets of the Asian region, with their fast growing economies, caught the eye of investors. Singapore, again, was a natural place for fund managers to locate themselves to oversee the regional investments of their clients.

The Singapore financial sector has been able to develop successfully and achieve its present proportions because it has focussed on serving international investors. Given the small size of the Singapore economy, it has been imperative that the financial sector, like the manufacturing, commerce and other economic sectors, be strongly outward-oriented. This preponderance of offshore transactions vis-à-vis domestic transactions is reflected in the various sectors of our financial market. For example, offshore assets comprised 80% of aggregate assets of banks and merchant banks in Singapore. In our foreign exchange market, Singapore dollar transactions accounted for only 5% of total turnover. On SIMEX, more than two-thirds of the customers are based outside Singapore.

Developments in the Future

What of the future? I see two developments which have significant implications for the growth of the Singapore financial sector.

First, the growing liberalisation of financial markets in Malaysia, Indonesia, Thailand, as well as Taiwan, South Korea and Japan, will increase the volume and range of financial activity in these countries. Although this trend must result in increased competition for some segments of the Singapore financial sector, the overall result need not be a zero sum game. The increase in financial flows generated by liberalisation in these markets would strengthen cross-border financial linkages, and will stimulate the overall growth and development of the region's financial markets. With its strategic location, Singapore should be in a good position to participate.

Second, the Asia-Pacific region will play an increasing role in world trade. The sources of rapid growth in the region have expanded from the NICs to include countries such as Malaysia, Indonesia and Thailand. This has been reflected, among other things, in the rapid rise in intra-regional trade and investment flows. Countries such as Taiwan, Korea, Hong Kong and Singapore have become more important investors in the developing economies of the region, in addition to traditional foreign investors such as Japan, US and the EC. Growth in manufacturing and other real economic activity in the region should provide a significant source of demand for financial services.

Against this background, the prospects for continued development of Singapore's financial centre look promising. However, there is no such thing as a free lunch. Singapore's viability as a regional financial centre would depend crucially on her ability to be competitive, and to maintain high professional and prudential standards. I remain confident that this can be done.

Derivatives Trading and the Importance of Risk Management in Banks

Mr Lee Ek Tieng
Managing Director, MAS
22nd Association of Banks in Singapore Annual Dinner
27 June 1995

Overview of Financial Sector

The financial sector's growth has moderated from 10.2% in 1994 to 2.2% in the first quarter of this year. However, like most broad statistical measures, the estimate for financial sector growth does not offer a full picture of developments in the financial sector. The decline in the growth rates of the financial sector has reflected mainly the consolidation of the stock market. However, other areas of the financial sector, particularly domestic banking, foreign exchange, financial futures and insurance activities, have recorded strong growth.

Non-bank customer loans of commercial banks continued to expand robustly at 23% in the year ended May 1995, similar to the rate in the preceding period. Loans to the manufacturing sector recovered strongly in the last few months, reaching 18% in May this year compared with single digit growth rates last year. Loans to the building and construction sector, and to individuals, although continuing to increase at about 30% on a year on year basis, have begun to moderate. The slowdown in loans to individuals was a result of the measures introduced earlier this year to limit personal borrowing. These trends are a healthy development as it would lead to better balance and diversification of banks' loan portfolios.

Banks' Asian Currency Unit (ACU) lending activities have also registered a recovery, with total ACU assets growing at a faster rate of 17% in May. Such ACU asset growth was due to strong loan demand from non-bank customers, which expanded by 19% in May. The volume of foreign exchange trading registered double digit growth to reach a daily average of US$116 billion in January to May 1995. Trading activity on SIMEX surged by 50% to a daily average of 110,000 lots for the first five months of this year. Although the amount of funds managed by fund management institutions in Singapore rose at a slower pace from S$63 billion at end-1993 to S$66 billion at end-1994, we expect more funds to be transferred for management in Singapore in the near future. The recent Government measures to promote the fund management industry have resulted in considerable interest from foreign fund managers to manage their Asian portfolios from Singapore. Since October 1994, 11 international fund managers have established fund management operations in Singapore and a number of others have also expressed interest. To further encourage the fund management industry, the Government introduced two new tax incentives in this year's budget. The first is a further concessionary rate of tax of 5% on incremental profits earned by fund managers who manage above S$5 billion of funds. The aim of this incentive is to encourage fund managers to expand the amount of funds managed. From our surveys, a number of fund managers in Singapore manage above S$5 billion of funds and hence qualify for this incentive. The second is the introduction of an alternative tax scheme for domestic unit trusts to allow foreign and domestic investors to invest in the same unit trust, and for the foreign investor to enjoy tax exemption on investment income from the unit trust.

Derivatives Activities of Financial Institutions

Last year I spoke to you about exercising prudence when undertaking financial derivatives activities, and suggested some key principles which financial institutions should observe in the conduct of financial derivatives activities. It would appear that our worst fears may have come true with the recent Barings debacle. Fortunately, the Barings incident did not have a systemic effect on the financial market. Although some MAS and SIMEX staff lost some sleep during the episode, no other financial institution, as far as we are aware, has lost money. It is however a timely reminder to banks of the vital importance of having strong internal controls in all areas of their operations, and not only in their derivatives trading area. As most of you would be aware, the Barings collapse can primarily be attributed to the lack of basic internal controls both at the local and head office level.

As senior bank management, it is your responsibility to institute rigorous internal control and risk management procedures and systems to ensure that all aspects of your bank's operations are conducted in a sound and prudent manner; in other words, management should exercise corporate governance. With more banks adopting the matrix or functional management structure, CEOs of such banks should ensure that they understand and properly supervise all aspects of the Singapore branch's activities as they will be held responsible for the entire branch operations regardless of the reporting structure. In particular, there must be strict segregation of duties between your bank's dealing, settlement and revaluation activities. There should also be clear and independent reporting lines, limits and guidelines set for all staff. Such procedures should be clearly documented and communicated to all your employees. In addition, we would encourage all banks to establish independent risk management or compliance units to ensure compliance with established policies and procedures.

One other important factor which I might suggest is the need to change the mindset of bank management concerning the role of internal and external auditors. As bank management, it is in your interest to view the auditors' role as complementary to yours in ensuring that your bank operations are being conducted prudently. Enlightened CEOs would not merely view auditors as expense items or inconveniences, but rather appreciate their assistance in detecting control weaknesses which if left unchecked, could lead to losses or the perpetration of fraud. Internal auditors on their part should ensure that they conduct regular comprehensive audits, preferably on a surprise basis, and should also focus on the risk management of the bank and the vulnerability of its operations. They should report their findings independently to senior bank management, conduct independent verification and reconciliation, and follow-up independently to ensure that the deficiencies and unsatisfactory practices are promptly rectified. Should the internal or external auditors' audit standards be found lacking, it is your prerogative as bank management to replace them.

I would like to reiterate that we expect the foreign banks to post chief executives with impeccable integrity and proven competence to head the Singapore operations. Head Offices should establish limits for branch management and staff and send internal auditors to check that they are complied with.

MAS has recently drawn up a set of guidelines on derivatives risk management. The guidelines, which draw from similar guidelines issued by other regulators, serve as a source of reference for banks and financial institutions to evaluate the adequacy of their internal control systems with regard to derivatives activities. I urge senior management of banks to ensure that all staff involved in derivatives activities are familiar with MAS guidelines. MAS will be conducting a survey of such systems in the coming months.

Singapore Dollar Loan Limit for Offshore Banks

It is MAS' policy to review its regulations regularly and if necessary to ensure that they are kept up to date with international developments. The robust economic growth rate in the last few years has led to an increase in demand for funds from the commercial sector. In order to allow offshore banks to continue to meet the needs of their corporate customers in Singapore, MAS has decided to increase the Singapore dollar loan limit for offshore banks by S$20 million to S$120 million with effect from 28 June 1995. This is in line with our policy of gradually liberalising the Singapore financial sector to increase participation from international financial institutions. Offshore banks which intend to utilise the new limits should note that under the Banking Act, any bank with above S$100 million of Singapore dollar loans is required to comply with the 25% limit on loans to a single customer and the 50% substantial loans limit.

Conclusion

For 1995 the prospects for the financial sector remain bright. Continued economic growth and liberalisation in Asia will provide a plethora of opportunities in financial services. The Asian Dollar Market is expected to grow as a result of lending to companies in the region. The foreign exchange market and SIMEX are also expected to expand strongly with the increased sophistication of investors in Asia in managing their risks and as a result of the increased volatility in financial markets. Asia will continue to attract inflow of funds in the capital markets. This would foster Singapore's development as a centre for managing investments in the region. Financial institutions should therefore continue to invest in manpower training as a vital resource in delivering their financial services efficiently and competitively.

New Approach to Regulating and Developing Singapore's Financial Sector

Mr Lee Hsien Loong
Deputy Prime Minister and Chairman, MAS
10th Anniversary of SESDAQ
4 November 1997

Introduction

I am happy to celebrate with you SESDAQ's 10th anniversary. SESDAQ has established itself as a second board on the Stock Exchange of Singapore (SES). It has provided small and medium enterprises with a useful source of funds, which are a critical supporting factor for entrepreneurship. Eighty companies have listed on SESDAQ over the past decade, of which 20 have since made it to the Main Board. Its total market capitalisation is now almost $5 billion.

However, despite SESDAQ's achievements, it has still not clearly established itself in investors' minds as a high risk, high return play. The SES should now study ways to expand SESDAQ's role, for example, how to develop SESDAQ into a source of seed capital for startup firms, well before they have built up a track record.

Such a review would fit into the Government's current comprehensive study of its strategies and approaches towards regulating and promoting the financial sector. Our aim is to develop the sector further, and make

Singapore one of the key financial centres in our time zone, and in the world. We need to modify the style and balance of regulation and supervision, strengthen our domestic financial institutions, encourage the private sector to play a bigger role in developing the financial industry and place greater reliance on market forces. Incremental improvements to established policies will not suffice. We need to rethink fundamentals and chart new directions.

The Development of Singapore's Financial Sector

The financial sector has played a major part in Singapore's success story. Financial services have consistently grown faster than the rest of the economy, and now account for 12% of GDP. The Asian dollar market has made us a dominant offshore banking centre in Asia. Our foreign exchange market is the fourth largest in the world. Fund management activities have also grown rapidly in recent years, as has the trading of foreign securities. Singapore International Monetary Exchange (SIMEX) has made a niche for itself as the leading futures exchange in the region.

Growth has been not only dramatic, but also orderly and well-controlled. Our local banks have some of the best debt ratings in South East Asia. No bank has failed. We have avoided most of the problems experienced by other financial centres in the region. We learnt from the Pan-El crisis in 1985, and tightened up management and regulatory controls. In 1987, we took Black Monday in our stride. Later we avoided the Bank of Credit and Commerce International debacle, and prevented Barings' spectacular collapse from inflicting any losses to SIMEX or other Singapore financial institutions.

The regional financial turmoil is the most recent testimony to the soundness of our financial system. The signs are that despite this external instability, our economy grew strongly in the third quarter, although our growth is bound to be affected somewhat over the next year or two. Because of our prudent macro-economic and financial policies, confidence in the Singapore dollar and our financial institutions remains unshaken.

Dramatic Worldwide Change

However, we cannot simply extrapolate this success, or the policies which have produced it, into the future. The financial industry worldwide is undergoing rapid change and ferment. The rules of the game are changing, and so are the players. The current World Trade Organisation negotiations to open up the financial sectors in member countries to foreign participation will hasten a process which is in any case already well underway.

The first driving force behind this revolution is technology, especially information technology and telecommunications. These allow financial institutions to introduce new products and techniques to arbitrage markets and manage risk, and new distribution channels like online banking. They enable, indeed strongly encourage, institutions to go for huge economies of scale, and to operate globally to survive and thrive.

Technology is breaching geographic, industry and regulatory barriers. Markets are becoming globalised. Trading takes place around the world and round the clock. Capital moves in and out of markets and financial instruments nearly anywhere in the world. The current regional disturbances illustrate this vividly. Thailand's problems set off a chain of events that contributed to pressure on Hong Kong stocks and the Hong Kong dollar. This in turn rattled stock markets in the US and Europe. And when Wall Street crashed on Monday 27 October, the convulsion and the aftershocks shook stock markets on every continent.

The second driving force for change is fierce borderless competition. This is fostered by both technology and the lifting of regulatory barriers, and is leading to more efficient financial systems worldwide. Gone are the days when institutions were protected by government regulation and barriers to entry, and could monopolise a geographic market and earn comfortable profits collecting economic rent.

Banks are facing increased competition in financial markets, because of new sources of funds for companies, and new channels for individual savings. The traditional functions of banks — to collect money, lend it out and earn a profit on the interest spread — are being split up among different institutions, each carrying out specialised functions more efficiently and with narrower margins.

In America and Europe there has been a surge in mutual funds, as more people have channelled their retirement savings into these funds to earn better long-term returns than bank deposits. Companies are raising funds in increasingly sophisticated ways on the capital markets, instead of borrowing from banks. And bank loans such as mortgages are being securitised, to take them off balance sheets.

Institutions are finding that their competitors are not across the street, but across the globe. In the US, online brokers like Charles Schwab are already doing stock trading on the Internet, at one quarter the usual cost. Software companies like Microsoft now offer transactions online.

Financial institutions are being driven in an unceasing quest for higher efficiency and lower costs. Margins are being shaved, especially in traditional activities like plain vanilla loan syndication and under-writing, and the trading of securities.

The result is a wave of mergers, acquisitions and corporate restructurings, now sweeping financial institutions in the US, Europe and Japan. Commercial banks are marrying up with investment banks. Insurance companies have been acquiring securities firms. The consolidation will lead to the emergence of new mega-players, with the economies of scale, market power, IT capability and expertise to dominate whole regions, or specialist services worldwide.

The new technology-driven strategies, increased competition and globalisation have also encouraged a consolidation of financial activities within fewer major centres. In Europe, London is the pre-eminent centre, eclipsing Zurich, Frankfurt and Paris. In and around the City of London, 600,000 people work in the financial industry, or businesses related to it. It is not a British industry, but a global, cosmopolitan one.

A similar consolidation will happen in our time zone. We cannot tell how many major centres the Asia Pacific will eventually have. But whatever the final count, we want to be in that number.

This bracing environment opens many exciting opportunities in financial services that embody innovation and expertise, such as fund management products and complex derivatives. But it also brings new risks to individuals, institutions and the financial system as a whole.

There have been numerous accidents, some involving new instruments, some caused by obvious lapses of internal controls. They have occurred even at some of the most well managed and respected banks. The potential consequences of failure are now far graver. When something goes wrong in an institution, losses can mount exponentially, almost by the hour. In the case of Barings, a 233-year-old merchant bank, Nick Leeson ran up most of his losses in the final few weeks before the collapse.

Barings was a small institution by international standards, so the damage was relatively easy to contain. But the collapse of a mega-institution poses a real risk of systemic failure. And with more tightly coupled global markets, the problem will very likely cascade across the international system.

Rethinking and Debate

This dramatic worldwide revolution in the financial industry is causing governments and regulators everywhere to review their approaches to regulating and supervising the industry. In the US, the separation between commercial banks and investment banks has become more porous. The Glass-Steagall Act will continue to be loosened by market forces, even if Congress does not repeal it.

In Britain, the new Labour Government has shifted responsibility for banking supervision away from the Bank of England, but left the Bank still responsible for the stability of the financial system as a whole. Britain is setting up a new omnibus regulatory agency, the Financial Services Authority, combining nine different existing regulators, to oversee all components of the financial industry. The industry is watching with fascination and apprehension how this will all work out.

In the developed countries, there has been substantial questioning and debate on how governments should manage financial institutions and markets. There is broad consensus on the goals of public policy: at the macro level, to protect the stability of the financial system and at the micro level, to protect individual investors and depositors. Now the debate is on how to achieve these two goals in a way which ensures the maximum effectiveness and efficiency of the financial system.

The debate is difficult, because there are tensions and trade-offs between the macro and micro goals. For example, if policies go too far in protecting all depositors and investors, it creates a problem of moral hazard, that virtually ensures that institutions and markets will not function efficiently and effectively.

Implications for Singapore

As a major financial centre, Singapore cannot isolate itself from these global trends, or ignore the issues which they raise. Tried and tested formulas will not necessarily be best in the next phase. We need to develop new principles and strategies to enable our financial sector to prosper into the 21st century.

Our review must cover not only the offshore financial institutions, but also domestic banking. Both must keep track of what is happening around the world and stay up to date. It is not tenable to keep the world outside our door. Firstly, technology will make this less and less feasible. Secondly, Singapore consumers and corporations need financial services that are up to world standards, otherwise the rest of our economy and our overall competitiveness will be affected. Thirdly, a major growth area for our domestic institutions is offshore, in the region. Unless our institutions can hold their own against the competition domestically, they have little hope of competing without home ground advantages in the far more difficult regional environment.

Our Traditional Principles

Up till now, our approach to regulating and supervising the financial sector has been to set high standards, establish strict rules, and take minimum risks. When we started, we were an improbable place to develop a financial centre. We had no track record or credibility. We had to earn it the hard way, by establishing a reputation for honesty and competence.

In this we were unlike Hong Kong. Hong Kong had a British umbrella, and hence could afford to be more tolerant of failures of institutions and ambiguous market practices. It is said that in Hong Kong anything not expressly forbidden is permitted, whereas in Singapore anything not expressly permitted is forbidden. This is an exaggeration, but it captures an important difference in the two systems. Had Singapore been lax and then run into difficulties or scandals, bankers would have lost confidence in us, and we would have failed to grow into a major financial centre. This has happened to many other aspiring financial centres.

Therefore we set out to attain and maintain the highest possible standards of professional integrity and sound financial management. We established strict rules and enforced them vigorously. We sought to protect not just the financial system as a whole, but even individual institutions from failing. We did our best to protect the public from fraud and sharp practice. We even crafted regulations to shield the public from risky ventures and business losses.

Because of this general approach, we have regarded innovative products and ideas warily, in the interest of preserving stability, minimising risk and protecting investors. We have tried to manage new developments in a gradual and orderly way. Sometimes we have imposed our judgment of what risks individuals and institutions should be allowed to undertake. For example, we have not encouraged trading of covered warrants, or investments in unit trusts covering unfamiliar parts of the globe.

We have been especially careful to protect Singaporean depositors and investors. We have kept the domestic and offshore banking sectors separate, and regulated the domestic sector more stringently. Local entities have been partially insulated from the bracing international environment, although our domestic market is more open to foreign institutions than most other countries in the region.

So far, this approach has promoted rather than hindered our growth. However, the trade-off has been that we have sometimes been slower than others to introduce new products and develop new markets. More important, we have not fully exploited the expertise and enterprise available in the private sector. Too often the industry has waited for government to signal its acceptance of change or even to take the initiative, rather than leading developments and actively contributing their ideas.

New Directions

What I have described has been the Government's long-standing policy, which MAS has faithfully and successfully implemented. But the global trends in banking and finance make a review imperative. Besides our financial sector is more developed, and our competence and credibility no longer in question. And Singaporeans are better educated and more financially savvy, wanting to manage their own wealth and make their own decisions, financial or otherwise.

We must shift our emphasis. We need to regulate the financial sector with a lighter touch, accept more calculated risks and give the industry more room to innovate and stretch the envelope. This process should start now, notwithstanding the current regional uncertainties. It is a strategic shift, not dependent on short-term ups and downs of economic fortunes. Indeed by starting now, our financial sector will be more ready to play a significant role as the region recovers.

We need to promote a more competitive, dynamic and innovative environment. In a dynamic global industry, Singapore can only stay near the leading edge if it too has that climate of ferment and innovation. This is not just having bright ideas, but being willing to break new ground and create fresh opportunities.

The private sector must play a larger role in developing the industry. We welcome constructive feedback, proposals and initiatives from practitioners. The Government will support and nurture, but it cannot direct the industry. In a fast-changing and dynamic business, the government cannot know, let alone control, everything that is going on.

Human resources will be crucial. Singapore has very good hardware — telecommunications, Changi Airport, computer systems for trading and settlement. We must continue to improve on these important advantages over our competitors. But our most urgent constraint is people rather than hardware. The key success factor is intellectual capital. Singapore must be the marketplace of choice which gathers the best financial talent, both domestic and foreign. We need to nurture promising participants, encourage talent to work in Singapore, and get them to play in a conducive and freely competitive environment.

New Principles

What new principles should guide the Government's policy towards the financial sector? What will the "lighter touch" consist of? The old approach was to maintain high standards, establish strict rules and take minimum risks. We must keep the first of these principles, and modify the other two.

We must maintain high standards of integrity and sound financial management, which have become associated with Singapore. These standards must never be compromised. There is no contradiction between keeping standards high and creating a more dynamic and vibrant environment. The regional economic problems underline the critical importance of maintaining both international and domestic confidence in the soundness of our financial system. If banks, and also their regulators in their home countries, lose faith in Singapore, they will take their business away.

We are now in a stronger position to take risks. But we are still unable to recover from a banking scandal as effortlessly as say London. MAS must continue to do the things it has done well, overseeing the financial sector professionally, vigilantly and proactively.

We need to shift emphasis from regulation to supervision. In banking jargon, regulation means establishing capital requirements and setting rules on prudential standards and practices, what can and cannot be done. Supervision, on the other hand, means monitoring and inspecting individual institutions for compliance with these requirements and rules, and ensuring that internal management controls are in good shape.

If we rely heavily on regulation to maintain high standards, we will need more rigid rules. And since these rules will apply to all institutions, they will hinder growth and innovation in the good institutions.

By depending less on regulation and more on supervision, we can deal with good and bad institutions differently. We should not impose onerous requirements which penalise many good institutions, just to safeguard against a few bad ones. Our supervisory style should incorporate a greater understanding of business needs, and be more tolerant of business imperatives. This will also help reduce regulatory costs.

This change is crucial, but it will take considerable effort and time to realise fully, because it requires changing operating procedures, and, more difficult, expectations of both participants and the authorities.

Our attitude towards risk must change. MAS has to take a less conservative approach to risk. It should allow financial institutions to assume the risk profiles which they themselves are comfortable with, within prudential limits. Sound standards are necessary, to provide the basis for prudent risk taking. But we must recognise a trade-off between safety and business opportunity. For example, it is riskier to lend and invest in regional markets than in the domestic market, but we cannot therefore avoid going regional.

We should focus more attention on systemic risk, rather than protecting individual participants, products or projects. The supervisor's primary responsibility is to avoid major disruptions to financial markets and a loss of confidence in the financial system as a whole. While the supervisor needs to protect depositors' interests, he also has to enable financial institutions to take considered business risks. We need a judicious balance between avoiding risks and grasping opportunities. Ultimately what risks to accept in our financial system is a matter of judgment, not a technical issue with a right and wrong answer.

Sometimes taking risks will result in unanticipated losses — that is what risk means. Deciding what risks a bank should take is the job of the bank's management and board of directors, who are responsible to the shareholders. The supervisor will not stop a bank from taking what he might himself consider a doubtful risk, so long as bank management controls are working, the bank is meeting appropriate prudential requirements, and it discloses adequate information to shareholders and the market.

We should allow investors to judge and take business risks for themselves. We must distinguish clearly between business risk on the one hand, and fraud and sharp practice on the other. We will protect investors from the latter, for example, by acting firmly against insider trading. But that should not extend to second guessing business decisions, whether by individuals or firms.

This requires a change of mindset. The public must learn to make investment decisions for themselves, and take responsibility for the outcomes, good or bad. Just because a stock is listed on the SES, and Central Provident Fund savings can be used to buy SES stocks, does not mean that all SES stocks are good investments, much less that the SES or the Government has endorsed the stocks. In exercising judgment and taking risks, there are bound to be mistakes and failures. Success means learning from mistakes and failures, without ceasing to try.

The man in the street will never become a sophisticated investor or financial analyst. He will not understand the ins and outs of calls and puts, warrants and futures. But he should at least know that there are risks that he does not fully comprehend, and refrain from venturing onto risky ground. We should signpost risky ground with danger signs, not cordon it off with triple barbed wire fences.

It is neither possible nor desirable to decide on behalf of Singaporeans what they can or cannot invest in. Some Singaporeans use their savings to buy properties abroad, often in countries where the laws are unclear. Others, more adventurous, even invest in ostrich eggs! Yet we do not propose to bring ostrich egg trading under the MAS Act. The rule must be *caveat emptor* — let the buyer beware, and watch out for his own interests.

What we can do is to develop a sub-industry which provides the public with reliable and unbiased information and advice, from independent advisors who have no vested interest in selling their own products. We should also encourage sector groups to develop and enforce industry standards. Such standards of good practice will help protect consumers against unethical conduct.

We should rely more on market discipline and full information disclosure to protect investors, rather than extensive regulation, formal or informal. The regulator's role is to make sure there is transparency and full disclosure, so that the playing field is level. Then the public can decide which institutions are soundest, and which companies are worth investing in.

For example, when a listed company seeks shareholders' approval for some proposition, the regulator's duty is only to ensure that the issue has been honestly and fairly put to shareholders, and that the facts and numbers are correct. It is up to the shareholders to decide to accept or reject the proposition, and for the markets to judge whether the shareholders have decided wisely.

Similarly, we must raise the standards of information disclosure for banks, to bring them fully in line with the major industrial nations. Currently they even lag behind some countries in the region. Shareholders and customers need adequate information about banks, to assess for themselves what risks the bank is exposed to, and how safe their investments and deposits are.

If investors and depositors are to have more freedom of choice, and market discipline and disclosure standards are to play a large role, then financial institutions must have very robust internal risk management, control and audit systems. This will allow us to minimise micro-management of financial institutions and activities and allow more free play, for example, freer entry and exit from businesses, and movement of professionals within the industry.

To quote Alan Greenspan, "we must be assured that with rare and circumscribed exceptions we do not substitute supervisory judgments for management decisions. That is the road to moral hazard and inefficient bank management."[1]

Our regulations should provide greater transparency. Rules should be as clear as possible. Things which are not expressly forbidden, but are informally and administratively discouraged, should be kept few. The authorities should also avoid having to approve individual transactions

---

1 Remarks at the International Conference of Banking Supervisors in Stockholm, 13 June 1996.

case-by-case. There will be times when the central bank cannot explain why it took certain decisions, even though it has good reasons. And moral suasion, or as Americans call it "jaw-boning", must remain an instrument in MAS' armoury. Every central bank needs this. But we can make the rules clearer — what can and cannot be done, the penalties for infringement and the avenues for appeal.

Rules will always have some unclear areas, particularly when new products are introduced which were not foreseen at the time the rules were drafted. Not every grey transaction is suspect. Sometimes the rules will be out of date, or will have been deliberately framed broadly so as not to be quickly overtaken by developments. Institutions need some leeway to operate in such areas, pending new rules. They must have the confidence that should they do something in good faith which is later ruled out of order, they will not be penalised.

It is the duty of the regulator to be sceptical of human motives. But it is also our policy to distinguish between a traffic and a capital offence, and not to treat everyone as a sharp operator until proven otherwise.

We must build a closer partnership between Government and the industry. The Government will promote a more open and friendly operating environment. It will actively consult the industry for views. The relationship between the regulator and the regulated should be arms length but not adversarial. Market practitioners are in the best position to help regulators keep abreast of new developments in the industry. Candid, thoughtful feedback, including dissenting views, is essential to help the regulatory authorities fine tune policies and avoid mistakes.

What SES did with the latest proposed amendment to Chapter 9B of the Listing Manual, circulating it widely to the financial community for comments, should be standard practice whenever we make a major change to the rules. In this spirit, I have invited SES to work with us on a comprehensive review of the regulations and structure of the securities industry.

The whole approach towards risk which I have described — to emphasise systemic risk, to allow participants to judge their own risks, to depend on transparent regulations, disclosure and market discipline, and to build a partnership with the private sector — rests on one more fundamental point. The primary responsibility for ensuring that financial institutions function in safe, sound and efficient manner rests with the institutions themselves, and their managers and directors. The supervisor will guide and aid these institutions towards these goals. This is already the prevailing wisdom in the developed economies. As always, greater freedom brings with it heavier responsibility.

Promotion and Development

Besides supervising the financial sector, MAS is also responsible for policy thinking, development of the sector and client servicing of institutions. The Government must have a clear idea of how the sector is developing, gather industry views on promising growth areas and help bring desirable activities to Singapore. Although it will not micro-manage, it will often have to play an active role, for example, in promoting the use of IT for finance, and designing policies and tax incentives to develop promising sectors.

In a competitive environment, the businesses with the most potential will not always come to Singapore by themselves. We have to market ourselves and bring them here. The financial sector is unlike manufacturing, because most of the major players in the world are already here. We are therefore promoting new activities rather than new entities. But offering innovative products and services also requires modifying rules and redefining boundaries. This can only happen expeditiously if the innovators, the regulators and other parties involved work together to bring it about.

Financial institutions also need help to deal with the many government departments and agencies, for instance, to bring in key people who are experts in these new areas, or to settle tax issues with the Inland Revenue Authority of Singapore (IRAS). This is how the Economic Development Board (EDB) looks after its clients who have invested in manufacturing operations in Singapore, providing them with one-stop service.

MAS has all along been providing one-stop service to financial institutions. But the scale and scope of the industry has expanded, and MAS needs to reinforce and strengthen the team responsible for policy and development. We must do more to institutionalise these non-supervisory functions in MAS.

Many bankers have suggested to me that regulation and development are incompatible functions. They worry that MAS will be too cautious in development, because its primary mission is regulation. They propose that some other agency instead of MAS be put in charge of development.

I am not convinced. There is a tension between these two functions, and the officers inspecting institutions should not also be charged with client servicing. But intimate cooperation between the regulator and developer is vital. This is easier achieved within one organisation rather than by splitting the functions between different agencies. MAS should continue to be responsible for developing the financial sector, of course working closely with other agencies like the Ministry of Finance (MOF) and IRAS, and even outside the MOF family, with EDB and National Computer Board. But how to build up this capability within MAS is something we will have to consider.

The Financial Sector Review Group

The Financial Sector Review Group has not yet completed its work. Nonetheless let me sketch briefly how it is proceeding.

Firstly, MAS has briefed us thoroughly on the present policy thinking and rationale on regulating, supervising and developing the financial sector. This has been an especially valuable education to me personally, as I have had little direct experience of this sector.

Secondly, we are tapping the Ministry of Trade and Industry's Committee on Singapore's competitiveness, particularly the working groups under Mr Peter Seah's financial sector sub-committee. We have met several groups to discuss their recommendations. I have encouraged them not to confine themselves to incremental improvements, but to make bold proposals where justified. I have told them that if all their proposals are accepted, it probably means that they have not been radical enough.

Thirdly, I have been meeting individuals from the financial sector, both Singaporeans and non-Singaporeans, to get a direct feel for the people in industry and their views. Many of those I have met have taken the trouble to set down their views in writing, putting forward ideas and suggestions. Their many lucid insights and valuable proposals have complemented what I have learnt from the regulators. I wish to thank publicly all those who have contributed so far, and encourage more to come forward with their views.

Fourthly, we have engaged external advisers, and are in the process of commissioning a strategy consultancy firm to do a study. The study will assess Singapore's strengths and weaknesses, identify promising areas for development, recommend policies and strategies and review our approach to regulating, supervising and developing the financial sector.

The Review Group will not publish a comprehensive final report. As we reach conclusions on individual areas, we will announce and implement them, beginning early next year. There will be many issues, because there is no single magic potion for developing and supervising the financial sector. But all the issues will fit into the major themes of the review — developing Singapore as a financial centre; developing our domestic financial system; modifying the style and balance of regulation and supervision; involving the private sector more and relying more heavily on market forces. The principles outlined earlier will give coherence and consistency to the programme.

Conclusion

Changing policies is never easy. It is harder to change policies which have been extremely successful and which continue to yield results, than policies which have failed and must clearly be abandoned. Yet we have to look ahead and prepare for major changes in our operating environment.

We must develop the new approach fully, apply broad principles to specific rules and policies and most importantly shift the mindsets of the regulators, the industry and the public. This speech is the start, not the fruition, of our efforts. The changes will take several years to work through. There are many difficult decisions and much hard work ahead. But if we persevere, we will eventually arrive at a new paradigm.

In many countries, dramatic financial deregulation packages have led to severe problems several years later. If we move late, we will be forced to make major changes in a hurry. Both regulators and participants will have less time to adjust to the new environment. More mistakes and accidents may happen.

By moving early, we can choose the timing and pace of the changes. Then through a series of controlled adjustments, we can navigate a major policy shift, build on the success of our last quarter century, and make Singapore one of the major financial centres in the world.

Financial Supervision in the New Millennium

Mr Koh Yong Guan
Managing Director, MAS
Millennium Law Conference
10 April 2000

Introduction

The organisers had asked that I speak on issues related to the Internet challenge. This is not surprising. Financial services is among those sectors that stand to be radically transformed by the world wide web phenomenon.

The Internet is more than just another delivery mechanism or cost-effective platform for financial providers to launch a global strategy. The Internet will alter the competitive dynamics of the financial sector in a fundamental way. By expanding the richness in consumer choice, the Internet is playing a powerful role in driving consumer education and shaping their expectations. This in turn accelerates the pace by which financial products and services are engineered and rolled out.

All these forces mean that the financial market place today is constantly and continually changing. Some have noted that technology deregulates markets faster than regulators are ready to do. As regulators, we can ill-afford to do our job in the same way if we are not to hinder the growth and development of the financial sector in the new economy.

The revolution in IT has been the key driver behind these rapid changes. It has sped up disintermediation and automation in many ways. The sale of products through Internet portals and extension of day trading to retail investors are among the more obvious developments to date. There is intense competition, not just from traditional rivals, but also from non-financial players.

The new competitive financial landscape ignores geographical and sectoral boundaries. Banks are acquiring insurance companies and vice versa. Stock exchanges around the world are demutualising and forging alliances. Many now offer competitive products on a single platform. Traditional mortgages are being securitised and the credit risks are spread to the capital markets. Catastrophic risks from the insurers are being offered to investors in the form of futures and options. You can even buy derivatives to hedge against specific weather conditions.

These are challenging times. No one can predict how financial markets will develop over the next five to 10 years. The fact is that the typical regulatory structure no longer mirrors the market structures. We are seeing the emergence of international financial conglomerates. These powerhouses not only exercise massive international reach, they have global expertise in banking, securities and insurance all within one entity.

To make sense of this financial revolution, we need to understand the motivations beneath these changes. We have to look ahead and see where the problems and opportunities lie. It is not just going to be a race among businesses. One might even envisage increased competition among regulators as well. To succeed, we need an effective and flexible regulatory approach that is conducive to the development of new business models. Institutions today can relocate rapidly in the face of legal or regulatory obstacles. Financial centres that do not respond to the new environment will simply lag behind.

MAS has articulated its five-year vision to propel Singapore into a world-class financial centre by 2003. We aim to be a global financial hub offering the full range of financial services. We were mindful of the financial revolution when we started our liberalisation process two and a half years ago. But change is happening even faster than what we initially anticipated. The challenge for MAS is to ensure that our supervisory framework keeps pace with the changes so that a conducive environment is in place for a thriving hub.

Against this backdrop, I would like to share my thoughts on a key issue in financial supervision that is consuming the attentions of regulators worldwide — the convergence of financial services. There are four main areas that I will touch on this afternoon. I will first elaborate on the underlying trends and change factors. Second, I will speak on the implications and challenges for regulators, and in particular, the fundamental questions that regulators must ask and objectives that regulation and supervision must continue to address in the midst of rapid technological change. Third, I will discuss the integration of regulation and supervision across the financial markets. Lastly, I will share some thoughts on how MAS intends to respond to these challenges.

Underlying Trends

By convergence of financial services, I refer to convergence at both the institutional and product levels.

Consolidation of Institutions

For many years, banks, insurers and securities brokers have pursued and developed their expertise in their respective fields. In many markets, regulatory barriers protected incumbents from competition. Financial institutions enjoyed good profit margins and had little incentive to venture beyond their traditional domains.

But things are changing. Customers are no longer satisfied with going to a bank to open a checking account, then seeing an insurance agent for retirement planning and then turning to a broker to buy shares. He prefers a one-stop financial service provider. He wants convenience and an integrated approach to money management. Many will want to ride on the new technology to do all these things from home or office.

Markets are also shifting. With financial liberalisation and globalisation, intense competition has led to falling margins. Banks, insurance companies and stock broking firms compete for the same savings dollar. They have to look for ways to improve cost efficiency, explore synergies and meet customer demand. Regulatory barriers are also breaking down, marked by the repeal of the 66-year-old Glass-Steagall Act in the US. The introduction of the Gramm-Leach-Bliley Act allows bank holding companies in the US to undertake the full range of financial activities including insurance and securities. Similar developments are expected in Japan.

Financial institutions are seeing the benefits of merger. The new entity is able to leverage on the expanded customer base and expertise of the combined entities. It can exploit cross-selling opportunities and cut costs by consolidating branch networks. It will enjoy economies of scale in terms of capital expenditure for IT infrastructure and even branding. In short, there are compelling business reasons for financial institutions to restructure and adopt new business models.

We have seen waves of mergers and acquisitions among global financial institutions. The Citicorp-Traveller's merger was only the precursor. It created a global brand for retail financial services and started what some analysts called the race to become the Coca-Cola of financial services. The merger will help Citicorp realise its ambition of having a billion customers worldwide. Insurance companies have not been idle. In Europe, the French financial giant AXA Group has been very aggressive in acquiring insurance and asset management companies in different parts of the world. Similarly, Japanese financial institutions have not been immune to the pressure to merge.

If competition is the impetus, then the Internet would be the accelerator. With its seamless and interactive nature, the Internet is an ideal medium for financial product aggregation. Firms find it easier and cheaper to broaden customer reach, and to distribute a whole array of financial products via the web. The focus has shifted from selling individual products to meeting customers' total financial needs. Customers find that having all their financial needs met at a single contact point is no longer a dream. Information can now be disseminated in real time. Price discovery and comparison of product features heighten competition and customer demand. "Consumer empowerment" is something that will increasingly have to be contended with. Financial institutions are poised to provide every service for global clients and offer more personalised services in the industry. Some firms even offer financial planning tools through the Internet for free.

Merging of Financial Products

The transformation of financial products is no less dramatic. Advances in computing power and applications have supported product innovations and improvisations. Financial engineering, sophisticated risk modelling and simulations allow financial instruments to be broken down into their basic constituents. This leads to insights into the pricing of risks, and allows re-grouping of basic building blocks. Products that straddle banking, capital markets and insurance, are now common.

For some time now, insurance companies have packaged investment-linked policies, combining the financial protection of life insurance with the investment returns of a mutual fund. Recently, banks issue credit derivatives, which bear the characteristics of insurance. They also sell index-linked notes and market funds, a hybrid of banking and securities products.

Implications for Regulation

How should regulators react to such a flood of changes? We have to stay sensitive to market developments, but not be overwhelmed by them. The instinct is to return to fundamentals. I begin by asking three questions that I think all regulators should ask:

- Who and what are we protecting?
- What are we protecting them from?
- Why are we protecting them?

The answers to these questions are interrelated. To put it succinctly, there are two key issues. Regulators protect the real economy from the ramifications of financial systemic failures. We also have to preserve the integrity and credibility of the financial market so as to safeguard the interests of depositors, investors and policyholders. In the latter, this arises because of the information asymmetry between providers and consumers. These objectives remain relevant, but their complexion is bound to be altered by these trends.

First, concern with systemic risk is heightened. Huge and complex financial institutions may pose a threat to systemic stability when they fail. With their global nature, risks can spread quickly to otherwise sound markets in different regions. Regulators have to be equipped with new skills to oversee and supervise complex institutions. Greater international cooperation among regulators is also needed.

Second, national regulators have mainly guarded against systemic risk arising from the banking system. This is too narrow now. Financial markets are now more integrated and globalised. More funds are being channeled into capital markets. Insurance is also claiming a growing share of personal savings. As bank deposits shrink, the management of systemic risk must extend beyond the banking system.

Third, the notion of depositor protection is also being re-examined. In the wake of the Asian financial crisis, Asian regulators are questioning the wisdom of bailing out individual banks in the name of depositor protection but at a large public cost. An efficient bankruptcy regime and prudential safety nets, such as deposit insurance and policyholders' protection fund, have now gained acceptance.

Finally, national regulators are finding it more difficult to shoulder the sole responsibility for safeguarding consumer interests. The Internet transcends national boundaries, and exposes consumers to a myriad of suppliers and products. It is increasingly difficult for national regulators to block out all unlicensed service providers. Consumers have to be empowered to exert market discipline on service providers.

Many national regulators are advocating a disclosure-based regime, so as to provide investors with sufficient information to make their own judgement. Such a regime requires a strong regulatory framework and high standards of disclosure. There has to be increased transparency. Accounting and reporting standards need to be harmonised too. This will improve comparability of financial statements. Regulators also need the legislative powers to carry out enforcement and provide appropriate remedy or restitution. It will be even better if we can have a lively educated investor community imposing discipline on financial intermediaries to meet high disclosure standards.

Integrated Regulation and Supervision

The regulators' response to market developments has been at two levels. The first is to re-model the way regulators are organised. The second is to re-align the regulatory framework across different sectors. Let me address them in turn.

Traditionally, regulations have been structured along sectoral lines. Different types of institutions are regulated under different legislation for banking, insurance and securities. In many countries, separate financial regulators administer the various laws. It is therefore not surprising that regulators for the individual industries have pursued the core regulatory objectives with varying emphasis and approaches.

Bank regulators have focused on depositor protection and systemic stability. They have guarded against bank failures, put in place deposit insurance schemes and given depositors priority ranking. Securities regulators on the other hand, have relied on market discipline to achieve investor protection. They have emphasised disclosure standards, fair market practices and strong enforcement. Systemic issues have been dealt with by ensuring stable exchanges and reliable settlement. Insurance regulators have been primarily concerned with safeguarding the interest of policyholders.

The blurring of institutional and product boundaries has questioned the effectiveness of the existing regulatory structure. We foresee at least two problems with integrated financial entities.

First, there will be regulatory overlap when these entities are required to comply with multiple sets of regulations. This increases compliance costs. Second, where there are different regulatory requirements for similar products, an institution will structure itself in such a way to deliver a product via an entity in the group that is subject to the lowest regulatory demands. Regulatory arbitrage will become a concern.

Shifts in regulatory model have already begun. The UK has restructured its regulatory framework by bringing nine industry regulators (including three self-regulatory bodies) under one consolidated body, the FSA (Financial Services Authority). Australia has two consolidated regulators — APRA (Australian Prudential Regulation Authority) for prudential regulation and ASIC (Australian Securities and Investments Commission) for regulating market conduct. We have been more fortunate in Singapore. MAS has been a single financial services regulator since 1984, overseeing the banking, securities, futures and insurance industries.

But putting different regulators under the same roof is only a start. Having an integrated supervisor is not the same as having integrated supervision. Even under MAS' umbrella, we have adopted the same silo approach in regulating different industries. Each industry has its own legislation and MAS adopts international best practices in each. The challenge ahead is to integrate financial regulation and supervision. This means aligning the regulatory approach across industries to mirror the convergence of individual markets. A more holistic view in supervising financial institutions and markets will also become essential.

The trend, regulators are moving towards, is best described as an "objective based" approach to financial regulation. This means that rules and regulations are no longer designed along product lines or types of entities but along fundamental regulatory objectives that we have identified earlier. Unlike entities and products, these objectives are less likely to change with time. An "objective based" regulatory framework will afford more flexibility to cope with the rapid transformation of institutions and products.

At this point, the global best practice for integrated regulation and supervision is still nascent. The UK has recently begun to consolidate all its financial services legislation into one omnibus Bill. This includes the creation of a single licensing regime and compensation scheme.

I believe this is a sensible approach for us to consider. MAS is on track. We are already a consolidated financial regulator. Our next milestone will be to integrate financial regulation across industries in a cohesive and meaningful way. I do not expect any easy solution. The issues are complicated and will involve difficult judgement of costs and benefits. It is also going to take some time. And refinements along the way would be necessary. But we have to start work now.

What would such an approach look like? I doubt anyone at this moment has all the right answers. Let me share some thoughts with you. I hope this will generate awareness and discussion among professionals. It will help in our search for an appropriate formula.

Harmonisation of Regulations Across Industries

I have touched on the need to harmonise regulations across the different industries. This does not mean that we intend to tear down sectoral distinctions completely. We will recognise the inherent differences in the nature of banking, securities and insurance businesses.

Guiding Principles

There are two key principles that will guide us in developing an integrated regulatory framework. The first principle is consistency. We want regulation of similar financial functions, products or services to be consistent across all types of institutions. Risks of the same nature should be treated similarly. For instance, the rules that apply to unit trusts should be comparable to those of investment-linked policies, since both are essentially investment products — one offered by fund managers and one by life insurers. This consistency will help level the playing field for market participants, and prevent regulatory arbitrage.

Second, the regulatory framework should be flexible. It is difficult to predict how financial markets will evolve. Bearing in mind the fundamental regulatory objectives that I mentioned earlier, we need a regulatory framework that can safeguard financial soundness, and yet be sufficiently flexible to allow firms to respond to market developments.

At the institutional level, we need to consider how regulations can be applied consistently across the entire market. This includes licensing as well as ongoing supervision once the institutions are admitted. To have flexibility, regulators should focus on risk-based parameters instead of dictating rigid rules for the conduct of activities and product offering.

Many new financial entities do not fit nicely into the existing licensing regime. Let me give you one example. In Singapore, if a merchant bank intends to engage in investment banking, securities and futures dealing, it will need to hold three separate licences, one for each activity. We need to ask if there can be a more streamlined licensing regime without compromising prudential standards.

The British have noted that the logic of a single regulatory framework would point strongly in the direction of a single authorisation process. This will ensure consistency at the licensing stage across all financial activities. The FSA commented that there are at least three methods of implementing the single authorisation process. At one extreme, a firm initially authorised would be able to vary or change the nature of its financial activities without requirement to seek further permission. At the other extreme, the authorised firm must apply for permission to undertake each and every line of business.

The FSA is inclined to adopt an authorisation approach that falls between the two extremes. Authorised financial institutions would need to apply for subsequent permission if they make substantial changes to their activities. This approach seeks to balance prudential concerns with developmental objectives.

Our proposed Omnibus Securities and Futures Act is a step in this direction, consolidating regulations in two activities that have the closest linkage. The new Omnibus Act will merge and streamline the Securities Industry Act and Futures Trading Act into one statute. Provisions currently contained in the Companies Act which relate to corporate fund raising, as well as unit trust regulations will also be transferred to the new Omnibus Act. This will have the effect of streamlining the licensing, prudential and market conduct requirements for the securities and futures industry. We hope to have the Omnibus Bill ready for Parliament debate in the year 2001.

Prudential regulation should also be consistent across different industries, where possible. One example is capital requirement. Regardless of the nature of business, the objective is to ensure that financial institutions hold adequate capital commensurate with the risks assumed. Banking regulators use the concept of risk-based capital. Securities and insurance regulators, on the other hand, prescribe adjusted net capital or leverage limits. Regulators are now studying the feasibility of adopting a common risk-based capital framework for all these businesses.

MAS' adoption of risk-based supervision has been timely. It is a more effective and efficient way to oversee larger and more complex institutions. The focus is on the review of an individual firm's risk management processes and control systems. But MAS examiners will have to equip themselves to understand the nature and source of risks in different activities, how these risks interplay and can get transmitted across activities.

In particular, we need to examine the guidelines for intra-group exposure. This addresses the concern of contagion within a conglomerate where the operations of individual entities may affect the liquidity and profitability of the entire group. Silo regulation may overlook this. Ownership and corporate governance rules need to be tightened.

Consumer

Regulators have always been concerned with protecting consumer interests. But we realise the increasing difficulty of shielding consumers from risks in the new environment. Financial products are becoming more complex, and unlicensed service providers can reach them using new channels such as the Internet. The best means to protect them is to raise consumer awareness and professional standards. Where the risks to consumers are alike, it is sensible to give consumers the same degree of protection across the board.

In Singapore, many consumers expect the regulator or government to take care of them. We have to moderate this expectation and shift the responsibility for making financial decisions onto themselves. In this regard, MAS has been raising disclosure standards across all industries. For disclosure to be meaningful, they need to be consistent, comparable and comprehensive. We will continue to work with the industries to educate the investing public, including raising their financial literacy.

Another step is to harmonise risk disclosure for different products. This will allow consumers to compare substitutable products. As integrated products become prevalent, disclosure is even more important, so that consumers can understand the risk-return profile.

International Cooperation

Today, having a strong, well-regulated domestic market no longer guarantees a sound night's sleep for the regulator. The Asian financial crisis and Long-Term Capital Management (LTCM) debacle illustrate the reality of a global market, and its contagion effect. Singapore was not spared even though we were fundamentally sound. Furthermore, with the Internet allowing ready and easy cross-border access, there is a need for greater regulatory cooperation. This includes the sharing of information and ideas, and working towards a harmonisation of standards across countries.

Regulators have entered into bilateral agreements to share information, and to render assistance for regulatory purposes. International forums, such as the Joint Forum and the Financial Stability Forum, have put in much effort to address some of these issues. MAS participates actively in these discussions.

Concluding Remarks

Looking ahead, the increasingly integrated financial landscape will bring about greater complexity as well as uncertainty. Yet no matter how radical we see the transformation, the principles that guide the regulator remain clear. The regulator must also continue to maintain high standards of integrity and impartiality.

Regulations will have to keep pace with market reality. It will take great skill to define the targets of regulation and to draw lines within the regulatory framework that are at once clear and yet sufficiently flexible.

There is no final solution, we have to update and adapt continuously.

We have to work hand in hand with market players and legislators to ensure that our regulatory framework continues to achieve these ends in a changing environment. We have benefited from the insights of the legal profession in crafting rules and regulations and shaping our policies. We will continue to consult you.

Institutions and consumers will also have to play a bigger role. We expect high standards of corporate governance from the board and management of financial institutions. They should stay on top of changes and put in place sound risk management practices. Ultimately, they have the primary responsibility for managing their institutions' risks and are accountable to their stakeholders. Consumers will also have to take on greater responsibility for making their own investment decisions. MAS will continue to work towards greater transparency in our markets, raise disclosure standards and foster market discipline in the financial services industry. We would also work with and encourage industry groups to develop and enforce standards of good market practice.

The new millennium holds invaluable opportunities for Singapore's financial sector. There is much work to be done in creating a forward-looking and dynamic regulatory environment for Singapore to thrive as a financial hub. Such an environment would accommodate new business models like Internet-only banks. MAS intends to introduce the regulatory framework for Internet only banks in a few months. So long as we gear ourselves up to meet new challenges, we can look forward to an exciting and prosperous future.

Separation of Financial and Non-Financial Activities of Banking Groups

Mr Lee Hsien Loong
Deputy Prime Minister and Chairman, MAS
27th Association of Banks in Singapore Annual Dinner
21 June 2000

Introduction

I last attended the ABS annual dinner two years ago. I spoke then on the need to free up our banking sector, and to allow competition a greater role in shaping the industry. Last year, MAS announced measures to improve corporate governance and institutionalise the management of the local banks, and the first phase of a five-year programme to liberalise the banking sector. We sought to strengthen Singapore's banking system, provide Singaporeans with quality banking services and further enhance Singapore's position as an international financial centre.

These reforms have brought about visible changes. The next step in strengthening the local banks is now to separate financial and non-financial businesses within the banking groups, and to further improve corporate governance through a clearer and more transparent ownership and control structure.

Separation of Financial and Non-Financial Activities

What ought to constitute the permissible activities for a banking group is an issue which all financial regulators have to consider carefully. If we took a purely *laissez faire* approach, we could leave banks to structure themselves as their owners and management saw fit. What businesses banks chose to be involved in, and what business entities chose to own a bank, would be matters for themselves to decide. Over time, banks with the right configuration and mix of activities would succeed, while those without would fail or be eliminated by the competition.

But regulators cannot leave it entirely to the market to sort out such matters, especially where the banks involved are not peripheral players but perform key roles in deposit taking and the payments system. Strong banks are important to the health of the financial system and to the entire process of credit intermediation. Regulators cannot guarantee that individual banks will never fail, but they have a duty to minimise the chances of a mishap and to maintain the integrity and overall stability of the financial system.

A clear source of potential problems in this regard is the commingling of financial and non-financial activities within the same corporate group. Many regulators regard it as good banking and sound supervisory practice to require clear separation of the two.

Firstly, separation will limit the risk of contagion from non-banking businesses to the bank. Banks with significant interests in non-banking activities are exposed not just to credit and market risks — which are the primary risks of their business, and which the banks should assess and manage as part of their core competence. These banks will also be taking on the business risks of their non-financial activities. If their non-financial activities run into trouble, the banks may feel compelled to support them beyond normal commercial considerations, to protect their own reputation. In so doing the banks may undermine their own soundness; yet if they did not extend the rescue, the problems of the affiliates may trigger a loss of confidence in the bank itself because of the close association.

Secondly, with banking and non-banking activities intermeshed within a conglomerate, there will be a strong tendency to stretch any safety net intended for the banking system also to cover non-bank operations in the group. If failure of an associated non-bank threatens the bank and systemic stability, the regulator or government may be forced to rescue both. We have seen this happen in the recent Asian crisis. An implicit safety net for the banking system may be a necessary evil; but extending it to non-banks compounds the problem of moral hazard. It also tilts the playing field against non-bank competitors who are not associated with banks.

Thirdly, separation minimises the risk of non arms-length transactions between banks and their non-bank affiliates. When a bank lends to a related entity at more favourable terms than market, or invests in an affiliate in order to control it even though the investment does not perform, minority shareholders of the bank are disadvantaged, and so are depositors.

Some economists have argued that in less developed financial markets, it is in fact a rational and practical strategy for a group of companies sharing common ownership or cross-shareholdings to lend to and invest in one another. Information about companies is often less than complete, and company accounts and business plans are hard to interpret. Family networks or *guanxi* are then efficient ways to establish a basis of trust for doing business, and to avoid the high costs of obtaining reliable knowledge about the other party's activities and finances.

But the non-transparency of this approach can lead to serious difficulties and abuses. Cross-shareholdings diminish the influence of minority shareholders, dilute market pressure on the companies in the group and weaken the internal discipline to appraise rigorously the risk of each investment.

The ongoing reforms in many Asian countries are as much about tightening corporate governance in this regard as they are about re-capitalising weak banks. The way forward for banks is therefore not to rely on family networks or *guanxi*. It is to strengthen their ability to assess credit risks and investment propositions rigorously, on arms-length, commercial considerations and to deploy their assets in a diversified, optimal manner.

Finally, separating out non-financial activities will focus management attention on their core business of banking and finance. The need to concentrate on core competencies is not unique to banking. Globalisation and technology are causing many world-class companies to focus on their core competencies, and to outsource parts of their value chain for which they have no particular competitive advantage. This is especially true for banks, which are operating in an intensely competitive and dynamic environment. They need to muster all their talents and energies on the financial business, instead of dissipating them over many different businesses.

For these reasons, banks should not commingle financial and non-financial activities. However, this does not mean that banks must refrain from engaging in venture capital or merchant banking business, which involves taking an equity interest in a diversified portfolio of non-financial companies for some period. It is not uncommon for the merchant banking business of well-run, international banks to take stakes in non-financial companies for three to five years. These activities are natural extensions of the lending business of banks. They are, however, quite different from taking long-term strategic stakes in non-financial companies which tie a bank's reputation to these companies.

In addition to the separation of banking and non-banking activities, regulators in several developed markets have also advocated dispersed ownership of banks. Often this has been achieved by legislation or via the bank's own memorandum and articles of association, which sets limits on shareholdings to prevent any single shareholder or group of shareholders from dominating the bank. The result has been a "clean" corporate structure for their banks, i.e. there are no cross-shareholdings between banks and non-banks, and there is clear separation of ownership from management.

Practice in Other Countries

The US is an example of a financial system which has prohibited commingling between banking and commerce, and required dispersion of bank ownership. For many years, the Glass-Steagall Act restricted commercial banks even from certain other financial activities, particularly investment banking and insurance, much less non-banking business. Now that Glass-Steagall has finally been repealed, allowing for more competitive banking institutions, the US Federal Reserve Board is proposing that US financial holding companies (FHCs) should only undertake a well-defined range of approved activities.

In the UK, there is no legal prohibition on banks participating in non-financial activities. But in practice few of the banks do so. This is partly the result of stringent treatment of capital adequacy by the regulator — banks are required to deduct from their regulatory capital dollar for dollar of any investment they make in non-financial activities. It is also because the banks are widely held, with no dominant shareholder who has other non- financial interests. The banks therefore have little incentive to control non-financial companies through their investments.

Germany has had a different approach. German banks have traditionally held major long-term equity stakes in industrial groups, such as Daimler-Benz or Thyssen. This arrangement gave the industrial groups long-term strategic shareholders, who could look beyond the next quarter's financial results. But it has also frozen the structure of the industrial groups, and prevented them from merging, restructuring and rationalising, as US companies have done. It has made it harder for the banks to deploy their assets flexibly, to maximise their own returns and to become as spry and competitive as US banks.

The Germans have recognised these structural weaknesses and are taking steps to rectify them. However, one major obstacle to German banks divesting their industrial holdings has been the prohibitive capital gains tax. Now a Social Democrat government has proposed tax reforms that will remove this obstacle, and pave the way for banking and industrial conglomerates to untangle their web of cross-shareholdings.

In Asia, both South Korea and Japan relied on close association between banking and commerce in the earlier stages of their industrialisation. South Korean *chaebols*, and the banks that lent to them, are now facing painful reforms. Poor lending practices by Korean banks disguised the deteriorating finances of the *chaebols*, and eventually nearly brought the whole system down in the Asian crisis.

In Japan, the pre-war *zaibatsu* system became the post-war *keiretsu* system. Each major *keiretsu* or industrial group consists of companies linked together through a web of cross-shareholdings, including a main bank. *Keiretsu* members support one another financially and in terms of direct business. The bank in the *keiretsu* plays a pivotal role, facilitating the financial transactions of the group.

While the *keiretsu* system helped Japan to rebuild and industrialise its economy after the war, many of the problems of corporate governance and unsound banks that now plague Japan are rooted in this structure. The prolonged crisis of the Japanese economy since 1990 has forced a fundamental rethink. The Japanese are now gradually starting to make basic structural changes. The banks are less willing to lend to associates without independently assessing their risks and charging the appropriate risk premiums. And both banks and non-banks within the group are no longer willing to maintain shareholdings in each other which yield low returns. The changes will enhance transparency and corporate accountability. They are essential to Japan's economic recovery, but will have far-reaching social and cultural implications.

Existing Structures of Singapore Banks

In Singapore, the local banks (other than DBS) started as family-owned banks and built up a successful financial business on that basis. Over time they have merged and consolidated. Today the founding families remain the principal shareholders, and are in several instances also involved in the management of the bank.

Besides banking, the principal shareholders have also built up diverse non-banking businesses, especially in property. The local banks participate in these non-financial activities of the group, both by lending and through equity ownership. The banks and non-banks in the same group have developed significant cross-shareholdings. A mixed conglomerate structure has evolved.

The commingling of financial and non-financial activities will potentially expose Singapore banks to the same problems that banks elsewhere have experienced. We have not run into serious problems, so far. This is because the principal shareholders have run the banks prudently and properly. MAS has also been stringent in monitoring related party transactions. Strict laws govern such transactions; for instance, bank directors are jointly and severally liable to indemnify the bank for losses arising from unsecured loans to related companies.

But problems will manifest themselves only in times of stress, as the Japanese and Korean experiences have shown. For the future, we need to restructure the banks' participation in non-financial activities before potential vulnerabilities become actual problems. We have the luxury of acting now while the banks are sound; we must not delay or put off changes which are essential for their long-term well-being.

The banking environment in Singapore will only become more open and competitive, and less forgiving of weaknesses or under-performance. Banks must concentrate on their core competencies and build strong and institutionalised management structures to compete in a globalised industry. Ultimately, their improved performance will benefit all depositors and shareholders, and strengthen the financial system as a whole.

New Structure

The Government has therefore decided to require the local banking groups to segregate their financial and non-financial activities, and unwind the cross-shareholdings between the two. This will mean changes to their present corporate structures. These measures will apply to all local banks — OCBC, UOB and OUB, as well as DBS and KTB.

There will be four key elements in the separation between the financial and non-financial entities: ownership, cross-shareholding, management, and name-sharing.

Ownership

MAS will require all the financial activities in each banking group to be grouped together, either under the bank or under a non-operating FHC. The non-financial activities must be segregated from the banking group and divested. They can be sold to third parties, or alternatively to the principal shareholders of the bank, so that the principal shareholders own them directly, and not through any of the entities in the financial arm of the group. MAS will regulate the bank or FHC, but it will not regulate the non-financial activities.

Currently, all the local banks are listed, and so are many of the non-banks in the groups. The banks and non-banks already have separate sets of shareholders. In fact, the minority shareholders, i.e., the shareholders other than the principal shareholder, typically account for about 70% of the ownership of the bank.

MAS will require this separation of ownership to be retained. The bank or FHC in the existing banking groups must continue to be listed on its own. For example, it cannot be subsumed as a 100%-owned subsidiary of a listed top-level holding company, which owns both the bank as well as the non-financial entities.

Having distinct groups of shareholders for the financial and non-financial activities will strengthen market discipline on the bank, and facilitate clearer accountability of its performance to minority shareholders. It will help to ensure that the separation of the financial and non-financial activities is substantive and not just pro-forma.

There are many ways for banking groups to reconfigure their corporate structure. In the end, what counts as a FHC is a matter of substance, and not of the form of the organisation chart. MAS reserves the right to declare any company which owns a substantial share of a bank, directly or indirectly, as a FHC. Such a FHC will be subject to MAS regulation and will not be allowed to own non-financial activities.

Cross-Shareholding

The financial entities will not be allowed to own, directly or indirectly, the shares of non-financial firms affiliated to the same principal shareholder.

Within the financial arm, shareholdings should only be in one direction. We will not allow two companies in the financial arm to have mutual shareholdings in each other. For example, if a bank takes a stake in an insurance company or securities firm, then the insurance company or securities firm would not be allowed to hold a stake in the bank. The Companies Act already prohibits subsidiaries of banks from owning shares in the bank. We will extend this principle to all entities below the bank or FHC, whether or not they are subsidiaries of the bank or FHC.

Ideally, we should also disallow the non-financial entities from owning shares in the financial entities. However, we do not start from a clean slate. Requiring the banks to divest themselves of the non-financial activities will already be a major structural change. Therefore, in the present exercise MAS will allow the principal shareholders to continue owning indirect stakes in the banking groups through the non-financial entities that they control. MAS will review this arrangement later.

Management

To avoid conflicts of interest, the management of the financial entities should be separate from the management of its non-financial affiliates. There should be no sharing of executive directors and management staff, such as the chief financial officer and chief operating officer. On the board of directors of a regulated financial entity, a majority of the directors should not be holding directorships on the boards of the non-financial affiliates as well.

Name-Sharing

Mixed conglomerates usually leverage on common brand building. Many of the non-financial affiliates of local banks share the name of their parent banks. Financial and non-financial entities alike have built up goodwill in the brand name over the years.

But reputational and contagion risks can result from sharing of names and corporate badges between the bank and its non-bank affiliates. Where an unregulated entity sharing a name fails or falls into disrepute, the public may attribute its problems to the bank, causing a bank run.

MAS will therefore disallow the sharing of names and logos between the financial and non-financial entities. We are considering amending the Banking Act, to prevent the use of names or acronyms by companies that may confuse the public, or give the impression that a company is related to or associated with any Singapore-incorporated bank.

Scope of Permitted Activities

MAS will determine the scope of activities which the bank or FHC will be permitted to undertake. Besides financial activities, they will include activities which have clear synergies with the bank's financial business. We will not have a fixed list of permitted activities. Instead we will exercise flexibility to allow banks to undertake business ventures that are related to their core competencies, such as e-commerce activities that are changing the banking industry worldwide. These include providing payment services in support of e-commerce, and leveraging on banks' IT competencies to provide IT services, especially in building infrastructure and applications for B2B e-commerce.

Banks will also be allowed to undertake equity portfolio and venture capital investments. We will define an equity portfolio investment to be one where the bank and its financial affiliates do not have control over the investee company, e.g. by being the largest shareholder. An equity portfolio investment should generally not exceed 10% of the investee company's capital. Furthermore, each equity portfolio investment will be subject to a single security limit of 2% of the bank's capital funds. We will amend Section 31 of the Banking Act to remove the existing aggregate limit on portfolio investments, and replace it with this new single security limit. We will also exclude debt instruments from Section 31 because they are generally less risky than equities.

Venture capital investments will be treated separately. MAS is drafting separate rules to allow for venture capital investments by banks, and will consult them on these guidelines soon.

The local banks have significant property holdings. This is partly because over the years the banks have grown together with the property business of their principal shareholders, and also because property has been seen as a good and safe investment in Singapore. Some of these property holdings were acquired many years ago, and have been kept on the banks' books at book values which are well below their present market values. This has provided a comfortable cushion of reserves for the banks against uncertainties. But it has also failed to reflect the true cost of holding these properties and therefore reduced the pressure on the banks to optimise returns on assets.

Property assets that earn competitive returns have their place as one component of the investment portfolio of the local banks. MAS will therefore allow the banks to hold properties, solely for investment purposes, and subject to a limit aimed at preventing excessive risk concentration. How much property a bank actually holds within these prudential limits is for its management and shareholders to decide.

However, banks should not be engaged in developing or managing hotels or other properties, whether directly or through companies they control. Banks are not property companies. MAS will therefore require banks to divest all properties held for development, and shareholdings in property development companies beyond the portfolio investment limits.

The aggregate net book value of permitted property holdings will be subject to a revised Section 33 limit of 20% of a bank's capital funds (reduced from the existing 40%). The 20% limit translates into less than 5% of each of the local bank's total assets currently. It will apply on the basis of both bank and group capital. As with the present Section 33, properties held for the purpose of the bank's business premises will be excluded from this limit. But whilst the present Section 33 applies only to properties directly held by banks and their subsidiaries, the new limit will also include properties held by companies in which the banking group has shareholding of 10% or more.

Investments Made by Insurance Funds

Most of the local banks have insurance companies within their groups. These insurance companies present a slight complication. They invest two separate types of funds: the equity in the company belonging to its shareholders, and the insurance funds managed by the company but belonging to the policyholders, for example, the life fund of life insurance companies.

Portfolio investments made using the shareholders' funds of the insurance companies will be subject to the same single security limit of 2% of the group's capital funds and the limit of 10% of the investee company's capital. The portfolio limits for the banking group as a whole will therefore include the investments using these shareholders' funds of their insurance companies.

MAS recognises that the insurance funds are different in nature from the equity of the company or the group because they belong to the policyholders and not the shareholders. Therefore in principle investments using the insurance fund should be treated separately from the investments of the company and the group. Nevertheless the insurance fund should also be used only for portfolio investments, and not for the purpose of controlling other companies in the group, especially non-financial companies, whether by itself or together with other investments by the group.

Currently, some banking groups have used these insurance funds as the vehicle for owning and controlling their investee companies. For example, the bank itself may own only 5% of an investee company, but the insurance fund of the insurance company may own another 15%, giving a total stake of 20%. This is not satisfactory, because it presents the same problems of contagion, non-transparency and dilution of management focus as the bank itself investing directly in these companies.

MAS will study the appropriate investment limits of insurance funds for both bank-related and independent insurers. The limits set should protect the interests of policyholders through adequate diversification, and ensure that the investments do not amount to controlling stakes. These measures will be developed in consultation with the industry, and are expected to be finalised by the end of the year.

Whatever the precise portfolio investment limits for the insurance funds, MAS will take the governance and deployment of these insurance funds into consideration, when assessing whether the banking group has de facto control of an investee company, and thus whether an investment meets the portfolio investment criteria for the banking group.

Time Frame and Potential Impact

The separation of the financial and non-financial activities will be a major change for the banking groups. There will be significant corporate restructuring and divestment of assets. We must do this in an orderly manner, over a reasonable period. There is no reason to force a fire sale, which would weaken the banks and diminish confidence, and would be against the interests of shareholders and depositors.

Local banks will be given three years to complete the restructuring and comply with the new requirements. The three years will commence from the passage of the relevant legislation, which should take place by the end of the year. MAS will work with the banks on a phasing-in schedule, so that the restructuring and divestments can take place in an orderly manner and be completed within the three-year deadline.

Tax Treatment for Divestment

The divestment of non-permitted assets will have significant tax implications. In order to avoid uncertainty as to how the Inland Revenue Authority of Singapore (IRAS) will treat these transactions, and to minimise the tax impact on the banks of changes which have been mandated by MAS, the Government has decided on a set of one-off administrative concessions to facilitate this exercise.

All gains arising from disposals of shares and real properties which have been held for more than 10 years will be treated as non-taxable capital gains. For assets held for less than 10 years, IRAS would look at the facts of individual cases to decide whether capital or income treatment is appropriate. The Government will also waive stamp duty on sales of all shares and properties where the gains are considered capital in nature.

These concessions will not apply to gains arising from the disposal of shares which have previously been claimed as trading stock for tax purposes, or gains on disposals of real properties by banks' property development companies. However, where income tax is payable arising from a mandated sale of assets that does not qualify for capital gains tax exemption, the Government will give the banks three years to settle the amount.

This package will apply only to assets required to be disposed of under the restructuring exercise, and will only cover disposals made within the three-year period allowed by MAS for the restructuring.

Conclusion

MAS has discussed our plans with the local banks. They agree with the policy direction proposed. They have suggested some modifications to MAS' proposals, which wherever possible MAS has incorporated.

Our approach is pragmatic, not purist. Our circumstances are different from other countries. We need to strike the right balance, to find the framework that suits our economy, and which recognises the historical developments that have brought about the present situation. The principal shareholders remain a source of strength to the banks, and it is not our intention to conscribe their contributions to the future banking business.

The separation of financial and non-financial activities will be another major step forward in strengthening the local banks. As one analyst wrote in March:

> "The MAS is expected to announce soon rules requiring banks to dispose of non-core assets. We consider this to be very important — as part of re-engineering the banks into more profitable and competitive entities would be to require them to concentrate on their core business rather than act as conglomerates with low-yielding assets".[1]

I urge all the banks to continue to upgrade their capabilities and build up their management teams, in order to prepare themselves for the new opportunities and challenges arising from the rapid changes of technology and the market. MAS will continue to work with the local banks to foster closer co-operation and strengthen the culture of openness as we liberalise the banking industry.

---

1 "Singapore Banks: Impact of Sale of Non-Core Assets", Theme Piece by Warburg Dillon Read Global Equity Research, 17 March 2000.

Capital Markets in the New Economy

Mr Lee Hsien Loong
Deputy Prime Minister and Chairman, MAS

25th Anniversary Dinner of the Singapore Investment Banking Association

6 September 2000

Introduction

I am happy to celebrate with the Singapore Investment Banking Association (SIBA) your 25th anniversary.

For many years, SIBA has actively provided industry feedback on government policies, especially on capital market regulations and developments. These inputs have helped MAS to create a conducive environment for all financial players.

Last November, your association broadened its charter, reconstituted itself to include a wider spectrum of activities and financial institutions, and changed its name to SIBA. This was a timely move.

I am pleased to note that you have formed the SIBA Debt Capital Market Committee. As an MAS survey[1] shows, corporate debt issuance more than doubled last year to S$19.5 billion. In the first half of this year, corporate debt issuance is already S$21.2 billion, exceeding the volume for the whole of last year. More diverse issuers are tapping the debt market, and interest from local investors has grown. An industry body to champion the development of the debt market, and institutionalise a feedback channel to MAS, will therefore play a useful role.

1 1999 Survey of the Singapore Corporate Debt Market.

Global Trends in Capital Markets

In the financial industry, globalisation is proceeding apace. There has been a worldwide wave of consolidation among financial institutions, stock and derivative exchanges, and even regulatory bodies. In 1999, there were 900 merger-and-acquisition (M&A) transactions among banks, worth US$300 billion worldwide.[2] The securities industry has been no less active, with exchanges and clearing houses in a flurry of mergers and alliances.

While globalisation and integration are established features of capital markets, two more recent trends are noteworthy: firstly, stronger linkages between capital market and treasury activities and secondly, the impact of technology and the Internet on capital markets, particularly in the securities industry.

MAS' Guidelines on Treatment of Credit Derivatives and Securitisation

The links between capital market and treasury activities reflect an increase in cross-border transactions. In the US and Europe, the spate of mergers and acquisitions has boosted the volume of foreign exchange flows. The mergers have also led to greater use of securitisation and credit derivatives, and caused European credit derivative markets to expand significantly.[3]

In Singapore, the burgeoning capital market has similarly benefited our treasury industry. Increased debt issuance has led to more swaps and other money market activities. Participants are using more sophisticated treasury and capital market products. We must keep our regulatory framework up-to-date, so that it provides clarity, and allows growth and innovation.

Credit derivatives form one potential growth area. Credit risk is an important issue for banks, particularly in Asia. Before credit derivatives were invented, banks generally had to stop extending new loans or services to customers to whom they had excessive exposure. This worked against the banks' efforts to maintain valued client relationships. Credit derivatives

2 "European Banking Turns Decisive Corner on Road to Consolidation", *International Wealth Management*, July 2000.

3 "Use of Credit Derivatives in Bank Mergers Soars", *International Financing Review*, March 2000.

provide banks an alternative. Banks can now repackage and divest excess credit risk exposures, and continue to service their clients.

MAS has studied how credit derivatives should be captured under the existing capital adequacy framework for banks. It has circulated draft guidelines to industry players and associations for comments. MAS has now finalised the guidelines,[4] which address capital treatment for three main credit derivative products: the credit default swap, the total rate of return swap and the credit-linked note.[5]

The guidelines reaffirm the principle of maintaining capital for risk exposure. If banks assume credit exposure via the use of derivatives, they will be subject to capital charges. But if banks use credit derivatives to hedge their underlying risk exposures, they will be granted relief, depending on the degree of risk transfer. For example, where the hedge is imperfect, because of mismatches in maturity, asset or currency, regulatory relief will still be available, albeit to a smaller extent.

A second promising area is that of securitisation. Like credit derivatives, securitisation allows banks to manage their credit risk and capital more effectively. In its basic form, securitisation involves pooling assets in a special purpose vehicle, which is then funded by issuing securities.

MAS has circulated draft prudential guidelines for securitisation to industry participants for comments. The guidelines for banks have been finalised. These take into account feedback from the industry and existing securitisation transactions. They set out the capital treatment of securitised assets, as well as disclosure, separation and other requirements for the various roles that banks take on in a securitisation transaction.

The guidelines seek to define clearly the roles, responsibilities and risks that banks retain or undertake, when they participate in a securitisation transaction. They also ensure that banks hold appropriate capital against the risks they accept. Thus, a bank that has securitised its assets will be granted capital relief only where the transfer of risks and rewards of the securitised assets has been effective and complete.

[4] To be published as Notice 627.

[5] To be published as Notice 628. Similar guidelines will be issued to finance companies and merchant banks.

The Internet and Its Impact on the Securities Industry

The second major issue is the impact of technology and the Internet on capital markets.

In the securities industry, the Internet has caused fundamental change, slicing the value chain more and more finely, and recombining it in novel configurations. Functions previously offered as a package by brokers, such as analysis and advice, recommendation and order routing, are being separated and broken up. New entities, such as aggregators or navigators, have emerged, offering hitherto-unseen types of services.

These changes will bring major benefits to the industry and investors.

Firstly, the Internet has fostered a free flow of investment information. With a surfeit of news, financial institutions are rethinking their business models. Research and analysis previously available only at substantial fees to institutions and high net worth individuals are gradually becoming available to online retail investors as well.[6]

Secondly, the Internet offers increased business opportunities and potentially limitless reach.

Thirdly, the Internet offers increased scope for cross selling financial products. Successful online firms like Charles Schwab and E*Trade are leveraging on their huge customer base to diversify into banking, bill payment and other areas of services.[7]

Lastly, do-it-yourself finance facilitated by the Internet allows institutions to cut whole layers of customer administration costs. The Internet is reducing the cost of capital, at the expense of the spreads that intermediaries traditionally enjoyed from a proprietary informational edge. This reduction of what has been called "knowledge float" will benefit both lenders and borrowers.

But at the same time, the Internet means new challenges. The same borderless nature can mean footloose customers and businesses. Cyberspace

---

6 For instance, Merrill Lynch provides its online clients access to some of its research and videos of analysts' daily briefings. From *The Economist*, 20-26 May 2000.

7 Charles Schwab offers bill payment facilities, while E*Trade has set up an online bank, E*Trade Bank. In May 2000, E*Trade acquired an ATM network to cross-sell E*Trade bank, brokerage, mutual fund and asset management products.

so blurs physical distinctions and facilitates convenient access that financial institutions can uproot themselves, go elsewhere and yet seamlessly offer the same services online. Jurisdictional boundaries become harder to enforce, while new business models potentially raise new operational, strategic and systemic risks.

Evolving the Infrastructure for Electronic Finance in Capital Markets

MAS has been closely monitoring these developments and scrutinising their implications for our financial centre.

As financial activities consolidate globally into fewer centres, and services spill over traditional borders, we need to constantly move up the value chain, in order to capture and root intellectual content creation in Singapore. A flexible and responsive supervisory framework is critical to accommodate rapidly changing business profiles of e-finance.

In prescribing rules to regulate new activities, we are unable to run ahead of innovation, because we cannot tell for sure which way technology, or the industry, will develop. Instead, we will monitor technology and market developments closely, and craft and update our rules in step with the market place.

Securities Licensing in the Electronic Realm

Two months ago,[8] MAS announced its intention to regulate securities and futures trading activities under a single licence, and the provision of personal investment and financial planning advice, also under a single licence. We shifted towards a unified licensing regime and a more holistic approach to personal investment advisory services, because the distinction between securities and derivative markets is blurring. Financial products are converging, and one-stop distribution channels are emerging.

Those changes were part of a broader framework of review we have

[8] These announcements were respectively made on 6 July 2000 by Minister Lim Hng Kiang at the third annual conference of the Investment Management Association of Singapore and on 7 July 2000 by DPM Lee Hsien Loong at the first anniversary dinner of the Securities Investors Association (Singapore).

undertaken for the securities and futures industries. MAS has now completed a study of another facet of the securities industry. We have reviewed securities licensing requirements in the electronic realm for market intermediaries: investment advisers and dealers.

Objectives in Supervising Intermediaries

Our key objectives in supervising intermediaries are:

- To reduce systemic risk in the securities market;
- To keep markets fair, efficient and transparent; and
- To safeguard investors' interests by requiring high professional standards among financial service providers and investor disclosure.

These objectives are in line with the principles of the International Organisation of Securities Commissions, and principles adopted in other developed markets.

Current Interpretation of Investment Advice and Dealing in Securities

Our current securities legislation relies on broadly worded definitions like "investment adviser" and "dealing in securities" to bring certain activities under our regulatory ambit.

Under present laws, "dealing in securities" covers any activity relating to transactions in securities, which contain an element of inducement. A broad spectrum of activities could possibly constitute "dealing in securities": broking in securities, referring customers to open accounts with licensed dealers for the purpose of trading in securities or providing prospectuses and application forms to prospective customers.

As for "investment advice", our current interpretation accepts that the provision of factual information does not constitute investment advice.

What constituted dealing or investment advice used to be fairly clear-cut and well-established. But the breakdown of the securities value chain has blurred the distinctions between fact and investment advice, and between dealing in securities and merely providing information. We therefore need to refine our interpretation of these terms, institute basic safeguards and spell out how to treat new entities.

Licensing Approach

In licensing investment advisers and dealers, our approach is to require persons conducting securities activities in Singapore to possess suitable qualifications, relevant professional experience and good character. This would give comfort to investors that they can expect competent advice and reliable execution from investment advisers and dealers.

Our licensing requirements for the new electronic market intermediaries should not be unduly onerous. They will not impose heavy prudential capital requirements. The main focus will be on website disclosure of credentials, physical addresses and other relevant information. In lieu of a corporate track record, licensees need only demonstrate individual qualifications and experience.

Bona fide intermediaries who subscribe to the objective of providing financial services of high standard should be pleased to come under our licensing ambit. With qualified intermediaries operating within an environment based on transparency and disclosure, investors would have a suitable basis for making well-informed decisions. This is another step towards realising the "*caveat emptor*" philosophy.

New Licensing Principles

MAS will therefore adopt the following licensing principles for securities activities conducted through the Internet:

Interpretation of the Activities of an Investment Adviser and a Dealer

Context and Circumstance

Our first principle is that MAS will examine the context and circumstance in which activities are conducted, to determine whether licensing is required. This applies to both investment advice and dealing in securities.

Suppose, for example, a web page of a business school provides a tool for calculating the value of shares. Should we require the business school to be licensed? In deciding this, MAS would take into consideration the fact that the business school's primary mission is education, not investment advice. In this context, we are unlikely to require the business school to be licensed to provide such a tool on its web page.

Interpretation of the Activities of an Investment Adviser

Fact versus Opinion

Our second principle relates to investment advice. In determining what constitutes investment advice, MAS will use the "fact versus opinion" test as a general guide, supplemented, where appropriate, by the context and circumstance principle. The presence of interpretation, selectivity or subjectivity will require licensing.

Let me explain. A wealth of information on securities is available on the Internet. It ranges on a continuum from pure factual statements, to calculated parameters, to outright buy/sell/hold recommendations.

While investors often use factual information concerning securities to guide their decisions, MAS takes the view that factual information itself is not investment advice. Data based on historical time series are facts, whereas forecasts would be considered subjective. Further, filtering data through the choice of parameters, for example, to display only shares with favourable financial ratios, would be considered selective, and would require licensing.

The "fact versus opinion" principle sets out quite clearly what would require licensing as investment advice. Nonetheless, in this information continuum, there remain some grey areas involving implicit advice. For instance, where the interpretation and presentation of facts leads to a specific conclusion, MAS would need to review the context and circumstances, such as other information on the website, to decide whether licensing is required.

Analytical Tools: A common device which challenges our interpretation of "advice" is an analytical tool, for instance, computer software aimed at facilitating investment decisions. Such a tool may require licensing. In making this judgment, we would consider the output of this tool, subjecting it to the "fact versus opinion" test. If the output goes beyond factual information, and includes subjective or interpretative content, this tool would require licensing.[9]

Other securities regulators have adopted the same stance in regard to the provision of implicit investment advice.

Interpretation of the Activities of a Dealer

Referrals for Opening of Trading Accounts

A third principle associated with dealing activity relates to referrals for the opening of trading accounts. MAS will not require the licensing of portals which refer investors to open trading accounts with stockbrokers, provided the stockbrokers themselves are licensed by MAS. This is so, even if the websites offer incentives for account opening. The reason is that trade orders will be handled by licensed dealers supervised by MAS.

Passive Distribution Conduits for Advice and Dealing

Our fourth principle relates to websites acting as what we consider to be passive distribution conduits. Passive conduits, whether for investment advice or for dealing in securities, will not require licensing. Some examples include the following:

- Hypertext Links and Reproduction of Investment Research Reports: Portals often provide hypertext links to websites of licensed or exempt financial institutions, for example, in advertisements. Or they may reproduce investment research reports from such institutions directly on their own websites.[10] Such portals would be considered passive conduits, akin to a newspaper or TV advertisement.

---

[9] To avoid attracting licensing requirements, analytical tools should operate within the following guidelines: they a) should not go beyond factual information; b) should disclose analytical processes transparently; and c) provide sufficient disclaimers to the effect that the tools are for informational purposes, and should not be relied upon as investment advice concerning securities.

[10] Portals which reproduce investment research reports should a) attribute the report sources accurately; b) should not exercise editorial control over, or modify contents of reproduced reports; and c) should not endorse or otherwise comment on the reports.

- Investment Advice by Persons Not Carrying on a Business:
  A growing number of online discussion fora, chat-rooms and bulletin boards allow persons to post their opinions concerning securities. An entity providing a platform for public discussion of securities would not attract licensing.[11] Neither would a participant, as long as he is not deemed to be "carrying on a business" of providing advice.

In the context of dealing, we will treat two common practices as passive conduits. First, websites providing hypertext links to, or advertisements for, licensed dealers. But websites should not advertise for, or link users, to unlicensed dealers, including overseas dealers not licensed by MAS. Second, licensing is not necessary for providing prospectuses and application forms passively on websites, or via email upon the request of investors. These merely improve on the efficiency of paper distribution.[12]

Websites must not go beyond being passive conduits. MAS will consider portals or websites providing facilities for accepting or relaying orders to dealers as licensable. This is because such a facility carries the risk of failure to transmit trade orders in a timely and accurate fashion, potentially to the detriment of investors.

Overseas Websites Specifically Targeting Singapore Residents

Our final principle deals with overseas websites. MAS will apply the same licensing principles to overseas websites which specifically target Singapore residents, as it does to local websites. This is to ensure that foreign and local Internet players are treated on the same regulatory basis.

Going Forward

Several of the new licensing principles can be implemented based on the existing Securities Industry Act and licensing framework. Others will

---

11 The webpages of such entities should contain disclaimers to the effect that the views expressed are not those of the entities.

12 Websites providing prospectuses and application forms in a passive manner should display disclaimers to the effect that they do not have the intention of inducing investors to subscribe for securities.

require amendments to the legislation. The new provisions will be included in the forthcoming Financial Advisers Act and the Omnibus Securities and Futures Act, and announced in 2001.

MAS has already received a number of new applications which fall under the proposed securities licensing framework. These are currently being evaluated. As I have just discussed the licensing principles broadly, interested parties should approach MAS to discuss the details of the revised licensing framework in relation to their business models. MAS will also be seeking further comments from relevant industry players on these changes.

Conclusion

The vitality and dynamism of global capital markets have ushered in challenging times for the financial services industry. With technology breaking down geographic and sectoral boundaries, links between markets, institutions and instruments will flourish.

Experience in developed economies show that financial services, notably stock trading, can take rapidly to the Internet. This should be no surprise. As an Economist online finance survey recently described, financial institutions deal in a product — money — that has long been accepted as "virtual". Unlike a piece of clothing, account-holders are happy to accept their money represented as figures on an ATM screen, or by a credit or smart card.[13]

The new financial landscape calls for a tripartite, complementary response from regulators, industry and investors. MAS as regulator will foster healthy market practices, while maintaining a sound overall investment environment. At the same time, in a democratised environment, investors need to recognise that there is little substitute for self-education, and thereby exercise greater caution in making individual investment decisions. Finally, industry participants need to set high professional standards and observe an exemplary code of conduct, in order to retain their customers and build their reputations which, in the long term, are their most precious assets.

---

13 "Online Finance: A Virtual Threat", *The Economist*, 20-26 May 2000.

Regulating the Capital Markets: Making Market Discipline Work

Mr Tharman Shanmugaratnam
Deputy Managing Director, MAS
Investment Fund Awards 2001
16 February 2001

The capital markets are undergoing a sea change. Technology and the Internet have opened new channels for investors to access a wide range of investment information and to transact in securities, often without advice or assistance from market intermediaries. Market intermediaries themselves are consolidating, and exploring new business models to capture clients and add value to their decisions. It is a more competitive environment all round, and the margins from traditional financial intermediation have thinned.

Regulators are having to rethink their approaches towards the oversight of the markets in this new and rapidly changing environment. The objectives have not changed — to preserve confidence by maintaining fair, transparent and efficient markets, and to minimise the risk of disruptions that threaten the stability of the system. But the methods of achieving these objectives are being refashioned. It is no longer possible for the regulator to root out all that is evil, dangerous or vaguely suspicious before they get to the market. Greater emphasis is therefore being placed on discipline being exercised within the market, and by the market.

Making Market Discipline Work

We have embarked over the last three years on a shift in our approach to regulating the markets from what is loosely called a merit-based regime, under which the regulator judged the appropriateness of securities being made available to the public, towards a market-driven, disclosure-based regime of regulation. It is aimed at allowing market participants greater choice and the free play to take calculated risks. We have made it clear that the shift in approach will not compromise our reputation internationally as one of the most open, transparent and well-regulated markets in Asia. Market-based regulation will indeed raise standards of business conduct, as is necessary for a more open, competitive and innovative market environment.

Market discipline will not simply be a matter of "*caveat emptor*". The buyer cannot be expected to beware if he is not provided with accurate and accessible information so as to make a reasonable judgment of prospective risks and returns. Neither can he do so if the market is rigged without his knowledge. It follows that market discipline requires a system of laws, rules and standards to discriminate in favour of companies with high standards of corporate governance and disclosure, and to exact penalties on those who manipulate the market.

Making market discipline work is therefore the responsibility of all participants in the system. Let me briefly outline some of these roles:

- MAS, as the statutory regulator, will monitor compliance with the laws and regulations that govern the integrity of the markets, seek enforcement of the laws and propose amendments in order to keep them relevant in a changing market environment. We have undertaken a substantial review of our securities laws in the last year. Insider trading is now both a criminal and civil offence, and we have recently proposed to amend the laws to capture a wider pool of persons who seek to take advantage of inside information. The proposed new Securities and Futures Act (SFA), to be put to Parliament later this year, will contain other substantial changes.

I will elaborate on one of these, concerning the prospectus registration regime later in the speech.[1]

- The Singapore Exchange (SGX), with its frontline interface with the industry and markets, plays a key role in preserving fair and transparent markets. It is responsible for the listing rules for companies that raise capital and have their shares traded on the exchange. It is also responsible for ensuring that conditions exist for orderly trading of listed securities.
- The conduct of issuers themselves is at the core of a system of market discipline. Issuers must take it upon themselves to make full and prompt disclosure of material information. It is not just a matter of meeting the requirements of the law and SGX's rules. It is increasingly in the interests of companies to go beyond the minimum in disclosure standards, as investors become more discerning to the quality of information available to them. A number of studies have shown that the markets have attached an increased premium in recent years to companies which demonstrate sound corporate governance and who are more forthcoming and open with information on their businesses. The so-called "corporate governance dividend", previously not easily discerned in Asian markets in particular, is now fully visible.
- Market intermediaries play an important supporting role. Investment banks, accountants, lawyers and other professionals who advise issuers have a duty to provide high standards of professional advice, and to exercise thorough due diligence to ensure that issuers comply with laws and rules, as well as adopt high standards of disclosure. Brokers and investment advisers likewise, have a duty to provide their investing clients with objective advice that is in their clients' best interests.

1 The SFA would also incorporate the provisions concerning the raising of capital that are presently found in the Companies Act, thereby creating a single compendium of laws governing the securities industry.

- Finally, it is for investors themselves to take advantage of higher standards of disclosure in making their decisions. Investors and the media also contribute to effective market discipline by calling for more and better quality information from listed companies. Institutional investors such as fund managers play an important role in this regard. They have greater resources to monitor and analyse information, and typically greater leverage on companies to encourage them to improve on standards of corporate governance and disclosure.

The move towards market-based regulation will be given a significant push by the recommendations of two private sector-led committees that were appointed by the Government last year — the Corporate Governance Committee and the Disclosure and Accounting Standards Committee. The committees have recently completed an exercise of public consultation on their preliminary recommendations, and aim to publish their final reports by April.

The development of a market-driven, disclosure-based regime is in progress. It will be naive to expect an effective system of market discipline to have arrived in a day, or in three years. The transition will cause some uncertainties initially, and even the occasional revanchist call for a return to the regime of the past. Market participants will take time to develop high standards of corporate conduct and disclosure, and to discover the new boundaries. We can expect some of them to test the boundaries in the process, either wittingly or otherwise. But the boundaries of what is permissible to preserve fair and transparent markets should become quite apparent through a few salutary cases, which will help define the new dispensation.

MAS and SGX themselves have reviewed their respective roles in the new regulatory environment. I will touch now on a number of issues concerning the regulatory functions of the SGX as a demutualised, profit-oriented and listed exchange, and its relationship with MAS as the statutory regulator.

Can a Demutualised, Listed Exchange Regulate the Market?

As a focal point of market activity, exchanges have traditionally been accorded the role of frontline regulator of the securities markets. With the demutualisation and public offering of shares by a growing number of exchanges — most recently the Deutsche Borse — questions arise as to whether a listed for-profit exchange is able to discharge its role as frontline regulator competently and effectively.

Conflicts of interest in the regulatory functions of an exchange are not new however. They existed before demutualisation. Members of the former Stock Exchange of Singapore (SES), a mutual body, had to set and enforce rules in the public interest that could negatively affect their commercial interests. The exchange was also expected to conduct effective and impartial supervision of its member-owners. The potential conflicts of interest in these respects were mitigated by the fact that the SES had only a small number of members, accentuating the financial risks that they each faced from a failure of the exchange to properly regulate.

More importantly, the potential conflicts of interest made it necessary for MAS to take a heavy hand in the affairs of the exchange. The folklore sometimes exaggerated this, so much that some observers attributed every decision of the SES to the mysterious ways of MAS. But the hidden hand of the regulator was not ideal for developing a mature and dynamic capital market.

Now that the SGX has been demutualised and listed, a new set of potential conflicts arises. While profits were never irrelevant to the SES, they are the primary motive for shareholders of the listed SGX. Share values and dividends also give greater transparency to the business performance and prospects of the SGX, providing the management with greater incentive to raise operational efficiency, and seek competitive advantage. This is as it should be, and is indeed a principle benefit of demutualising and listing the SGX. There will however be concern from time to time as to whether the greater drive for commercial success will reduce the commitment and resources deployed by the exchange to fulfil its responsibility to regulate in the public interest.

MAS believes that the interests of the SGX are more aligned than divergent with public interest as represented by users of the exchange. A fair, transparent and efficiently-regulated market is indispensable to the vibrancy and sustained business success of the SGX. Serious investors will not trade on an exchange that does not have internationally acceptable rules of listing, trading and settlement, or does not enforce the rules fairly and effectively. The examples of exchanges that have failed to meet such standards and suffered the consequences of investor shunning their markets are well-known. Without the interest and liquidity provided by investors, no exchange will find it easy to attract issuers and to build its business.

Credibility in regulation is therefore a vital commercial asset for the SGX. The board and management of the SGX recognise this fully. Corporate governance of the SGX is not designed to favour short-term revenue objectives at the expense of long-term gains. Shareholders of SGX themselves have it in their interests to hold the exchange to high standards of market regulation, so as to achieve sustained returns on their investments.

MAS-SGX Regulatory Relationship

A demutualised, listed exchange however requires an enhanced role for MAS in some respects, even as the functions of the SGX and MAS are more clearly delineated than in the past. The Exchanges (Demutualisation and Merger) Act passed in 1999 was drafted to give MAS the power to issue directives to SGX in the interest of ensuring fair and orderly securities and futures markets, and the proper management of systemic risks. MAS is the backstop. It is in the position to put things right, where any potential conflicts of interest become real.

The regulatory relationship between MAS and SGX may be broadly defined as follows. MAS, as the statutory regulator, will administer the corpus of statutory law regulating the capital markets. We also maintain oversight of SGX's regulatory responsibilities and seek to ensure that there are no gaps in the overall regulatory framework. The SGX has direct and frontline regulatory responsibilities of the securities and futures markets, and over the broker-dealers who trade on the exchange. This MAS-SGX regulatory relationship applies to all the major areas of regulation:

Regulation of Capital Raising

- SGX defines and enforces the rules that apply to companies that seek to raise capital on the exchange through primary or secondary issues.
- MAS' approval must be sought for any changes to SGX's listing rules. Under the proposed SFA, the SGX will have to notify MAS of any rule changes 21 days before its announcement. MAS will be able to approve, alter or stop any rule change during that 21-day period.

Continuous Listing and Disclosure Requirements

- SGX enforces the continuous listing requirements on companies, to see to it that listed companies maintain timely and adequate disclosure of material information. SGX has the power to suspend and even de-list a counter if a company fails to meet the standards set out in the listing rules.
- Continuous disclosure by listed companies will also become a statutory obligation under the proposed SFA. This means that non-disclosure or late disclosure of material information will be a breach of the law, not just a breach of SGX's listing requirements, and carry either civil or criminal penalty.

Market Surveillance

- SGX carries out market surveillance to detect unusual trading activities that could reflect attempts to manipulate the market. Such surveillance efforts could also lead to discovery of parties trading on privileged insider information. SGX has the power to suspend or de-list a counter if conditions for orderly trading are found to be absent.
- MAS will carry out independent surveillance on a selective basis, to ensure that SGX is performing its responsibilities effectively.
- MAS will have the power under the proposed SFA to pursue civil prosecution of listed companies which fail to make timely disclosure

of material information, and of any participants suspected of market misconduct. The recently introduced civil remedy regime for insider trading will be extended to cover other forms of market misconduct such as market manipulation, or the employment of fraud and deceit in dealing. Civil remedy, which lowers the burden of proof against offenders, will complement the present framework of criminal remedy for offences under securities law.

Supervision of Brokers

- SGX supervises and inspects brokers to ensure that they comply with SGX's rules, are prudentially sound, and uphold high standards of market integrity. SGX has to act swiftly and firmly to deal with any unprofessional conduct by brokers and their representatives.
- MAS conducts continuous off-site review of brokers' operations to check if they comply with statutory licensing requirements. Such off-site reviews will be complemented by MAS' selective, on-site inspection of brokers to assure itself of the competence and effectiveness of SGX's supervision.

Regulation of SGX as a Self-Listed Entity

When the SGX was listed on itself (on its Securities Trading subsidiary), MAS assumed the role of frontline regulator for the listing and trading of SGX's shares. MAS was the approving authority for SGX's listing, and was directly responsible for vetting SGX's prospectus. We are also conducting surveillance of trading in SGX's shares, and monitoring the continuous disclosure of material information by SGX. MAS has powers under the Exchanges (Demutualisation and Merger) Act to issue directives to SGX to resolve any conflicts of interest arising from its self-listing. Such conflicts are also addressed in a Deed of Undertaking to MAS. In keeping with the Deed, SGX has appointed a Conflicts Committee to deal with such issues, and MAS is the approving authority for the composition of the Committee.

Revisiting the Regulatory Structure Will Be Necessary

The relationship between the regulator and the exchange is evolving internationally. Regulators are monitoring the effectiveness of self-regulation by the exchanges, and the division of responsibilities between regulators and exchanges. No single model has gained universal acceptance, and no model is regarded as good for all time in any jurisdiction.

The present MAS-SGX regulatory arrangement has major elements in common with that in the major jurisdictions which have seen the exchanges demutualised, and in particular with arrangements in Australia. The UK approach is also similar, except that the Financial Services Authority (FSA) has taken over the listing authority from the London Stock Exchange (LSE). That decision was shaped by the inappropriateness of leaving the listing authority with the LSE when other competing exchanges are emerging in the UK.

We believe that the current arrangements for the regulation and supervision of the securities markets between MAS and SGX, with an enhanced oversight responsibility for MAS and powers to pursue civil prosecution, will prove robust. But we will continually review the arrangement, keep in touch with international practices, and re-calibrate the roles of MAS and SGX where necessary to ensure effective oversight of the local markets.

I would now like to touch on two features of the regulatory arrangement that we have recently reviewed. The first concerns the approval of substantial shareholdings in the SGX; the second, proposed changes in the prospectus registration regime.

Approval of Substantial Shareholdings in the SGX

The Exchanges (Demutualisation and Merger) Act requires anyone who wishes to acquire 5% or more of SGX to seek prior approval from MAS. This provision recognises the unique and important role of SGX in providing the infrastructure and marketplace for the trading, clearing and settlement of securities and derivatives in Singapore.

Strategic Investors

As announced previously, MAS will allow suitable strategic investors who can promote SGX's growth and development to acquire substantial stakes of 5% or more in SGX. How large a stake these strategic investors will be allowed to take will depend on what they are able to contribute to the exchange in terms of business alliances, technology or other ways of supporting the business and infrastructure of the exchange.

Fund Managers

In addition, SGX has received indications from fund managers that they would like to hold more significant stakes in SGX than is currently permissible under the 5% cap. Fund managers are key institutional players on the buy-side of the capital markets, and will, as shareholders, add to the diverse range of groups with an interest in SGX's business. MAS will therefore generally allow fund managers who invest pools of customer funds to hold SGX's shares beyond the 5% limit. They will have to apply to MAS for approval first. The combined holdings of such a fund manager will be capped at 10%. A fund manager, however, cannot expect to be represented on the SGX Board unless it has a substantive, strategic relationship with the Exchange.

Proposed Changes to the Prospectus Registration Regime

The Companies Act requires every company seeking to raise funds via a public offer to issue a prospectus to inform potential investors of the financial status of the company, its business plans, the risks of investing in the company, and all other material information which will enable them to make informed investment decisions. Currently, companies submit their draft prospectuses to the Registry of Companies and Businesses (RCB) to be vetted for compliance with the Companies Act. Companies applying to list on the SGX will also send their draft prospectuses to the exchange for vetting to ensure that they meet SGX's disclosure requirements.

When the capital-raising provisions in the Companies Act are transferred to the new SFA later this year, MAS will take over from RCB as statutory regulator for prospectus registration. We are now reviewing the prospectus registration regime with a view to enhancing market accountability, and raising the standards of prospectus disclosure.

Under the proposed regime, MAS will register a prospectus not earlier than 14 days and not later than 28 days after an issuer has lodged the prospectus with MAS. This period will allow for both regulatory review by MAS and SGX, and public scrutiny and comment. (Currently, there is no public scrutiny before a prospectus is registered.) The prospectus will be published on the Internet to give investors the opportunity to scrutinise the prospectus prior to its distribution, and raise any issues of concern. This model is similar to that which has been introduced in the Australian markets.

There will be a more measured approach to prospectus review by the regulator. I was told that SGX currently vets an average of five drafts for every prospectus that gets published. This is clearly not desirable going forward. The review of prospectuses by MAS and SGX will focus, respectively, on compliance with laws and SGX's listing requirements on prospectus disclosure. MAS and SGX will no longer vet prospectuses with a view to determining if they contain inaccuracies in information or factual errors. Issuers and their advisers have to bear greater responsibility for ensuring accurate and adequate disclosure.

After a prospectus has been registered, it is proposed that MAS be empowered to issue a stop order and prevent further issues of securities if a prospectus is found to contain misleading or incorrect statements, or to have omitted material information. Investors who have subscribed for securities on the basis of the deficient prospectus can withdraw their applications and have their monies refunded.

The new prospectus registration regime is aimed at placing greater responsibility on issuers and their advisers to meet the high standards of disclosure necessary for the development of more effective market discipline, and a more mature capital markets environment. MAS will be seeking feedback on the proposed prospectus registration regime shortly, as part of our public consultation on the draft SFA.

Conclusion

Approaches to regulation worldwide are evolving with the times. An effective system of market discipline is necessary to sustain and promote the growth of open, transparent and competitive markets. Singapore is making substantial changes to its laws, rules and standards to support enhanced market discipline. It will be a process of evolution, but we have made good progress. Succeeding in this endeavour will require effort by both the regulator and all market participants, including issuers, their advisers and investors themselves. It is an indispensable part of our efforts to make Singapore a premier financial hub in Asia, and we have every confidence in getting there.

Consolidation and Liberalisation: Building World-Class Banks

Mr Lee Hsien Loong
Deputy Prime Minister and Chairman, MAS
28th Association of Banks in Singapore Annual Dinner
29 June 2001

Introduction

Two years ago, MAS embarked on the first phase of a programme to liberalise the banking industry. The aim was to strengthen our local banks through competition, provide Singaporeans with quality banking services and enhance Singapore's position as an international financial centre. We phased in the liberalisation measures progressively, to give local banks time to upgrade themselves to meet the competition, and maintain the stability of the financial system.

The first package of measures in 1999 comprised a few main elements. MAS permitted four Qualifying Full Banks (QFBs) to establish up to 10 locations each, relocate their existing branches and share ATMs among themselves. We granted eight new Restricted Bank licences to banks that wanted to expand their wholesale S$ business. We also gave Offshore Banks more flexibility to lend in Singapore dollars and engage in S$ swaps, and even wider leeway to eight Qualifying Offshore Banks.

These measures marked the start of a major and irreversible process of change. We could not foresee exactly how the industry would respond and develop. So MAS committed to reviewing progress at the halfway mark before deciding on further liberalisation measures. We have now completed this review.

Local Banks' Upgrading and Consolidation

Since the first liberalisation package was announced, the local banks have made progress in building up their capabilities. They have generally strengthened their management teams, and invested heavily in infrastructure to provide banking services more efficiently, especially via electronic channels. They have improved their customer relationship management systems, which will allow more effective data mining of their customer databases and cross-selling of multi-sector products. Local banks have also been seeking opportunities and expanding their presence in the region.

An important and more visible sign that local banks are gearing up for competition is of course the process of consolidation that is underway. The opening gambit was made on 12 June when OCBC announced that it was making a voluntary general offer for Keppel Capital Holdings which owns Keppel TatLee Bank. Ten days later, DBS made an unsolicited bid for OUB. And just three hours ago, UOB made a competing bid after reaching agreement with the controlling shareholders of OUB. All the local banks are now busy reassessing their positions. It is likely that a new configuration will quickly crystallise.

MAS views this as a very positive development for the banking industry, and more importantly for Singapore. If the consolidation is well executed, a stronger group of local banks will emerge, able to hold their own domestically, provide Singaporeans with better services and compete in the region. Let me elaborate.

The Importance of Consolidation

Economies of scale have become critical in banking today. Banks in the developed countries have been merging and consolidating, globally, in search of greater scale and efficiency. Their customers are demanding faster access to more customised and integrated financial services. Banks can now deliver one-stop service through faster distribution channels, and develop sophisticated customer relationship systems to customise products. Technology has made this possible. But the cost of investments in technology is high, and can only be justified and recovered if it is spread over millions of customers. Banks like Citicorp have spent tens of billions of dollars, developing IT systems to support their consumer banking services.

Being a big bank is no guarantee of success, as shown by the persistent difficulties of the Japanese banks over the last decade, which in the 1980s were among the biggest banks in the world. But being a small bank is definitely a significant handicap. The logic of Singapore's position is inescapable: if we want strong banks, then they have to be big banks, and if they are to be big banks, then we must have fewer banks. This is the reality in many small countries. Switzerland, with a GDP and population about twice our size, now has only two big banks — UBS and Credit Suisse — both of which are world-class players. The Netherlands, four times as big as Singapore, has three: ABN-AMRO, Rabobank and ING, plus Fortis which is partially Belgian. These have become major international players.

Australia, which is slightly bigger than the Netherlands, also has four big banks, but they are mainly domestic, smaller than the Dutch although bigger than the Singapore banks. The Australian government maintains a "Four Pillars" policy, under which it will not allow any of the four banks to merge or take over any of the others, in order to maintain sufficient competition in the domestic market. But there is debate in Australia over whether this "Four Pillars" policy is sustainable, or whether it will cause Australian banks to lose out in the long run, by preventing them from becoming large enough to be truly viable.

Singapore's economy is 1/4 the size of Australia's. Singapore cannot afford a "Four Pillars" policy. If we tried that, our banks would be like bonsai plants, root-bound by the small pots in which they grow. Our biggest bank, DBS, even after the merger with POSBank, is ranked only 115th in the world by asset size. In banking, size is not everything, but size is important.

If the local banks fail to achieve enough scale, they will not be able to invest in cutting-edge technology and management systems, or to attract the talent necessary to compete with the best players. Their service standards and product range will not be able to keep up with their foreign competitors. They will find it difficult to diversify their earnings by competing in fee-based businesses, like asset management and cash management. Customers, especially the more sophisticated ones, will take their business to the foreign banks already in Singapore.

The local banks cannot rely on Government protection forever. Even if we had not liberalised the banking industry, the foreign banks here would still have been able to use technology and new delivery channels to compete for retail business. In fact, the most innovative foreign banks have been growing their market share despite the restrictions that we have placed on them. Over time, local banks that cannot compete would become marginalised.

This would not be a good outcome. In the event of a crisis, we want to be able to count on strong institutions with a major stake in the country, whose interests will be aligned with those of the long-term interests of the Singapore economy. Banks which are tied more closely to Singapore will be more likely to act in support of financial and economic stability. That is why MAS remains committed to building strong local banks with a significant share of the domestic market.

This is the reality that Singaporeans must understand and accept, as we debate the pros and cons of bank mergers. If small banks were economically viable, we would not be meeting tonight with every Singaporean bank either a bidder or a takeover target. The fact that they are bidding and being bid for proves not just that the smaller local banks are vulnerable, but also that the bigger ones themselves feel insecure, and rightly so. If the local banks stay small and weaken over time, we will be worse off for it. In the longer term, stronger and larger local banks offer far better assurance of Singapore's interests.

MAS' Approach to Consolidation

While MAS welcomes the process of consolidation, it will remain strictly neutral, and will not seek to influence the outcome. We have made it known to all the participants that we will allow the local banks to bid for one another. The new configuration should be determined by the free play of the market. MAS will leave the banks and their shareholders to decide whom they should merge with or acquire, subject to five conditions being met:

a. First, the banks should have the capability to achieve effective integration following the merger. The management of the acquiring bank must understand the financial, operational and cultural issues involved in integrating two entities and have a credible plan in place.
b. Second, the merger must not impair the bank's financial soundness. In particular, the bank must meet MAS' capital adequacy requirements at all times. Consolidation should not compromise the safety and soundness of the bank.
c. Third, we will consider the impact of the merger on competition. Consolidation should not lead to the emergence of one or a small group of overly dominant banks, which are in a position to engage in monopolistic or other anti-competitive behaviour.
d. Fourth, the consolidation should not lead to loss of service for small depositors, for whom affordable banking services are a necessity.
e. Fifth, any cross-border partnerships should not result in the foreign partner taking control of a Singapore bank.

I will elaborate on these five considerations in turn.

Managing the Integration

Consolidation, whilst necessary for the local banks to be competitive, is not in itself sufficient to produce strong banks. Having merged, the banks will have to integrate and rationalise different management teams, information and risk management systems and internal control procedures. The reality is that some mergers work while others do not. Good execution of a merger will produce a stronger bank, by yielding the expected synergies and cost savings. Poor execution will only lead to a more unwieldy and riskier bank.

A larger scale and wider range of activities will demand stronger and more institutionalised management. Singapore banks have benefited from having their principal shareholders, including family shareholders, play an important role in overseeing the banks, although most no longer run the management. The controlling families have had the entrepreneurship and business acumen to build up the banks, and their long-term interests were substantially aligned with those of the banks. This situation currently serves us well, but is not likely to endure over the longer term. The ongoing consolidation, the lifting of foreign shareholding restrictions, the separation of banking and non-banking activities and the process of generational change will result in a reduction in the relative shareholding of the major shareholders. Succession planning is critical.

The transition from the present framework to the new landscape will need to be carefully managed. The banks have already started taking steps to enhance corporate governance and professional management. MAS has also implemented measures to ensure that the Boards and key committees of the banks have sufficient representation of independent directors, and to encourage the Boards to appoint qualified professionals to run the banks. MAS will continue, by moral suasion and prescription, to encourage the banks to strengthen and institutionalise their managements, especially those merged banks which emerge from the consolidation.

Safety and Soundness

While bigger banks are likely to be stronger and more diversified, they pose a larger risk to systemic stability if they run into difficulties. MAS will intensify its supervision of the merged banks, placing stronger emphasis on evaluating the banks' internal risk management processes and control structures. In the US, the Federal Reserve Board installs examiners almost continuously in the large and complex institutions under their purview, in order to monitor and supervise the banks more closely. MAS does not expect to have to do the same, but more frequent inspections and closer supervision of the banks will be necessary.

While MAS will intensify its supervision, the first responsibility for soundness and prudence lies with the Board and management of the bank itself. Bank management must ensure that they have in place robust, group-wide risk management systems adequate to the new scale and risk profile of the combined entity. This again underlines the importance of top quality institutionalised, professional management for the banks.

Competition

We should not allow an enlarged bank, or a few banks in a consolidated banking industry, to use their market power to engage in monopolistic or other anti-competitive practices that raise prices, diminish consumer choice or erect barriers to entry by other players. MAS does not think this will happen. It is unlikely that the largest bank in the system will have an over-dominant share. For example, if OUB merges with one of the larger banks, their combined market share of non-bank deposits will be at most about 30%. This will still be significantly less than the share of the largest banks in other small countries, like the Netherlands and Hong Kong.

Secondly, the competition will not just be among the remaining local players. The banking liberalisation programme will continue to introduce greater competition from foreign banks, in the range and pricing of products they offer and quality of service.

Thirdly, the Government will be vigilant against any abuse of market power. The Competition Act that the Ministry of Trade and Industry is now considering will help us to do that.

Small Depositors

Given the prospect of mergers and rationalisations, it is natural that many bank customers are apprehensive and worried about how they will be affected. A merger will result in rationalisation of branch and ATM networks, which will inconvenience some customers. But overall, customers should have access to more branches and ATMs after the merger, even though not every existing branch and ATM can necessarily be retained. And because a larger merged bank can operate more efficiently and realise revenue synergies, it should be able to provide better service and greater choice to customers. Of course, the bank will have to handle the implementation carefully and sensitively, giving customers adequate notice of changes and helping them to adjust. It is in the bank's own interest to do this, and I am sure they will make every effort to do it well.

Unfortunately, this does not mean that as a result of a merger, every bank service will become cheaper or free. This is not possible, not because of mergers, but because of competition. Competition will force banks to watch their bottom lines more closely, and to make each service and product break even. It will become harder for banks to continue cross-subsidising services that they used to provide for free or below cost. That was a luxury that they could only afford in a protected and languid market where profits came easily, a state of affairs which was unsustainable in the long run. DBS is already facing this pressure, the public is upset that some branches have been closed, but analysts and investors are criticising DBS for not rationalising the branch network and extracting cost synergies fast enough.

Furthermore, as banks focus more on returns, they will tend to concentrate on the middle and upper segments of the market, where they can sell a wider range of services and earn better margins. However, if all banks neglect small depositors, this would cause a problem to lower income Singaporeans, in a society that is increasingly cashless.

Other jurisdictions like the US and Australia also face the same problem, and either have implemented or are studying requirements for basic banking accounts. In the State of New York, banks are required by legislation to provide such accounts, while in some other US states the banks have voluntarily offered such services so as to avoid the heavy hand of legislation.

Banks have to be allowed to recover their costs, just like utilities and public transport companies. But they should not simply opt out of the responsibility to service the mass market. The Government will therefore ensure that in this competitive environment, low-income Singaporeans continue to have access to basic banking services at affordable prices.

This is not an immediate problem, even after consolidation among the local banks. DBS already has an obligation to play a social role, and service the mass market, because that was a condition of the sale of POSBank to DBS. Most of the local banks also service small depositors. This will continue. However, over the longer term, the conflicting pressures on banks on the one hand to provide a public service, and on the other to earn competitive returns for shareholders, will persist and intensify.

The Association of Banks (ABS) has encouraged banks that engage in consumer banking to provide affordable basic banking services to lower income Singaporeans. MAS welcomes this, and hopes that these banks will find ways to meet this need. MAS will monitor the situation closely, together with ABS and the banks. When it becomes necessary, MAS will require all banks with significant retail operations in Singapore to provide basic banking accounts with defined minimum features to low income Singaporeans.

Cross-Border Partnerships

As the financial industry continues to change rapidly and the global banks grow even larger, consolidation among the local banks alone may not be sufficient. Apart from seeking growth and acquisitions abroad, the local banks may also seek out foreign partners. Strategic partners can bring expertise and market discipline to Singapore banks. MAS has encouraged the local banks to explore such strategic alliances and is prepared to approve significant stakes by foreign banks, provided three conditions are met:

a. One, the foreign player must be more than a financial investor. It must become a strategic partner bringing specialised skills, new technologies, or business strategies to the bank. The outcome must be in the long-term interests of the bank;
b. Two, the strategic partner must be a sound and well-managed entity. The alliance should not result in a higher risk profile for the

Singapore bank through, for example, increased contagion and reputation risks; and

c. Three, the Singapore character of the bank must be retained. Foreign parties cannot become controlling shareholders, even if the controlling stake is less than 50%. To allow this would circumvent a key objective of our liberalisation programme, that is to build strong local banks which can underpin the stability of the banking system.

Some of the local banks have already had initial discussions with prospective foreign partners, although so far nothing has materialised. These proposals have not failed because of regulatory objections. MAS' stand is clear: as long as the foreign partner is not seeking to take control of the local bank, we are open to discuss all possibilities.

Banking Liberalisation — The Second Phase

The consolidation being played out among the local banks is a clear indication that they understand the urgency of strengthening their competitiveness. Overall, the local banks have responded well to the liberalisation programme, upgraded their capabilities and maintained their market shares. This has given us confidence to proceed now with the second phase of liberalisation. The second package of measures has three main components: freeing up entry to domestic wholesale banking, enhancing competition in retail banking and instituting prudential safeguards necessary for a more liberal banking environment.

Freeing Up Entry to Wholesale Banking

First, we will significantly broaden participation by foreign banks in the domestic wholesale market. We have to do more to encourage quality international banks to use Singapore as their Asian base. Granting them more access to corporations and high net worth individuals will strengthen their business case to develop their operations in Singapore.

Opening up the wholesale market to international banks will also benefit industries in Singapore. It will give our industries better access to world-class financial products and services that will help them develop their businesses.

MAS will make a fundamental shift, towards a licensing regime that distinguishes between retail and wholesale banks, away from the three-tier licensing regime of Full, Restricted and Offshore Banks. We will rename the existing Restricted Bank licence as the "Wholesale Banking" licence to better reflect the wide range of activities that can be already conducted under the licence. We will phase out the Qualifying Offshore Bank (QOB) and Offshore Bank (OB) licence, and upgrade all existing QOBs and OBs to Wholesale Bank status over time. The upgrading will allow these banks to accept S$ fixed deposits above $250,000 and operate S$ current accounts. It will also remove limits on the amount of S$ lending that they otherwise face as offshore banks.

We plan to grant some 20 Wholesale Banking licences over the next two years. Banks will be admitted to Wholesale Banking status in priority of their financial strength and ability to contribute to Singapore's financial industry. The eight QOBs will be given priority in the upgrading. Existing OBs as well as banks that do not yet hold a banking licence in Singapore are encouraged to apply. After these 20 licences are granted, we will review the pace of upgrading the remaining OBs.

Enhancing Competition in Retail Banking

In retail banking, we will maintain the momentum of liberalisation by improving on the first package of measures. We will take applications for the two outstanding QFB licenses. We will also expand what a QFB is allowed to do:

a. With immediate effect, they will be permitted to establish up to 15 locations (previously 10), of which up to 10 (previously five) can be branches, and the rest off-site ATMs.
b. From 1 July 2002, QFBs will be allowed to provide debit services on an EFTPOS (Electronic Funds Transfer at Point of Sale) network. QFBs can negotiate with an existing EFTPOS network such as NETS, Visa or Mastercard, for access on fair commercial terms.

QFBs will then be able to provide debit services such as debit cards, and cashback at retail outlets. Using the Visa network alone to provide debit services will open up more than 23,000 terminals to the QFBs. With cashback services, each EFTPOS terminal, whether run by NETS or a credit card company, becomes a potential cash withdrawal point.

c. Also from 1 July 2002, QFBs may offer Supplementary Retirement Scheme accounts, accept CPF fixed deposits and offer agent bank accounts under the CPF Investment and Minimum Sum Schemes. Liberalising the CPF Investment Scheme alone will open up a large pool of funds that could be placed with the QFBs. About $62 billion of funds in CPF Ordinary and Special Accounts are still available for investment under the CPF Investment Scheme.

These measures will significantly enhance competition in retail banking in Singapore. With six QFBs permitted to share ATMs among themselves, the increase in locations could result in a QFB ATM network of 90 or more locations across Singapore. Together with access to a nationwide EFTPOS network, this provides QFBs with significant scope for expanding their presence in the domestic market. For consumers, these changes will mean more choice and greater accessibility.

The only part of the retail payments system not yet liberalised will be access by the foreign banks to the local banks' ATM networks. Foreign banks have not been allowed to provide their customers with ATM services on the local banks' networks. We will maintain this restriction for now.

Safeguards

These changes to the wholesale and retail banking markets represent a substantial opening up of the industry. We expect foreign participation in Singapore's banking industry to increase as we liberalise. More people will invest and deposit their money with foreign banks. MAS is therefore looking into two measures to safeguard depositor interests — subsidiarisation of systemically-important foreign banks and deposit insurance.

Subsidiarisation of Systemically-Important Foreign Banks

Local banks are required to maintain a minimum of $1.5 billion in paid-up capital and meet MAS' capital adequacy ratio (CAR) requirements to ensure that they have adequate resources to support and expand their operations. MAS' requirement of a minimum of 8% Tier I capital and 12% Tier I plus Tier II capital exceeds the international standards set by the Basel Capital Accord. However, QFBs and foreign banks can operate as branches, and accept retail deposits without any paid-up capital in Singapore.

This has led local banks to complain that the playing field was tilted against them. It was tenable in the past when individual foreign banks had a small share of the domestic market and we placed greater reliance on the home supervisor. But as we open up further, we need to make sure that the prudential safeguards that apply to foreign banks are commensurate with their increased role in the retail deposit market.

MAS is considering requiring systemically-important foreign banks with a large retail presence to subsidiarise their operations in Singapore. This means that the foreign bank will have to incorporate in Singapore and meet MAS' minimum paid-up capital of $1.5 billion, as well as MAS' CAR requirements. Subsidiarisation will provide greater clarity and certainty in supervision. A subsidiary is a separate legal entity from the parent. It will have its own assets and will have to maintain its own capital. This will allow us greater flexibility to ring-fence the subsidiary, and minimise contagion arising from problems that may emanate from the bank's home market or global operations, especially where the home jurisdictions have laws which favour depositors in the parent bank over depositors in overseas branches.

Subsidiarisation will not turn the subsidiary into a local bank. The foreign parent bank will in most cases own 100% of the subsidiary and want full control over its activities. MAS will continue to treat the subsidiary as a foreign bank, and will exempt it from a requirement placed on local banks to maintain a majority of Singapore citizens or permanent residents on their board of directors.

MAS is studying this issue and will make a decision later this year.

We would not be the only jurisdiction with a subsidiarisation requirement. Several reputable jurisdictions, such as Australia, the US and Canada, go even further and require that in order to accept any retail deposits at all, foreign banks must incorporate locally and meet the minimum capital requirements imposed on locally incorporated banks.

Deposit Insurance

We will study the need for a deposit insurance scheme in Singapore. Unlike most countries, Singapore does not have a deposit insurance scheme. In the past, sound management and conservative practice by the local banks, coupled with strict regulation and supervision by MAS, helped to avoid problems in our banking system. On the few occasions when a foreign bank has run into difficulties, MAS has managed to ring-fence the banks' Singapore operations in time — as we did during the Asian crisis — so that Singapore depositors did not suffer losses.

However, as we liberalise, foreign banks will gain market share. Local banks will also venture abroad. The safety and soundness of both local and foreign banks will increasingly be affected by factors beyond our control. We have seen how in other countries even well-run international banks supervised by highly-regarded authorities can nevertheless run into financial trouble. Even as we strengthen MAS supervision, we cannot expect our supervisors to always be in time to pre-empt any difficulties that the bank has not prepared itself for.

No government can promise to bail out depositors whenever a bank runs into trouble. If a government did so, depositors would lose the incentive to seek out sound banks, and banks would lose the incentive to lend prudently, knowing that even if they run into trouble their downside risks will be absorbed by the government. This is what bankers call moral hazard. However, in the absence of a deposit insurance scheme, there will be an implicit expectation, both by depositors and banks, that if something goes wrong, particularly with a large bank, the government will be there to pick up the pieces. And should a mishap happen, the government may come under strong political pressure to do so. This can be destabilising.

Deposit insurance makes clear where depositors stand: depositors know exactly how much of their money will be protected if a bank fails. Government statements that it will not bail out depositors beyond the insured amounts become more credible. However, deposit insurance is not without its downside. If its coverage is too broad, or it insures too large a proportion of deposits, it can cause the same problems as a government guarantee. A poorly designed deposit insurance scheme may make the banking system less rather than more stable. These problems can be mitigated if the deposit insurance scheme only insures small deposits, or sets premiums in line with the relative riskiness of banks, or discriminates between banks and subsidiaries that are incorporated here from those that are not. These are complex issues that need careful study, which MAS has begun.

Conclusion

This liberalisation package will provide further impetus for upgrading and progress in the local banks and Singapore's financial sector development. We will review the progress made in another 2–3 years, before deciding on further moves.

Consolidation and continued liberalisation are important in building strong banks. But they are not in themselves sufficient. Banks must press on to upgrade their capabilities. They must keep abreast of international best practices, new products, technological developments and new ways of doing things, while retaining the support and confidence of consumers. ABS can play a part to help the banks do this. The Government will do its best to maintain a sound regulatory framework, conducive to competition and innovation. But finally, success will depend on the quality and passion of the people in the financial industry. Together we have to build the skills, develop the businesses, and enhance the regulatory framework to make Singapore the premier financial centre in Asia.

Deposit Insurance and Managing the Liberalisation Process

Mr Lim Hng Kiang
Minister for Health and Second Minister for Finance, and Deputy Chairman, MAS
29th Association of Banks in Singapore Annual Dinner
25 June 2002

Introduction

The last five years have been challenging ones for our banking sector. Whether facing the direct impact of the Asian financial crisis or the aftershocks of the South American and Russian financial crises, it is clear that financial services is a global industry. Singapore emerged relatively unscathed but the lesson was clear. No country can insulate itself. Least of all, a small country like Singapore.

MAS began to liberalise the domestic banking sector in 1999, and introduced further liberalisation measures in 2001. We had to move away from the protected environment in which our local banks operated. Protection was unsustainable and incompatible with the long-term interest of Singapore. It was far better to proactively manage the introduction of competition. The local banks would be spurred to upgrade without being overwhelmed by the competition, and the economy would benefit from world-class banking services provided by quality international banks.

Three years later, liberalisation has permanently changed the landscape of the banking sector. We now have six Qualifying Full Banks (QFBs) with the ability to reach out more widely to retail customers through branches and offsite ATMs. Our local banks have responded to the competition by improving their product offerings and investing in new technologies and systems. They have consolidated into three larger entities with greater scale to compete at home and abroad.

Impact of Liberalisation on Consumers

Competition in the new, liberalised environment has brought consumers many benefits. Technology has been harnessed to produce new service channels such as internet banking, phone banking and self-service banking centres. In some instances, these provide consumers with a suite of services exceeding those available at branches.

Competition has also driven down the prices for many banking products and services. In the mortgage loan market, for example, intense competition has meant lower mortgage interest rates for homebuyers. But in some other areas, fees and charges have risen. This is because competition also means that banks have to watch their costs and bottom lines more closely. Banks have also had to rationalise their branch networks, to achieve greater cost effectiveness.

This is a process of adjustment for both banks and consumers. Consumers are entitled to expect banks to provide high standards of service while keeping prices affordable. But they must gradually get accustomed to paying for services which used to be provided free. On their part, consumer banks — especially the local banks and the QFBs — must realise that they have an obligation to service the mass market, so that lower-income Singaporeans have access to affordable banking services, just as nearly every household in Singapore can afford a telephone and utilities services provided at market rates.

I commend the Association of Banks in Singapore (ABS) for taking the initiative to develop the banking code of practice and to set up the Consumer Mediation Unit. These are important steps to reassure the public of the industry's commitment to quality service and high standards of fairness and transparency. In particular, the Consumer Mediation Unit will assure customers that they have an independent avenue for redress outside the courts that is impartial, quick and affordable. The industry now has to ensure that the standards in the banking code are effectively enforced by member banks and the mediation unit functions well to meet the needs of customers. The industry should also continue to periodically review its service standards to ensure they are in line with international best practices.

Last year, MAS called on the industry to address consumer concerns on costs and access. I am pleased that ABS has reached a consensus on the main features of an affordable Basic Bank Account. I understand that ABS has put this initiative on the fast track, with details to be announced within the next two months, and implementation early next year. I would encourage ABS to make use of this time to have discussions on the account with key stakeholder groups such as Consumer Association of Singapore (CASE) and National Trades Union Congress (NTUC) to explain the underlying economic rationale and ensure that the features meet the needs of customers.

These voluntary initiatives by the industry to assure customers of continued access to affordable quality banking services are positive steps which merit encouragement. A banking sector that understands its role in the market and is responsive to the needs of its customers offers the best assurance that the interests of consumers will be met. The alternative to this is government regulation, compelling banks to provide by law a specified package of services to the public. A number of other countries have chosen this path, but its disadvantage is inflexibility: once the package is fixed, it cannot easily be changed to adapt to changing needs and conditions. This will impose burdensome costs on the industry, and ultimately will serve the interests of neither banks nor consumers. In my view, the banking industry should be given the opportunity to make the various industry initiatives announced today succeed.

Deposit Insurance in a Sound Banking System

Just as the liberalised banking sector has prompted calls for an assurance of quality basic banking services at affordable cost, it has also prompted a review of whether depositor protection should be further strengthened.

Last year, MAS announced that it was studying whether a deposit insurance scheme would be desirable and feasible in Singapore. Deposit insurance schemes have been implemented in over 70 countries, including the US, UK, Canada, and most European countries. The features vary, but they all share the common purpose of providing an assurance to depositors. This takes the form of a guarantee to depositors that they will be compensated up to a maximum specified amount of their deposits in the unlikely event that the bank they had placed their deposit with fails. This guarantee is backed by an insurance fund that is built up through premium contributions from each participating bank, and which will be drawn upon to meet payouts to depositors.

Why would we need a deposit insurance scheme when our banking system is stable and sound? Indeed, might the mere act of introducing a deposit insurance scheme give depositors the mistaken impression of some heightened risk in our system? MAS considered these issues very carefully.

Depositors with banks in Singapore have always been secure in the knowledge that our banking system is strong and well-supervised by MAS, which has acquired a reputation over the years for being a strict regulator. The three local banks are well-managed and amongst the best-capitalised in the world. The QFBs operating here have met high prudential standards for admission. MAS remains steadfast in maintaining high standards of regulation and supervision even as we take a more consultative and risk-focused approach to supervision.

Whilst our banking system remains sound, we are operating in an increasingly challenging global and regional environment. The business of banking has grown more complex, and so has risk management. As foreign banks gain greater market share in Singapore and local banks further develop their presence abroad, the soundness of banks operating here will increasingly be affected by factors beyond our control.

Vigilant supervision can minimise the probability of bank failure but cannot eliminate the risk of failure entirely. Even in reputable foreign jurisdictions with highly-regarded supervisors, bank failures occur from time to time. With sufficient warning signals, a supervisor may be able to ring-fence assets in Singapore of an ailing bank, and so reduce the losses suffered by its creditors, but this may not always be possible. Depositors cannot assume they will always be protected from losses.

MAS has concluded that a deposit insurance scheme is suitable for Singapore. A deposit insurance scheme will provide a further layer of protection to depositors and complement the role of prudent bank management and MAS supervision in minimising risk. Indeed, studies by the IMF have found that an increasing number of countries have established deposit insurance as an integral part of their financial safety net, and that a well-conceived deposit insurance scheme reinforces confidence in the banking system.

MAS also believes that this is a good time to implement deposit insurance in Singapore. A recent study by the Financial Stability Forum covering more than 100 countries has found that the introduction of a deposit insurance scheme will be most effective when the country's banking system is healthy. Thus, far from being a measure that is necessary only in bad times or in a weak banking system, a deposit insurance scheme should be put in place when the banking system is strong and sound. This is the same with any insurance policy. We take out medical insurance when we are hale and hearty and so enjoy low premiums. By the time we are sick, insurance cover will not be available or it will be provided at a prohibitive cost. Many of us will consider the premiums well spent for the extra peace of mind even if we hope never to make use of it.

A deposit insurance scheme also makes explicit the extent of protection that depositors can expect. It dispels the mistaken impression that depositors may have, in the absence of an explicit deposit insurance scheme, that the government has provided an implicit guarantee and will bail them out in the event of a bank failure. Such a guarantee can pose risks to the stability of the banking system by undermining market discipline. Depositors would lose the incentive to seek out sound banks, and banks would lack discipline to manage their business prudently, taking comfort that public funds will be made available to bail them out. This is what economists call "moral hazard". The consequence is a less stable banking system, and a greater likelihood of something going seriously wrong. Clearly, this would be against the interests of both banks and depositors.

Having explained why a deposit insurance scheme is desirable, I now turn to the objectives that this scheme should serve. First, it should provide a basic financial safety net aimed at small depositors. Second, the cost of this scheme should be kept low for banks and depositors. Third, it should differentiate between stronger and weaker banks so that incentives are created for banks to improve their risk profile. I will elaborate on each of these in turn.

A Basic Safety Net

As is the case in many other countries, Singapore's deposit insurance scheme should be aimed at small depositors and therefore provide specific and limited protection. This can be achieved by setting a maximum coverage amount. A depositor is assured of getting back in full his deposits with a failed bank up to this maximum coverage limit. Deposit amounts above this coverage limit are not guaranteed. Thus, while small depositors can expect to enjoy full protection of their deposits, large depositors may experience some loss beyond the maximum guaranteed amount.

The vast majority of small depositors maintain relatively modest balances with their banks. About 80% of individuals maintain balances below $15,000 to $20,000. Hence, a coverage limit of this amount would afford adequate protection to the majority of small depositors. Large depositors on the other hand can reasonably be expected to make their own assessments and be subject to the *caveat emptor* principle when putting their money with a bank of their choice. Also generous coverage weakens the incentive for large depositors to exercise market discipline on banks and encourages banks to take excessive risk.

A Low Cost System

MAS is very mindful of the need to keep deposit insurance affordable. Like all insurance plans, deposit insurance is not free. Participating banks have to contribute towards building up the deposit insurance fund to stand behind the guarantee. The higher the level of coverage, the higher the cost. Banks might find the Singapore market commercially unviable to operate in or they could pass on the additional costs to depositors. It is therefore critical to keep the cost of deposit insurance low whilst achieving the objective of providing effective protection to the majority of small depositors.

A coverage limit of between S$15,000 and S$20,000 can be provided at a relatively modest cost and should not significantly impact the cost of deposit-taking.

Differentiating Between Banks

Apart from keeping the cost of deposit insurance low, MAS is also mindful of the need to allocate the funding of deposit insurance equitably among contributing banks. Some deposit insurance schemes levy flat rate contributions on banks. Under a flat rate regime, all banks are charged a uniform rate on the deposit base. A flat rate contribution structure, while simple, has its disadvantages. First, it does not recognise differences in the risk profiles of banks and hence the differing level of expected losses that each bank exposes the deposit insurance fund to. Well-managed, highly-capitalised banks would in effect be subsidising riskier banks for the insurance cover the latter enjoy. Second, flat rate contributions do not provide an incentive for banks to improve their risk profiles in order to enjoy lower contribution rates.

MAS is studying a system of risk-based contributions. Deposit insurers in the US and Canada have implemented risk-based contribution systems. Under a risk-based system, insured banks are assigned to different contribution categories in accordance with their risk profiles and their ability to manage their risks. Each category of banks is charged a different contribution rate, with banks in the best category paying the lowest rate.

Public and Industry Consultation

Deposit insurance is a major initiative. Although deposit insurance is already well established in many mature economies, the concept and mechanics of an explicit but limited guarantee on deposits is new to Singaporeans and will require careful explanation. It will be effective only if it is well understood by depositors. Thus, even though the study is on-going and may take another year to complete, MAS will communicate key concepts and features of the deposit insurance scheme to the public periodically. MAS will also actively consult with banks on the design of a scheme that is cost-effective, equitable and bolsters confidence in our banking system.

The first phase of MAS' deposit insurance study will make preliminary proposals on participating deposit-taking institutions, coverage limit, fund size and risk-based contributions. MAS expects to complete the first phase by August and will consult extensively with the industry and the public on these issues.

Conclusion

Three years ago, MAS embarked on a process to liberalise the banking sector. The aim was to develop a more competitive and dynamic environment that promotes innovation and enterprise. Whilst this has brought many positive changes, it has also raised concerns about the quality and affordability of basic banking services to small depositors. I am happy that the ABS has responded positively by developing the banking code of practice, setting up the Consumer Mediation Unit and offering the Basic Bank Account. In addition, the introduction of a deposit insurance scheme will strengthen our banking sector further. With all of us working together, I am confident we can develop a competitive banking sector that can hold its own in the global market.

Best Practices in Insurance Regulation

Mr Lee Hsien Loong
Deputy Prime Minister and Chairman, MAS
38th Annual Seminar of the International Insurance Society
15 July 2002

Introduction

These are trying times for the insurance world. Insurers are coping with extraordinary losses arising from the September 11 tragedy. High profile corporate scandals involving household names such as Enron and Worldcom are depressing market sentiment. Sustained declines in asset values mean that insurers can no longer rely on investment returns to offset poor underwriting results.

New Risks Facing Insurers

Over the past decade, insurers have forayed deeper into financial markets in pursuit of higher profitability — both as investors and as intermediaries.

As investors, they are exposed to the vagaries of volatile capital markets. As intermediaries, they are taking on new financial risks. Insurers investing in credit derivatives effectively take on bank credit risks. Insurers who underwrite professional indemnity policies for bank directors and officers, effectively assume banks' operational risks.

Insurance company managers must keep abreast of these developments. They must understand how their companies' risk profiles have changed, and how new activities can have opposing effects on both sides of the balance sheet. All insurance industry professionals need to become more astute at assessing risks, and competency needs to be upgraded at all levels in the company.

Regulators must also keep pace. In supervising individual insurers, regulators need to look beyond insurance risks and protecting policy-holders. From a broader systemic perspective, greater engagement of insurers in financial markets raises important questions concerning their impact on financial stability. How well are insurers managing this new portfolio of risks? What are the spillover effects of an insurance company failure in this environment of inter-linkages?

Traditionally, regulators associate systemic risk with the failure of large banks. The events of September 11 have turned the spotlight onto the importance of the insurance industry as a whole, and even of individual insurance players. A number of recent failures and near failures of insurance companies have revealed just how wide an economic impact insurers have. The high-profile collapse of a few major insurers such as HIH and Independent, left businesses without essential insurance coverage, and critical services without professional indemnity coverage. Economic activity in these sectors might have ground to a halt, had the government not stepped in. But by stepping in, the governments created a new source of moral hazard.

These issues have been extensively debated. The IMF has concluded that the insurance industry, while not systemically critical, has taken up a definite systemic relevance. We need to understand better the nature of insurance companies' financial activities and their possible impact on global financial stability.

In Singapore, the supervisors of banks, insurance companies and securities houses are housed under one roof in MAS. This has given us a head-start in dealing with current industry trends, with financial product boundaries blurring and insurance companies crossing over into banking and capital market territory. The pressure is on to bring integrated supervision to an even deeper level.

Singapore's Response

In today's new risk landscape, MAS aims to develop sound and efficient markets where risk can be effectively spread and mitigated. We need to make sure that best practices prevail in the management as well as regulation of insurance companies. Strong players will make for a resilient industry.

Two years ago, Singapore opened up completely the direct life and general insurance market. The earlier closed-door policy had insulated both local and foreign incumbents from competition and engendered complacency. Creating an open and competitive environment was the first step to raising standards and strengthening resilience.

Since we opened up the industry, insurers in Singapore have taken various measures to enhance their competitiveness. They have sharpened their business focus, moved into higher-value added and higher-growth areas and improved professional standards. This will stand our insurers in good stead to meet new challenges and opportunities.

Meeting New Challenges and Opportunities

Entering New Growth Areas

Globalisation of markets, advances in technology, changing demographics and socio-economic patterns are some trends that will result in new or changing needs for insurance protection and financial planning. Insurers should hone their skills in these new areas and take advantage of emerging opportunities.

One important opportunity is in health insurance, especially financing the health care needs of the aged. This is a challenge that is facing governments around the world. It is no different in Singapore where the population is aging rapidly. Health insurance can play a greater role in financing old age medical care than it now does. MAS plans to introduce in 2003 a regulatory framework for this specialised area of insurance. We will be seeking feedback from local industry on this.

The government recently announced the launch of Eldershield, a national long-term care insurance scheme to be underwritten by private insurance companies. Eldershield provides a basic level of benefits, which many Singaporeans will wish to supplement. This will create opportunities for insurers to structure and market appropriate Long-Term Care policies.

Credit insurance and political risk insurance are two other promising areas. Globalisation and lower barriers to cross-border trade will spur continued internationalisation of trade and support strong demand for credit and political risk insurance.

Being located in Asia, a region that has traditionally witnessed strong trade flows, Singapore is well-placed to develop further as a hub for such activity. Several new specialist insurers and brokers have in recent months set up a presence in Singapore, including financial guarantee insurers and trade credit insurers and brokers.

Another growing area of business is bancassurance activity. Life insurance products sold through the bancassurance channel now account for 25% of new life insurance business.

Two new specialist bancassurance players have established operations in Singapore, and contributed significantly to this trend.

Increasing Resilience

Amidst these new opportunities, more than ever, we now need to strengthen the resilience of the insurance industry. MAS has for some time, been working with the insurance and reinsurance industry to raise standards of corporate governance, internal controls and professionalism. Many of our companies are already at international best practice standards. However, as in all countries, practices vary, and we aim to have all our insurers to attain best practice standards by 2005 if not earlier.

Risk-Based Supervision

In 1998, MAS embarked on a strategic change in our regulatory philosophy. We moved from a bottom-up, audit-based inspection approach to a top-down, risk-based supervisory approach. This approach, being prospective in nature, is well suited to today's world of new and increased risks.

Risk-based supervision evaluates the major risks faced by an institution and assesses how well these risks are being mitigated. This will help both regulators and companies to identify and, importantly, to pre-empt problems. Well-managed institutions will be given greater flexibility, while less well-managed ones will be subject to closer scrutiny.

Singapore's Risk-Based Supervisory Framework for Insurers

The basic framework for risk-based supervision of insurers in Singapore has been set up.

MAS is now developing risk profiles for each Singapore-based insurer. We have devised a five-step "supervisory ladder of intervention", and will use it to classify insurers according to their risk rating. The five steps range from "Normal" to "Viability at Risk" and terminally, "Winding Up or Closure".

Insurers assessed to be on the more critical steps will receive more stringent and intrusive supervisory actions. MAS draws the analogy between the risk classification of an insurance firm and the medical assessment of a patient's health. If an insurer is classified as being on the "Viability at Risk" step, it will probably be admitted to MAS' Intensive Care Unit.

However, MAS is not regulating for a no-failure regime. We encourage industry consolidation. In today's competitive environment, size brings financial strength and facilitates diversification on both sides of the balance sheet. But it is not possible, and also not desirable, to operate on the basis that we will never, under any circumstances, allow a financial institution to fail. That way lies moral hazard.

Improving Corporate Governance and Internal Controls

A risk-based supervisory approach relies heavily on the strength of company leadership and management. Corporate governance is thus critical. MAS expects the Board of Directors to provide clear strategic leadership and set consistent corporate values. Management teams must operationalise these strategies while upholding the spirit of the corporate values.

Given the nature of the insurance business, corporate values need to be guided by risk management concerns. What is the company's risk appetite? What should be its risk tolerance limits? What is the level of risk management skills in the company? How profitable is the underwriting of various classes of risks? Apart from answering to shareholder interests, the board of directors and management also have a fiduciary duty to their policyholders. Sound internal risk management and controls are needed to protect policyholders' interests.

Currently, our regulations oblige the Appointed Actuary to take responsibility for monitoring the financial soundness of life insurance companies. But the Board and management cannot just sit back and rely on the actuaries. Board and management themselves must acquire a better awareness and understanding of actuarial assessment.

We need to set clear expectations of the role that the Board and management play, in ensuring the financial soundness of their companies. MAS will work with industry and professional associations to set out guidelines for this important area.

In Singapore, we established the Corporate Governance Code for listed companies last year. MAS has tightened corporate governance standards for local banks. We recently required auditor rotation for local banks, a policy which we had been considering for some time, even before the latest wave of accounting scandals.

For insurance companies, we are currently working on a draft corporate governance framework. MAS is consulting the industry and will issue guidelines for internal governance for local Boards of Directors, as well as guidelines for the roles and responsibilities of Principal Officers of insurance companies.

The guidelines for internal governance will deal with the main responsibilities for the Board, stress the importance of transparent and performance-linked compensation; emphasise the need for the integrity of financial information; encourage fair dealings with the members of the public who are policyholders and urge insurers to engage in regular communications with policyholders.

Life insurance companies are entrusted with the management of long-term funds. We are considering more rigorous corporate governance requirements for life insurers. We intend to formally introduce and enforce the corporate governance framework for the insurance industry later this year.

Imposing Risk-Based Capital Requirements

In a world of new and increased risks, appropriate levels of capitalisation are necessary. Insurers face mounting complexities, given the increased volatility of asset risks and the diversity of liability risks.

In Singapore, as in many other countries, the existing statutory framework of solvency and capital adequacy for insurers is essentially a "one-size-fits-all" approach. This is clearly no longer appropriate, since different insurers have acquired different levels of exposure to financial risks and developed different underwriting specialties.

In banking, a risk-based capital approach is well-established. There are clear guidelines from the Bank for International Settlements, and a new standard is undergoing extensive worldwide consultation.

For the insurance industry, the same level of regulatory consensus does not as yet exist. MAS has formed two workgroups comprising industry practitioners, representatives of professional associations and regulators to develop risk-based capital models for life and non-life insurance.

Besides refining the treatment of liability risk, we will also look at capital charges for asset risks. This will help to level the playing field between banks and insurance companies, and minimise opportunities for capital arbitrage. The new capital requirements should also provide an early indicator of financial weaknesses, and thus facilitate progressive intervention by regulators. These risk-based capital requirements will be introduced by end-2003.

Raising Professional Standards in Insurance

To improve corporate governance and internal governance, it is critical to raise insurance professional standards. All insurance professionals should constantly upgrade both their technical and management skills.

In 2000, MAS appointed a private sector committee, the Committee for Efficient Distribution of Life Insurance Products (CEDLI) to recommend minimum standards of transparency, competition and efficiency in the distribution of life insurance products. MAS accepted CEDLI's recommendations to enhance the sales advisory process and professional training.

To date, industry practitioners have adopted these minimum standards enthusiastically. Many have gone further, and set their own requirements that exceed the prescribed standards, because they realised that this makes them more competitive in the market. This has improved the level of professionalism among life insurance agents and greatly enhanced the reputation of the industry, which in turn, is helping the industry to attract higher-calibre talent.

Training and competency requirements should apply across-the-board to all insurance professionals, and not just to life insurance intermediaries. MAS is currently reviewing the manpower capabilities of the insurance industry and will identify the main competency gaps and areas of weakness. Apart from upgrading professional competency, consideration will also be given to the technical competency of company directors and other staff involved in the insurance business. We will work with industry to formulate an insurance manpower development strategy. We envisage industry players, training providers and tertiary institutions cooperating to develop programmes that will enhance professionalism in the insurance industry.

Conclusion

MAS will continue to work together with the insurance industry to achieve international best practices and standards. Over the past two years, MAS has worked hard to build a closer partnership with the financial sector. We will continue to promote an open environment and consult actively with the private sector for its views. The relationship between the regulator and the regulated should be arms length but not adversarial. The regulator has to be firm, but also friendly. Market practitioners can help regulators generate ideas, keep abreast of market developments, anticipate global trends and review our financial sector strategies. Candid, thoughtful feedback, including dissenting views, goes a long way to ensure that policies are pragmatic and remain relevant.

We hope that such a regulatory environment will help to develop well-managed insurers in Singapore, who will take up new challenges, and play a more active and productive role in upgrading our insurance industry, and thus our financial sector as a whole.

Sensible Rules, Effective Supervision, Industry Partnership

Mr Heng Swee Keat
Managing Director, MAS
The Asian Banker Summit
19 April 2010

Introduction

The inaugural Asian Banker Summit was held in Singapore about 10 years ago. At that time, Asia was staging a strong recovery from the financial crisis which shook the region in 1997. Today, we find ourselves at a similar inflection point.

Emerging From the Crisis

The worst of the global financial crisis appears to be over. Global financial conditions have since improved markedly and prospects for the world economy have brightened. Asia ex-Japan is leading the recovery, with its GDP already surpassing the pre-crisis level by nearly 8%. For the whole of 2010, the region is expected to grow by 8% over the previous year. The Singapore economy has rebounded strongly and is expected to grow by 7%–9% this year.

While the immediate outlook is positive, we need to remain vigilant. The structural headwinds to growth in advanced economies remain. The transition from government-led stimulus to sustained private-sector driven growth may be more difficult in those economies which face rising sovereign debt levels. As global liquidity conditions are normalised —

following the unprecedented easing of interest rates by major central banks — financial markets could experience bouts of volatility as a range of asset classes are repriced and this could impact negatively on various interest-sensitive industries.

In addition, the reform of the global financial system has to be carefully thought through, calibrated and sequenced. It is important that regulatory reforms do not become politicised, with a rush to adopt simple rules that seem to solve the problems. Specific measures, each of which is sensible, may collectively create unintended outcomes and stymie the nascent economic recovery. In this regard, the Basel Committee's Quantitative Impact Studies will provide an important basis for us to take a more holistic view of the required changes.

So far, most of the discussions have been framed around the theme of "how do we prevent a similar crisis from happening again." Clearly, we must look back and learn from the crisis. But we must not fight the last war. We must also look forward. In the years ahead, significant restructuring of the global economy is necessary. Hence, I believe a more fundamental question to frame the discussion is: "Given the economic changes and challenges ahead, how do we make the global financial system more resilient and at the same time support economic restructuring and sustainable global growth?"

It is therefore critical to get the nexus between the financial system and the real economy right. In this regard, Asia's needs are likely to be different from those in the advanced economies. Economies in rapid transition need responsive banking and capital markets. Bankers need to appreciate the changing needs of the economy, build new capabilities and develop new products and services, to support the needs of companies, large and small, in both mature and new industries. The financial industry needs to build up capabilities to understand the requirements of new industries in the technology and services arena, and to efficiently fund long term infrastructure needs. To sustain Asia's growth trajectory, we need to further develop and deepen national financial systems and regional financial integration. MAS is studying several ideas in these areas, and we look forward to working with our counterparts in the region and with the industry to advance this.

Let me now share the measures that MAS is taking to respond to the challenges from the international reform agenda and the evolving new financial landscape. Our measures are based on three key pillars.

Sensible Rules

The first pillar is establishing sensible rules. MAS seeks to establish sound rules of a high standard that allows well-managed risk taking and innovation, and which emphasises the stable and sustainable development of the financial services sector. The effectiveness of a regulatory framework is not determined by whether it is stringent enough to prevent any kind of shortcoming or failure of any firm. Neither is it determined by how dynamic and innovative the financial services sector is. A regulatory framework focused on stringency alone would impose undue costs and constrain innovation without the assurance that it would be effective. A regulatory framework focused on dynamism alone may not offer sufficient protection to investors, depositors and customers, and may experience more disruptive consequences in a crisis.

MAS' approach to rule-making is outcome-focused. This recognises that the design of regulation should take into account market realities so that unnecessary disruption to well-functioning markets is minimised. For example, in current proposals for a new liquidity framework for banks, having too narrow a definition of acceptable liquid assets is likely to adversely affect the operations of banks in countries without an active sovereign debt issuance programme. We believe that there is a good case for high quality, widely circulated non-sovereign debt to be included as acceptable liquid assets, without undermining the prudential intent of the new liquidity rules. In this regard, the results of the Quantitative Impact Study conducted by the Basel Committee will have to be studied carefully in finalising the list of eligible liquid assets.

Having outcome-focused rule-making also means that where appropriate, MAS may seek to reign in potential risk-spots through more prescriptive rules, even if such rules are not commonly accepted international best practices. A good example would be the macro-prudential rules in some Asian countries, including Singapore, to cap loan-to-value ratios for mortgages, which are not common in the US and Europe. In Singapore, we have also disallowed innovative financing schemes for mortgages. Drawing such "bright lines" in regulation — simple, clear "out-of-bound" markers — has been very useful in targeting excessive build-up of risks in certain situations.

Our approach to rule-making has to strike the right balance of having a financial system that is both sound and progressive, so that it can fulfil its function as a conduit of capital and a facilitator of trade and economic activity. MAS will shortly publish a monograph on our approach to effective regulation.

Effective Supervision

The second pillar is effective supervision. Globally, there has been much discussion on having better rules, but not enough on strengthening day-to-day micro prudential supervision.

An eminent ex-central banker once likened this financial crisis to a massive accident on the highway. To prevent future accidents, if we assess that all drivers are irresponsible, we would have to drastically reduce the overall speed limit. But if we assess that we could also do a better job to take errant drivers to task early, we would have to also focus on strengthening the effectiveness of enforcement. We can then afford to be more measured and targeted in our rule-making. I believe reinforcing sensible rules with good supervisory judgments achieves a better outcome than acting on just one or the other.

However, effective supervision is not easy. The spectrum of supervisory issues will continue to expand and evolve. The economic and financial landscapes are changing rapidly, and interactions remain complex even as we seek to simplify the system.

Globally, financial supervisors are responding to this challenge in two ways.

First, many countries are now considering changes to the institutional structure of their supervisory authorities in the aftermath of the crisis. In this regard, MAS is rather unique in combining financial sector regulation and supervision, central banking and development responsibilities under one agency. This structure has served us well. Building on this, MAS recently implemented a revised organisation structure. Aimed at broadening and deepening our management bench, this structure would also serve to enhance our ability to respond more effectively to supervisory challenges ahead, and to derive greater synergies from the combined structure.

Second, many financial supervisors are stepping up their investment in building up and enhancing their supervisory resources and capabilities. The crisis has underscored the need for financial supervisory authorities to have adequate and well-trained staff, so as to cope with the demands of supervising financial institutions in a fast-moving, complex and challenging operating environment. To maintain a high degree of confidence in the quality of supervision, we recently set up the MAS Academy and devote considerable resources into training and developing our central banking and supervisory staff.

Working in Partnership With Industry: Shared Outcomes and Responsibility

However, sensible rules and effective supervision are not enough. We need a third pillar of partnership, where authorities and financial institutions each take on specific responsibilities to develop a shared ownership of supervisory outcomes. Indeed, the design of regulation and the supervisory approach taken should allow for financial institutions to take on responsibility in contributing towards desired supervisory outcomes where appropriate. Let me highlight two of these areas, namely the industry's role in improving corporate governance and in capability building.

Corporate Governance

One lesson from the recent crisis is that good corporate governance matters. The failure by Boards to exercise effective risk management oversight had damaging consequences for many institutions. Boards play a vital role in safeguarding the safety and soundness of their institutions by setting the risk appetite, remuneration policies and strategic direction, amongst others. For directors to discharge their responsibilities, they have to have the requisite knowledge, skills and experience.

MAS will place increasing emphasis on the quality of the board of directors of financial institutions. Among the proposals to enhance our Corporate Governance Framework for locally incorporated banks and significant life insurers is the requirement for financial institutions to assess the current skills of their Boards on an ongoing basis, and to establish a continuing development programme for all their directors. Given the important role that the banking industry plays in our economy, MAS is also considering developing a mandatory training programme for bank directors.

But let me add that rules, and mechanical compliance with rules, can only go so far in encouraging good corporate governance in organisations. What matters most is for Board and management members to embrace not just the letter of the rules but the spirit of the rules, to take ownership of outcomes, and to internalise the essence of these rules in the ethos and practices of the organisation. Corporate governance in our financial institutions has improved over the years. We must continue this partnership between the authorities and the corporate sector to seek continual improvements in corporate governance which will underpin Singapore's reputation as a trusted financial and business hub.

Capability Building

The other area for collaborative partnership is in building up the capabilities of financial industry professionals. Asia's financial services industry is likely to grow rapidly. If this is not underpinned by an equally rapid growth of capabilities, whether it is in the front office or the mid-back office, we risk a major disruption ahead. It is essential that we act preemptively to address this.

MAS has been working closely with the industry and with organisations such as the Institute of Banking and Finance (IBF) and the Workforce Development Agency (WDA) to increase the supply of skilled talent and to build professional capacity. It is heartening to see that the industry-led initiative in developing the Financial Industry Competency Standards or FICS for short is gaining traction, and despite the financial crisis, investment in training has not become an easy target for cost-cutting measures.

Such efforts should continue apace. Now that financial conditions have improved and firms are hiring again, financial institutions must invest in recruiting and developing their own staff. Taking the easy option of poaching staff from competitors to meet business expansion will undermine the collective strength of the industry in the long term, with adverse consequences on growth prospects for the industry as a whole.

To complement industry efforts in capability building, MAS would be prepared to consider regulatory initiatives to bring about a better-trained and more competent financial sector workforce. In the area of consumer banking, for example, some industry players have suggested the idea of a national examination to test the competencies of relationship managers serving customers in this segment. This could include topics such as ethics and conduct, so as to further promote fair dealing outcomes between industry players and end-consumers. MAS is now studying the idea and will work with the industry to develop this further.

Conclusion

Let me now conclude. Asia's financial systems and institutions are facing considerably less pressure for financial restructuring and regulatory reform in the current crisis. While Asia has not emerged unscathed, significant structural changes made after the Asian Financial Crisis have enabled the region's financial systems to weather this crisis relatively well.

But there is no room for complacency. Even as we recognise the need to continue development of our financial markets, considerable risks and policy challenges still remain for the region. MAS will continue with our three pillar approach of sensible rule-making, effective supervision and partnership to achieve the desired outcome.

We should take advantage of the global reform agenda to strengthen our regulatory and supervisory regimes, consistent with international standards and best practices, but at the same time, doing it in a manner that is sensitive to our regional environment and needs. I am confident that with financial supervisors and the industry working together in partnership, we can further enhance the resilience of our financial system to better serve the economic aspirations of Asians going forward.

Singapore's Approach to the Regulation of Capital Markets

Mr Ravi Menon
Managing Director, MAS
Thomson Reuters 2nd Pan-Asian Regulatory Summit
28 September 2011

What Do Capital Markets Do?

Two thousand years ago, in ancient Rome, enterprises contracted with the government to build temples and collect taxes. The enterprises funded these ventures by selling ownership or equity stakes in the form of shares which were readily transferable among the Romans. Later, the Italian city states sourced for funds from their citizens in the form of bonds to finance wars, while merchants sought financing from individuals to procure better vessels for sailing over ever increasing distances. Over time, a market developed to enable holders of bonds and equities to sell their holdings to other interested buyers. Thus was born — what we now call — capital markets.

Since those early days in Imperial Rome, capital markets have spread far and wide across the globe. But the fundamental function of capital markets has remained unchanged — to allocate capital to those who need it and transfer risk to those who are able to bear it. It is the ability of capital markets to efficiently mobilise financial resources that has made possible the large investments needed for the Industrial Revolution of the 18th century, and the risk capital that funded the global Internet Revolution more recently.

Like other markets, capital markets are prone to volatility as demand and supply fluctuate. But unlike other markets, turbulence in capital markets can have far wider consequences on the rest of the economy. From the Wall Street Crash of 1929 to the Global Financial Crisis of 2008, we have seen how dislocations in capital markets can have devastating effects on financial stability, economic growth, and the welfare of citizens.

Capital markets must therefore be regulated, but in a way that does not unduly undermine their efficiency and effectiveness.

This morning, I want to share with you Singapore's approach to the regulation of capital markets.

Why We Regulate Capital Markets

We can think of the capital market as an ecosystem comprising four key components:

- One, issuers — those who issue securities to raise capital;
- Two, investors — those who invest in these securities;
- Three, intermediaries — those who advise issuers or investors and facilitate the trading of securities;
- Four, infrastructure — the platforms or systems through which securities are traded.

Each component of this ecosystem is prone to market failure — hence the need to regulate.

- First, there is information asymmetry between issuers/intermediaries and investors, and investors may be unable to make informed judgments about financial products.
- Second, there is a principal-agent problem, and intermediaries may not act in the best interests of their clients, be they investors or issuers.
- Third, investors are sometimes prone to herding behaviour, exaggerating price movements and thereby precipitating market instability.

- Fourth, if issuers and intermediaries take on too much risk or liability that they cannot manage, there will be loss of confidence and market instability.
- Fifth, critical infrastructure may fail, again leading to market instability.

The purpose of regulating capital markets is to safeguard the interests of investors, ensure that risks are kept to an acceptable level, promote efficient price discovery and maintain confidence in the market.

In Singapore, the regulatory framework for capital markets is underpinned by the Securities and Futures Act (SFA) and the Financial Advisers Act (FAA). Consumers who invest in products or deal with entities that are regulated under this framework will enjoy the safeguards provided under these laws. Together, the SFA and FAA cover each of the four components in the capital markets ecosystem.

Issuers — Dissemination of Material Information

Let me begin with issuers.

A key tenet of capital market regulation is that relevant information is transmitted efficiently for price formation and discovery. Like most reputable regulators, MAS imposes stringent rules requiring issuers of securities to disclose and disseminate all material information. We conduct ongoing surveillance of market practices and undertake rigorous enforcement actions to ensure compliance.

Disclosure

The SFA requires exchanges to develop rules for reliable and unhindered price formation and discovery. First, disclosure must be ongoing. Post-listing, material information likely to affect market prices must be disseminated in a timely and organised manner. For example, a company that makes an acquisition which is likely to have a material impact on its share price must immediately announce it on the website of the Singapore Exchange (SGX). Second, disclosure must be accessible to all. Listed companies are prohibited from disclosing material information on an individual or selective basis. These disclosure requirements complement Singapore's statutory provisions on market manipulation and insider trading.

Enforcement ... and its limitations

Issuers and investors alike must have confidence that the ground rules are adhered to when they transact in our markets. Constant surveillance and strict enforcement are therefore critical. MAS takes a serious view of any false statement or omission of material information that misleads the market. We will not hesitate to impose stiff penalties on issuers who have made misleading statements in initial public offerings, or IPOs.

But no regulator can totally prevent fraud or misconduct. Take for instance our experience with S-chips, or Chinese companies listed on the SGX. Many of them are reputable companies and add breadth to our equity capital market. But some of them are not. Since 2006, accounting irregularities or outright frauds have been discovered in 14 such companies listed on the SGX. Most of these cases came to light when the auditors were unable to confirm the companies' cash and account receivables. The counters were suspended pending investigations by special auditors, and investors had to bear the losses. I still get letters from investors who had lost money in these shares. I can understand their frustrations.

Many have asked MAS to do more to bring the full force of our law to bear on the wrongdoers. Let me state the position categorically: MAS will leave no stone unturned to take rigorous action against those who break our laws. But there are real challenges when the fraud is perpetrated by parties outside our jurisdiction. Cross-border investigations and enforcement are intrinsically difficult.

Singapore is not alone in facing challenges with international listings. Cooperation among securities regulators and enforcement agencies in different jurisdictions is therefore critical.

We cannot eliminate fraud. But we can and must ensure that companies that are brought to the market are of good quality. SGX must be rigorous in evaluating the suitability of listing applicants before admitting them.

Other stakeholders must play their part too.

- First, directors of the company seeking a listing must exercise adequate oversight of internal controls and ensure the veracity of information disclosed.
- Second, IPO advisers have a legal and professional responsibility to conduct proper due diligence when bringing companies public. They must have a healthy dose of scepticism, and never place their commercial interests above the need to ensure that a company is suitable for a public listing. MAS will not hesitate to take advisers to task for poor due diligence work.

If the regulators, issuers and advisers each do their jobs well, we can reduce the likelihood of poor quality companies gaining access to our markets.

Investors — Safeguarding Their Interests

This brings me to the second component of the capital market ecosystem — investors.

Well-informed and empowered investors are at the core of a well-functioning capital market. Investors will lose confidence in a market where disclosure is misleading and where selling practices are irresponsible.

Safeguarding the interests of investors, particularly retail investors, is therefore a key focus of MAS regulation. But this objective has to be balanced against the need for investors to take ownership of their investment decisions. A regulatory approach that requires issuers or intermediaries to bear all the risks and losses will not work. If investors expect their losses to be always made good, there will be moral hazard and it will encourage reckless investing.

MAS safeguards the interests of investors in five ways:

- First, we demand stringent disclosure of information by issuers;
- Second, we require transparency in the information disclosed;
- Third, we set standards for intermediaries who sell investment products to provide quality financial advice;

- Fourth, we promote investor education, so that investors are empowered to make informed decisions; and
- Fifth, we provide affordable and accessible dispute resolution mechanisms for investors who feel aggrieved by the investment process.

Let me take each of these aspects in turn.

Disclosure

There is nothing like disclosure to instill market discipline. In the words of US Supreme Court Justice Louis Brandeis, "Sunlight is said to be the best of disinfectants; electric light the most efficient policeman." Disclosure is about shining that light so that all can see and make informed decisions.

Investors are entitled to accurate and timely disclosure of material information so that they can assess the risks and rewards of their investment. Disclosure works not because all investors understand every word that is disclosed. Disclosure works because it facilitates scrutiny by experts in the market; it is this professional scrutiny that acts as a check on issuers and helps to inform the broader investor base.

Take for example an IPO prospectus. It can typically run into hundreds of pages, with detailed descriptions about the company's business operations, its competitive environment, governance practices and risk exposures, not to mention a full set of financial statements. Most retail investors cannot easily digest all this information. But the scrutiny of the prospectus by analysts and institutional investors helps to bring to light any significant weakness in the company.

Having said that, I must acknowledge that greater disclosure does not always improve our understanding of investment products. While all material and relevant information must be disclosed, there is a tendency for disclosure to be voluminous and legalistic — often made for the purpose of limiting legal liability rather than facilitating understanding by retail investors. MAS therefore seeks to ensure that information disclosed is not only adequate but also transparent.

Transparency

MAS has sharpened the focus on providing investors information in a clear and concise manner to aid understanding. Earlier this year, we introduced a new regulatory requirement for a Product Highlights Sheet to accompany offers of investment products that come with prospectuses. Its purpose is to convey key risks and product information in plain language and in a simple question-and-answer format. Let me give an example. In one recent prospectus, the right of the investors to cancel their subscription within seven days was spelled out in two rather technical paragraphs using a total of 170 words. In the Product Highlights Sheet, the same point was made in two simple sentences.

Financial advice

The third aspect of investor protection is the provision of sound financial advice by intermediaries when they sell investment products. The Fair Dealing Guidelines issued by MAS require intermediaries to conduct their own internal assessment to ensure that a new product being launched for sale is suitable for its targeted investor base. Intermediaries must also ensure that their representatives have the competencies to understand and explain the product features to their customers.

MAS has introduced new rules requiring intermediaries to assess their customers, investment knowledge or experience before investing in complex products. The rules will come into effect in January 2012. Where an investor does not possess the requisite knowledge or experience, intermediaries must provide appropriate advice. Investors who choose not to heed their advice or insist on buying a product which has been assessed to be unsuitable for them must take responsibility for their decision. This approach recognises that investors' capacity to understand complex products is uneven, while respecting their right to invest as they see fit.

Over the last two years, MAS has conducted surveys and inspections to assess intermediaries' delivery of these fair dealing outcomes. We will use our findings to fine-tune the Guidelines on Fair Dealing.

While MAS has taken these steps to ensure that the financial advisory industry is able to help investors make informed decisions, the best way to instill discipline on the industry is for investors to demand good advice. Singapore's investing public should seek good financial advisers who are prepared to even advise them against buying an unsuitable product. They should be prepared to pay a fee for such advice.

Investor education

Even with the best of disclosure and transparency, investors can make informed decisions only if they have the knowledge and skills to do so. This brings me to the fourth area of investor protection — education.

The centrepiece of Singapore's investor education efforts is the MoneySENSE national financial programme. It was launched in 2003 to raise consumer understanding of basic money management, financial planning and investment products. Through various seminars and media initiatives, MoneySENSE has reached a large segment of the population since its launch. In the last year alone, MoneySENSE events attracted close to 100,000 attendees while media initiatives reached more than two million people. These events are conducted by industry practitioners, academics, and investor advocates. To date, MoneySENSE has published more than 230 educational articles on its website and in the media. More than 30 consumer guides have been issued and are available online.

While we have made steady progress, much more needs to be done. Most Singaporeans have sound savings habits and are generally responsible in managing credit, but many still do not have a good understanding of common investment products. Every month, MAS receives, on average, about 10 complaints from the public involving the sale of investment products.

I read many of these letters. Sure enough, there are indeed a few cases of inadequate disclosure or mis-selling, which the financial institution concerned should remedy. But there are others where the customer has failed to exercise basic due diligence. These are the most painful letters to read:

- of investors who were attracted by headline returns and purchase products without reading any of the product documentation;
- of investors who willingly signed blank sheets of product assessment forms without realising what they were buying; and
- of investors who insisted on buying risky products even though they were advised that the products were not suitable for them.

It is very difficult to help in cases like these.

MAS will continue to explore ways to equip investors with core financial capabilities. We are currently studying the feasibility of establishing a financial literacy institute to complement existing MoneySENSE initiatives through talks and workshops to reach a larger segment of the population.

We are also reaching out more to students, through the schools. The objective is not so much to instill technical expertise in investment products, but to inculcate good money habits from a young age — being prudent, being alert to risks, being clear about the objectives of investing.

Dispute resolution

Even with well-informed consumers, occasional disputes with those who sell investment products will be inevitable. Hence the final area of investor protection is to provide an affordable and accessible dispute resolution mechanism for aggrieved investors.

MAS has set clear expectations that financial institutions must establish a robust process to resolve customer grievances independently, effectively and promptly. We also expect financial institutions to investigate and rectify issues related to any widespread complaints on a particular product or selling practice.

This dispute resolution mechanism within financial institutions can be effective only if parties to a dispute act fairly. Financial institutions must police their relationship managers and enforce internal guidelines. Recently, we were alerted to a case where a financial institution tried to salvage its reputation by denying that its relationship manager had recommended a highly risky investment product to an elderly retiree with a low risk tolerance. This is not acceptable. MAS will take firm action against financial institutions for such behaviour.

On the other hand, investors should not make unreasonable demands and expect financial institutions to accede to them. For instance, a consumer demanded that her bank accept her mobile text instruction to reverse a transaction when the message was sent a day after the transaction was executed.

Where disputes cannot be resolved through the financial institution's internal processes, investors can approach the independent Financial Industry Dispute Resolution Centre (FIDReC). FIDReC provides access to an independent and affordable dispute resolution process through mediation or adjudication. This provides the consumer a low-cost alternative to litigation. FIDReC awards are binding on the financial institution, but the investor can choose to reject the award and pursue other options for recourse.

Intermediaries — Safety and Market Conduct

I turn now to the next key component in the capital markets ecosystem — intermediaries. The objective of regulation with respect to capital market intermediaries is twofold: their safety and soundness, and market conduct.

Safety and soundness

We want intermediaries to be safe and sound, in the interest of preserving systemic stability. Intermediaries connect the various parts of the capital market ecosystem. They stand between buyers and sellers, underwrite risks, act as counterparties in risk transfers and participate as members of clearing houses. The failure of a major intermediary can transmit risks across the system, causing severe market disruption and undermining confidence. Lest we forget, Lehman Brothers was principally a securities firm, not a bank.

MAS regulation cannot rule out the failure of an intermediary. But we can seek to ensure an orderly winding-down process.

The segregation of customers' funds from the intermediary's own funds is a key feature of our regulatory regime. Unlike banks which can freely deploy the deposits they collect, capital market intermediaries are required to segregate customers' assets from their own monies. This acts as a safeguard for customers' funds should the intermediary fail. Fund managers are required to appoint independent custodians and fund valuation firms, and be subject to regular audits.

Market conduct

The second regulatory outcome we expect from intermediaries is fair conduct. Trades that give a false or misleading appearance of market activity, actions to rig the prices of securities or futures, are all prohibited under our law and severely dealt with.

MAS works closely with the Commercial Affairs Department to take enforcement actions ranging from civil penalties to criminal action. Last year saw the fruition of MAS' first civil penalty court action. We secured civil penalties against a fund manager who was found by the High Court to have window-dressed his portfolio by creating a false appearance relating to the price of one of the component shares. The fund manager and its CEO were ordered to pay a civil penalty of S$250,000 each to MAS, as well as costs of the court action. The decision was upheld by the Court of Appeal.

The assistance that we sought, and obtained, from our foreign counterparts was vital to our success in this case. Similarly, MAS stands ready to assist our international counterparts in their enforcement efforts. Earlier this year, the Australian authorities successfully prosecuted a former fund manager of an Australian bank for insider trading. MAS had referred this case to the Australian Securities and Investment Commission (ASIC) and provided ongoing assistance during ASIC's investigations.

Infrastructure — Sound and Stable

The final component of the capital market ecosystem is the infrastructure that supports the trading of securities and futures. Capital market participants trade either on a multilateral basis through organised exchanges, or bilaterally with each other over-the-counter or OTC.

Exchanges

The Singapore Exchange and the Singapore Mercantile Exchange operate the systemically-important securities and futures markets in Singapore. They constitute critical infrastructure that must function properly to preserve stability and efficiency. Our laws require the exchanges to maintain sufficient financial, human and system resources, have frameworks and processes to manage their risks, and to regulate and supervise their participants.

OTC derivatives

The OTC derivatives space has traditionally been the preserve of sophisticated financial institutions which are well placed to assess and negotiate trades among themselves. These financial institutions are regulated by MAS and the risks associated with their OTC derivatives positions are taken into account under the respective regulatory frameworks for these institutions.

OTC derivatives, unlike their more standardised counterparts on futures markets, enable customised hedging of risks. Properly employed, they confer significant benefits to the financial intermediation process and hence the wider economy. For example, interest rate swaps enable companies to convert floating rate loans to fixed-rate loans. Companies with large capital investments over a long horizon, such as airlines, shipping companies and infrastructure builders, rely on interest rate hedging tools to manage their financial risks.

But with the rapid growth of OTC derivatives globally, weaknesses in the market structure can contribute to a build-up of systemic risk. We saw this during the global financial crisis. The interconnectedness of OTC derivatives market participants and the limited transparency on counterparty risks can trigger rapid contagion. Under stressed market conditions, this can potentially threaten the stability of the financial system.

The G20 has called for changes to improve transparency and mitigate risks in OTC derivatives markets. The Financial Stability Board has made recommendations under four key thrusts. Singapore is fully committed to implementing these recommendations.

The first thrust is to standardise derivative contracts. MAS is working with the Singapore Foreign Exchange Markets Committee to encourage standardisation of derivative products. The Committee will formulate a code of conduct for financial institutions operating in the OTC market.

The second thrust of the reforms is to mandate central clearing of all standardised contracts. Central clearing mitigates systemic risk through multilateral netting and ensures that the failure of a counterparty does not affect other participants. Since 2006, the SGX has operated a clearing facility for OTC derivatives, covering derivatives contracts for commodities, energy and freight. It started clearing interest rate swaps in November last year, and will clear foreign exchange forwards by the end of this year.

But comprehensive implementation of central clearing is not without challenge. We need to determine carefully the products for mandatory central clearing, particularly those employed by commercial end-users. The cost of clearing can potentially increase their hedging cost, causing a cut-back on needed investment or an increase in unhedged positions. We also need to be mindful that while central clearing removes counterparty risks, it adds to concentration risks. It is therefore critical that central clearing platforms be subject to robust supervision to ensure that they manage their risks effectively. To the extent that these platforms operate across geographical borders, appropriate arrangements for cooperation among national supervisors must be in place.

The third thrust is to move derivatives trading to platforms where appropriate. This will help to improve price transparency. Singapore is a major centre for exchange-traded derivatives in Asia. We are well placed to move more derivatives trades to organised platforms, but the extent would have to take into account the local context, such as product characteristics and participant profiles.

The fourth thrust is to report trades. Mandatory trade reporting enhances supervision of derivatives markets by addressing information gaps. For this to be effective, regulators need timely access to relevant data that can be aggregated. This requires cross-border supervisory cooperation on data access and harmonisation of reporting requirements and standards. But national concerns have led to some jurisdictions setting up their own trade repositories, which could make data aggregation more challenging. MAS is assessing the need for a local repository and the appropriate regulatory regime to avoid duplication.

In recent months, there has been a notion in some quarters that as tighter regulations are proposed for OTC derivatives in the US and EU, activity will flow to centres in Asia that are purportedly less tightly regulated.

This is mistaken. Leading centres in Asia — like Singapore, Hong Kong, and Australia — are very much part of the G20 initiative and there is no room for regulatory arbitrage. MAS is fully engaged in the OTC work of the Financial Stability Board, the International Organisation of Securities Commissions, and the Committee on Payment and Settlement Systems. We will fully implement the OTC derivatives reform agenda.

There must be consistency in implementation across jurisdictions, but there cannot be precise equivalence. The OTC derivatives landscape in Asia and Singapore differs considerably from that in the US and Europe. We have smaller markets and less complex derivative instruments. We have to consider how to implement the G20 reforms effectively while taking into account enforcement issues and the characteristics of our markets. MAS will consult the industry on its proposals for OTC derivatives market reforms by the end of this year. We aim to meet the G20 target to implement the reforms by end-2012.

Conclusion — Shared Responsibility

Let me conclude.

In regulating capital markets, we are not dealing with a particular industry or a particular type of institution. We are trying to create the conditions within what is essentially an ecosystem, so that its risks are managed and its economic benefits sustained.

But these benefits cannot be achieved by regulation alone. As Winston Churchill puts it, "If you have ten thousand regulations you destroy all respect for the law." There is a limit to how far regulation can go without undermining compliance, not to mention efficiency and innovation.

All components of the capital market ecosystem must play their part. A well-functioning capital market is a shared responsibility. If all stakeholders do their part well, not only will we have fair and efficient capital markets that everyone has confidence in, but we will also make Singapore a competitive and vibrant financial hub in Asia.

Ensuring Strong Anchors in Our Banking System

Mr Tharman Shanmugaratnam
Deputy Prime Minister and Minister for Finance, and Chairman, MAS
39th Association of Banks in Singapore Annual Dinner
28 June 2012

The Continuing Lessons from the Crisis

Four years after Lehman Brothers collapsed, the global financial crisis is still with us. Its new epicentre, as we all know, is in Europe. The combination of weak banking systems and overstretched government balance sheets in several European economies has proved toxic. It has led to a loss of confidence and unsustainably high borrowing costs, not just for Greece but for a few other larger Eurozone economies. It has also resulted in the virtual disappearance of the unsecured interbank market, which is the lifeblood of any financial system.

Each major crisis yields lessons for all countries, and there will be many lessons arising from the crisis in Europe. In several European economies, as in the US, entitlement spending by government has outrun future revenues, and it is no longer possible to borrow away the problem.

But there are major lessons too in banking, and the main ones are in fact the old lessons. Spain, the current focus of attention in the markets, is a case in point. Its government finances were in fact in better shape than in many other advanced countries. But troubles had been accumulating in its banking system, caused especially by small and medium-sized banks having made excessive loans to a property sector that has now crashed — a familiar problem repeated almost in cycles, across a range of countries. The result is a cutback in credit, a deeper recession, greater strain on government finances both as revenues decline and the government is forced to bail out banks, and worsening bank balance sheets as banking assets lose further value and borrowing costs increase. We are therefore seeing a vicious cycle of economic decline and a loss of confidence.

The situation is not unique to Spain. The specifics of the balance sheet problems vary from country to country, but a self-reinforcing cycle of feedbacks between falling economic activity and weak bank and sovereign balance sheets is now taking place in several countries in Europe. It is complicated by an increasing fragmentation in politics, which makes the journey to a credible and lasting solution in the Eurozone all the more complex and challenging in the years to come.

The problems in the Eurozone and the US underline the absolute necessity for consistently sound banking practices and governance by banks. The crisis also provides lessons for regulators and the supervision of banks. The IMF has found that regulatory intervention in Spain lacked timeliness and effectiveness, even though the problems in banking had been identified early on. Regulators must be prepared to take early and decisive corrective actions to forestall a build-up of risks in individual banks and the banking system as a whole.

Further, contagion amongst banks is a fact of life. Financial systems can be severely stressed by their weakest points, even if it involves a single bank or a group of small banks. The Northern Rock episode in the UK was an example in the earlier phase of this crisis. The Spanish *cajas* or regional savings banks are now another. The largest Spanish banks are widely acknowledged to be well capitalised, to have lower exposure to the property sector and to have well diversified earnings internationally. But until the troubles in the *cajas* are resolved, even sound Spanish banks are being penalised by higher funding costs, and citizens and tax payers too are exposed. Confidence is therefore about banking systems, not just about individual banks. This is all the more why regulators have to be vigilant in spotting weaknesses and requiring corrective actions, both across a system and in individual banks. The weakest point matters.

International Regulatory Reforms

The global financial crisis has prompted a major review of international regulatory standards. We have achieved much, with the new rules developed through the Basel Committee on Banking Supervision and the Financial Stability Board — new rules on the quantity and quality of capital and liquidity and the ongoing work to strengthen cross-border supervision and resolution frameworks for global banks.

The Basel Committee has proposed several reforms to minimise the risk of failure of global systemically important banks (G-SIBs), and to minimise the impact if any of them should fail. It is also recognised that some banks are systemically important within their own domestic markets even if they are not internationally active to the same extent as the G-SIBs. The failure of these domestic systemically important banks (D-SIBs) can have a major impact on an economy, and indeed unpredictable consequences for a broader region. Bankia, for example, is not a G-SIB. The Basel Committee has recommended higher loss absorbency requirements for G-SIBs, and is studying an appropriate regulatory framework for D-SIBs. MAS is very much part of that discussion.

However, in order to keep to the spirit and intent of the new measures, sensible judgment will be the key to implementing the new rules. Sensible implementation requires national regulators to take into account the impact of their actions on economic growth and international finance even as they exercise national discretion to address prudential issues in their banking system. There are two risks of a broader nature that we have to keep clearly in focus in international discussions, so that what we do now to strengthen our respective national systems does not lead to new problems and vulnerabilities internationally, further down the road.

First, we have to ensure that the cumulation of enhanced capital and other requirements on global banks do not impede them from playing their critical roles in global finance. The global banks play a major role as providers of liquidity in home, host and international markets. Even in emerging markets, debt and equity market liquidity often relies on active participation by global banks. Enhanced regulatory requirements should therefore be targeted, risk appropriate and applied in a non-discriminatory way on banks posing the same level of risk, be they domestic or global banks.

The safety buffers for global banks, which clearly need to be enhanced, cannot therefore rest too heavily on premiums in upfront capital, liquidity and other regulatory requirements. We should strengthen supervision and crisis resolution capabilities to complement and avoid an over-reliance on regulation. Strengthen continuous supervision rather than rely excessively on upfront regulatory requirements. Effective international coordination among supervisors requires more open and transparent sharing of information between home and host supervisors — home supervisors will want to be well informed about the requirements imposed on significant overseas subsidiaries, and host supervisors need to be kept apprised of developments at the parent bank. Cross-border supervisory colleges and crisis management groups are therefore critical, and they have to be strengthened to ensure that national policy measures are globally consistent and mutually supportive. So that is the first risk, of going too far with respect to global banks such that the global financial system is impaired.

The second risk is that of the fragmenting or balkanising finance. We are already seeing signs of this, and most especially in the wake of the European crisis. Deleveraging by some international banks is leading to a pull-back into home markets. But some regulatory responses, not just market responses, may reinforce this pull-back, by restricting the flow of capital and liquidity outside home markets. Not only will this ring-fencing of national systems weaken international banking and trade, it may introduce new risks to financial stability when global banks are not able to deploy liquidity from one part of the banking group to other parts in need. Better international coordination in the implementation of rules is therefore needed to ensure that they serve their intended national objectives without weakening the global system as a whole and introducing new vulnerabilities.

A Sound Financial System Anchored by a Core of Strong Local Banks

Just as we derive lessons from troubled banking systems, it is worth looking too at those that have not run into problems. It is notable that among the jurisdictions with systemically important financial centres, Canada, Australia, Hong Kong and Singapore have held up well during the global financial crisis. A little remarkably, the top 10 banks in Bloomberg's latest annual ranking of the world's strongest banks included four Canadian banks, the three Singapore local banks and two Hong Kong banks. There is no room for complacency — the financial crisis has shown how volatile financial markets can be and the speed with which contagion can spread. Banks have to be constantly vigilant against the build-up of risks and maintain strong buffers against contingencies.

But let's look at these four banking systems for a moment, Canada, Australia, Hong Kong and Singapore. They share two characteristics in common:

(i) They are anchored by a handful of banks with a significant share of the domestic market.

(ii) These "anchor" banks are closely supervised and regulated.

Several economies, including some in emerging countries, which had completely opened up their banking systems and left themselves without local anchors, have now found themselves to be vulnerable. Banking systems need strong anchor players, who are well regulated and diligently supervised, and are able to take the long-view, enabling their interests to be closely aligned with that of the economy. In a crisis too, strong anchor banks may be needed to acquire distressed financial institutions whose failures could otherwise have a systemic impact.

But having anchors with a substantial share of the domestic market is not sufficient to ensure resilience. Without adequate competition, they will earn what the economists call oligopolistic rent, rather than serve the needs of an economy by innovating and introducing efficient services. Anchor banks have to be competitive.

This is why we have progressively opened up Singapore's domestic banking sector since 1999. We have allowed greater competition, particularly in wholesale banking where local players are not protected, and increasingly in retail banking too. It has involved some risks. We took a risk. But the result is now widely acknowledged to be stronger and more dynamic local banks, with much improved systems of management, risk controls, technology and expertise. Banking liberalisation provided the spur for our local banks to raise their game and compete with some of the world's largest banks while maintaining high prudential standards and they have done well.

We had previously announced the Government's policy of maintaining the local banks' market share at no less than 50% of total resident deposits. This remains our position. We are committed to having strong local banks at the core of the banking system. In a very real way, our three strong local banks also give Singapore the confidence to continue opening up the banking sector to foreign competition.

Encouraging Foreign Banks to Deepen Their Singapore Roots

A diverse international presence and global connectivity must remain key strengths of Singapore's financial centre. We host many international banks, who conduct an increasing share of their activities out of their Singapore offices. Some banks have moved their global heads of business to Singapore, or hubbed specific business lines or IT operations in Singapore. Consumers and corporate customers have benefited from the wider range of products and services, offered at competitive rates.

The majority of foreign banks in Singapore operate as branches, taking advantage of the cost efficiencies arising from branching within an international bank. We continue to support the use of branches for the vast majority of banks in Singapore, which are in the wholesale and investment banking businesses.

Additional measures may be appropriate for retail banks that are important to the domestic market. At the individual depositor level, additional safeguards such as a deposit insurance scheme (which we already have in place in Singapore) and local incorporation will provide better protection for depositors from problems emanating from other parts of the banking group.

Local incorporation can also bring benefits to a bank, especially where it has a significant retail presence. Liquidity rules under Basel III will require long-term stable sources of funding to comprise a larger share of a bank's total funding. Competition for deposits is expected to intensify, and banks that can attract stable funding will gain an advantage. Local incorporation can therefore demonstrate a bank's long-term commitment to depositors and other stakeholders in a world of possibly permanent heightened volatility and uncertainty. Beyond local incorporation, encouraging strong international banks to sink deeper roots in a domestic economy will allow them to play a greater role in contributing to financial resilience. Let me elaborate on this important objective of encouraging strong international banks to sink deeper roots in a national economy.

One of the key features of our banking liberalisation has been the Qualifying Full Bank (QFB) privileges that have been granted to foreign banks. The number of QFBs has increased from the initial four in 1999 to six in 2001 and eight today. QFBs have also been allowed more places of business from 10 in 1999 to 25 today.

MAS will continue to liberalise the domestic banking sector in a progressive and calibrated manner. We will allow greater foreign bank participation in Singapore's domestic financial system in a way that strengthens financial stability and that encourages foreign banks to deepen their roots in Singapore. MAS will make several refinements to the QFB programme:

(i) We will require existing QFBs that are important to the domestic market to locally incorporate their retail operations. The key objective for requiring local incorporation is to strengthen depositor protection. One indicator of importance to the domestic market will be the share of domestic deposits. MAS is also evaluating other factors that may be relevant to individual QFBs and will consult them on the criteria for requiring local incorporation. Not every QFB needs to be locally incorporated.

(ii) A very small number of QFBs may become significantly rooted in Singapore over time. For these significantly rooted QFBs, MAS will consider granting an additional 25 places of business, of which up to 10 may be branches, as part of an overall package negotiated with the home countries of these QFBs which are free trade agreement (FTA) partners with Singapore. This will bring the total to 50 places of business for such QFBs. Being significantly rooted entails both additional privileges as well as responsibilities to contribute to the stability of the Singapore financial system.

A significantly rooted bank will be determined by both qualitative and quantitative attributes. For example, whether:

(a) the bank is locally incorporated with majority Singaporean/ Permanent Resident Board representation, and what types of businesses are conducted by the locally incorporated entity;
(b) Singapore is one of the major markets for the bank group, constituting a substantial part of group profits and assets;
(c) major business lines and key decision makers are headquartered in Singapore; and
(d) the bank serves a comprehensive spectrum of the local community in Singapore.

A bank that demonstrates these and other characteristics can be considered significantly rooted.

(iii) MAS will consider awarding new QFBs only under FTAs where there are substantial benefits to Singapore. New QFBs that are granted under future FTA offers will have to first locally incorporate before they may establish up to 25 places of business.

This evolution of our QFB scheme, and it is an evolution, should ensure that our local banks continue to have majority share of domestic deposits, while banks awarded QFB privileges can build a deeper presence. Given the size and maturity of Singapore's domestic retail banking market, we have to calibrate our moves to ensure that greater foreign bank participation does not result in a fragmented and inefficient market, but instead leads to a more robust and competitive system. Banks with a meaningful market share will be in a better position to reap the benefits of scale from a more extensive network, to respond to customers' changing needs and at reasonable cost, and to be better rooted in Singapore to contribute to our financial stability and growth.

Taken together, this latest phase in our banking liberalisation and the refinements we are making in regulation and supervision together with our international counterparts, will ensure that Singapore remains both a vibrant global financial centre and one of the rocks of stability in global finance.

Building a Culture of Trust in the Financial Industry

Mr Ravi Menon
Managing Director, MAS
MAS-Singapore Academy of Law Conference
23 January 2015

Bad Behaviour in Finance

Six years ago, the Global Financial Crisis tipped national economies into recession and brought to their knees some of the most hallowed names in the financial industry. But the biggest casualty of the Crisis could well be trust:

- trust between regulators and financial institutions;
- trust among financial institutions; and
- trust that the public places in the financial industry — that their bankers are honest and their financial advisers are acting in the best interest of their clients.

And six years after the Crisis broke, the global industry continues to be dogged by shocking revelations of financial malfeasance, mis-selling, and dishonesty. In the US, large banks are paying billions of dollars to settle charges against them for mis-selling mortgage-backed securities which led to massive losses for their buyers. In the UK, over 13 million complaints have been made against retail banks for the aggressive mis-selling of so-called Payment Protection Insurance (PPI). We read of traders in banks circumventing internal rules to make outsized market bets that subsequently resulted in large losses for these banks. And in financial centres across the world, including Singapore, regulators have uncovered attempts by traders at several major global banks to manipulate key financial benchmarks used to set rates for loans and foreign exchange contracts.

Little wonder that global surveys show that levels of trust in the financial industry are lower than ever. According to Edelman, a public relations firm, banking and financial services ranked last among 15 industries that the public trusted "to do what is right".[1] In countries most affected by the financial crisis and its aftermath, levels of trust are lower still — barely 30% of the public in Europe trust their banks.

Why Trust Is Critical to Finance

Financial products and transactions can be quite complex and information asymmetries often place financial institutions in a more advantageous position compared to their customers. Trust that the bank is sound is critical for savers to keep their monies in bank accounts and for borrowers to make long-term investment decisions. Trust that financial advisers and insurance agents are dealing fairly is important for consumers committing large portions of their savings for a long period of time. Trust that asset managers and investment brokers are acting in the clients' interest and not front-running them is key to the investment process.

The licensing and regulation of financial institutions confers a degree of legitimacy on them. But being a bank, an insurance company or a capital markets intermediary is not just about holding an official stamp to collect and manage funds. As Mark Carney puts it, financial institutions also need a social licence to operate.[2] They earn this social licence through a track record of exemplary conduct and a reputation for integrity and prudence. Their obligations towards their customers and counterparties must be based on not just a contractual obligation but a moral one as well.

1 Edelman Trust Barometer, 2013 and 2014.

2 Mark Carney, "The Future of Financial Regulation", MAS Lecture, Singapore, 2014.

Getting the Culture Right

What accounts for the repeated cases of misconduct in the global financial industry? Weaknesses in governance, risk management and operational controls have allowed unbridled risk-taking and encouraged some individuals to push, and in several cases, break the bounds of what is permissible. Since the financial crisis, the international regulatory community has issued directions and guidance to tighten financial institutions' governance standards and curb excessive risk-taking.

But weaknesses in governance and control, grave as they were in some financial institutions, cannot fully account for the spate of misconduct. There are deeper issues of trust, ethics and culture in the financial industry that we need to confront.

First, finance is at risk of becoming more "de-personalised". Long-term relationships with customers are being replaced by more transient transactions with counterparties. Raghuram Rajan observes how increasing product complexity and reliance on technology has created a detachment from the customer. It ultimately leads to a reductionist view of finance where "money is the measure of all worth", a state that is hardly conducive for ethical conduct.[3]

Second, compensation structures tend to over-emphasise profits as performance measures. Excessive focus on sales targets and commissions has incentivised a "trading mentality" which is often associated with too much risk-taking or scant regard for client interests or the sustainability of relationships.

Third, and more fundamentally, departures from ethical conduct are too easily tolerated as the norm. In a global survey of financial sector executives by the Economist Intelligence Unit, more than half the respondents felt that their career progression would be difficult without being "flexible on ethical standards". If you look at the email and chat room messages between traders involved in the rigging of financial

---

[3] Raghuram Rajan, "Where Money is the Measure of All Worth" in *Fault Lines: How Hidden Fractures Still Threaten the World Economy*, 2010.

benchmarks, they betray a lack of any sense of guilt or wrongdoing. In fact, traders were congratulating and complimenting each other on their manipulation. And when subsequently questioned by their superiors or regulators, they offered an array of self-justifications, chief of which is "everybody does it".

But everybody does not do it. I believe the vast majority of people working in the financial industry are committed to serving their clients or customers fairly and with integrity. But the unethical actions of a few have undermined trust and created instability.

Reform of the financial industry will not be complete until this issue of trust and ethics is addressed. This requires "getting the culture right". And by culture, I mean the shared values, attitudes and norms that guide actions.

There is increasing international regulatory guidance to improve risk governance and align compensation schemes with long-term sustainability and customer interests. This is necessary but not sufficient. There are limits to what externally imposed rules can do to promote the right values in financial firms. Because culture develops from within a firm, it invites a certain resonance from the members of that firm — in a way that will be difficult for an externally imposed set of rules to achieve. For the same reason, the behavioural norms that a firm's culture and value system promotes are more amenable to internal governance and self-policing than rules that rely on external enforcement.

In short, rules tell us what we can do, but values tell us what we should do. A mechanistic compliance with rules cannot be an adequate substitute for an internalised sense of responsibility and basic morality that a finance professional owes to his client or counterparty.

How can we build a culture of trust and strong values in the financial industry? We need an ecosystem to do so — with a role for regulators, the industry, and most important, the firm itself.

What Can Regulators Do?

First, the role of regulators. The international regulatory community has been intensifying efforts to ensure that financial institutions foster a sound risk culture and conduct themselves in a prudent and socially responsible manner. But instituting a good risk culture is not merely about slapping on more rules or adopting a perfunctory, checkbox approach to compliance.

MAS therefore takes an intensive supervisory approach to risk governance and culture in financial institutions. We prefer this to an overly prescriptive regulatory approach based on one-size-fits-all rules that may be less effective in addressing idiosyncratic risks. Financial firms differ widely in goals, activities and culture.

Instead, close supervision — consisting of both onsite inspections and offsite reviews — provides MAS with a good view of a firm's risk governance and culture and practices on the ground. This allows us to assist the board and management in identifying emerging areas of vulnerabilities and to take pre-emptive corrective actions where necessary. Let me cite two areas we focus on: compensation and fair dealing.

Compensation is an important mechanism to shape incentives and behaviours. Compensation structures must motivate not only high performance but also high ethical standards. Some jurisdictions have placed restrictions on bonus payments — how much can be paid or over how long a period.

MAS has put in place rules and guidelines that are consistent with the Financial Stability Board's principles for sound compensation practices. They require the compensation of a bank executive to be aligned with not only the risks that the bank undertakes, but the time horizon of those risks. But we have chosen not to cap bonus payments or be overly prescriptive in our rules. Such measures may have unintended consequences or could be easily circumvented.

Instead, MAS has stepped up its supervisory intensity of financial institutions' overall compensation policies and practices. We assess the effectiveness of the firm's compensation system, its relationship with the firm's governance framework, and its impact on risk-taking behaviour. We intend to conduct deeper-dive reviews, to examine how a firm makes compensation decisions in practice, as well as the extent to which the firm's board and management deal with issues relating to compensation and risk culture.

A second area of focus is fair dealing: Are firms dealing fairly with customers? MAS has issued guidance on fair dealing principles and outcomes that financial firms should achieve. We assess whether the board and management have put in place initiatives to foster a corporate culture of fair dealing. We evaluate the processes in place to ensure that clients and customers are offered products and services that suit their needs. We monitor the volume of customer complaints of mis-selling and examine how complaints are dealt with.

What Can Industry Do?

But even the most intrusive supervision can only go so far in promoting a culture of ethics. The industry must itself take collective responsibility to promote higher ethical standards. It is better that industry develops codes of good conduct that take into account operational realities that they know best and that holds firms accountable to their peers, than wait for the regulator to set rules that may be impractical or too onerous.

The industry has already begun to do so. In the UK, high street banks have set up the Banking Standards Review Council (BSRC), which aims to work with the industry to improve banking practices in three broad areas: culture, competence and customer outcomes. Participating banks will be required to commit to a programme of improvement and report to the BSRC on their performance every year. In the Netherlands, the Dutch Banking Association is exploring plans for a disciplinary system for ethics violations, similar to what the medical profession is subject to.

I am pleased to note that in Singapore, our industry associations have not lagged behind. The Association of Banks in Singapore (ABS) has published guidance for its member banks and minimum service standards that customers can expect from their banks. The Code of Consumer

Banking Practice commits member banks to treat their customers "fairly and reasonably". A separate Private Banking Code of Conduct sets out standards for financial advisers, not only for professional competency but ethical conduct as well.

The Singapore Foreign Exchange Market Committee (SFEMC), an industry association of major foreign exchange market participants, has published a guide to conduct and market practices for treasury activities. More commonly known as the Blue Book, the guide has recently been updated with instructions on the governance, requirements on professional conduct and best practices for participants in benchmark rate settings.

The industry could consider going further in promoting and reinforcing ethical standards and good practices:

- Industry may want to consider a mechanism or process by which firms could be benchmarked against and held accountable to industry standards on ethical behaviour and professional conduct.
- Industry may also want to conduct periodic surveys on stakeholders' views on risk culture, governance and market conduct, to help identify potential blind spots and emerging areas of risk.

What Can Firms Do?

But ultimately it is the financial institution that must bear responsibility for getting the culture right. This requires setting the right moral tone from the top. Many financial firms have issued values statements and codes of conduct espousing principles, norms and behaviours that apply universally across the firm. It is important to have such a tangible point of reference for standards of conduct, but setting the right tone requires more than lofty exhortations for good behaviour.

First, lead by example. Management must take time and effort to clearly articulate the firm's core values and purpose. They have to demonstrate commitment and credibility by "walking the talk" with concrete policies, processes and actions. The firm's leaders must themselves be seen to be guided by those same qualities they want their staff to emulate. And programmes to build a culture of trust and ethics cannot be a one-off exercise to fend off bad publicity or to placate the regulator. Shaping culture demands a sustained effort.

Second, create a safe environment for whistleblowing. This means providing the necessary mechanisms to challenge, question, and report ethical breaches. A number of banks in Singapore have put in place new channels for whistleblowing and enhanced the escalation and investigation processes to facilitate staff reporting.

Third, align human resource policies to a culture of trust and ethics. I have already mentioned compensation as being an important way to create incentives for the right behaviour. But the incentives for ethical conduct must go beyond compensation and encompass all HR policies: recruitment, on-boarding, appraisal, training and coaching, promotion, and career development. An organisation's HR policies and practices are the clearest demonstration of its value system, the qualities it regards as important. In financial firms, it is important that these policies and practices dispel the perception of good ethics as a constraint on profitability or hurdle to career advancement.

We are beginning to see some progress. Performance appraisals in some banks now take into account how an employee's conduct is consistent with the banks' avowed principles and values. Others have developed balanced scorecards for remuneration that go beyond traditional measures of financial performance to include indicators relating to culture and controls. Yet others take into account a business unit's record on compliance, customer experience, internal audit findings and other relevant considerations to underscore the organisation's behavioural expectations of staff.

Conclusion

Let me conclude.

The global financial industry's standing with the public is at an inflection point. It could continue a downward spiral of mistrust with yet more egregious misconduct, or it could seize this opportunity to restore high ethical standards.

Thankfully, we are in a better place in Singapore. The financial industry here is generally well regarded and trusted. But we have not been immune to some of the egregious practices in global finance, for example, attempts to manipulate financial benchmarks and the mis-selling of financial products. We must be on our guard, and work to further strengthen ethical standards and a culture of trust in the industry. We must foster a culture in the industry that looks beyond the question "is this legal?" to the larger question "is this right?". For without sound ethics, there can be no trust. Without trust, there can be no confidence. And without confidence, there can be neither growth nor stability.

We are gathered here to discuss the future of financial market regulation. May I suggest that restoring a culture of trust based on strong ethical standards is imperative to securing a bright future for a purposeful financial industry.

FinTech – Harnessing its Power, Managing its Risks

Mr Ravi Menon
Managing Director, MAS

Singapore Forum
2 April 2016

FinTech is fundamentally transforming the financial industry. The smartphone is becoming our bank. Computer programmes are offering investment advice. People can now lend directly to one another online.

Technology will replace many jobs in finance but will also create exciting new jobs. Calls for new and different skill sets — understanding technology and the ability to work with and harness the power of machines and algorithms. As someone in Silicon Valley put it, "the geek shall inherit the earth".

Unregulated FinTech companies are now providing many financial services. They will challenge traditional financial institutions (FIs), disrupt and even displace some of them, but will not replace them. Banks and insurance companies have something that unregulated entities do not have — trust. Trust based on a track record of performance. FIs are not sitting still. They are actively harnessing technology to enhance product offerings and improve efficiency. They are setting up in-house FinTech units to replicate the start-up mentality. Many global banks have set up "innovation labs" in Singapore: Citibank, StanChart, UBS, HSBC, to name a few. And insurance companies too: Aviva, Aeon, AXA, Allianz, MetLife. They are also collaborating with or buying over FinTech companies to tap their technologies.

Financial technology, or FinTech, may well be the best hope for the future of finance. The financial industry is facing many headwinds. Slower economic growth, narrower margins, tighter regulation and greater competition from outside. FinTech can potentially help the financial industry regain its dynamism and at the same time purposefully serve the economy and the people.

But the FinTech phenomenon is not without risk. The rapid pace of innovation and adoption throw up many questions for the industry and financial regulators. What should be the policy approach? I will speak from the perspective of MAS.

First — take a differentiated approach to different technologies and their applications.

FinTech encompasses a wide range of technologies: we cannot take a "one-size-fits-all" approach. The nature of technologies, their benefits and risks are very different:

- Digital payments, digital currencies — they pose issues of authentication, identity.
- P2P lending platforms, crowdfunding — there are implications for consumer protection and fraud risk.
- Cloud computing, big data — there is the issue of cyber security.
- E-trading platforms, algorithmic trading — there are implications for market functioning, both good and bad.
- Blockchains and distributed ledgers systems (DLS) — this is potentially the most transformative innovation, at least until artificial intelligence comes along in a big way.

Many new technologies intelligently used can help to reduce risk. For example, DLS. Decentralisation reduces concentration risk. A cyber attack cannot bring down the entire system because every player has a copy of the ledger. Speed of transaction verification reduces counterparty risk. This could potentially translate to lower collateral requirements, better capital optimisation. Imagine clearing and settlement in seconds rather than days. But mind you, these are still at proof-of-concept stage. There is still no scalable market-wide solution in place.

But contrary to what DLS advocates proclaim, it is not without risk and may even introduce new ones. The public DLS is susceptible to malware being uploaded into the system. Blockchains are not hack proof. And as all data are replicated to every node in the system, there is a risk of compromise of privacy.

So, each technology must be evaluated on its own merits. And we must also consider which financial activity it is being applied to. Blockchains in clearing and settlement systems are very different from blockchains in trade finance or e-KYC.

Second — adopt a risk-based approach to FinTech innovation in the unregulated sector.

Regulation must not front-run innovation. Introducing regulation prematurely may stifle innovation and potentially derail the adoption of useful technology. MAS applies a materiality and proportionality test. This means when the risk posed by new technology becomes material, then regulation comes in. And the regulation must be proportionate to the risk posed.

For example, Internet-based payments or P2P lending that takes place outside regulated banks. We regulate banks chiefly because they take deposits. When they get into trouble, they have systemic consequences. So, we supervise their lending activity and their payments systems. We do not regulate P2P lending platforms — as long as they do not take deposits. But if they get very large and pose macroprudential concerns, then we may consider regulation.

Likewise, a payment service through the Internet will not automatically attract regulation. These are typically small payments, often in connection with e-commerce. Only larger, more significant players that cross the materiality and other thresholds are regulated. Even then, we do not regulate them as banks and throw at them the whole kitchen sink of capital and liquidity requirements under the Banking Act.

We regulate them under the Payment Systems Oversight Act or the Remittance Agents Act — modular regulation customised to address the specific risks or concerns they pose. But I must acknowledge we do not have ready-made regulations for all new technology solutions; often we must improvise the use of existing legislation, even as we draw up new ones.

Third — actively promote the FinTech ecosystem and seek to harness its potential for good.

While regulation must not front-run innovation, regulators must run alongside innovation. We must know what's going on and be ready: either to promote or to restrain. There are three ways in which MAS does this.

One, we actively engage FinTech firms to better understand emerging innovations and help them design their solutions for financial services. For example, cloud computing. Our traditional approach was to deal only with regulated FIs, not their service providers. But with cloud solutions proliferating, we changed tack. Many of these solutions offered strong efficiencies and cost savings but not all models met our regulatory requirements for data integrity and protection. So we engaged in dialogue directly with cloud service providers to explain our concerns and at the same time understand the technology. The service providers then came up with solutions that met our concerns. And we modified our requirements to take account of new business models and technological capabilities.

Two, we allow our FIs to experiment with new technologies in a safe environment. FIs do not have to seek MAS' permission to try new things. Responsibility lies with boards and management to assess the risks and put in place adequate safeguards. But with many innovations, it is not always possible to anticipate every vulnerability or whether there is a risk of breaching regulation. Sometimes, as Nike puts it, you have to "Just do it".

MAS will therefore introduce a "regulatory sandbox" approach that aims to give FIs more confidence to experiment and launch their innovative products or services within controlled boundaries. The idea is not to remove all risk. Failure is an inherent part of innovation. Rather, we want to create an environment where if an experiment fails, it fails safely and cheaply, without larger adverse consequences. MAS will soon issue guidelines for public consultation on how the regulatory sandbox will work.

Three, we promote greater interoperability within the industry to harness the full potential of technology. An innovative environment proliferates a wide range of technologies and solutions. But if the solutions cannot interact with one another, we sub-optimise efficiency gains or customer experience. While we should allow a hundred flowers to bloom, we should also take care we create a garden.

Greater interoperability across data systems is therefore a key priority. Let me give two examples of what MAS is doing together with the industry:

- One, common standards for payments systems to realise more seamless payments across a range of platforms. We are working towards a unified point of sale (POS) terminal — a single terminal that can read all kinds of cards at retail and hospitality outlets. We are also exploring an "all-in-one" addressing system that will enable us to pay someone electronically using the payee's mobile number, email address, social network account, or other proxies. No need to know the payee's bank account number.
- Two, seamless data sharing through publication of open application programming interfaces, or APIs. We just had a two-day API conference earlier this week, where industry players shared their views on how we can take the API strategy forward. MAS is working with FIs to leverage on new technologies to share aggregated data to improve market and risk analyses, forecasts and projections.

We are committed to building a Smart Financial Centre, where innovation is pervasive and technology is used widely to:

- Increase efficiency,
- Manage risks better,
- Create new opportunities, and
- Improve people's lives.

Singapore's Financial Centre: Resilience, Dynamism, Trust

Mr Ravi Menon
Managing Director, MAS
Foreign Correspondents Association of Singapore Lunch
6 September 2016

This afternoon, I want to share my thoughts with you on how the MAS sees the financial sector. Many of you, especially from abroad, are sometimes intrigued by MAS' role as both regulator and developer of the financial sector.

As one of you put it recently, the adjectives used by bankers to describe the MAS are "no-nonsense", "business-friendly", "pragmatic". You will be forgiven to think that we are sometimes schizophrenic. In my meetings with foreign bank CEOs, I have sometimes, in the same breath, said we would like to see an improvement in the bank's risk management and internal controls and then asked what we could do to encourage the bank to expand its operations in Singapore — safely of course!

Let me explain why we are both "no-nonsense" and "business-friendly".

The financial services sector is one of the key pillars of the Singapore economy. It accounts for about 13% of GDP and has strong positive demand spillovers on the rest of the economy. The sector employs about 200,000 people, 84% of them are Singapore citizens and permanent residents. It creates good jobs. The median wage for Singaporeans in financial services is $6,400, compared to the national median of $4,000.

Financial services will become even more important in the future economy. The sector grew by an average of 8.6% p.a. during the last five years (2011–2015), two times faster than the overall economy at 4.0%. If the sector continues to grow twice as fast as the economy over the next five years — not easy but we aim to — financial services will make up 14% of the economy in 2020, compared to 11% in 2010.

Now, the bad news.

The financial sector is inherently vulnerable to risk and volatility. As crisis after crisis has shown, problems in the financial sector quickly become problems for the entire economy. The Global Financial Crisis imposed a tremendous cost with the global economy estimated to have lost 5 percentage points of growth between 2007 and 2009, not to mention the human dimension in jobs lost and companies closed. As an international financial centre — connected to the global network of financial flows and playing host to hundreds of foreign financial institutions — Singapore is particularly vulnerable to contagion and shocks from abroad.

The global financial industry is facing unprecedented headwinds. We are looking at a prolonged period of low growth and low interest rates — a combination that spells reduced earnings and increased risks for most financial institutions. The regulatory and compliance burden has increased significantly, following wide-ranging regulatory reforms in the wake of the global financial crisis. The reforms were necessary to help make global finance safer; but their cumulative effects do pose a challenge for the profitability of financial institutions, especially banks. Unprofitable banks are not necessarily safe banks.

Finally, the financial industry in many parts of the world is facing a crisis of trust. Financial institutions have come under increasing public scrutiny over their business conduct. Globally, we have seen repeated cases of mis-selling financial products, manipulating benchmark rates, and using the financial system for illicit transactions.

Singapore's financial sector has to overcome these headwinds and manage these risks as it develops further. And it must do this while seizing on opportunities presented by a growing Asia and technological change.

Let me touch on three attributes that our financial sector needs to maintain and strengthen in the years ahead: resilience, dynamism and trust.

A Resilient Financial Centre

I will start with resilience.

We cannot insulate our financial sector from the stresses and turbulence in international financial markets. We must remain open but be able to absorb shocks from abroad and bounce back.

High prudential standards have therefore been a hallmark of Singapore's financial sector since the very beginning. In recent years, we have further strengthened the resilience of the system through higher capital requirements and enhanced liquidity rules.

Singapore banks operate well above the regulatory capital minimums. The Basel Committee prescribes a minimum Tier 1 capital adequacy ratio of 6%. MAS has set a regulatory minimum of 8%. The three local banking groups have Tier 1 ratios in excess of 13%. Singapore banks are well-placed to meet the Basel III leverage ratio requirements, currently proposed as 3%. In fact, the three local banks have leverage ratios above 7%.

MAS has had a liquidity requirement long before an international standard was developed and has recently increased the risk sensitivity of our liquidity rules. The three local banks' Liquidity Coverage Ratio or LCR is already well above 100%, the target set by the Basel Committee for 2019.

These strong buffers — built up in good times — are now serving us well as we enter a soft patch in economic conditions. The banking system's ratio of non-performing loans went up to 1.9% in Q2, from 1.3% a year ago. But the banking system has set aside provisions to cover more than 100% of its non-performing loans (NPLs).

There have been concerns raised about the impact of the oil and gas (O&G) sector. The O&G industry has been under pressure from low global oil prices for some time. We expect to see some of that pressure showing up in our banks' NPLs. The banks have been actively managing the risks from the O&G sector. The banking system's exposures to the O&G sector as a proportion of total exposures (i.e., including non-bank loans, debt securities and contingent liabilities) is less than 10%. Among the local banks, O&G exposures are even lower, at about 6%.

It is also important to appreciate that there is no systemic problem across the O&G industry. The problems in the O&G industry are concentrated in the upstream marine and offshore engineering segment which makes up less than one-fifth of the industry. About 60% of the surveyed banks' O&G exposures are to the more resilient downstream, oil trading and integrated firms, which are less impacted by the decline in oil prices. Firms focusing on oil refining have also fared better on account of regional demand for refined petroleum products and lower feedstock prices.

The most recent stress tests conducted by the MAS indicate that the banking system would not do too badly even under some pretty severe scenarios. The stress scenario assumed:

- the US, EU, Japan and several emerging Asian economies slipping into recession and China's economic growth falling below 3%;
- sharp depreciation in regional currencies and oil and commodity prices falling by another 50% over three years;
- a protracted recession in Singapore with resident unemployment spiking to more than 6%;
- property prices falling by another 50% over three years, with similar declines in China and Hong Kong; and
- the banks' top O&G counterparties failing.

Under these rather dire conditions, the banks' NPL ratios could rise to 8% to 10% by the end of 2018. That should not be surprising. What's important is that the banking system will be able to absorb these losses. Banks will continue to meet the Basel minimum capital requirements comfortably. And they will have sufficient liquidity to meet their cash flows.

This resilience did not come about by accident. It reflects prudence and sound financial management in the financial industry:

- building up capital and liquidity buffers;
- identifying and managing risks proactively;
- provisioning against losses conservatively.

A Dynamic Financial Centre

I have talked about imagining the worst and preparing for it — that is resilience. Let me now talk about seizing opportunities — that requires dynamism.

Our financial sector has been able to grow handsomely because it is plugged into the region — which is growing two to three times faster than our own economy. But the continued growth of the financial sector is not a given. MAS and the financial industry have been working hard together to realise this potential.

A key priority is to strengthen infrastructure. Let me give an example.

Emerging Asia has enormous infrastructure needs. At the same time, global investors are seeking investment projects with good, long-term yields. There ought to be a good match. Yet, for all the promise and rhetoric, infrastructure finance has not really taken off. The basic problem is this: infrastructure projects are not structured in a way that would draw investors.

MAS has been working closely with stakeholders to improve the bankability of projects. There is now a recommended template to help regional governments structure meaningful public-private-partnership agreements for infrastructure projects.

The latest innovation is an infrastructure debt takeout facility. By providing a guaranteed takeout arrangement, the facility will enhance banks' ability to originate, arrange and provide infrastructure project finance loans. At the same time, it will make it easier for institutional investors to invest in long-term infrastructure debt instruments as an asset class.

Second, we need to deepen our markets.

Take the asset management industry, where Singapore plays the role of a regional hub with S$2.6 trillion of assets under management. To deepen our market, we are embarking on several initiatives:

- To add diversity and resilience to the industry, we are seeking to anchor sovereign wealth funds and pension funds.
- To fund managers who use Singapore as their hub for Asian growth, build their investment capabilities and strengthen their local talent pool, MAS is giving out more investment mandates.
- To facilitate the domiciliation of funds in Singapore, MAS together with the Ministry of Finance is putting in place a more efficient corporate fund administration structure for asset managers.
- To meet the growing demand for family offices, we are providing greater clarity on the regulatory treatment of single family offices.

The third way in which we build dynamism in the financial sector is by enhancing connectivity.

One of Singapore's key roles as a financial centre is to connect investors and markets across Asia and beyond. Our expanding financial ties with China is a good example.

Singapore is one of the top three offshore RMB centres globally. Singapore's financial centre has played a constructive role in supporting the internationalisation of the RMB. This has in turn helped to forge stronger trade and investment links between China and Southeast Asia.

Singapore also offers a gateway for the expansion of Chinese corporates into the region. More than 6,500 Chinese enterprises are established in Singapore. Many of them have based their regional headquarters in Singapore to cover their Southeast Asia portfolio — well-known firms like Xiaomi, Alibaba, Haier, Baosteel and Qingjian, to name a few.

As an international financial centre, Singapore offers Chinese corporates the necessary breadth and depth of banking and capital market services — from advice on regional markets to funding solutions.

A Trusted Financial Centre

The third key attribute for the success of Singapore's financial centre is trust. Financial institutions from all over the world come to Singapore because this is a jurisdiction they can trust. There is rule of law, clarity and consistency in regulation, rigour and fairness in supervision, and no tolerance for misconduct.

Upholding high standards of integrity in the financial industry is an absolute priority. This means having an effective regime against: market misconduct and misdemeanours; and illicit finance, namely money laundering and terrorism financing.

MAS is stepping up enforcement action against misconduct such as insider trading, false trading and front running by individuals and traders in the securities market. We have sought criminal actions or higher civil penalties to send the right deterrent message. In April last year, MAS imposed a civil penalty of close to $12 million for insider trading — the highest quantum in a single case so far.

When it comes to anti-money laundering and countering the financing of terrorism (AML/CFT), the rules are strict and in line with international standards. Financial institutions must know their customers; assess the risks and perform additional due diligence where the risks are higher; and monitor transactions on an ongoing basis and report any suspicious activities.

Supervision of financial institutions is rigorous. In recent years, MAS has stepped up its onsite supervision of AML/CFT controls — increasing the number of inspections by six-fold. This is resource-intensive business: each AML/CFT inspection of a bank takes about four to eight weeks and involves four to six supervisors.

We have now set up a dedicated AML Department. We will:

- make more robust risk assessments of financial institutions' business activities, client profiles, geographical connections, transaction volumes and quality of controls;
- intensify supervision of financial institutions that pose higher risks;

- conduct thematic inspections of activities that pose higher risk across financial institutions; and
- step up engagement with financial institutions to promote deeper understanding of emerging risks and typologies as well as best practices to mitigate these risks.

But MAS cannot inspect every bank every year. Nor can we go through all transactions. And we certainly do not set out to detect fraud — which would take months of intense scrutiny.

Responsibility for AML/CFT rests with the board and senior management of financial institutions. They must:

- put in place robust monitoring mechanisms to detect suspicious activities;
- promote strong risk awareness and constant vigilance among all staff; and
- empower their compliance and risk management people.

My advice to senior managers in our financial institutions is this: keep your risk and compliance people close to you. They are often seen as hindering opportunity and profits. But when things go wrong, you wish you had heeded them. When they say "I think something's not right here", listen to them.

Ultimately, trust and conduct boil down to culture more than any externally imposed rules. By culture, I mean the shared values, attitudes and norms that guide behaviour. Financial institutions must get the culture right.

This requires setting the right moral tone from the top. Boards and senior management in particular must send a clear signal that profits do not come before values and ethics. Compensation structures must motivate not just high performance but also right conduct.

Conclusion

Good fortune has played a role in the growth of Singapore's financial sector. Our financial centre has benefited from connecting one of the fastest growing regions in the world with global markets.

But fortune can be fickle and economic cycles will turn. To stay relevant and thrive as a financial centre requires us:

- to remain resilient through good times and bad;
- to be dynamic in serving the changing needs of the region; and at all times
- to be trusted as a clean and credible place to do business in.

MAS is committed to working with the industry and all our stakeholders — including an inquisitive and fair media — to ensure that.

A Flexible Framework for the Regulation of Payment Systems and Payment Service Providers

Mr Ong Ye Kung
Minister for Education and Board Member, MAS
Second Reading Speech in Parliament
Payment Services Bill
14 January 2019

Technology is transforming the world of payments. In particular, FinTech, or Financial Technology, has opened up opportunities for more convenient, faster and cheaper payments.

At the same time, new payment methods give rise to new risks. This has necessitated a review of our regulatory framework. Further, services that were previously provided separately and regulated separately are now merging.

MAS currently regulates various types of payment services under two Acts, first, the 2006 Payment Systems (Oversight) Act — or PS(O)A — and the 1979 Money-Changing and Remittance Businesses Act — or MCRBA. The Bill combines the PS(O)A and MCRBA into a single Payment Services Act.

The Payment Services Bill provides a forward looking and flexible framework for the regulation of payment systems and payment service providers in Singapore. It provides for regulatory certainty and consumer safeguards, while encouraging innovation and growth of payment services and FinTech. In drafting the Bill, MAS has taken reference from regulatory frameworks in various other financial centres — Australia, Hong Kong, Japan and the United Kingdom.

Overall Approach

Let me outline the broad approach underpinning the Bill.

First, we are adopting a regulatory structure that recognises the growing convergence across payment activities which I just mentioned. For example, payment and remittance services are now often provided as one product to customers.

Second, we are expanding MAS' regulatory scope to include more types of payment services, such as digital payment token services and merchant acquisition. The Bill includes provisions that level the playing field for banks and non-banks, and that enhance user protection.

Third, we have adopted a modular and risk-focused regulatory structure, so that our rules are tailored to the scope of services being offered by any provider. A modular approach gives MAS the flexibility to regulate payment service providers that offer one, two or more parts of the payments value chain. It also enables MAS to respond quickly to fast changing payment solutions and business models. A risk-based approach enables MAS to impose proportionate regulatory measures on each type of payment service provider, depending on the scale of their activities.

MAS has conducted public consultations on the Bill, and engaged extensively with the industry. It has been well received. MAS has considered all the feedback and, where appropriate, has taken them into account in preparing this Bill. Mr. Speaker, let me now take the Members through the key areas of the Bill.

Regulatory Frameworks for Designation and Licensing

The Bill comprises two regulatory frameworks: a designation regime and a licensing regime.

The designation regime enables MAS to designate significant payment systems, to ensure the stability and market efficiency of the financial system.

Designating payment systems for financial stability reasons is a power that is already provided for in the PS(O)A, and it will be retained. However, the Bill provides for an additional basis for designation, which is to ensure efficiency and competition in the financial system. This is because a payment system that becomes widely used and dominant can be used to shut out competition and new, innovative players. Hence for competition reasons, MAS can designate a payment system if it is widely used in Singapore, or its operations have an impact on the operations of other payment systems in Singapore.

The second framework is quite a complex one — it is a licensing regime to allow MAS to regulate a wide range of payment services in a manner that matches the scope and scale of services provided by each provider, and that can respond flexibly to market developments, as I have explained.

The services can be grouped into seven types: account issuance, domestic money transfers, cross-border money transfers, merchant acquisition, e-money issuance, digital payment token dealing and exchanges, and money-changing.

Service providers may offer different combinations of these services, and the licensing regime will regulate them according to the risks they pose.

Three Classes of Licences

MAS will not impose requirements uniformly across all licensed payment service providers. We will have three classes of licences — a licensee may be a money-changing licensee, a standard payment institution or a major payment institution. These three classes will be broad enough to deal with the different combinations of payment services that a service provider may offer. Each service provider needs to hold only one of the three licences. And in line with our risk-based approach, the regulatory requirements for each class of licence differ according to the risks posed by the scope and scale of services provided by the licensee.

This is how it will work:

a. First, money-changing licensees can provide only money-changing services. They will continue to be regulated under the Bill in largely the same way as it is under the existing MCRBA, as the attendant risks have not changed. The regulation is quite narrow in scope, as these are over-the-counter services often offered by small businesses such as sole proprietors, with limited risks.

b. Second, standard payment institutions may provide any combination of the seven defined payment services, but below specified transaction flow or e-money float thresholds. They will be regulated more lightly, and the regime mimics a "permanent sandbox" environment to encourage innovation and enterprise. So this is where FinTech companies will play.
c. Third, major payment institutions can go above the specified thresholds. As the scale of their operations would pose more risk, they will be subject to more regulation.

This new licensing regime is a more comprehensive and robust framework than what current legislation provides. We will be regulating new services, as well as expanding the scope of activities under the services we currently regulate.

Services that MAS will now be regulating are domestic money transfers, merchant acquisition, and digital payment token services. We will be among the first few financial services regulators in the world to introduce a regulatory framework for digital payment token services, or what are commonly understood as cryptocurrency dealing or exchange services. As we have stated in Parliament before, while there may be some potential in these digital payment token services, they also carry significant money laundering and terrorism financing risks or ML/TF risks due to the anonymous and borderless nature of the transactions they enable. Under the Bill, all providers of digital payment token dealing or exchange services in Singapore will have to meet anti-money laundering and counter financing of terrorism requirements — this is abbreviated "AML/CFT". So AML/CFT is to counter ML/TF. I will be using more of that later; so just to be clear.

We are also recognising new activities under the services we currently regulate. The definition of e-money in the Bill will go beyond stored value or pre-paid services, such as public transport cards, to include e-wallets — i.e., any monetary value that is held for future payment transfers between individuals or with corporates. This means that e-money issuers have an obligation to protect the value held in major e-wallets for consumers and merchants.

Further, under the Bill, we will regulate inward remittance services in addition to outbound remittance services that are currently regulated.

The Bill will also clarify that a person will be presumed to carry on a business of providing a payment service even where the payment service is only incidental to the person's primary business. The intent is to disapply the 2017 Singapore High Court decision in Chinpo Shipping Co (Pte) Ltd v. Public Prosecutor, which suggests that the undertaking of remittances that are purely incidental to a primary business of ship agency and ship chandelling would not have constituted the carrying on of a remittance business under the MCRBA.

Mitigating Key Risks in Payment Services

Mr. Speaker, I will now elaborate how the Bill will mitigate the four key risks that are common across many payment services: loss of customer monies; ML/TF risks; fragmentation and lack of interoperability across payment solutions and technology risks including cyber risks. Proper oversight of these risks will both protect the public and facilitate a vibrant payment services sector.

One key risk is that customer monies entrusted to payment service providers may be lost, such as when the service provider becomes insolvent. The Bill requires major payment institutions to safeguard customer monies from loss through the institutions' insolvency using any of the following means:

a. An undertaking or guarantee by any bank in Singapore or prescribed financial institution to be fully liable to the customer for such monies;
b. A deposit in a trust account; or
c. Safeguarding in such other manner as may be prescribed by MAS.

However, we also want to ensure that measures are not too onerous or stifling. That is why we adopted three classes of licences. For example, standard payment institutions are not subject to the safeguarding requirements for major payment institutions, but they must disclose this to their customers so that the customers can make informed decisions on which payment service or provider best suits their needs.

The second risk is that payment services may be used for ML/TF, such as through illicit cross-border transfers, anonymous cash-based payment transactions, structuring of payments to avoid reporting thresholds or the raising or layering of assets or funds for ML/TF purposes. MAS studies the business model of each payment service to determine where regulatory measures should be imposed. The appropriate AML/CFT requirements will be imposed on relevant licensees through Notices issued under the MAS Act. MAS will also provide guidance to the industry.

A third risk is that payment solutions in Singapore become fragmented. We have deliberately allowed many e-payment solutions to come on stream in Singapore. This provides choice for consumers but the downside is that it can also be confusing. MAS has been persuading the industry to undertake various measures to ensure that the solutions are interoperable, within an open architecture. For example, we worked with the banks to implement PayNow, to make instant payment transfers more convenient for consumers and businesses. So today I can use the PayNow feature from the app of one bank to pay someone who is banking with a different institution. And the money I transfer goes directly into his bank account and that is open architecture, interoperability at work. We also worked with the industry to introduce SGQR, which allows different e-payment schemes to be accepted via a single standardised and unified QR code.

This Bill will give MAS formal powers to ensure interoperability of payment solutions, in the interests of consumers and market development. The Bill will provide MAS with the powers to mandate the following outcomes:

a. One, a designated payment system operator or major payment institution must allow third parties to access any payment system it operates, and the access regime imposed must be fair and not discriminatory;
b. Two, a major payment institution must participate in a specified common platform or equivalent arrangement to achieve interoperability of payment accounts; and

c. Three, a major payment institution must adopt a common standard to make widely used payment acceptance methods interoperable.

MAS will exercise these powers judiciously. MAS will continue to employ its powers of persuasion with the payment players, before using its interoperability powers as a last resort.

Finally, technology risk. The Bill will give MAS powers to impose technology risk management requirements, including cyber security risk management requirements, on all licensees. We will require payment service providers to ensure there is adequate risk governance and implementation of adequate controls, particularly in areas such as user authentication, data loss protection and cyber-attack prevention and detection.

Right-Sizing Permissible Activities

Mr. Speaker, this Bill right-sizes regulations depending on the risks posed by the payment service provider. This means tailoring our regulations to the activities of the licensees, such as opening accounts, issuing e-money, transferring money within Singapore and overseas and providing e-payment solutions to consumers and merchants.

It must follow that if the licensees wish to do more, then they must be subject to more regulatory measures. Licensees therefore cannot engage in consumer lending or banking activities such as accepting deposits and granting loans, unless they hold the appropriate licence under the Banking Act or the Moneylenders Act.

Banks perform a vital economic function of intermediating savings. They take in deposits and on-lend these funds back into the economy to help it grow. To protect depositors' interests, banks are subject to much more stringent prudential regulation and supervision, such as on the amount of capital and liquid assets they must hold, how much concentration risk they can take and how they manage repayment risks and make provisions against these risks.

Non-bank payment service licensees do not perform similar economic functions, and do not face similarly stringent regulations. Accordingly, e-money issuers will not be allowed to on-lend any customer money or use any customer money to materially finance their own business activities.

Additionally, withdrawals of Singapore dollars will not be allowed from e-money accounts held by Singapore residents. This is consistent with the objective of the Bill, which is to promote greater adoption of electronic payments, in lieu of cash services. It will also preserve the privileges of our Free Trade Agreement partners, whose banks have been accorded access to ATMs and cashback services.

Finally, personal payment accounts will be subject to a stock cap, which is the maximum amount of funds that can be held in a personal payment account at any given time. They will also be subject to an annual flow cap. This is the maximum cumulative amount of yearly outflows from the personal payment account, other than to the user's designated bank accounts. The stock and flow caps were calibrated with due regard to consumer needs and existing industry practices, and will be set initially at $5,000 and $30,000 respectively. These caps will not apply to merchant payment accounts that cater to business uses.

These caps help to further protect customers by limiting a customer's potential loss from his e-money account. This also enables the e-money safeguarding measures to be simple and low-cost, different from deposit insurance that banks have to undertake.

More importantly, the caps will ensure continued stability of the financial system, by reducing the risk of significant outflows from banks deposits to non-bank e-money which can undermine the stability of our banks.

Conclusion

The Bill is a necessary piece in Singapore's Smart Nation journey. It will help us build a technologically robust smart financial centre, that preserves stability while facilitating innovation and growth in the payments landscape.

Mr. Speaker, I beg to move.

Singapore Parl Debates; Vol 94; Sitting No 87; 14 January 2019.

Banking Liberalisation's Next Chapter: Digital Banks

Mr Tharman Shanmugaratnam
Senior Minister and Chairman, MAS
46th Association of Banks in Singapore Annual Dinner
28 June 2019

Our Objectives in Liberalising Banking

I would like to talk this evening about our next steps in liberalising our banking system, and in taking advantage of the ongoing digital revolution in finance.

It will be a new phase in our banking system. But the spirit of what we intend to do, and the calibrated way in which we will move forward, is similar to the approach we have taken over the last 20 years, from the time we began liberalising the industry.

MAS embarked in 1999 on a major programme to open up and liberalise Singapore's financial sector across the board, in banking, our securities markets and in insurance.

We did so to ensure we remained a competitive and growing centre for finance in Asia and globally. But enhanced competition was also a way to spur our local banks themselves to upgrade and innovate so that they remained strong anchors in our banking system, and to expand into markets abroad.

We took a calculated risk. The risk was not trivial, as we began opening up in the midst of the Asian financial crisis. The changes in banking in particular had to be paced out, to ensure that confidence in our local banks and the system as a whole was not shaken, and to give the banks time to regear and to grow new capabilities.

The liberalisation of the banking industry to date has achieved its key objectives. Singapore is one of the leading financial centres in Asia, and plays an enhanced role in financing the region's growth. We have also retained a core of strong and increasingly innovative local banks, as anchors of the banking system. Critically, trust in our local banks and the MAS as regulator remains high. We have avoided the sharp decline in trust seen in many financial centres.

MAS has consistently held the view that banking systems need strong anchor players, competitive and well-supervised, who can take the long view and have interests closely aligned with both the growth and stability of the system as a whole.

- The experience of the global financial crisis and its aftermath vindicated our view. A common feature of jurisdictions with systemically important financial centres that held up well through the crisis — notably Canada, Singapore, Hong Kong and Australia — was the presence of a handful of strong anchor banks in each of their systems.

We have continued to liberalise the system, a decade after the first major steps that introduced Qualifying Full Banks (QFBs) and enhanced the space for wholesale banks.

- In 2012, we took steps to encourage foreign banks to deepen their roots in Singapore. MAS will allow a significantly rooted QFB to operate an additional 25 or up to 50 places of business, as part of an overall Free Trade Agreement package negotiated with the home countries of these QFBs.
- In September 2018, we announced that FinTechs and other non-bank financial institutions will be granted access to the Fast and Secure Transfers (FAST) network for real-time payments. This is a major step towards making our payments system open, accessible and competitive.

But we are in fact at the threshold of a further and more fundamental transformation in banking. The far reaching effects of digitalisation are stimulating a fundamental re-think of the role of banks, in most advanced financial centres. The ramifications go well beyond those ushered in by the technologies and business models of a decade or two ago.

We must take advantage of these opportunities that digital finance brings, and not be overtaken by the wave of changes taking place globally.

We must allow for greater competition and spur greater innovation in finance — competition between new and traditional business models, new players and incumbents and different ways of using technology to serve business and individual customers better. We must also retain strong local anchors and trust in the banking system. These dual objectives have guided our past liberalisation initiatives, and motivate our next moves.

As we embark on this new phase, however, it is worth reminding ourselves of our real purposes in finance. Innovation in finance is not an end in itself. And competition in finance has to be more than a zero sum game — it has sometimes looked like that, as trading desks compete against each other to be a fraction of a second faster and to knock the other out. Competition and innovation has to be aimed at serving the needs of society and the economy better, here in Singapore and abroad. So it is worth reminding ourselves of these larger purposes and opportunities. I will highlight five:

- First, financing the growth of infrastructure in emerging Asia, and increasingly of climate-resilient, low-carbon investments. Both banking and capital markets should seek to meet what is still a huge financing gap in the region for critical and sustainable infrastructure.
- Second, financing growth enterprises and small and medium-sized enterprises (SMEs). SMEs are the backbone of all our economies. Besides finding new ways to meet their financing needs, banks can also help to raise their productivity by helping them adopt digital services.

- Third, reducing costs and improving convenience for consumers. We are already seeing major changes here, especially in cheaper, more convenient and seamless payments.
- Fourth, in helping people to plan early and achieve financial security in their later years. Singapore has recently come up top in the world for life expectancy. It is to be celebrated, but it also increases the need for good financial advice, and for those with savings outside their Central Provident Fund (CPF) accounts to be able to invest in products that will help them achieve greater retirement security. This is in fact going to be a growing challenge in much of Asia too.
- Finally, creating good jobs. In Singapore, the financial industry employs close to 200,000 people, most of them in relatively well-paying jobs. Technology will replace many tasks and even whole jobs in finance. But with proactive upgrading of skills to keep pace with new technologies, and with the continuing growth of our financial centre, we must and will provide good jobs in finance for many years into the future.

How Finance Is Being Transformed

The digitalisation of finance is picking up pace, and will transform banking.

There are essentially three key forces driving this transformation: pervasive mobile internet access, the rise of big data and the growth of platform ecosystems as a major new business model in finance. The three forces are also reinforcing each other, and together transforming banking in more fundamental ways than we have seen before.

Smartphones and tablets are ubiquitous. Pervasive broadband access has coupled mobility with connectivity — so interaction is real-time and unconstrained by where you are. The smartphone is now our grocery store, our restaurant, our bank and much more.

Second, big data. We have unprecedented computing power, coupled with cloud technologies that allows us to store and retrieve large volumes of information at low cost and on-demand. Firms are also gathering a lot more data from a wide variety of sources, including social media and e-commerce platforms. Advanced data analytics and machine learning are allowing them to analyse this data to derive much richer insights into customers' financial needs. Incorporating big data into lending decisions, for example, can in fact help SMEs access finance more easily.

These first two forces — mobile connectivity and big data — have enabled the rise of platform ecosystems as a major new business model in finance. Armed with the goldmine of data generated by millions of connected users, these technology platforms are able to exploit huge network effects. They operate an ecosystem of diverse services, from retail to healthcare, savings to lending. They are providing integrated, end-to-end solutions, often customised to individual preferences. And the more users that engage with the platform ecosystems, and more extensively to meet their needs, the more data is generated. The platform ecosystems are using this competitive advantage to expand into new markets.

The march towards digitalisation is having a profound impact on consumers, who themselves have become a force for change. Younger or "digital-native" consumers have come to expect the same lower costs, greater convenience and more customisation from financial services as they already obtain from other services, from online shopping to transport to food delivery. The days when transferring a bit of money involved taking a brisk walk to the bank's branch during lunch hour are now a quaint memory.

Embracing a Digital Future with Strong Anchors

The changes we are already seeing in banking will very likely accelerate in the next 10 years. We must take advantage of these changes, and guard against the risks. Cyber risk is foremost among them, as cyber incidents are growing in number and sophistication in banking.

MAS welcomes the innovation and competition from new models. We are doing so while ensuring that we maintain the trust and stability that are the hallmarks of the Singapore banking system.

First, we have been working with the industry and other government agencies to put in place the enabling infrastructure to help banks to better harness the benefits of new technologies.

In payments, we have built up the national electronics payments infrastructure to provide instant, seamless digital payment services that is more convenient and intuitive to users.

- FAST allows fast and secure payments for both consumers and businesses.
- Building on the FAST infrastructure, we were able to introduce further initiatives such as PayNow, which allows real-time payment with the convenience and speed of mobile texting for the customers of all major retail banks, including the three local banks and six QFBs.[1]
- As mentioned, MAS has also announced that it will be working with the industry to open FAST access to non-bank players.

In customer identification, MAS has worked with the Ministry of Finance and the Government Technology Agency (GovTech) to introduce MyInfo for the financial industry.

- The MyInfo platform allows banks to more effectively and efficiently obtain authenticated and updated information for account opening and other applications, doing away with the tedium of manual physical authentication and resulting in time saving of as much as 80% for banks and their customers.

Second, we are reviewing our regulatory framework to balance the tension between encouraging innovation and managing risk.

- The Payments Services Act is a forward looking and flexible framework for the regulation of payment systems and payment service providers in Singapore. It gives regulatory certainty to new players to pursue innovation and growth, while at the same time providing sufficient safeguards for consumers.

[1] These include Bank of China, Citibank Singapore Limited, Hongkong and Shanghai Banking Corporation, Industrial and Commercial Bank of China, Maybank and Standard Chartered Bank.

Third, we are creating more channels to promote the exchange of ideas and collaboration among financial and technology firms.

- Since 2016, MAS has partnered industry players to bring together financial and technology players from all over the world in the week-long Singapore FinTech Festivals. Turnout has more than quadrupled over the past three years with 45,000 participants from 130 countries in 2018.
- It is early days yet, but the results of our efforts are encouraging. Singapore is widely regarded as one of the leading FinTech hubs in the world. A report by Ernst & Young finds that nearly seven out of 10 Singaporeans have made use of FinTech solutions in 2019, making us a leader in the Asia-Pacific region.

Another important development has been among our local banks themselves. They have been expanding their digital platforms to better cater to customers' needs, and grow markets abroad.

- They have partnered with FinTechs to harness the capabilities of new technologies and deliver more customised solutions. For example, United Overseas Bank (UOB) has partnered with Personetics to use artificial intelligence to identify individual transaction demands and enable UOB to provide customers with real-time and personalised guidance on their financial decisions.
- Second, they have built digital banks in overseas markets, leveraging a lower-cost operating model to quickly acquire new customers. For example, DBS launched digibank in India and managed to acquire over 2.5 million customers in its initial two years of operations. The bank has also recently replicated its digibank strategy in Indonesia. DBS was ranked by Euromoney as the world's best digital bank last year.
- Third, they have adopted more customer-centric approaches, integrating solutions for their financial and non-financial needs. For example, Oversea-Chinese Banking Corporation (OCBC) has built a niche marketplace to provide curated products and services

for mothers and their babies. The bank also launched the OCBC Silver Years programme to provide seniors a one-stop solution for financial advice, insurance products and lifestyle options.

Digital challengers with innovative business models can add diversity and choice to banking systems. They can often serve the needs of traditionally underserved segments, such as the credit gap faced by young and micro-enterprises. They could also bring with them deep digital know-how and insights from operating non-bank businesses.

- In China, for example, MYBank, has broadened financial inclusion, with 80% of its clients being first time borrowers like mom-and-pop shops. 99% of its customers repay on time.
- In Korea, Kakao Bank has in its first year of operations attracted more than six million users.

The success of our banking liberalisation to date gives us the confidence to manage the entry of digital banks in our next phase of liberalisation. In time, successful digital banks in Singapore can also complement the local banks in anchoring domestic financial stability.

New Digital Bank Licences to Facilitate New Business Models

Eligibility conditions

MAS will therefore issue up to five new bank licences to digital players that can add value to the Singapore banking sector and the economy. This is in addition to any digital banks that the local banking groups may also establish. The local banks are already allowed to set up standalone digital banks under our internet-only bank framework.

We welcome firms with innovative value propositions to apply for the new digital bank licences, even if they have not yet established a track record in banking. They may apply for a digital full bank licence or a digital wholesale bank licence, as follows.

MAS will issue up to two digital full bank licences, to companies headquartered in Singapore and controlled by Singaporeans. Foreign companies are eligible for these full bank licences if they form a joint venture with a local company, and the joint venture meets our headquarter and control requirements.

We are starting with two digital full bank licences, so as not to fragment Singapore's small domestic retail banking market. We are also restricting the new licences to players anchored in Singapore for two reasons. First, so that we maintain a strong local core in our banking system, which must remain our objective as I explained earlier. Second, to avoid an unintended unilateral liberalisation of our full bank regime as a result of our WTO commitments.

MAS will also issue up to three digital wholesale bank licences, which will be open to both local and foreign players. The digital wholesale banks will be introduced as a pilot, and MAS will review whether to grant more such licences in the future.

Safeguards

To ensure high-quality applicants, MAS will set prudent baseline requirements on track record and sustainability of business models. MAS will not allow value-destructive competition to the detriment of long-term financial system stability. We will also put in place safeguards to protect depositors, mitigate the risk of untested business models and minimise costs to the financial system in the event of a failure. We will also ensure that digital banks will compete with incumbents on a level playing field.

As digital full banks will have access to retail deposits, MAS will phase in their permissible activities via a two-stage process to minimise risks to retail depositors. It will also be required to be a member of the deposit insurance scheme.

- A digital full bank will commence as a restricted digital bank to build up its business model and internal processes, and gradually progress to become a full functioning full bank. MAS will not prescribe a time period within which graduation to a digital full bank must be achieved.

- When the restricted digital bank first commences operations, it will be subject to an initial deposit cap of $50 million, an individual depositor cap of $75,000 and generally be allowed to accept deposits from only a small group of depositors such as business partners, staff, related parties and selected customers.

MAS is prepared to award up to five new digital bank licences — two full and three wholesale. We will only award all five if the applicants meet the eligibility and admission criteria, including demonstrating a tangible proposition that is innovative and sustainable.

MAS is working on implementation details, and expects to invite applications in August this year.

Conclusion

Today in 2019, we are continuing the process of transforming our banking sector with a progressive opening to new digital banks. We are in a strong position to do so today, as local banks have responded well to changes in the competitive landscape and have in fact become leaders in some areas of innovation. I am confident that they will hold their own against the new competition. This new phase of banking liberalisation will add diversity and help strengthen the resilience of our banking system in a new digital era in finance.

FINANCIAL CENTRE DEVELOPMENT

Financial Centre Development

The speeches in this section provide an overview of Singapore's development as an international financial centre which Mr Tharman Shanmugaratnam has described as "an act of volition", or sustained, deliberate effort by MAS and the Singapore government working closely with the financial industry. The speeches cover the key asset classes of growth, such as offshore banking, foreign exchange, capital markets, and wealth management; as well as the key cross-cutting priorities of skills, technology, and sustainability.

Key Asset Classes of Growth

Singapore's development as an international financial centre began in 1968 with the establishment of the Asian Dollar Market (ADM). Leveraging on Singapore's favourable time zone between the close of US markets and opening of European markets, the ADM facilitated offshore US dollar borrowing and lending activity and substantial growth in foreign exchange trading in Singapore. The Singapore International Monetary Exchange (SIMEX) was set up in 1984 to enable investors to hedge interest and exchange rate risks with futures contracts.

In a 1972 speech, Mr Hon Sui Sen laid out the key policy thrusts to develop Singapore into a financial centre to serve the region. MAS would encourage reputable financial institutions to grow their presence in Singapore. To support an environment conducive to growth and innovation, MAS relaxed exchange controls and interest rate restrictions.

From the outset, MAS recognised that a highly skilled and professional workforce was critical to sustaining the growth of Singapore's financial centre. At the opening of the Institute of Banking and Finance (IBF) in 1976, Mr Hon stressed the importance of raising standards and capabilities and fostering a sense of professional pride and ethics.

In the 1990s and 2000s, MAS focused its attention on the development of capital markets, re-insurance, wealth and asset management activities. A vibrant financial ecosystem took root with a critical mass of reputable financial institutions across various asset classes and deep financial markets to serve the region, international businesses, and global investors.

Under the chairmanship of Mr Lee Hsien Loong, MAS made several policy shifts and strategic moves to position Singapore as one of the leading international financial centres of the world. In 1998, Mr Lee announced measures to grow the asset management industry, including streamlining the regulatory structure for fund managers and unit trusts and developing the equity and bond markets to tap the burgeoning demand for fund management products in the region.

That same year, Mr Lee announced the demutualisation and merger of the Stock Exchange of Singapore and SIMEX to form the Singapore Exchange, to exploit synergies between the cash and derivatives businesses and spur the development of the capital markets.

Mr Goh Chok Tong shared in 2009 his observations of key trends in the financial landscape as a result of the changes wrought by the global financial crisis and how Singapore's financial sector was in a good position to capture emerging opportunities, especially in helping to meet Asia's growing wealth management and infrastructure financing needs.

In 2013, observing the continued growth of the Asian economies and financial markets, Mr Shanmugaratnam encouraged the financial industry in Singapore to tap on regional opportunities, especially those presented by the growth and internationalisation of the Chinese renminbi.

Later that year, Mr Ravi Menon recounted Singapore's journey to become a leading reinsurance hub in Asia and the strategies going forward for Singapore's insurance industry to become a global marketplace.

Skills, Technology, Sustainability

Besides helping to develop various asset classes, MAS also played an active role in promoting cross-cutting priorities such as skills development of the financial industry; the adoption of technology in the industry and the growth of the FinTech ecosystem; and embedding sustainability and green finance as new capabilities in the financial sector.

MAS worked closely with IBF on the jobs and skills agenda for the financial sector. At IBF's 40th anniversary celebrations in 2014, Mr Shanmugaratnam reiterated the importance of developing strong workforce capabilities to take the financial industry into the future. These included deep functional expertise in specialised areas of finance; technological skills; leadership competencies; and adaptability to thrive in a rapidly changing environment.

In 2017, Mr Heng Swee Keat highlighted that harnessing technology was key to maintaining the competitiveness of Singapore's financial centre and outlined measures to position the financial sector for a technology-driven future.

Speaking at the third Singapore FinTech Festival in 2018, Mr Menon described the key components for a vibrant FinTech ecosystem: common standards, open architecture, inter-operable infrastructure, and strong public-private collaboration. He took stock of the progress that the financial industry had made in technological capabilities; infrastructure, for digital identity and electronic payments; data governance; applied research; and innovation platforms.

With climate change emerging as an existential threat, MAS saw green finance as a key enabler to support the global transition to a lower carbon future. Mr Ong Ye Kung outlined in 2019 how Singapore's financial sector could play a key role in catalysing Asia's decarbonisation efforts and become the leading hub for Green Finance in Asia.

In 2020, Mr Menon elaborated on MAS' Green Finance Action Plan to strengthen the financial sector's resilience to environmental risks; develop green financing solutions and markets; harness technology for trusted sustainable financing flows; and build knowledge and capabilities in sustainable finance.

Development of Singapore as a Financial Centre

Mr Hon Sui Sen
Minister for Finance and Chairman, MAS
International Chamber of Commerce Luncheon
5 May 1972

On a similar occasion last year, I had the opportunity in speaking of Singapore in the Seventies to draw attention to the likely development of two major characteristics in the economy in this decade. One was the developing situation in respect of employment where labour would become more and more of a scarce resource. The other was that the economy would move towards a greater involvement in regionalism. Both these characteristics emanate from the healthy growth of the economy during the past decade. Economic growth and to a large measure the consolidation of our economic position must change our policy perspectives. Whatever residual feelings of inequity some of your Members may have about a general application of the National Wages Council guidelines, I am sure that a policy of orderly and progressive wage increases after tripartite consultation and agreement is basically correct. The good employer in a tight labour market will find that it pays sometimes to err on the side of generosity. We should also now be pursuing more qualitative goals and be able to take a regional view. One of our main objectives in this decade will therefore be to evolve a meaningful economic role in the regional context and contribute towards the economic development of the region. Whilst careful and practical planning has within the past decade enabled us to build a more solid manufacturing base beneath the already flourishing commercial superstructure, we are intent within this decade to further develop and extend both base and superstructure to accommodate the great increase in economic activities which are required to service the region.

In planning our restructuring programme, we shall be greatly assisted by a dialogue between the public and the private sectors. In this connection, I am glad to note that stimulated by the remarks — I would not call it a challenge — which I made on the last occasion, your Chamber has now produced the interesting and comprehensive report entitled "Trade Programme for the Seventies" but ranging over a much wider economic area than merely trade. As I received the Report only two days ago and have not been able to do more than glance very briefly through it, I will not at this time comment upon it other than to say how grateful I am to the Chamber and in particular to all those responsible for the hard work of preparing the Report for giving us such a valuable insight into how the private sector views Singapore's economic development.

Mr Chairman, I do not propose today to speak in terms of plans and broad perspectives as I did last year, but will concentrate on one aspect only of Singapore's economy which we are planning for the Seventies — namely, the Development of Singapore as a Financial Centre.

Singapore, by virtue of its entrepot trading activities, has always had a traditional function in financing trade within the region. The policy question for the Seventies is how to add new dimensions in financial and allied activities in Singapore not only to service the region but even outside it — to develop Singapore into a sophisticated international financial centre, in the same way as the older established financial centres of the world located in Europe and the United States. Despite a world reduced considerably in size today by excellent communications, there could still be a need for new centres in other regions with different time zones. A financial centre could be developed in this region if an acceptable financial environment is combined with the availability of specific expertise which is in a better position to service the surrounding region. In Asia, Singapore now offers the best prospects for developing into a financial centre, if not for the whole of Asia, at least beyond the South East Asian or ASEAN region. The early development of a financial centre in Singapore would enable us at a later stage to complement any development of the Tokyo market.

The financial centre in Singapore must provide a comprehensive range of financial services to the surrounding region. It is necessary therefore to promote the establishment of sophisticated financial institutions of all types and the speedy growth in the size and depth of money, capital, gold, securities and exchange markets. It would mean also that certain changes must be made in a number of banking and financial practices to which the financial community here has been accustomed. In short, the environment has to be made conducive to both growth and innovation in financial activities.

The Monetary Authority, in consultation with the Ministry of Finance, has now formulated plans to nurse the growth and development of the financial markets. Some measures have already been taken. The Government will create the conditions for markets to flourish leaving the actual development largely to private enterprise, local, overseas or in joint ventures.

The Asian Dollar Market mirrors Singapore's potential as a financial centre. The first syndicated Asian dollar bank credit made to the Private Investment Company for Asia (PICA) and the issue of an Asian Dollar Bond by the DBS signified an important development of the market. Yesterday, the US$27.5 million consortium loan to Brunei LNG Limited took that development further forward. We anticipate that this development marks the beginning of more bonds issues and loan flotations in the market to be made by international corporations operating in the region. We hope that in due course, international organisations like the World Bank and the Asian Development Bank will also consider floating bonds in this market.

Originally, when we authorised banks to operate Asian Currency Units, they were required to maintain a 20% liquidity ratio. On 1 January 1972, this requirement was abolished so as to bring the Asian Dollar Market in line with the Eurodollar market and thereby enable our banks to be competitive.

There has also been a measure of liberalisation in exchange control. Applications by resident companies to borrow from the Asian Dollar Market have been permitted, particularly in the case of export-oriented industries. Furthermore, the Monetary Authority will begin to consider applications by insurance companies, approved provident and pension funds who may in future be permitted to invest up to 10% of their funds in the Asian Dollar Market and certain specified Asian Dollar Bonds. Every encouragement will be given to institutions who can assist in the development of both the primary and secondary markets in Asian Dollar Bonds.

It is also our intention to maintain a liberal attitude in the licensing of more Asian Dollar Market participants. Naturally such participants must be of absolutely first class financial standing and reputation.

High priority is also accorded to the creation of an active and sophisticated domestic and regional money market. I announced in my Budget Statement the abolition of stamp duty on bills of exchange and certificates of deposit. This is to encourage the growth of an acceptance market and a secondary market in negotiable certificates of deposits denominated both in Singapore and in Asian Dollars. A discount market set up on the lines of the London discount house system will be in operation soon and the Monetary Authority will foster the growth of the market by providing "lender of last resort" facilities to discount houses. In addition, the Government is considering the issue of Treasury Bills of varying maturities, and short-dated bonds to increase the volume and variety of money market instruments.

Consideration is also being given to measures to create a more active foreign exchange market. As a first step, the foreign exchange limits of banks have been liberalised to give flexibility to them to engage in more active foreign exchange trading on their own account. The Monetary Authority is also working towards a more active intervention policy.

In order to develop the financial markets to their full potential, a number of changes will have to be made in the existing financial infrastructure. Commercial banks have been operating under a system of fixed rates regulated by the Association of Banks. There are fixed maximum rates of interest for deposits and a fixed minimum rate to be charged for loans and advances. Rates for foreign exchange transactions are also uniformly fixed. Whilst these arrangements have served the purpose of imparting a degree of stability into the banking system in the past, I believe that their rigidity is inimical to the growth of expertise and the development of financial markets. I suggest to our bankers that this is a matter which should be reviewed to see if we can move to a more flexible situation where banks operating in Singapore would be free to quote competitive rates on deposits. The cartel agreement on exchange rates should also be examined as the practice has discouraged the development of the skills and expertise necessary for the development of an active foreign exchange market. The authorities will play their part by encouraging the establishment of exchange, money and deposit broking companies. We have already given approval for one such company to be established. It also appears that foreign exchange brokerage rates will have to be reduced considerably to be internationally competitive. I hope that the Association of Banks instead of perpetuating restrictive banking practices will rise to meet the demands of modern banking and finance by channelling its efforts into providing banking and financial expertise necessary for a sophisticated financial centre. I hope also that the Association will pick up the hints which I have perhaps too gently dropped from time to time to its members, that they could play a major role in the establishment of a reputable banking training centre to fill a domestic and regional need.

The growth of the gold market has enhanced Singapore's position as a financial centre and encouragement is being given to its further development. The Monetary Authority is looking into the feasibility of the creation of a wholesale market for transactions in standard size bars and the establishment of a possible market in forward gold transactions.

The capital market will be broadened and deepened. The Government is considering the flotation of loan stocks of varying maturities to stimulate the market for fixed interest securities. Public authorities at the appropriate time may be encouraged to obtain their financing requirements by floating bonds in the market. The Monetary Authority, for example, will be liberalising the exchange control regulations to allow companies resident in Singapore but controlled by non-sterling area residents to borrow freely in the domestic market. The development of the domestic market will run parallel to the market for bonds denominated in foreign currencies such as Asian dollars issued by foreign corporations operating in the region or even by local borrowers.

To enable Singapore to provide the wide range of financial services to the surrounding region and beyond, favourable consideration will be given to financial institutions with international connections to set up offices in Singapore. Merchant banking activities have started in Singapore and though some are at present domestically oriented, a number of applications have been received which have wider, regional, operations in mind. It is hoped that merchant banks will in time tap the potential for regional financing instead of being geared heavily to the Singapore economy. Other institutions being encouraged are international firms of stockbrokers, money and deposit brokers and insurance companies with the capacity to develop regional and inter-regional activities.

I have outlined our plans and policies to develop Singapore into a centre for financial activities to service the surrounding region. The Government will do the spadework and prepare the ground but our efforts would have to be matched by private enterprise. As is evidenced from the wide ranging recommendations in banking and finance in your Report on "Trade Programme in the Seventies", the International Chamber of Commerce which represents international and overseas business in Singapore with wide financial business and commercial interests in the region should, I think, enthusiastically respond to our policy initiatives. I confidently expect that the development of a sophisticated financial centre in Singapore will facilitate the flow of trade and investments and promote the economic development of Singapore, of the surrounding region and of the world.

Inauguration of the Institute of Banking and Finance

Mr Hon Sui Sen
Minister for Finance and Chairman, MAS
Official Opening of the Institute of Banking and Finance
30 April 1976

In the last few years, we have witnessed a period of unprecedented growth in the banking and finance industry in Singapore. There are now 70 banks, 36 finance companies, 21 merchant banks and 38 representative offices in Singapore.

We have obviously travelled quite a long way towards our objective of establishing ourselves as a major financial centre. However, notwithstanding the progress in the past, the end is not yet in sight. Banking is an ever expanding business, with increasingly more complex financial transactions. Many of our banks have been extensively reorganised to adjust to the changing business environment.

To keep pace with such expansion and, indeed, even to maintain our present position, we need also to have a continuing programme for manpower planning and development.

Thus the setting up of the Institute of Banking and Finance (IBF) is both timely and crucial. To maintain the level of efficiency necessary to match our growth, we must develop greater professionalism.

My choice of the term "professionalism" is deliberate. In a profession, practitioners have not only to be proficient but also to maintain at all times high standards of ethics and integrity. A certificate of attendance at a training institution does not automatically make the trainee a banker, whether of the commercial, merchant or other variety. Nor for that matter, does the possession of recognised degrees or diplomas. It is only when the trainee puts into practice what he has learned and, more important, when he has acquired the standards the profession calls for that he can call himself a banker.

We have just emerged from the worst recession since the Great Depression of the Thirties and right now, there are still debates on how it happened. One major cause has been stated as too much liquidity provided by the banking system. Whatever faults the system may have made, there is no doubt that it has been under strain over the last few years. In the pursuit of growth and profits, the traditional standards of prudence, ethics and common-sense may have been sacrificed far too often by some errant members of that system, though happily not in Singapore.

Now that we are coming out of the recessionary cycle, we shall be looking again to the banking and finance industry to lubricate the wheels of the economy. It has therefore a responsibility beyond the confines of routine banking and it is to be hoped that in furthering the interests of their own financial institutions, bankers should not forget their other responsibilities.

I am given to understand that during the short space of five months, the IBF has completed more than 20 courses, organised several talks and seminars, implemented a survey of training requirements in the financial community and started on its publication programme. This is indeed highly commendable. In view of what I have said previously about errant bankers under the pressures of the last few years, it may not be too early for the IBF to attempt yet another task — that of fostering a sense of professional pride, ethics and standards in its members. The job is difficult, more difficult than merely imparting banking knowledge and techniques. But it is necessary to be done for banking's future development. And there is no better place to start than in the classroom.

The IBF must also keep abreast of modern methods of manpower development and training, and learn especially from the successful experience of other similar institutes around the world. At the same time, the IBF will need also to work closely and in parallel with our local institutions of higher learning to ensure that there will be suitably trained graduates to meet the ever growing needs of the financial industry. In the final analysis, the level of expertise of our banking manpower will influence our future position in the financial world. And the task of ensuring that the highest standards of skill and ethics are realised will fall upon all our training institutions collectively. I have no doubt that both the IBF and our tertiary institutions will be equal to the challenge facing them.

And now it gives me great pleasure to declare the Institute of Banking and Finance officially open.

Fund Management in Singapore: New Directions

Mr Lee Hsien Loong
Deputy Prime Minister and Chairman, MAS
Investment Management Association of Singapore Seminar
26 February 1998

Introduction

I am happy to address this seminar jointly hosted by the Investment Management Association of Singapore (IMAS) and the Stock Exchange of Singapore (SES). This is the first major public event organised by IMAS. It takes place at a significant moment, both externally and domestically. The region is facing its most serious economic crisis since the 1960s. In Singapore, we are reviewing our policies and strategies towards the financial sector, to make Singapore a key financial centre in an increasingly dynamic and competitive global environment.

Over the last few months, MAS has worked intensively with industry players and other Government agencies to review the regulatory framework and formulate strategies to develop specific industries within the financial services sector. Last week, the Government responded to Mr Peter Seah's Finance and Banking Sub-Committee Report. We accepted nearly all the recommendations, other than those involving tax issues.

This is only part of our review of the financial sector. In parallel with the Finance and Banking Sub-Committee, MAS had set up a group led by Mr Tharman Shanmugaratnam to study in detail the fund management industry. The group has drawn on the views of the Finance and Banking

Subcommittee, IMAS and numerous fund managers. The group has proposed a set of strategies for developing the industry, which MAS has accepted. I shall outline the key strategies today. But first let me touch on the regional economic crisis and its implications for our financial sector.

Implication of the Regional Crisis

The financial turmoil in Asia has yet to run its course, but some lessons are already clear. The crisis confirms the importance of our long-standing fundamentals. But it also points to potential risks that we have to manage as we further liberalise and open our system to more competition and external influence.

We must continue to maintain macroeconomic stability. This means pursuing sound fiscal and monetary policies, spending prudently within our means and keeping inflation low. But this crisis has shown that macroeconomic stability alone is not quite enough. The Asian countries' fiscal positions were on average much better than the OECD economies. Inflation rates were mostly as good as or only slightly higher than the OECD average. Yet a crisis was precipitated.

The problem was not so much wrong macroeconomic policy as structural and institutional weaknesses. These weaknesses caused resources to be misallocated to unproductive purposes. Fixed exchange rates and easy access to foreign capital encouraged financial institutions to borrow foreign funds at low interest rates, and expand domestic credit excessively. When economic conditions turned, borrowers could not repay, credit quality deteriorated and domestic banking and financial institutions were severely weakened. Tighter regulation and supervision of the financial sector might have pre-empted this breakdown of the financial intermediation process.

In Singapore, rigorous regulation has helped to prevent excessive credit growth and risk concentrations, and the build-up of large unsustainable positions that could endanger the whole financial system. The strong capitalisation of our financial institutions has been a valuable buffer, helping them to absorb problems in their loans and investments to the region.

Liberalisation does not mean lowering supervisory standards. Indeed, as we review our regulations to allow market players greater room to innovate and take risks, we must strengthen our supervisory system further. Regular on-site examination of financial institutions will become an important part of our supervisory framework.

The crisis has also shown the risks involved when countries and companies raise funds from global financial markets. Financial institutions need to constantly review and update their internal risk control mechanisms, to keep up with changes in external conditions and business strategies. Countries need to build better systems to assess and manage these risks. Governments should track foreign borrowing by financial institutions and companies, and assess how vulnerable they are to changes in external factors under various scenarios.

Disclosure standards of countries, financial institutions and companies must all be raised. Lack of transparency about the operations and exposure of financial institutions was a major factor which first allowed a dangerous situation to develop, and then aggravated the crisis of confidence when problems emerged. Investors who do not know enough fear the worst. The result is herd behaviour and market over-reaction.

Nevertheless, all these precautions cannot guarantee that a similar economic crisis will not recur sometime in the future. Manias, panics and crashes are intrinsic to financial markets. But the precautions will make a recurrence less likely, and perhaps if it does happen again make it less disastrous.

The ongoing crisis should not cause us to slow down our reform and developmental efforts. Rather, we must take this opportunity to build on our strengths to further enhance our role as a financial centre. We should look beyond the current problems, and prepare ourselves now so that we can prosper together with the region again when it recovers.

Longer-Term Prospects

Fund management is one activity with good potential when the region picks up again. We do not expect quick results in the current climate. Fund managers and investors have reduced their Asian exposures and are not in a hurry to build them up again. A few are cutting back on staffing. The total volume of Asian fund mandates has declined since the middle of last year, and may well shrink further. But the longer-term trends give cause for optimism.

First, global demand for fund management services will increase significantly over the next 20 years. Working adults in the US, Europe and Japan are increasingly investing their retirement savings in professionally managed funds that are more diversified globally and offer higher risk-adjusted returns than traditional investments.[1]

Second, East Asia has strong potential once again to grow faster than the developed countries when it gets back on its feet. The high savings rates, the drive for education, the dynamism sparked off by China's economic reforms, will continue. Growth will once again create attractive investment opportunities. Mutual funds and institutions in the US and Europe will want Asian assets in their portfolios, even if they invest more judiciously than before.

Third, American and European fund management companies are locating their investment teams across the globe, to be nearer to the markets they invest in and to interact more actively with their clients. Asian clients want direct access to investment managers based in Asia. Our time zone offers scope for at least two major fund management centres.

Singapore started actively promoting fund management in the early 1990s. Since then the industry has grown strongly.[2] But still it manages only a small fraction of the funds sourced from Asia or invested in Asia. Only 10 fund management companies here manage more than $3 billion. We need to attract more internationally reputable fund management companies to establish here. We will encourage those already here to expand their operations. We will also provide room for indigenous fund

---

1 According to some estimates, US pension and mutual funds will invest more than US$2 trillion outside the US over the next 10 years. The deregulation of the Japanese corporate pension fund industry could release an additional US$100 billion over the next few years.

2 Total funds managed here at the end of last year amounted to $123 billion, compared to $18 billion in 1990. The number of fund management companies almost tripled from 58 in 1990 to 157 in 1997.

managers, including boutique firms, to grow.

Our vision is to develop Singapore into the premier fund management hub in Asia over the next 5–10 years. We start with well known advantages: our reputation as a safe haven, our record of political stability and macro-economic soundness, our well-established airlinks, telecommunications network and IT infrastructure. But we also face some natural constraints: a small domestic market, and distance from the major investment markets of America and Europe.

Our target is therefore twofold. First, to become a centre for managing the Asian investment portfolios of both Asian and Western clients. And second, to manage global investments of clients in Asia. The industry is already developing in this direction.[3]

Regulatory, institutional and policy weaknesses have held us back from realising our full potential. Our strategies for developing the fund management industry focus on these areas.

Strategies

Improve Regulation

First, we will improve and streamline the regulatory structure for fund managers and unit trusts. Fund management companies are exposed to lower risks than securities companies, and therefore generally need less capital. But our financial criteria for obtaining an Investment Adviser's (IA) licence are set too high. This has kept smaller but well-managed fund management companies of good repute out of Singapore.

We can relax the financial requirements to qualify for an IA licence without compromising prudential standards. MAS will reduce the minimum shareholders' funds required for an IA licence from $500 million to $100 million. It will also lower the minimum amount of global funds

[3] In 1990, funds sourced from American and European investors accounted for less than 13% of total funds under management. By 1997, this had grown to almost half. At the same time, the importance of America and Europe as a destination for funds managed here has declined relative to the ASEAN countries. In 1990, 29% of total funds managed were invested in the US and Europe, while the ASEAN economies accounted for less than 6%. By 1997, US and Europe bonds and equities accounted for only 11%, while ASEAN bonds and equities had grown to 21%. This clearly reflects Singapore's growing role as a base for investing funds sourced from America and Europe in the Asian region.

that the parent company must manage from $5 billion to $1 billion. However, the admission criteria in terms of track record, management expertise and licensing status will remain.

Firms that fall below the threshold, but whose managements have established a strong track record and shown that they can contribute to the development of the industry in Singapore, will also be considered for IA licences by the MAS. This is especially to help some of our indigenous boutique firms to grow. In time, a few may develop into larger players. Perhaps not on the scale of Alliance Capital, Templeton, Fidelity or Warren Buffet's Berkshire Hathaway, but those too all started off as small firms. We should support talented fund managers who venture forth to startup on their own, and not subject them to onerous conditions.

At the same time, we must strengthen supervision of the fund management industry. We need to verify that IAs comply with securities regulations and disclose their activities to investors fully and accurately. MAS already has the authority to inspect IAs. But hitherto it has concentrated on inspecting banks rather than IAs because of lack of manpower. MAS will undertake on-site inspection of IAs, and build up its inspection capabilities to cope with the additional workload.

For unit trusts, we will make our regulatory requirements and approval procedures more transparent. For instance, guidelines for trust deeds and prospectuses are currently issued as administrative requirements. We will give legal effect to these requirements by amending the relevant sections of the Companies Act and Companies Regulations.

Currently, the Registry of Companies and Businesses (RCB) approves unit trusts, with MAS giving its input on policy matters. Yet fund managers deal only with the RCB, and not MAS. If the issue is not legal or procedural but arises from MAS' policy requirements, RCB has to refer it back to MAS. The industry is not aware of these arrangements. This has caused some confusion and delayed the processing of applications.

We will make MAS' role in reviewing trust deeds and prospectuses more transparent. Documents will be sent simultaneously to MAS and RCB. MAS will discuss any queries it has directly with fund managers and their lawyers. RCB will continue to approve unit trusts under the Companies Act, but eventually we will transfer the statutory responsibility for regulating unit trusts to MAS, so that the agency setting the policy is also charged with implementing it.

It currently takes 2–3 months to process applications to launch unit trusts. The industry has told us that Hong Kong is much faster. Through these measures, we aim to cut down the processing time to 4–6 weeks, as recommended by the Finance and Banking Sub-Committee.

We will also free up the current restrictions on regular savings plans (RSPs). RSPs are an optional feature in some unit trusts. The subscriber commits a certain capital sum which is paid in monthly instalments. Currently, we require the monthly contributions and total ongoing investment in RSPs to exceed a certain minimum figure. By removing these limits, we will level the playing field for lower-income investors and further promote the fund management industry.

Place Out More GIC Funds

Next, GIC will place substantially more funds with private fund managers based in Singapore. Ultimately, the growth of our fund management industry depends on overseas funds. But having a sizeable core of domestic funds to manage will help attract major international fund management companies to make Singapore their regional centre. The domestic funds will provide these companies an initial source of business and encourage them to invest in infrastructure, build up their teams and expand.

Since 1994, GIC has been placing out more funds to private fund managers with offices in Singapore. So far, it has placed out a total of $10 billion. GIC has reviewed the progress. It has made a policy decision to step up the pace significantly, and place out a larger proportion of its funds to external fund managers.

Specifically, GIC aims to farm out up to 50% of its Asian portfolios to private fund managers. Almost all of this will be placed with fund managers who have Singapore offices. The extent to which GIC's target is met will depend on how well these fund managers perform and how much they contribute to the development of the industry here.

In the next three years, GIC will increase the amount placed out to fund managers with Singapore offices from $10 billion to $35 billion. This will comprise both global and regional mandates. Not all of this need be managed from their Singapore offices. But we would expect fund managers receiving GIC mandates to bring in additional funds to Singapore for management, to meet MAS' development objectives. They should bring in talent to Singapore, as well as build up their team of Singaporean fund managers. Those receiving global mandates should involve their Singapore-based managers in the global investment process, and give them responsibility for the Asian investment portfolio.

The total volume of funds managed out of Singapore will probably not expand much over the next year or two. But the incentive of additional funds from GIC should encourage firms to shift funds to Singapore and moderate any downturn.

Liberalise the CPF Unit Trust Scheme

Our third strategy is to further liberalise the CPF Unit Trust Scheme, and encourage CPF members to invest in professionally managed funds. This will increase the pool of domestic funds available for professional management.

In October 1994, the Senior Minister announced a set of measures to promote the fund management industry and allow CPF members to invest their savings in CPF-approved unit trusts. But the response from CPF members has been modest. They have so far invested only $400 million in CPF-approved unit trusts and discretionary fund management accounts. This is despite successive relaxation of the rules for CPF-approved unit trusts, most recently in January.

One reason the scheme has not been popular is that Singaporeans prefer to punt individual stocks on their own, rather than entrust their money to professional managers. Unfortunately the record shows that few individual punters make money. This is a process of education, as people learn by experience and gradually become older and wiser. The industry should mount programmes to encourage CPF account holders to use professional managers to diversify risk rather than invest in individual stocks themselves.

Another reason is that CPF-approved unit trusts have generally not performed well. In fact, on average they have done worse than non-CPF unit trusts. Fund managers have told us that one reason is that the CPF investment limits for fund managers are too restrictive, and prevent them from diversifying their portfolios properly to maximise risk adjusted returns. This is probably also why few fund managers have applied to set up CPF-approved unit trusts.

We have reviewed the CPF Unit Trust Scheme with the help of the industry. We will modify it as follows:

a. First, we will widen the selection of CPF-approved fund managers, so as to offer CPF investors more choice.
b. Second, we will rewrite the investment guidelines for CPF unit trusts, to give fund managers the flexibility they need to diversify their portfolios. We will remove the current caps on asset types and foreign investments, restrictions on the universe of permitted foreign markets and strict liquidity requirements. Instead we will require CPF unit trusts to diversify their portfolios in order to reduce portfolio risk. We will allow them to invest in a wider range of assets, excluding only risky instruments like unlisted shares.
c. Third, we will raise disclosure standards so that CPF investors can compare the performance and charges of different unit trusts and fund managers, and make informed decisions.

We are now finalising the changes and will announce the revised CPF Unit Trust rules within two months.

Enhance Distribution Channels

Our fourth initiative is to enhance distribution channels for unit trusts. The network for marketing and distributing unit trusts and fund management products in Singapore is inadequate. The extensive branch and ATM networks of local banks and POSBank are not being fully exploited to benefit investors or the fund management industry. Foreign fund managers based in Singapore have found it particularly difficult and expensive to distribute their unit trusts.

Improving distribution channels will give investors a wider choice of unit trusts. It will promote competition among financial institutions, and drive fees lower. MAS will therefore permit foreign fund managers in Singapore to market their products to Singapore investors through local financial institutions, including POSBank.

In the US, banks use their branch networks to distribute a wide range of third-party funds. Our banks should view asset management and distribution as separate businesses, and treat client servicing and the marketing of third-party funds as a source of revenue in its own right. Some banks are already starting to do this.

MAS will evaluate the foreign fund manager's contribution to Singapore's financial sector, and whether it is adequately regulated by its home supervisory authority, in deciding whether to allow it to sell its products through the local banks. But it is up to each local bank to decide what unit trust it wants to distribute, and whether to recommend a unit trust to its customers. And of course it is up to individual investors to decide for themselves, given full information, whether to buy a unit trust.

We also need to develop a class of independent investment consultants in Singapore to service institutional clients, both local and overseas. They will add depth and professionalism to the fund management industry. In the US and UK, most institutional investors have independent consultants to advise them on how to allocate their assets, which fund managers to place their money with and how to measure and evaluate performance. In so doing they provide a channel for fund managers to market their services. Some of the consultants manage a fund of funds, which provides an additional vehicle for corporate clients to diversify their investments.

Retail customers in the UK and Hong Kong are also advised by independent advisors on which unit trusts to purchase. We should develop this sub-industry so as to serve the investing public better and reduce marketing and distribution costs for unit trust managers. Our stockbrokers are beginning to play a role in distribution of unit trusts. They can be among the key players in this regard.

Develop Equity and Bond Markets

A fifth area of focus is to develop a broad range of domestic investible instruments. Fund management companies seek financial centres that have deep and broad capital markets offering a wide array of instruments. We are currently studying ways to develop our equity and debt capital markets so as to make Singapore the leading corporate funding centre in the region.

In equity markets, we will continue to promote the listing and trading of international securities in Singapore, especially regional securities. We need to attract foreign listings, because Singapore's small base limits the growth potential of domestic listings. MAS is reviewing the rules governing the listing of foreign companies on SES. The SES Review Committee and the Corporate Finance Committee are also studying these issues.

In bond markets, the longest maturity Singapore Government Bond is now seven years. MAS will issue a 10-year Singapore Government Bond, to further develop the long end of our benchmark yield curve. Statutory boards will issue bonds to finance infrastructure projects, particularly statutory boards with major infrastructural responsibilities like Land Transport Authority (LTA) and Jurong Town Corporation (JTC). We are also considering measures to promote secondary market trading.

Foster a Strong Private Sector Role

Finally, we encourage a strong private sector role in promoting the fund management industry. IMAS is well placed to do this. Our study of the industry has benefited from valuable inputs from IMAS members. IMAS should continue to be an effective channel for such feedback, raising the industry's concerns to us and suggesting ways to improve the regulatory or fiscal environment.

IMAS can play a central role in helping to raise professional standards among fund managers. It should formulate an industry Code of Ethics that matches the best practice internationally. This will set the standard of ethical conduct in areas like compliance arrangements, fiduciary duties and disclosure of conflict of interest to clients.

IMAS and MAS can work closely together to design and run training programmes to produce a steady stream of high quality professionals for the industry. Fund management is a people business highly dependent on knowledge, skills and experience. The industry has often complained of the shortage of skilled local professionals, which forces them to import expensive foreign talent, pushing up operating costs. While we must continue to attract foreign talent who provide valuable specialist knowledge and expertise, we should also do more to groom promising local talent.

IMAS can also help to educate the public. It can organise investment fairs and seminars to educate the man in the street about the merits of collective, professionally managed investment schemes. It can also collate data on investor preferences, which will help fund managers to tailor their products. Where possible, IMAS should pool resources with the SES to avoid duplication.

Use Tax Incentives

One strategy that I have not touched upon is to use tax incentives to promote fund management. This is not an oversight. We are studying the matter. We already have various tax incentives for this purpose, but they can be further improved and enhanced. When we decide on any changes, we will announce them.

Conclusion

These initiatives to promote the fund management industry are designed to bear fruit over the next 5–10 years. We must not underestimate the current difficulties in the region. But the region will recover, and long-term investors will come back. And when they do, we will be well positioned to ride the next wave.

Building a Premier Exchange

Mr Lee Hsien Loong
Deputy Prime Minister and Chairman, MAS
25th Anniversary Dinner of the Stock Exchange of Singapore
4 November 1998

Introduction

I am very happy to join you this evening to celebrate the Silver Jubilee of the Stock Exchange of Singapore (SES).

The SES has come a long way from the Clifford Trading Rooms of the old Malayan Stock Exchange, and its subsequent premises in Clifford Centre, to the fully-electronic exchange now housed at The Exchange building. It has established a reputation in Singapore and abroad as an exchange where rules are upheld, investor rights are protected and transparency and integrity prevail. It has played a full role in developing Singapore's capital market and corporate sector, and proven resilient in weathering the regional economic storm. Over 370 companies are listed on SES' mainboard and SESDAQ, with a current total market capitalisation of $300 billion — 190% of Singapore's GDP.

Full credit must go to the successive SES Committees and management, whose professionalism and dedication have made this possible. I should especially mention the President of SES, Mr Lim Choo Peng, who has been with the SES throughout its 25 years. He has been instrumental in making the SES one of the first fully-electronic equities exchanges internationally, and in the continuous upgrading of the SES' trading and settlement systems to keep pace with advances in IT.

The question is how the SES can continue progressing. There is no simple answer. The Hong Kong Stock Exchange can always tap on and service the huge mainland Chinese corporate market. But the SES is in a different position. It therefore needs to take bold innovative steps to break through to a higher growth trajectory.

Reviews of Singapore's Capital Markets

One major focus of our financial sector review has been to develop strategies to broaden and deepen Singapore's capital markets. We set up two private sector committees to review our capital markets — the Corporate Finance Committee chaired by Mr Lim Yong Wah, and the SES Review Committee chaired by Mr Lim Hua Min.

The Corporate Finance Committee has submitted its final report. Its thrust is to shift from merit-based regulation to a predominantly disclosure-based regime, streamline our regulatory framework and improve our rules and regulations. Key recommendations include instituting a comprehensive legal obligation to disclose, consolidating securities laws and rules into a single piece of legislation, publishing regulatory policies and interpretations to facilitate appeals and empowering the regulator to take civil action in the public interest against companies which have failed to comply with rules, thus causing losses to investors. The Government has accepted all the recommendations of the Corporate Finance Committee, which will be publishing its Report next week.

Earlier, the Government had also accepted most of the recommendations of the SES Review Committee to liberalise stockbroking commissions, and progressively open access to the exchanges.

The SES Review Committee highlighted the need to fundamentally review the governance structure of the SES before we open up access. We therefore set up a third committee, the Committee on Governance of the Exchanges (CGE), to follow up on this basic issue for both our exchanges, SES and Singapore International Monetary Exchange (SIMEX), so as to keep them competitive. The CGE comprises MAS officers, SES and SIMEX members, the Presidents of the two exchanges, capital market participants and corporate lawyers. They have worked intensively over the last two months. The Government has accepted their recommendations. I shall outline our plans for the two exchanges arising from this review.

Global Forces Driving Change

Both SES and SIMEX have done well despite the regional crisis. On the SES, trading volume has held up despite the removal of Malaysian shares from Clob International. On SIMEX, this year's volumes of most key contracts are already at all-time highs. In a static environment, both would probably continue to hold their own when the economy picks up and the region recovers. But exchanges worldwide are finding themselves in an increasingly globalised and competitive environment.

Leading US and European equity and derivatives exchanges are competing furiously to link up into international networks, in order to combine liquidity pools, lower trading costs and become the dominant player. Almost daily there have been press reports of exchanges linking up in London, Frankfurt, Paris, New York or Chicago. Equity and derivatives exchanges are merging to develop complementary products, provide more integrated trading facilities and share overheads. Examples include the Deutsche Borse, Paris Bourse, Amsterdam Stock Exchange, Stockholm Stock Exchange and Tokyo Stock Exchange. Most recently, NASDAQ bought the American and Philadelphia stock exchanges to acquire new capabilities in equity-related derivatives products.

Electronic trading systems are rapidly replacing traditional trading floors. The DTB in Frankfurt wrested trading of German bund futures back from the London International Financial Futures Exchange (LIFFE) within a few months, because LIFFE was slow to abandon open outcry for electronic trading. LIFFE has just announced a major restructuring to reduce its operational costs by half, opening the way for partnerships with other exchanges and financial institutions.

Major financial institutions are increasingly seeking direct electronic access to exchanges and bypassing local intermediaries. If their needs are not met, they will bypass the exchanges altogether to trade amongst themselves.

Exchanges are competing more fiercely not only with one another, but increasingly with new non-traditional players. Information providers like Reuters and Bloomberg already provide trading services. Longer term even non-financial companies like Microsoft with its global distribution network may enter the fray.

The gap between the exchanges in the premier league and the rest is widening. Those which cannot keep up will be marginalised into servicing their limited national catchments, and risk seeing even their traditionally protected markets being eroded.

These trends have not yet affected Asia in full force. Access to most Asian equities exchanges is still far from open, Singapore included, and many still have non-negotiable broker commissions. Consequently, Asia has some of the highest "all-in" trading costs in the world.

This gives us a window of opportunity to act swiftly, in order to capture the first mover advantage, and build ourselves up into the premier exchange in the region. It is no longer tenable for us to maintain a closed, static arrangement, with commissions fixed at levels comfortably higher than would prevail under free competition. We need to attract a critical mass of global investors by opening access widely to international brokers and other market participants. We also need more competition, to bring trading costs down through greater efficiency and innovation.

Demutualising SES and SIMEX

The present structure of both SES and SIMEX are "mutuals", i.e. they are legally owned by their members. Access to the SES is restricted to its 33 members. As a result, a new player wanting access to trade on SES has to buy a seat from an existing member, unless the existing members agree to let SES sell additional seats. This acts as a barrier to entry, besides creating a scarcity value for the seat.

SIMEX is owned by the 35 clearing members, and access is restricted to them and to the non-clearing members, whose number is also controlled by a limited number of seats (presently 472). Access to SIMEX has been less rigid, as new seats have been issued periodically to meet new demand for trading rights.

The mutual structure of the exchanges is not ideal for the future development of our capital markets. The interest of existing members does not always coincide with the interest of the exchange itself, or indeed with the broader interests of the financial sector. The SES has partially addressed this problem by requiring non-brokers to sit on the SES Committee, and by coordinating closely with MAS on strategic issues. But open access is an increasingly critical success factor for our exchanges. To grow and compete, the exchanges must take bolder steps to liberalise access and deregulate commissions, and make more business strategy decisions themselves in response to investor and corporate needs. As they do so, the present arrangements will become increasingly problematic.

The solution is to demutualise the exchanges, i.e. change their governance structure to separate ownership rights from trading access rights. The exchange becomes a stock company with a more diversified shareholding structure, in which non-broker investors can own shares, and non-shareholders may participate.

This brings several important advantages:

- First, it lessens the potential for conflict of interest. An exchange serves not only brokers, but also other capital market participants such as issuers, fund managers, investors and those trading on the exchange. A stock company structure with broader ownership allows more diversified interests to be directly represented in setting the directions for the exchange.
- Second, in a stock company the share value and dividends will reflect more transparently earnings and prospects, maximising incentives for owners and management to raise operational efficiency and seek competitive advantage.
- Third, funding can be obtained more efficiently and flexibly directly from the capital market. This is important because the exchange

may need to make long-term strategic investments that will not always benefit existing brokers directly, and may require more funds than its limited membership can provide.

Several international exchanges have already demutualised. These include the German, Swedish, Dutch exchanges and the Australian Stock Exchange which recently publicly listed itself. The Toronto Stock Exchange and LIFFE have announced similar plans.

Merger of SES and SIMEX

The Committee on Governance of Exchanges has proposed, and the Government has agreed, that SES and SIMEX should be demutualised, as well as merged into a single integrated privately-held stock company. A new holding company will be formed, which will wholly own SES and SIMEX as subsidiaries.

Combining the cash and derivatives exchanges will yield significant advantages:

- First, it will align cash and derivatives business strategies more closely. Integration can spur the development of complementary products with international appeal like equity-linked options and synthetics. The derivatives market is set to grow faster than the cash market, as it introduces more new products, and links up with strong international derivatives partners. This has also been the experience of the merged Amsterdam and Stockholm Stock Exchanges, both of which serve small domestic markets like ours.
- Second, the combined entity will have more bargaining power to deal with prospective strategic partners. It will also be financially stronger to make the heavy capital investments necessary in future, for instance, developing common front-end trading workstations and back-office processing systems.
- Third, it will enable us to build one strong management team. The existing managements are highly capable and will remain integral team members. But because of the greatly expanded demands of

the new enterprise, and the competitive challenges in the business, we need to consolidate and reinforce the existing teams to compete against other international exchanges.

- Fourth, the combined entity can share overheads such as product development, technology management, marketing and risk management. The merging of administrative and backroom functions of the two exchanges should also yield cost savings, although this is not the main motivation.

SES and SIMEX will initially be separate legal entities under the combined exchange, and operate their trading and clearing functions substantially as they do now. There will therefore be no immediate impact on the way brokers or investors trade on SES and SIMEX.

In particular, the clearing processes for SES and SIMEX trades will initially be kept separate, as different divisions within one umbrella clearing subsidiary. This way the different risk profiles of cash and derivatives trading will be retained. SIMEX's "common bond" system will continue unchanged for the time being. Its clearing members will have the same rights and obligations, and earn clearing fees from derivatives trades. Existing qualifying criteria for clearing membership will also remain unchanged and SIMEX clearing members will continue to have a strong say in running the clearing function.

In the longer term, SES and SIMEX will probably become a single legal entity, and share a common trading platform when this becomes technologically feasible. No trading engine is yet operational to cater to both cash and derivatives. The exchange can also bring together the separate clearing and settlement functions of SES and SIMEX. This will create scale and allow the exchange to expand into the clearing of off-exchange products like OTC derivatives and fixed income instruments.

New Directions

Business Development

Combining the two exchanges into one is by itself not sufficient for the continued development of our capital markets. The combined exchange must grow its business. At present, the SES is domestically oriented, like most equity exchanges elsewhere. It is highly dependent on our local corporate base and retail investor pool. SIMEX is an important regional and international player, but it relies heavily on trading of non-proprietary products, like the Eurodollar and Euroyen interest rate contracts. SIMEX has started introducing a range of regional index futures contracts, and will need to further broaden its product offering.

The new exchange needs to develop a range of Singapore and Asian equity products and equity-linked derivatives, in order to become the equity centre in the Asian timezone. Only then can it attract Asian investors, as well as G7 investors wanting exposure to the Asian cash and derivatives markets.

Freeing Access and Commissions

The combined exchange will phase in the complete freeing of SES commissions, and fully open access to both SES and SIMEX. Open access means that any institution which meets standard requirements, such as capital and competence, will be admitted to trade on the exchange, regardless of local or foreign ownership, and without any quota on the total number of seats. I expect this process to take three years, completing by January 2002.

This is in line with the SES Review Committee's recommendation that the liberalisation take place within five years. Three years will give local brokers reasonable time to prepare to meet the multiple challenges of a more competitive environment, and develop new capabilities and areas of business.

Brokers

Sound capital markets also require a strong local broker community, fully committed to Singapore's financial centre vision, with the indigenous capability to provide value-added services to a wider pool of international investors.

To play this role, local brokers must take full advantage of the three years of transition to restructure the industry, expand their capabilities and build up their talent base. Those intending to stay in the industry need to take some hard decisions, work out their own business strategies and find new ways to add value in the new environment of deregulated commissions and free competition. Some may choose to become niche players, providing specialist services in research or asset management. Others may try to build up to compete with international securities firms.

Some local brokers have already begun to upgrade their range of services, like providing internet access and more investment advice. A few are planning to merge. They are conscious of the challenges ahead, and are already staking out their positions.

MAS supports the aspirations of local brokers to develop themselves. It will review its regulations to help brokers diversify into other financial services, and compete on a more level playing-field. SES and SIMEX will organise educational seminars and programmes to help brokers gear up for new opportunities.

Remisiers

The freeing up of commissions and increased competition in the industry will impact greatly the way retail clients are serviced. The changes will mean that like the broking companies, remisiers must upgrade themselves to provide more services to customers. For instance, rather than just transacting shares, remisiers may cover markets other than just local equities, and over time build asset advisory capabilities like US brokers.

Some may find these changes daunting, but they are not avoidable. For the innovative, there is still a world of opportunity to develop a good business and a viable future.

Implementation

Capital Structure

Government will pass legislation to effect the transfer of 100% of the shares of SES and SIMEX to the new holding company, which will be set up by the Government. The SES and SIMEX's entire existing assets and cash reserves will be transferred to the new company. In return, existing members of SES and SIMEX will be allocated shares in the new combined entity. The Government will sell its remaining shares in the new entity to new investors.

Awarding existing members shares is justified, because firstly they have contributed much to developing the two exchanges. Secondly, the Government is changing the rules to remove the brokers' monopoly franchises, which will substantially diminish the existing value of their seats. Thirdly, giving existing brokers a stake in the new exchange will ensure their commitment and vested interest in the success of the new enterprise. In all other cases where exchanges have been demutualised, similar arrangements have been made for existing members.

The Government has decided that the value of shares allocated to each SES member should be slightly below the current estimated market value of an SES seat. This is fair considering that the liberalisation of access and commissions will be phased out over three years, and will not take place immediately. Furthermore this liberalisation would have happened even if the exchanges were not demutualised, though perhaps not as quickly, so that the seat values in any case could not have remained at past levels. Each of the 33 members of SES will therefore receive $6 million worth of shares in the new entity.

SIMEX commissions are already freely set, but the SIMEX seats still command a scarcity value because their number is controlled. So for SIMEX members, the Government has also taken a small discount on the average seat and share values from January to October 1998.[1] We are using the average as the benchmark, to smooth out the highly volatile SIMEX seat

[1] The average price of seats and shares traded between January and October 1998 is about $190,000 and $125,000 respectively.

prices. SIMEX members will receive $115,000 worth of shares for each SIMEX share owned, and $170,000 worth for each seat owned. Clearing members (who typically own one share and three seats) will therefore receive $625,000 worth each. Non-clearing members, both individual and corporate, will receive $170,000 worth per seat.

The actual number of shares of SES and SIMEX members in the new entity will depend on the exact valuation of the new entity. This will be determined by a financial advisor. The net tangible assets of the new entity amount to about $600 million. A valuation range of $600–800 million would give SES and SIMEX members together a total of 40–50% of the new entity. Assuming a valuation of $700 million, for example, SES members will collectively receive shares amounting to 28% of the new exchange, and SIMEX members 15%.

To diversify the ownership pool, the remaining shares in the new entity will be offered to new investors including financial institutions, fund managers and listed companies. Brokers (both SES and SIMEX) may also purchase these shares. To ensure ownership stability and balance long-term financial sector interests with short-term profit motives, the Government will encourage a pool of strategic investors to take a significant stake in the new entity. These may include the local banks, and government-linked entities like Temasek Holdings.

Shareholders in the new exchange will be allowed to trade their shares immediately. The percentage of total shares owned by brokers will be subject to a ceiling of 75%, and a floor of 33 1/3%. This will ensure that brokers retain a significant but not an over-dominant stake in the new entity.

As other exchanges have done, single owner shareholding limits will be imposed to ensure a diversified ownership structure. Holdings beyond 5% will require MAS approval. For strategic investors who are allowed to go beyond 5%, we will set a further requirement to seek approval for shareholding beyond 10%.

The new entity will not be publicly listed immediately. It needs time to consolidate its resources and develop new strategies. We also want existing SES and SIMEX owners to maintain meaningful stakes during the transition. However, we do envisage an IPO in the medium term, within say five years. This will give an incentive for owners and management to commit to the success of the new enterprise.

You may want to know what will happen to the proceeds from selling shares in the new entity. They will not go into the Government's Consolidated Fund. Instead they will be placed in a Financial Sector Development Fund administered by MAS. This Fund will be used to promote training and upgrading, and to undertake projects to develop the financial sector, including of course helping brokers to train and upgrade their human resources.

Timing

A Pro-Tem Committee will be formed soon to oversee the formation of the new exchange. We need to engage a financial advisor to value the combined entity, place shares with new investors, pass legislation, complete pre-merger integration work and develop the new regulatory framework. Preparation for the corporate integration of SES and SIMEX as well as conversion to a privately-held stock company should take about nine months. We therefore expect to launch the new entity in late 1999.

Regulation

The new for-profit exchange will continue to be responsible for routine regulatory functions such as listing approvals and market surveillance, like other demutualised exchanges. However, MAS will enhance its regulatory oversight over the exchange. MAS will inspect the new entity regularly to ensure it performs its supervisory functions adequately and properly. We will also encourage the exchange to price its services competitively, especially in functions which are natural monopolies, such as depository services. MAS will study the necessary regulatory arrangements more fully.

Conclusion

I have focussed on the structural changes necessary for our exchanges to continue to develop, and to support our role as a regional financial centre. We will put in place the right incentives, but success will depend on growing our talent pool, and developing proprietary benchmark Asian products with international appeal.

This will be a challenging task, especially as we begin to build momentum. The development of regional business will not be a smooth path. In the present uncertain environment, many countries are preoccupied with immediate problems, and some are taking steps to restrict the free operation of capital markets. However, capital markets play a vital economic role mobilising funds for corporates, and providing liquidity to investors who might otherwise stay away from the countries altogether. As the region recovers, the countries will feel more keenly the need for free but well-regulated capital markets. Each country will promote its own capital markets, but in addition there will be a role for regional hubs servicing the whole region and deepening the overall pool of liquidity.

We should start to prepare ourselves now for this opportunity. SES' strong foundation, laid over the last 25 years, will help it and SIMEX to restructure and take the next major step forward together, to become a premier exchange and make Singapore a hub for capital markets in Asia.

The Future of the Financial Sector in Singapore — Riding the Challenges, Emerging Stronger

Mr Goh Chok Tong
Senior Minister and Chairman, MAS
36th Association of Banks of Singapore Annual Dinner
26 June 2009

The Annual Dinner of the Association of Banks (ABS) has always been an excellent opportunity for the financial community to catch up, discuss issues impacting the financial industry and look ahead at how the Singapore financial sector will develop.

As we look forward tonight, we do so with a measure of optimism, as economic and financial indicators have stabilised in recent months. For example, manufacturers' Purchasing Managers' Indices (PMIs) have rebounded globally. The Chinese PMI has remained above the 50-point mark for three months in a row, and Singapore's PMI rose above 50 in May. In financial markets, interbank borrowing rates have fallen, as have interest rates on corporate debt. Markets have thus shown signs of thawing.

However, optimism about a recovery must be tempered with an appreciation of the risks that remain. I will just mention two briefly.

First, while the global financial system has stabilised relative to the dramatic events of last year, the broad-based downturn in economic activity continues to pose challenges for financial sector earnings. Losses may even be higher than expected if defaults on consumer and corporate loans mount. If banking systems in the major economies are not fully restored to health, it would reinforce the downturn as companies and consumers who are unable to access adequate credit will further weaken economic activity. The prospect of further losses cannot be ruled out. We should stay vigilant to deal with negative surprises, should they arise.

Second, there are incipient signs of protectionism. Following the inclusion of "Buy American" clauses in the US stimulus plan in February, we have heard in recent weeks of similar "Buy local" initiatives by economies such as China and the Australian State of New South Wales. The commitment of governments and international bodies to combat protectionism looks set to be sorely tested. But it is important for governments everywhere to maintain their resolve, because global growth cannot return without the growth of trade and capital flows. Protectionist measures that reverse these flows will ultimately result in a lose–lose situation for all countries.

The present circumstances mean that we have to be on our guard as we move ahead to build a foundation for long-term growth. Charting our future course involves asking two questions. First, what are the trends that shape and drive the new landscape? Second, how can we position ourselves to capitalise on these trends? Let me address these questions in turn.

Trends Shaping the New Landscape

There is growing acknowledgement that the shape of the global economy will be permanently altered. Developed economies, which have been the drivers of global demand, will experience a period of balance sheet repair and deleveraging. After years of living on easy credit and now facing the prospect of having to rebuild their eroded retirement nest eggs, consumption in developed economies will remain depressed for a prolonged period.

In the global financial industry, we are witnessing a "back to basics" movement, while regulation shifts towards stringency. In banking, risk-taking and proprietary trading will be reduced, while core activities anchored on providing services to consumers and the economy will regain its former importance. In capital markets, investors will demand less complex products and more standardisation, with trading and settlement conducted on central clearing platforms to mitigate counter-party risks.

Internationally, regulators are considering tighter regulation, after several decades of liberalisation. Proposals such as those laid out in the de Larosière Report in Europe, the Turner Review in the UK and most recently in the US Treasury's Financial Regulatory Reform document, are speeding the reform debate. The changes being discussed go beyond more capital for banks and more stringent liquidity management. It includes bringing more entities, such as near banks, under the regulatory umbrella, as well as enhancing consumer protection frameworks. Better identification and monitoring of systemic risk are also high on the agenda.

Prospects for Singapore Are Good

Although the tone of discussions about the global financial industry has been rather subdued and introspective, the outlook for Singapore's financial sector remains bright. For a start, Singapore is situated in the heart of a growing Asia. Rapid urbanisation will bring about more infrastructure projects, which can spur the growth of project financing in Asia. Demographic trends in Asia are expected to drive the demand for greater wealth planning, including asset management, as well as life and healthcare insurance products. Also, growing trade within Asia and with the rest of the world will drive financing opportunities.

Moreover, the ever greater emphasis on building trust, good governance and competence plays to Singapore's advantage. We are ranked first in corporate governance standards in Asia by the World Economic Forum, and we have maintained a stable "AAA" sovereign rating from Fitch. The City of London's Global Financial Centres Index ranked Singapore the most competitive financial centre in Asia, and third globally, after London and New York. However, it is important not to be complacent as trust, good governance and our reputation for competence require continuous reinforcement as standards change and new demands arise.

Nevertheless, our strong fundamentals will give us a firm footing to tap the region's growth opportunities when they come. And to better position ourselves, we need to adapt to the realities of the post-crisis landscape. In particular, I would like to highlight five strategies going forward.

Sound and Progressive Regulatory Framework

First, we must continue to maintain a sound and progressive regulatory regime to provide an overarching framework for Singapore's growth as a financial centre.

MAS' regulatory framework has generally been regarded as stringent, and in some aspects it exceeds international standards. For example, Singapore's capital requirements were high relative to international standards, and our local banks maintained buffers in excess of the minimum. This approach of emphasising robust regulation and supervision has proven to be a prudent "through-the-cycle" policy. It has helped our financial system remain resilient through this crisis.

Should the current round of discussions on regulatory reforms result in a movement towards more stringent international standards, we should be in a good position to align ourselves with these standards. But we will also be mindful of maintaining a balanced approach and not to "over-swing" the regulatory pendulum.

While our financial institutions weathered the crisis well, a significant number of Singaporeans were adversely affected by losses suffered on structured products sold to them by banks and other financial institutions. Some have alleged mis-selling and misrepresentation by the financial institutions. Others have questioned if the products were suitable for retail investors.

Although emotions ran high, MAS addressed investor concerns in a calm, methodical and objective manner. This is as it should be for a regulator. Apart from setting out the three-step process for affected investors, MAS has required the relevant financial institutions to review each complaint in a serious and impartial manner.

Financial institutions that distributed the failed structured products have generally reviewed investors' complaints in line with MAS' recommendations not to take an overly legalistic approach, even though they are of the view that the documents signed by the customers afford them a legal basis not to offer redress in many cases. The three banks and one finance company concerned have informed MAS that as at end May, they have offered settlements on a no-admission-of-liability basis to over 3,600 investors for about $105 million. This means that of the 5,350 cases decided by these financial institutions, 67% have been offered a settlement. 25% of the cases decided received full compensation.

MAS has now completed its investigations into the sale of the structured notes. It will release its findings shortly. MAS has also recently consulted on proposed enhancements to the regulatory framework for the sales and marketing of structured products to retail investors. Broadly, the findings from MAS' policy review and investigations show that financial institutions will need fundamental changes in both business models and mindsets to win back the trust and confidence of consumers. This is true not only in Singapore, but across the globe.

This is where progress on the regulatory front can underpin the efforts by financial institutions to build strong relationships by adding real long-term value to their customers. MAS has recently set out in its Fair Dealing Guidelines the roles and responsibilities of Boards and Senior Management in driving some of the fundamental changes required to deliver good customer outcomes. MAS will also fine-tune its approach to supervision of market conduct of financial institutions, including greater probing of the Boards and senior management of the steps they are taking to embed fair dealing outcomes in all their processes, from product approval to staff incentive structures.

I am pleased to read in recent weeks that some banks have proactively been taking steps to revamp some aspects of their sales process, such as remuneration structures for frontline staff. I encourage all of you to step up these efforts in the interest of building the trust and confidence of your customers.

Consumers of investment products also have an important part to play as our system will remain one based fundamentally on personal responsibility for financial and investment decisions. Through the MoneySENSE programme, MAS will target consumers from all walks of life to assist them in becoming better equipped to make investment and financial planning decisions confidently.

Tap Growing Wealth in Asia

Our second strategy is to tap the growing wealth in Asia. Prior to the crisis, the asset management industry in Singapore had flourished, with growth averaging 20% per annum over the past 7 years. It has grown in diversity to include not just global traditional fund managers but also alternative investment managers. Most of the fund management firms here are from Japan, Europe and the US, reflecting the international character of our asset management industry. With the crisis and fall in global assets under management (AUM), Singapore's AUM for 2008 has fallen too. Nevertheless, the continued accumulation of Asian wealth will remain a key driver for longer-term growth.

What is more important is to recognise that falling asset values and wealth destruction during this crisis has created a shift in investor mindset. Investors are now also paying more attention to protecting their wealth, in addition to growing wealth. Investors are also asking for better transparency and risk management of their portfolios. The building of trust has now become a key component of the asset management industry, leading banks and wealth managers "back to basics" to restore client relationships.

This mindset shift plays to Singapore's advantage, as we have a reputation for a sound regulatory regime and a trusted legal and governance framework. We should build on this foundation to facilitate the growth of a trusted ecosystem for the asset management industry, encompassing high standards of risk management, transparency and industry competencies.

As investors shift towards demanding less complex and more transparent investment instruments, the industry should position itself to ride this shift. To this end, we are currently working to improve individual investors' access to one such investment instrument — Singapore

Government Securities, or SGS. Unlike in other jurisdictions, SGS are not issued to fund government expenditures, which the Government Securities Act explicitly prohibits. Instead, SGS functions as a useful pricing benchmark for local corporations issuing bonds, and many institutional investors favour SGS as a liquid and safe investment alternative.

Because of rising interest among individual investors to purchase SGS, from 1 July, individuals will be able to participate in SGS auctions by submitting bids through the ATMs, similar to bidding for an equity IPO. Similar to equities, we have also moved the custody of SGS from individual banks to The Central Depository (CDP). Eventually, we hope to work with SGX to list the SGS on the exchange so that it can be traded just like other stocks. By making SGS more accessible and more liquid, we hope to enhance the array of financial instruments that financial advisors can use to match their clients' needs.

Leverage on Infrastructure Needs in Asia

Our third strategy is to leverage on the massive infrastructure needs in Asia. A recent ADB study showed that Asia needs to spend about US$8 trillion on transport, power and communications infrastructure over the next ten years for Asia to emerge as a viably connected, integrated and competitive region. Such infrastructure investment will spur the region's growth, and will potentially add US$1.6 trillion or 10% to developing Asia's GDP by 2020.

Singapore can play a significant role in regional infrastructure financing due to our developed financial markets, urban infrastructure management expertise and strong legal and regulatory framework. I know that many banks already have established project finance teams based in Singapore, and are poised to expand in this area. So I encourage ABS member banks to do more Asian infrastructure financing out of Singapore.

On the government's part, we are actively working with multilateral agencies to attract more private sector investments into viable infrastructure projects. The launch of the Asia Infrastructure Project Development (AIPD) last year is one positive outcome. A joint venture by the ADB, Singapore

Cooperation Enterprise and three private sector participants — AIPD will assist municipal governments in sourcing for funds, from commercial banks and private investors, for commercially viable Public Private Partnership (PPP) infrastructure projects. Singapore also entered into a Memorandum of Understanding (MOU) with the World Bank last year, which would leverage on Singapore's developmental expertise to provide urban solutions for developing countries which will also have spill-over benefits to our financial sector.

Strengthen Risk Management Capabilities and Market Infrastructure

Our fourth strategy is to enhance our risk management capabilities and market infrastructure. Emerging from the crisis, industry players and governments are keen to see the introduction of enhanced risk mitigation platforms for derivative products. By working on initiatives to mitigate counter-party risks, we can enhance our lead position as a risk management hub for the region. One example is SGX's AsiaClear which will extend its current central clearing facility for OTC trades in energy derivatives and forward freight agreements to the clearing of OTC financial derivatives. This will no doubt enhance the market infrastructure for OTC clearing in Singapore.

Another initiative which will strengthen Singapore's market infrastructure is the ongoing industry effort to enhance the framework for the fixing of the Singapore Inter-Bank Offer Rate (SIBOR) and the Swap Offer Rate (SOR). The turmoil in the global interbank markets during the current crisis has raised questions about the robustness of the interbank rate fixing system and its reliability in representing market conditions. Banks were accused of underestimating the cost of borrowings to downplay their financial difficulties, prompting widespread calls for reviews of interbank rate fixings globally. In Singapore, the ABS has conducted a review of SIBOR and SOR fixings and found the methodologies and processes to be sound. Nevertheless, governance of the fixings can be strengthened by expanding the resources and scope of the oversight committee. These proposals will be circulated to members for comments shortly.

Build Talent Pool and Intellectual Capacity

Fifth, we should take advantage of the current environment to further build our talent pool and intellectual capacity. The economic downturn should not disrupt our efforts to look long term and strategically invest in manpower development. Doing so will prepare us for the upturn. As the global economy slows, we appreciate that managing costs has to be a priority for our financial institutions. So to ensure that our financial institutions do not lose sight of the critical need to continue to invest in developing a pool of skilled manpower, MAS announced up to 90% co-funding for training schemes supported under the Financial Sector Development Fund. MAS has also launched new schemes to spur the creation of job and industry internship opportunities for fresh graduates. This will ensure a ready pool of young talents, well-trained and ready to contribute to the growth of the financial sector when the economy recovers.

To contribute to enhancing Singapore's intellectual capacity in the financial sector, the AXA University Asia Pacific Campus and the SMU-Sim Kee Boon Institute for Financial Economics were established last year. Both centres will conduct research and training programmes to generate highly specialised and Asian-centric knowledge in finance.

Conclusion

Eleven years ago, the Asian financial crisis swept through the region. Seeing the economic wreckage that it caused, Asian governments were determined to avoid a repeat, thus spurring them to undertake the necessary reforms, and growing stronger as a result. Singapore, which was not guilty of the financial excesses then, was nevertheless affected. Pressing on with further reforms and liberalising our financial sector allowed us to emerge stronger from the Asian financial crisis. Witness the robust development of the financial sector in the last few years.

In the same vein, we must not waste the current crisis. Whether as financial institutions, regulators or as consumers, this downturn has not only taught us new lessons but also presented opportunities for the nimble and prepared. Today's challenges may be different and the future environment uncertain, but with the same willingness to adapt to new realities, we can build the foundation for stronger growth. I urge us all to take advantage of the current crisis to create new opportunities for our financial sector.

Key Issues in Asian Financial Markets

Mr Tharman Shanmugaratnam
Deputy Prime Minister and Minister for Finance, and Chairman, MAS
ACI 52nd World Congress
15 March 2013

The last time Singapore hosted the ACI Congress was back in 2001. In fact, it was just before 9/11. The world was in a very different place. Asia too was so different from today. The wounds of the Asian crisis of the late 90s were still fresh. Investor confidence in the various countries in the region was uneven. And Asian capital markets were by and large in their infancy.

The New Financial Landscape

We are now in a new phase in global finance. Global finance is deleveraging, after the great credit bubble that began more than a decade ago and came to an end in 2007. But deleveraging still has some way to go, and some years to go, before the overall level of leverage relative to economic activity gets back to a sustainable level.

The pace of deleveraging has been moderated so far by central banks, who have taken onto their balance sheets unprecedented levels of both public and private sector debt. Their actions have reduced the risks of catastrophe. But it also means we have a long way yet to go in reducing debts and returning to sustainable growth.

We are also seeing important shifts in the structure of global finance, besides the gradual contraction in global liquidity. It is too early to say where we will be five years from now, but some of the broad brush-strokes in this new landscape of global finance are already with us and likely to stay:

- The return on equity in global banking has fallen, and will not return to pre-crisis levels, given stricter capital and liquidity rules.
- Deposits have become more important as a source of bank funding.
- Banks in certain major jurisdictions have retreated from global markets, and worryingly, may stay in retreat for some time.
- The securitised debt markets should recover, but with less leverage underpinning them, and hopefully greater risk transparency.
- In the derivative markets, there will be greater standardisation of products, and much greater reliance on common market infrastructure — for trading, clearing and reporting of trades. High volume, low-margin platforms will likely gain in competitiveness.
- Wealth management will remain a growth industry, especially in Asia, where the pool of wealth is growing most rapidly and the need for diversification remains great.
- And outside of intermediated finance, companies will seek new ways of raising funds, including through private placements.

Will this mean a safer financial world? Maybe. That will depend on whether we persist in seeing through the regulatory reforms that began a few years ago. It will depend on whether we keep to a sensible balance in regulation — and that includes not over-doing bank regulation and under-doing the oversight of shadow banking. It will also depend on whether we all stay intensely alert to the risks of the future, including especially the risks that we do not yet see or know, rather than focus only on the last battle or on preventing the last crisis from recurring.

What of global capital flows? There too we see shifts, as global finance responds to a two-track world of economic growth. The prospect of sub-par growth in the advanced economies for a number of years, together with central bank actions to keep interest rates very low, have led to what is becoming a furious search for yield. Pension funds and insurance funds need better yields badly, and they are putting more monies in the emerging markets and other risk assets.

This is likely to be more than a cyclical trend. We are seeing a secular shift in assets towards the emerging markets. Advanced country funds in fact remain significantly underweighted in emerging market assets, and are gradually correcting for this. At the same time, sovereign debt ratings have been raised in several emerging economies, in Asia[1] especially, at the same time that a number of advanced economies[2] have seen their ratings lowered. Asia is certainly not free from risks, and there is much work ahead to preserve and improve sovereign ratings. But no one can assume that the recent rebalancing of risk assessments vis-à-vis the advanced economies is temporary.

What this continuing shift in global funds also means, however, is that there is critical need to add depth and breadth to Asian financial markets. It will not be possible to absorb a greater share of global savings without developing this depth and breadth in markets, and a robust market infrastructure. Otherwise, both global and Asian capital flows within the region will lead to recurrent bubbles, whether in equities, property markets or currencies, rather than find their way to the most productive investments in Asia's economies.

Asia's financial markets have grown significantly over the past decade. But the capital markets, and especially for bonds and securitised debts, remain small in relation to Asia's GDP. Further, the region's financial markets are still relatively small and fragmented.

There is by the same virtue, great potential to develop Asian financial markets and enable them to play a stronger role in promoting balanced and sustainable growth.

We will have to push ahead with reforms at two levels to develop these financial markets. Gradual and progressive financial liberalisation can bring about more liquid and broader domestic financial markets. It will

[1] For example, South Korea, Indonesia, Thailand and the Philippines

[2] Namely the US, Japan, France, peripheral Europe

also help spur domestic demand by households, and provide smaller enterprises with better access to capital in several Asian economies. Secondly, at the regional level, we have to inject greater momentum into improving cross-border market access and harmonising rules and standards.

Key Themes in the Development of Asia's Financial Markets

Let me now touch on three themes that will influence the development of Asia's financial markets in the decade ahead:

i. Firstly, the changes in the over-the-counter (OTC) derivatives markets as a result of global reforms;
ii. Secondly, the harnessing of technology to transform Asia's financial infrastructure; and
iii. Thirdly, the increasing international role of the RMB.

Structural Shifts in the OTC Derivatives Markets as a Result of Global Reforms

First, the structural shift in the global OTC derivatives markets. Most of you will be familiar with the changes that are coming into place, in steps, as a result of global reforms — more standardised products, and more robust market infrastructure: central counterparties for clearing, trade repositories for reporting, swap execution facilities for trading where appropriate. The global reform process is now shifting from rulemaking to implementation.

We are already seeing the shift in Asia's OTC derivative markets. The new market infrastructures are expected to provide greater transparency and allow risks to be managed more effectively among market participants. Market practices will be redefined, with the need to report and clear selected OTC derivative trades within more than one jurisdiction.

However, we are also seeing a proliferation of central counterparties (CCPs) and trade repositories being set up in Asia. While this will provide choice to Asian market participants, it may also increase risk and lead to higher costs.

Regulators will need a comprehensive view of risks in the cross-border, interconnected market. Having multiple CCPs and trade repositories in the region may risk fragmentation, and may hamper monitoring of systemic risks as regulators may see only their own segments of the market. Market participants will also face additional costs if CCPs and trade repositories lack economies of scale.

Asian regulators will therefore need to work closely together to enable infrastructural entities to offer their services across different jurisdictions. For example, the infrastructure of a DTCC global trade repository and AsiaClear CCP in Singapore offers the prospect of effective surveillance by regional regulators and economies of scale. We will continue to ensure that our market infrastructure operates in a transparent and accessible way so that the needs of regional regulators and the industry can be met under clear and robust guidelines.

At the global level too, there are real benefits for regulators to ensure inter-operability in market infrastructure to allow for more effective risk monitoring. However, inter-operability will require time and effort, as risk management practices such as margin eligibility standards have to be harmonised across CCPs in different jurisdictions.

As Asia's infrastructure is still at an early stage of development, we have an opportunity to harmonise practices while making the changes needed to respond to emerging global regulatory reforms. It is heartening to note that Asian regulators are working closely on OTC derivatives regulations. A good example was the joint letter from Singapore, Hong Kong and Australia to the US Commodity Futures Trading Commission (CFTC), expressing our concerns on the extra-territorial application of the US rules.

Harnessing Technology to Transform Asia's Financial Infrastructure in a Game-Changing Fashion

Regulators everywhere are confronted with highly connected global markets. Collecting and managing information is now a core competence in itself, for effective surveillance of the financial markets. Similarly, market participants are making greater use of technology in risk management — performing complex portfolio valuation and mitigating risks such as through intra-day margining at CCPs, and often across global books and in multiple time zones and jurisdictions. Moving collateral across markets swiftly and efficiently is also now a core competence.

Besides risk management, technology can be useful in developing liquidity in Asian markets. It can bring greater pricing efficiency and transparency, as we are seeing in the US and EU financial markets as trading moves to electronic platforms.

In Asia, there is room for our financial markets to embrace greater "electronification" of trading, notwithstanding our smaller markets. To illustrate, an estimated 80% of trades are executed in electronic platforms in developed country FX markets, whereas 85% of FX trades in Asia are still executed by voice. A reduction in transaction costs can promote greater liquidity for Asian asset classes, and broaden participation from investors including retail traders.

Growing Regional and International Role of the RMB

Let me go on to the third theme I wanted to talk about, which is that of RMB internationalisation, and how this will shape Asia's financial markets development.

The status quo will not last. Currently, only 0.6% of global payments are settled in RMB, vastly below China's share of global trade (10%) or investment flows. There is clearly room for growth.

In the long run, if we envisage China with deep and liquid capital markets, and a largely liberalised capital account, the RMB market will potentially play a transformational role in Asian finance. For now, even with limited convertibility, there is considerable potential for greater use of the RMB. The economic fundamentals are driving this. Besides China's growing share of global trade, there is a rapidly growing trade between China and the rest of the Asian region, and especially ASEAN. Further, China's foreign direct investments are expanding strongly, especially into Asian markets. Outbound foreign direct investment (FDI) from China has increased almost sevenfold in the last seven years (to US$77 billion in 2012)[3], and is expected to expand further in the coming decade. A growing part of this FDI is expected to be RMB-denominated, and this too will contribute to greater offshore use of the RMB.

The overseas expansion of Chinese corporates will be reinforced by the growing presence of mainland Chinese banks as they grow their regional and international presence. In Singapore, we extended Qualifying Full Bank (QFB) privileges to Bank of China and ICBC as part of the China-Singapore FTA. Both banks are growing their Singapore operations as Southeast Asian hubs. We are also seeing interest from other Chinese financial institutions.

The re-denomination of China's trading flows in RMB will allow Asian corporate and financial institutions to more effectively manage their exposures to China. While USD would remain an integral global settlement currency, RMB is likely to be increasingly used for trade denomination and contract pricing.

As we see greater acceptance and use of the RMB as a trade settlement currency, there will also be important implications for the interactions between China and Asia's financial markets, and indeed for global financial markets.

For one, it will be critical to facilitate the development of a single fungible offshore RMB market, as the market grows in multiple jurisdictions. (Currently, the industry has designated different currency codes, such as the CNH and CNY, to reflect these existing market frictions.) Regulators and market participants will have to work together to avoid fragmenting liquidity across markets, and to promote efficiency in the offshore RMB market.

In addition, China plans to launch its international payment system, known as CIPS, in 2014. The development of a single centralised cross-border RMB payments infrastructure also augurs well for market efficiency and standardised practices for RMB payments across the region.

[3] CNBC, 17 Jan 2013. "China's outbound investment leaps to record high in December".

Singapore's Role as an Offshore RMB Market

As an international trading and financial centre, Singapore will seek to support the growth of a resilient offshore RMB market in the Asian region by:

i. Building RMB liquidity;

ii. Enhancing access to RMB for funding and investment purposes; and

iii. Integrating the offshore RMB with existing Asian local currency markets.

Firstly, Singapore can leverage on its strengths as a key wholesale funding centre to increase liquidity and circulation of the RMB in Asia. We are already seeing good growth in RMB deposits, both non-bank and interbank. We are also one of the largest centres for RMB payments outside Hong Kong. As a major regional funding centre, Singapore has traditionally supported the liquidity of the Asian markets and can partner China in promoting sustainable offshore use of the RMB.

In February this year, ICBC Singapore was appointed by the People's Bank of China (PBC) as the RMB clearing bank in Singapore. The RMB clearing bank will be an important channel for RMB liquidity to circulate between China and Singapore.

In addition, PBC and MAS together announced an expanded Currency Swap Facility last Friday. This will see a doubling in the size of the swap facility from RMB150 to RMB300 billion. The scope of the Currency Swap Facility will also be expanded to allow MAS to provide RMB liquidity to banks in Singapore, where needed. This backstop facility will further strengthen confidence in Singapore's offshore RMB market, and encourage more financial institutions, corporates and investors to step forward and participate in the RMB market via Singapore.

Secondly, with a strong RMB pool, Singapore can provide enhanced access to RMB funding for corporates and investors. Singapore is a major source of FDI to China and serves as the Asia-Pacific headquarters for many multinational companies (MNCs) and Asian corporates with operations in China. We also serve as the regional treasury centre for a large base of Chinese corporates.

With the new RMB clearing arrangements, we can expect financial institutions based in Singapore to reach out to local and regional corporate and investors and encourage greater participation in the offshore RMB market.

Thirdly, Singapore can support the integration of offshore RMB with Asian local currency markets and act as a test-bed for new RMB products. The development of a wider range of RMB products will be healthy. It will create additional ways in which corporates can redeploy their RMB funds in the offshore markets, and provide additional products for investment.

The financial industry in Singapore has good expertise in developing FX and derivatives instruments, with several emerging Asian FX teams based here. It is well equipped to develop customised offshore RMB capital market instruments, especially for Asian market participants. For instance, banks in Singapore can explore how to encourage offshore RMB bond issuance in Singapore with longer maturity tenors and different issuer profiles.

Conclusion

Let me wrap up briefly. Global deleveraging is being accompanied by the continued inflow of funds into Asia's emerging market economies. This shift poses risks if not well-managed, but it is also an opportunity. The next phase of development in Asia's financial markets is therefore critical. We have to develop greater breadth and breadth in Asian markets, so that savings flows translate into sustainable economic growth rather than recurrent bubbles in asset markets.

Singapore as a Global Insurance Marketplace

Mr Ravi Menon
Managing Director, MAS
12th Singapore International Reinsurance Conference
6 November 2013

Asia's Changing Risk Landscape

These are interesting times for the insurance industry. The operating environment has become more challenging.

- Underwriting results are being pressured by a combination of sluggish economic growth, softening rates and rising claims.
- Investment returns are being depressed by the low interest-rate environment. In Europe, for instance, returns on long-term safe assets are at their lowest since the creation of the European Economic and Monetary Union.
- Regulatory and capital requirements are being tightened as the world shifts towards risk-based regimes like Solvency II.

At the same time, the growth potential has never been better. At a time, when questions are being raised globally as to whether the financial industry has grown too big, no one is asking the same of insurance. Much of the world remains under-insured.

The prospects in Asia are especially bright. The Asian risk landscape is transforming rapidly, generating robust demand for insurance and re-insurance.

- Over the next decade, the insurance business in Asia is projected to grow at about 8% per annum.
- By 2020, Asia is likely to account for almost 40% of the global market.

There are three large factors driving insurance demand in Asia.

First, Asia is growing. Developing Asia is still growing at double the global average. Rising affluence and a growing middle class will underpin a steady increase in insurance penetration rates that are still well below the global average. Continued industrialisation, expanding cross-border trade and infrastructure development will drive demand for insurance solutions to mitigate a variety of business risks.

Second, Asia is vulnerable. Asia is highly prone to natural catastrophes.

- Asia accounted for 41% of global economic losses from disasters between 2000 and 2009, and 81% in 2011 alone.
- Only about 35% of the economic losses from 2011 were insured, resulting in a heavy economic burden for affected countries.

A growing risk awareness, coupled with rising asset values, will lead to greater demand for catastrophe insurance and reinsurance, including alternative risk transfer solutions. Following the 2011 catastrophes, several Asian countries have already established insurance pools for key catastrophe risks.

Third, Asia is ageing. Asia is facing a rapidly ageing population. By 2050, Asia and the Pacific will be home to 62% of the world's elderly population, with one in four persons aged 60 and above. This will lead to greater demand for health insurance, annuity and other retirement security products.

As the leading insurance centre in Asia, Singapore is well-placed to serve the burgeoning insurance needs of the region. The insurance industry is one of the brightest stars in the constellation of Singapore's financial sector. The industry has done remarkably well, but its story is not well known.

I want to briefly sketch the journey of Singapore's insurance industry from writing pure domestic risks to becoming a regional underwriting hub in just 10 years. I will then share our vision and strategies for the next phase of the industry's growth — to become a global insurance marketplace at the heart of Asia.

The Journey to a Regional Underwriting Hub

In the early days, the Singapore insurance industry was focused on servicing domestic business, with life insurance being the mainstay. In fact, MAS had adopted a closed-door policy to direct insurers since 1990. In 2000, MAS liberalised the insurance industry, lifting the closed-door policy on direct insurers and the 49% foreign shareholding limit in locally owned direct insurers.

Singapore's development as a regional insurance hub took off.

- Since 2000, offshore business has been on a steady uptrend, growing an average of 13% per annum to US$5.4 billion in 2012. The share of offshore non-life business has increased from 50% in 2000 to 65% in 2012.
- Major insurance groups across different segments of the industry, from direct insurers to reinsurers and brokers, have sited their regional operating and business hubs here.

Today, Singapore is recognised as the leading reinsurance hub in Asia. Amongst the top 25 reinsurers in the world, 16 have regional hubs here.

The market has built up significant expertise in specialty insurance, namely marine, energy, catastrophe, credit and political risks. For example, Singapore is the second largest market for structured credit and political risk worldwide after London.

The number of global and regional positions in Singapore has grown. Most underwriting decisions can be made on the ground instead of being referred back to headquarters. This has enabled the Singapore market to respond more quickly to clients' needs. Most Asian risks, including entire large reinsurance programmes and specialty risks, can now be fully placed in Singapore.

Towards Becoming a Global Marketplace

Our vision is for Singapore's insurance industry to become a global marketplace by 2020, with the ability to accept not just regional, but global risks.

To achieve this, we are pursuing four strategies with clearly laid out initiatives.

- First, to increase supply-side capacity, in both volume and expertise.
- Second, to promote insurance demand, both locally and in the Asia-Pacific.
- Third, to develop a true marketplace, where sellers and buyers come together to negotiate and trade risks.
- Fourth, to foster a conducive business environment.

Increase Capacity

Let me begin with our plans to increase supply-side capacity.

We are focused on increasing the quality and diversity of underwriting expertise here. Having expert underwriters on the ground enables insurers to be more responsive to their clients and make underwriting decisions quickly. They will also have a better understanding of the market environment and underlying risks.

Recent events highlight the need to build up a deeper understanding of Asian risks. For example, prior to the devastating floods of 2011, Thailand had not been viewed as catastrophe-prone. The scale of the floods and the knock-on effects of natural catastrophes on global supply chains came as a rude surprise. The floods damaged more than 7,000 industrial and manufacturing plants in 40 separate provinces. This affected countries with significant manufacturing capabilities in Thailand, most notably Japan.

The majority of the insurance losses therefore came not from property damage, but from business interruption claims arising from the disruption to manufacturing and supply chains. It is therefore important that insurers have senior experts in the region who understand Asia's multi-faceted and inter-connected risks. This will enable the industry to better price and underwrite regional risks, and achieve sustained growth.

MAS will seek to increase the depth of expertise in Singapore by continuing to work with existing players to build up their specialty and reinsurance underwriting and broking capabilities as well as expand their regional hubs.

MAS will also seek to increase breadth in the industry by promoting growth in emerging business lines, such as cyber risks.

Lack of data is a key hurdle for cyber insurance in Asia. MAS is working with industry to create a test-bed for cyber risks where insurers and potential clients can come together to simulate loss events.

- Cyber insurers will be able to generate sets of valuable loss data and raise awareness about the value of specialty cyber insurance cover.
- Clients will get the opportunity to stress-test their systems, assess the responsiveness of existing coverage to losses and gain an appreciation of potential losses and the need for cyber insurance cover.

Promote Asian Demand

Next, we want to promote insurance demand in Asia.

Asia is already leading the world in premium growth. We seek to catalyse the development of insurance demand in the region via a three-pronged approach.

First, enhancing cross-border access to regional markets. The ASEAN economies are working together on a comprehensive insurance liberalisation framework.

- We aspire to achieve substantial liberalisation by 2020 for all insurance sub-sectors, namely life insurance, non-life insurance, reinsurance and retrocession, insurance intermediation and insurance auxiliary services.
- Insurers can expect to benefit from easier cross-border provision of services and substantial access across the ASEAN customer base from offices in any ASEAN member country.

- The framework is expected to be discussed at the ASEAN Finance Ministers' Meeting next year.

Second, increasing the pool of Asian risk data. Modelling and loss simulation are key tools to help insurers manage and price their exposures. Accurate and timely data are critical for risk models to predict the impact of a loss event. For example, to predict the vulnerability of an insured risk to catastrophes, a wide variety of data is required, such as geographic location, soil structures, rainfall, construction materials and urban density, just to name a few. However, there is a severe paucity of data on Asian risks.

Singapore is addressing this gap by setting up several research institutions to gather and analyse data in specific areas of risks.

- For example, the Institute of Catastrophe Risk Management (ICRM) at the Nanyang Technological University is currently undertaking research projects for flood and earthquake risk assessment in selected Asian cities.
- In addition to collecting and analysing the data, ICRM conducts on-site studies and risk assessments of the cities in question, and develops hazard maps and risk models.
- To ensure that its research is relevant to the industry, ICRM actively reaches out to industry players through seminars and workshops.

Third, increasing risk awareness. MAS supports efforts to raise risk management awareness in the region.

- I am pleased to note that Asia's first association for risk managers, the Pan-Asian Risk and Insurance Management Association (PARIMA), was set up in Singapore in April, with strong support from the insurance industry.
- As a platform for dialogue between risk managers and the insurance industry, PARIMA will help to enhance risk culture and risk management capacity in Asia.

Develop the Marketplace

I will now move on to our efforts to develop the insurance marketplace in Singapore. We have three key thrusts for marketplace development.

First, expanding the broker network. Singapore already has a vibrant broking cluster, which has played a central role in facilitating business flows. We play host to over 70 insurance brokers. Four of the top five brokers in the world have their regional hubs in Singapore.

Today, brokers are not just intermediaries, but also high-value service providers who drive innovation and collaboration in the industry.

- Many brokers provide a wide range of risk management services. These include dynamic financial analysis, risk management and actuarial consultancy, portfolio and financial modelling and catastrophe modelling.
- Some brokers have also begun to tap alternative risk transfer solutions to manage more complex and larger risk exposures and liabilities.

We are keen to encourage brokers to use Singapore not just as a placement centre, but also as a centre of excellence for innovation.

- A good example of this is Aon, which recently established its Analytics and Innovation Centre in Singapore to provide analytics solutions to the Group's business units on a global basis.

Second, encouraging a subscription market. To underwrite large and complex risks, insurers need to collaborate. Risk sharing enables market participants to diversify their portfolios. We want to promote a true subscription market, where insurers not only share risks, but also expertise. The subscription concept leverages both the deep expertise of the lead insurer and the supporting capacity of the other insurers to cover a variety of large and complex risks.

Such deep collaboration requires contract certainty. Contract certainty ensures the finalisation of terms and conditions of the policy prior to inception of risk and therefore, serves to minimise ambiguity and disputes over claim and coverage.

- I am pleased that our industry players have come together to form a workgroup, which issued earlier this year a set of guidelines and best practices for reinsurance contract certainty.
- The workgroup is now monitoring the industry's progress in achieving contract certainty via monthly submissions by industry players on the level of contract certainty in their reinsurance transactions.
- This is a sterling example of industry collaboration. MAS supports this initiative and has been working with the industry to implement the new standards.

Third, creating more platforms to bring buyers and sellers together. This conference is a good example. The Singapore International Reinsurance Conference has become Asia's version of the Baden-Baden Meeting and the Monte-Carlo Rendezvous. It is a key platform for insurance players not just to share knowledge, but also to negotiate renewals and explore opportunities for collaboration.

Foster a Conducive Business Environment

Finally, I will touch on our efforts to foster a conducive business environment for insurance. There are two critical success factors.

The first is Talent. The insurance industry already has in place some good talent development programmes at the undergraduate and fresh graduate levels.

- Take, for instance, the Global Internship Programme (GIP) offered by the General Insurance Association. This is a structured internship programme which gives selected undergraduates exposure in general insurance companies both locally and overseas.

MAS, in partnership with the industry, has recently developed an Insurance Talent Development Framework, which maps out training and career progression pathways for both new entrants and existing insurance professionals. New industry-wide programmes will be launched in 2014 across a spectrum of roles and seniority levels.

At the entry level, we will have two programmes.

- The Insurance Executive Assistant Programme (IEAP) will prepare diploma holders for junior entry-level positions. It will complement the GIP, which is targeted at university graduates.
- The Insurance Management Associate Programme (IMAP) will place and train top-tier fresh graduates through a structured apprenticeship programme.

For existing industry professionals, there will also be two new programmes.

- The Insurance Specialist Programme will deepen participants' specialist and technical knowledge in key functions such as underwriting and claims, as well as in specialist lines such as trade credit, political risks, aviation and marine risks.
- The Hi-Po Leader Programme will provide those with leadership potential with a series of programmes to prepare them for senior management roles in the insurance industry.

The second critical success factor is Regulation. Strong prudential and regulatory standards have always been a source of Singapore's competitive advantage as a financial centre. Through promoting sound risk management and a safe environment, regulation fosters confidence in the industry and helps attract business.

Singapore was one of the early movers to a risk-based supervisory and capital framework for insurance in 2005. Since then, MAS has been actively refining the regulatory framework and approach. We are currently undertaking a comprehensive review to enhance the risk-based capital framework, taking into account evolving international standards and market developments. In particular, we are seeking to improve the comprehensiveness of the risk coverage and the risk sensitivity of the framework.

Conclusion

Let me conclude.

The operating environment — be it for individuals or enterprises — is becoming more complex and uncertain. Managing risk has become an increasingly important part of our existence, and doing it well has become a key determinant of success. Insurance — at its core — is about managing risk. You are in an industry that serves a larger public purpose.

You are also in an industry that has great promise. Asia offers tremendous opportunity for the insurance industry. As the leading insurance and reinsurance hub in Asia, Singapore is well-equipped to serve the growing needs of the region. But to become a global marketplace for insurance, we have to continually reinvent ourselves.

The industry's support and partnership are critical to the achievement of this vision. Let us work together to build a truly global insurance marketplace in Singapore.

Building Capabilities for the Financial Sector of Tomorrow

Mr Tharman Shanmugaratnam
Deputy Prime Minister and Minister for Finance, and Chairman, MAS
40th Anniversary Dinner of the Institute of Banking and Finance
10 June 2014

I am sure I speak for everyone in saying what a pleasure it is for us to be here as the Institute of Banking and Finance (IBF) celebrates its 40 years — 40 years of building skills and capabilities for what has become a leading international financial centre, and financial activities that support consumers and businesses with a broad range of their needs. I congratulate IBF for its achievements. Credit must go to IBF's pioneers for your leadership and foresight, and the many individuals and financial institutions who have brought us to where we are today.

Singapore's Development as a Financial Centre

Major anniversaries are a good occasion for reflection. Singapore did not start out as a financial centre. In the early years of the nation's development, the finance industry mainly comprised a group of foreign bank branches and small local banks. They serviced the foreign merchant houses and local merchants involved in trade across the Causeway, and provided working capital to various domestic businesses. However, the corporate sector relied largely on internal finance. There was also very little consumer finance. Skills in finance did not need to be more than basic.

The key centre for international finance in Asia was Hong Kong. It was the Asian outpost of the City of London, and the gathering point for bankers. Further north, Tokyo was growing in pace with the Japanese economy, which was leading Asia.

There was no reason why a financial centre had to be located in Singapore in those days. Mr Lee Kuan Yew once called it a most "improbable start". Our development as a financial centre was always an act of volition — we made it happen.

We created a space for ourselves in international finance, starting with the Asian Dollar Market (ADM) in the late 1960s, followed in the early 1980s by the Singapore International Monetary Exchange, or SIMEX. They were building blocks for what is today the third largest foreign exchange centre in the world, and a leading Asian player in global derivatives markets. We developed a strong core of local institutions even as we opened up to greater competition from foreign institutions in the domestic market, especially in the last 15 years. Our local institutions have held their own, not only in the domestic market but in regional finance. And underpinning all of this, we developed the skills and capabilities that have made us a credible player internationally.

The development of skills was progressive. We lacked banking expertise when our development kicked off. MAS, itself a fledgling institution, together with the Association of Banks in Singapore (ABS), formed a Training Committee in 1972 to organise formal programmes to develop skills. This led to the creation of IBF in 1974, as a dedicated institute for financial sector training. More initiatives were introduced to deepen skills, such as the launch of the Chartered Financial Analyst (CFA) examinations locally in 1982 and the establishment of the Wealth Management Institute (WMI) in 2003. As the training landscape developed over the years, we subsequently evolved IBF into a standards-setter for financial sector competency.

Today, Singapore's financial sector comprises almost 12% of Singapore's GDP, with more than 1,000 financial institutions performing roles in Singapore, the region and globally. It employs almost 190,000 people, of which about 70% are Singaporeans. The jobs are now diverse and increasingly complex. Beyond traditional corporate lenders and retail bank tellers, many more jobs have been created in portfolio management and investment analysis, product structuring, risk management and technology.

Our financial sector has significant opportunities ahead of it. However, growth will demand deeper skills and expertise, rather than a large expansion of jobs. The deceleration in job growth in Singapore's financial sector in the last few years[1] is not a temporary happening. It reflects the slowdown in our local labour force growth, as well as major forces that are reshaping global finance. I will say a little more about these global forces, before going on to talk about what we have to focus on to remain a competitive and dynamic financial centre in the years to come.

The Evolving Global Financial Landscape

Globally, we are seeing countervailing forces. First, there is overall shrinkage in the global financial sector. Weak economic growth and higher capital requirements in the wake of the global financial crisis are forcing financial institutions to review their business models and restructure. Redundancies have been outpacing new hires by roughly two-to-one. Financial institutions have been particularly pressured to consolidate activities in trading and securitisation, which have higher capital charges.

Asian finance continues to grow. This is a solid story for another two decades at least, with increasing trade flows, rapid urbanisation and infrastructure development, as well as rising middle-class affluence and wealth creation in the region.

Thirdly, however, against this global and regional backdrop, there is a driving force that is transforming activity across all financial markets, and that is technological change. As early as the 1990s, technology has been transforming the way financial institutions competed and did business. But a bigger wave is coming.

[1] About 5,000 new jobs were created in the sector each year in 2012 and 2013, compared to about 10,000 a year in 2010 and 2011.

The relentless advance of computing power and internet speed has meant that many more financial transactions can now be done at lower cost, faster and to an increasing degree, automatically. In wholesale markets, electronic platforms are now dominant. This is most clearly seen in the FX industry, where 74% of global FX trading volume is executed electronically today, up from single digits in the early 2000s. The exponential growth in use of mobile devices is leading to profound changes in how financial institutions interact with their customers. Meanwhile, the potential for data analytics is leading to increasing sophistication in financial research and risk management. Algorithms are being developed to assess the impact of market-moving information on traded securities, replacing the role of junior analysts.

These changes will change the profile of jobs in finance, globally, in the coming decade and beyond. We saw an earlier wave of this during the IT revolution of the 1990s, when many typing and clerical jobs, and those in switchboard operations and routine production lines were lost. In the next wave, experts now foresee many more white-collar jobs at risk globally.

There are indications that this is already happening in the financial sector. Following the 37,000 jobs lost in the US financial sector as a result of the crisis, Wall Street announced further planned layoffs amounting to another 14,000 jobs in the first two months of 2014 alone. Analysts believe that a large proportion of these job cuts reflect the ongoing shift from branch to mobile banking, and replacement of voice trading jobs by electronic platforms. Some estimate that about 30% to 40% of spot traders are at risk of being replaced by this electronification of trading.

These are trends we have to respond to, and indeed take advantage of. We can do well in this new financial landscape, and ensure that Singaporeans have quality jobs that complement and take advantage of new technologies. Asia will grow, and the demand for quality in finance will grow. As global financial institutions restructure, and as technology transforms jobs in the next decade and beyond, we must ensure we are well prepared with the skills, depth of expertise and innovative capabilities to stay relevant and competitive. We have to continue to build globally competitive teams in Singapore, by proactively developing our Singaporean core while remaining open to foreign professionals with needed specialised experience and skill-sets.

Skills That Make the Financial Sector of Tomorrow

In short, we can excel in finance and build rewarding careers for Singaporeans. We move ahead from a solid base: a well-reputed financial centre with extensive links to the world, and a competent and skilled workforce. As we look to the future, we must develop capabilities in five areas, which I will touch on briefly in turn:

- Deep Functional Expertise;
- Cross-Functional Capability;
- Regional Knowledge and Experience;
- Technological Skills and Adaptability; and
- Leadership.

Deep Functional Expertise

First, we need to deepen functional expertise, across all areas of finance — in banking, capital markets and insurance. We are seeing a greater demand for specialised skills, for example, in structured trade finance, reinsurance and specialty insurance. Financial institutions need strong expertise in risk management and compliance. In wealth management, there is demand for more sophisticated investment strategies that better hedge risks, and for being able to execute these strategies efficiently. These are all areas in which Singaporeans can excel.

Cross-Functional Capability

Second, we are seeing greater demand for finance professionals with cross-functional abilities, besides a core competence in a particular business area. This is obviously helpful in small institutions, but is also in demand in large institutions as different financial services are being integrated and packaged together for the customer. Cross-functional knowledge and competence also enables financial professionals to take on larger responsibilities, and to achieve greater resilience in their careers in a fast-changing financial sector landscape.

Regional Knowledge and Experience

Third, regional knowledge and experience. It is now an essential for a good career in finance, not just nice to have. We must give it far greater emphasis, and encourage and support Singaporeans in building up this capacity. Cross-border solutions and transactions are increasingly the norm in the business. Strong regional knowledge is also necessary in meeting clients' needs, whether in relationship management, transaction banking, specialised finance or product structuring. It also enables financial institutions to manage their risks well, and operate effectively in Asia's still diverse regulatory frameworks and market environments.

Technological Skills and Adaptability

Fourth, technological adaptability. I spoke earlier about how technology is changing the business, and changing jobs. It is not a matter of defending ourselves against the onslaught of technology, but taking advantage of it. Financial institutions are increasingly using technology to gain an edge over their competitors, or to achieve cost efficiencies and free up resources for new growth areas. In consumer banking, we are now seeing new mobile payment products that enable on-the-go transactions. In private banking, banks are putting more investment tools at the disposal of their clients. For corporates, banks are using technology to facilitate end-to-end supply chain financing. And needless to say, cyber security is now a key risk, everywhere in the world. Across the business, from management to individual business units, technology skills and adaptability must be a strategic imperative.

Initiatives to Facilitate the Building of Competencies

IBF has a key role in ensuring that finance professionals are able to keep pace with these challenges of the future. IBF has been undertaking the strategic role of a standard-setting body for financial sector competencies since 2001. When we went on to launch the Financial Industry Competency Standards or FICS in 2005, IBF took on the role as the national accreditation and certification agency for the FICS framework.

FICS cannot be a static set of competency standards. It must evolve, to cater to new business opportunities and new regulations, and to encourage individuals to build up expertise continually.

We are thus unveiling today the "IBF Standards", which provide practice-oriented development roadmaps for all our financial sector practitioners. The IBF standards which will merge IBF's current offering of industry examinations and industry standards offered under FICS, into an integrated and seamless set of competency standards. They will provide clear pathways on how a practitioner can undergo accredited programmes to progress him or her from the first licensing examination through to foundational skills and subsequently, advanced-level specialist training.

IBF consulted the industry actively in the last year to ensure that the IBF Standards meet the demands of finance professionals of tomorrow. For instance, in risk management, the Standards will now encourage individuals to acquire deeper knowledge of the underlying businesses and their risk triggers. In compliance, individuals will learn to take on advocacy roles, so as to inculcate a stronger compliance culture within the organisation. In Technology and Operations, practitioners will be given core skills in project management and change management to better facilitate process re-engineering within their organisations.

Following last year's launch of foundation programmes for Compliance, Corporate Banking and Wealth Management, IBF will be adding two new foundation programmes this year, in IT & Operations as well as Risk Management. This will enhance the opportunities for graduates or individuals with no prior experience in these areas to be able to land in and excel in such roles.

In addition, IBF will launch a new integrated e-learning system over the coming year, which will help individuals use the revised Standards to undertake self-directed training and map out their professional development milestones.

Leadership

Let me go on to the fifth capability that I mentioned earlier, which is leadership in finance. We want to develop Singaporeans for positions of leadership in tomorrow's financial world.

It requires both depth and breadth, and will increasingly require both local and global experience and know-how.

MAS already has several initiatives in place to further this objective, including the Finance Scholarship Programme and the Finance Associate Management Scheme (FAMS) for Singaporeans early in their finance careers,[2] as well as the International Posting Programme (iPOST).[3]

To equip local practitioners with Asia-relevant leadership capabilities, MAS will be launching a new Asian Financial Leaders Programme (AFLP) later this year for Singaporeans who aspire to take on regional or global leadership positions. Through the AFLP, participants will be able to learn from regional policymakers, as well as interact with fellow financial sector leaders from other countries.

IBF will complement these initiatives by introducing a new IBF Fellows Scheme. Financial industry veterans will be recognised as thought leaders and serve as trainers, speakers and panel discussants, or as mentors. Many of our industry pioneers and senior professionals have a wealth of experience to share, having been through the ups and downs of the industry and various market cycles. This scheme will provide a structured way for us to transfer knowledge from past to future leaders in the industry, complementing what is done within individual financial institutions.

Financial sector skills and leadership development is a key priority for the industry, and MAS takes this very seriously. It will define our continued success as a financial centre. MAS will continue to invest in developing Singaporeans who are committed to a career in the financial

2 The Finance Scholarship Programme (FSP) builds expertise in specialist finance areas such as financial economics and actuarial science while the FAMS provides young talent with exposure to other business lines and overseas operations, through a structured fast-track programme. MAS aims to groom at least 200 young Singaporeans every year under FAMS to take on leadership positions in the future.

3 The iPOST supports the posting of high potential Singaporeans for overseas secondments, through which we hope that they return with managerial skills, a deep understanding of global best practices and strong business networks.

sector. We already fund up to 70% of course fees for training programmes. MAS funding support for manpower and leadership development has increased steadily over the last three years, with about $60 million set aside for 2014 alone. I would like to urge the industry to tap on these programmes actively.

Conclusion

To conclude, I would like to commend the IBF Council and staff, past and present, for your commitment over these past four decades. Going forward, the responsibility on IBF will be greater, as it delivers the IBF Standards and the various initiatives that will help our practitioners develop the capabilities of tomorrow.

I look forward to an even stronger collaboration between IBF and the industry. Let us work together to ensure that the financial sector is one that continues to enable meaningful and rewarding careers for Singaporeans.

I wish you all a happy 40th Anniversary and a great evening ahead.

Positioning for a Technology Driven Future

Mr Heng Swee Keat
Minister for Finance and Board Member, MAS
44th Association of Banks in Singapore Annual Dinner
28 June 2017

I last addressed the ABS in 2006. At the time, Singapore's economy and financial services sector registered robust growth. We successfully hosted the IMF-World Bank Annual Meetings that September. Then came the global financial crisis in 2008.

It was tumultuous worldwide, but in Singapore, our banks were well-capitalised and our system remained healthy throughout the crisis.

Fast forward to today, Singapore is one of the top international financial centres[1] and our regulation and supervision is rated as "among the best globally."[2]

Our banking system continues to be anchored by strong, well regulated banks which are ranked among the world's 10 safest commercial banks.[3]

Singapore's current standing as a respected and innovative global financial centre is a shared success — one that MAS and the industry have earned through your partnership.

---

1 Z/Yen and CDI (2017), "Global Financial Centres Index 21."
2 IMF (2013), "Singapore: Financial System Stability Assessment."
3 Global Finance (2016), "The World's 50 Safest Commercial Banks in 2016."

Innovation — a Key Trait of Singapore's Financial Sector

Innovation is at the heart of Singapore's economic and financial sector transformation. As Mr Hon Sui Sen said, back in 1972, to have a successful financial services sector, we must have an environment that is "conducive to both growth and innovation in financial activities."[4]

Two episodes come to mind in which innovation figured prominently: the launch of our financial sector and the liberalisation of the banking sector during the Asian Financial Crisis.

In the book *From Third World to First*, Mr Lee Kuan Yew recounted Dr Albert Winsemius' story on Singapore's improbable start to become a financial centre.

- In 1968, Dr Winsemius was in London where his friend, Mr Van Oenen, the vice-president of Bank of America Singapore, pointed to a globe and highlighted the gap in global trading hours. Zurich handed over to London, and London to US markets, with global trading stopping once San Francisco's market closed. Nothing could happen until the next day 9.00am Swiss time when Zurich reopened.
- At Dr Winsemius' request, Mr Van Oenen presented the concept of creating a financial centre in Singapore to Mr Hon Sui Sen, then-Chairman of the Economic Development Board and Mr Lee. Mr Lee decided that Singapore must capitalise on our geographical location and the available technologies to build a financial centre here. Singapore thus filled the gap in the trading hours and ushered in "for the first time, a 24-hour-round-the-world service in money and banking."[5]
- We started modestly, building an offshore Asian Dollar Market to intermediate the flow of global and regional funds. Over time, we enhanced our position as a foreign exchange centre, reviewed our policies to remove unnecessary controls and transformed into an international financial centre.

[4] Mr Hon Sui Sen, International Chamber of Commerce Luncheon Speech, 5 May 1972.

[5] Lee Kuan Yew (2000), *From Third World to First: The Singapore Story*.

The second episode was when I was Principal Private Secretary (PPS) to Mr Lee in the late-1990s. Mr Lee held extensive consultations with the industry and came away impressed at how other regulators and financial institutions welcomed innovation. Mr Lee appreciated how globalisation and technology were changing, and would continue to change, the global banking landscape.

- Our practice of protecting our banking system from competition was too domestically focused and would be detrimental in the long run. Mr Lee recognised that for Singapore to become a global financial centre, our banking system must adapt and be exposed to competition.
- With this goal in mind, MAS, under then-DPM and Chairman MAS Mr Lee Hsien Loong, took the bold steps to liberalise the banking sector in 1999.

We have not looked back. Singapore's financial sector has grown to become a key economic driver and will continue to be a lynchpin of Singapore's future economy.

Technology — Transforming Our Economy and Society

To maintain our competitive edge, we must ready ourselves for the next wave of change. Maintaining our innovation edge and harnessing technology will be key.

When I last spoke to the ABS, most of us would have had a mobile phone. But a smartphone? That came a year later in the form of the iPhone. It has changed our view on what it means to be "connected."

- Singaporeans now spend on average, 3 hours and 12 minutes a day on our smartphones.[6]
- We are one of the most connected societies in the world. Our mobile phone penetration rate is 150%. For wireless broadband, it is 200%.[7]

---

6 Straits Times (2017), "Digital Habits in Singapore."

7 Infocomm Media Development Authority (2017), "Mobile Penetration Rate."

The advent of mobile apps and e-commerce platforms have disrupted traditional business models and transformed consumer preferences.

- For instance, social media and messaging apps have usurped the traditional modes of communication. In Singapore, the volume of SMS fell by 70% between 2011 and 2016.[8]
- 60% of Singaporean consumers surveyed in 2016 said they would make purchases online at least once a month.[9]

Technology is also transforming financial services and the way banking customers consume these services.

- Non-financial companies, like WeChat, have created platforms that enable customers to chat, purchase and pay for goods and services, including financial products, all within one application.
- Financial and technology firms are leveraging on application programming interfaces (APIs) to create customised solutions to serve their customers better.

Singaporeans have embraced these changes.

- 94% of Singaporean survey respondents have used mobile and internet banking to access their financial accounts.[10]
- 1 in 5 consumers in the Asia-Pacific are using digital wallets, and Singapore is the top adopter in ASEAN.[11]

I am pleased to see MAS and the industry working closely together to promote innovation and use of technology. There is indeed strong interest to test-bed new ideas in Singapore.

- MAS has received more than 20 applications, and over 70 enquiries from financial institutions and FinTech players, to test their innovations in the MAS Regulatory Sandbox.
- More than 20 global banks and insurance companies have set up innovation labs in Singapore.

---

8 Infocomm Media Development Authority (2016), "Total SMS Messages Sent and Received Over Mobile Network."

9 PwC (2016), "Total Retail 2016 — Southeast Asia and Singapore Highlights."

10 McKinsey (2015), "Digital Banking in ASEAN."

11 MasterCard (2016), "Mobile Shopping Survey."

These are the right moves for us to keep pace with changes in the global economy.

Let me now focus on two important changes we are making to position our financial sector for a technology-driven future.

- First, MAS will be streamlining the anti-commingling framework.
- Second, to accelerate e-payments, we will establish a Payments Council to explore strategies and address cross-cutting issues. ABS will also be launching PayNow this evening.

Streamlining the Anti-Commingling Policy

MAS introduced the anti-commingling framework in 2001 to separate the financial and non-financial businesses of banks. It was a pre-emptive move to ensure that banks remained focused on their core financial businesses and competencies. This policy has served the industry well.

But the policy has not remained static.

In 2011, MAS took a first step to give banks greater allowance to carry on non-financial businesses that are related or complementary to the bank's core financial businesses.[12]

Since then, the outlook has changed further.

- The growing ease of accessing financial services over the internet and smartphones presents new channels for banks to deliver value-added services to customers.
- The line between financial and non-financial business is blurring. Banks are facing increasing competition from online and non-financial players that have leveraged their large user base to provide digital wallets, payments and remittance services.

MAS recognises that we can simplify our requirements to enable banks to embed banking services into consumers' day-to-day activities.

First, MAS will streamline regulatory requirements for banks seeking to conduct or invest in permissible non-financial businesses that are related or complementary to their core financial businesses.

12 MAS Banking Regulations — Regulation 23G.

- Currently, banks seeking to conduct or invest in non-financial businesses must comply with specific conditions and obtain approval from their parent supervisory authority.
- Going forward, banks will not need to seek prior regulatory approval before conducting or acquiring major equity stakes in permissible non-financial businesses.
- MAS will also remove detailed requirements such as conducting regular stress tests or external audits. However, MAS will continue to require banks and their boards to put in place the necessary risk management governance arrangements.

It remains important for banks to focus on their core financial businesses. Hence, MAS will limit such non-financial businesses to 10% of a bank's capital funds.

Second, MAS will allow banks to operate digital platforms that match buyers and sellers of consumer goods or services, as well as to conduct the online sale of such goods or services. These activities must be related or complementary to banks' core financial businesses and will be subject to the cap I mentioned earlier.

- Banks are currently prohibited from selling consumer goods. But non-bank digital players are now offering a seamless transactional experience in the sale as well as payment of consumer goods.
- Under MAS' proposal, banks may be involved in the sale of consumer goods and services on these platforms in a way that provides synergy to the provision of banking services.
- Beyond digital platforms, banks would need to seek case-by-case approval, as we do not want banks to engage in the sale of consumer goods and services as a business in its own right.

MAS will provide the operational details of these policy changes in a consultation paper that will be released by the end of September.

Fostering Innovation in Payments

As Singapore progresses to become a Smart Nation, the country needs a robust electronic payments system that allows individuals and businesses to send and receive money easily.

Let me recap the progress we have made to-date in our e-payments journey and provide an update on latest developments.

Unified Point-of-Sale, or UPOS, terminals are being deployed at major supermarkets and convenience stores across the country. They make payments easier for customers, and help frontline service staff be more productive and efficient.

Going beyond the established merchants, MAS and the National Environment Agency (NEA) are working to trial various electronic payment solutions in a few hawker centres, with a view to achieving mass adoption in subsequent years.

- For instance, hawkers can accept contactless cards or QR codes which consumers can scan with their phones to make payments.

MAS is also reviewing the regulatory regime for payments. Last year, MAS proposed an activity-based regulatory framework for payments that will right-size requirements to the specific payments activities that new players are undertaking.

- MAS is carefully reviewing the industry feedback provided in the first round of consultation, and aims to respond by November.
- MAS will also be conducting a second round of public consultation.

We will also establish a forum for the payments industry and businesses to come together to discuss payment strategies and cross-cutting issues as well as promote inter-operable payment solutions.

- MAS has invited 18 senior leaders representing banks, payment companies, industry associations and businesses to form a Payments Council under MAS' leadership.
- This is a unique opportunity for stakeholders in the payments ecosystem to collaboratively chart the future of Singapore's e-payments journey.

But the most significant development in our e-payments journey begins tonight with the official launch by ABS of PayNow.

I congratulate ABS and Banking Computer Services (BCS) for the many months of hard work, and also the seven participating banks for making PayNow a reality.

PayNow will make use of Singapore's real-time 24x7 Fast and Secure Transfers (FAST) payment system to allow PayNow users to, securely and seamlessly, transfer funds to each other using only their recipient's mobile or NRIC numbers.

The Government is also looking into the use of PayNow to make payments directly to citizens' bank accounts using their NRIC numbers. In the future, we would no longer need to update each government agency one-by-one when we change banks. We will just need to link our new bank account to our NRIC via PayNow.

Conclusion

I have recounted in brief the innovations that enabled us to develop as an international financial centre, from providing 24-hour trading to the liberalisation in the late 1990s.

Change is our constant now. The financial sector must be able to transform and adapt in time with changes in the economy and society.

- The Global Financial Crisis prompted regulators around the world to strengthen financial regulations, underscoring the significance of safety and soundness.
- Structural changes are happening in economies in our region, and around the world, in response to technological, demand-driven and demographic changes. In the midst of these changes, Asia remains well-positioned to grow.
- To enable growth, investment by firms and government will be critical. We just celebrated the 50th anniversary of the founding of the Asian Development Bank. Just before that, we witnessed the setting up of the Asia Infrastructure Investment Bank or AIIB.

> It is a recognition of the importance of infrastructure in development. In my discussions with the leaders of these banks, I am encouraged that they appreciate the importance of catalysing funding from private sector funders.

This is the very dynamic, fluid context in which we set up:

- first, the Committee on the Future Economy — to better appreciate the changes around us;
- and now the Future Economy Council — to move with these changes, adapt and innovate, and create value for and stay relevant to the world.

I am happy to see MAS and our financial sector responding swiftly and creatively to changes around us. Effective intermediation of the growing pool of savings to productive uses to yield sustainable returns will remain a key goal for our financial system.

How we navigate these two currents — one, the urgency for innovation in a world of flux and disruption; and two, the timeless goal of maintaining the safety and soundness of our financial sector — will be critical to our future. This will require all of us to work in close partnership.

The key is to watch the horizon for and adapt to changes, remember and honour our duty to our stakeholders, and work together in a spirit of collaboration. The Government will do our best to facilitate and support the industry in making these changes.

I wish you all success in working together in the years ahead.

Singapore FinTech: Innovation, Inclusion, Inspiration

Mr Ravi Menon
Managing Director, MAS
Singapore FinTech Festival 2018
12 November 2018

Financial Services Built Around Us

When we began our FinTech journey in 2015, we imagined a Smart Financial Centre where innovation and technology are pervasive. We said we want to increase efficiency, manage risks better, create new opportunities and improve people's lives. We didn't know — we still don't know — how the future will look like. But we imagined what we want it to look like, and set about trying to create it.

Imagine a world where financial services are built around us — around our life and our needs.

Imagine a world where identity is human. Imagine a world with no identity cards, no passwords, no mothers' maiden name. We are who we are, not just what we have or what we remember. This is how we have always identified one another throughout history — by recognition, more human, more natural. But when we have large numbers of people and we don't know one another, we had to resort to artificial means. But advances in biometrics are now making identity human again.Many banks are already letting us use our face as our new banking password. Here in Singapore, OCBC Bank is already doing this.

Imagine a world where payments are invisible. Our shopping experience will be transformed. Cameras and sensors identify us and the items that we place in and out of our shopping bag. And when we are done, we just walk out of the store! No more checkouts, no more lines, no more fussing with cash and credit cards. Fantasy? Just visit Amazon Go — it is already happening.

Imagine a world where insurance is intuitive. How many of us truly understand our insurance policies, or are fully confident they will pay out when we need them? Imagine a world where the payout is automatically triggered by events and is instantaneous. No more lengthy claims forms, no more waiting time, no more opaque processes. Science fiction? Not quite. MetLife's Lumenlab here in Singapore is already making this a reality for gestational diabetes insurance. They are testing this out in MAS' regulatory sandbox.

Imagine a world where financial advice is integrated. Imagine our own personal financial dashboard on our mobile devices giving us a complete view of our finances — pulling in data from banks we have deposits with, insurance companies we have policies with and broker-dealers we have investments with. Not to mention, our pension or social security funds, tax liabilities and mortgages. All in one place: a personal balance sheet, in real-time! And where financial advice is customised for us, based on an integrated view of our unique situations, at important milestones in our life — buying our first home, planning our children's education, looking for investment opportunity to grow our retirement nest. Many FinTech firms are already developing apps and solutions to do this.

This is the financial sector we want to create: customised for our needs, invisible to our eyes and an absolute delight. And I'm happy that Singapore's three local banks understand this well:

- That's why UOB Bank says it is Right By You!
- OCBC Bank says Simply Spot On!
- DBS Bank says Live More, Bank Less!

Innovation and technology are key to realising this future. But they are not enough. We need a FinTech ecosystem to make this happen. We need common standards, open architecture and interoperable infrastructure. We need collaboration across government, financial industry, research institutions and the FinTech community at large. We need a free flow of ideas, knowledge, investment, people.

And growing this ecosystem is what we have been hard at work for the last three to four years in Singapore with the private and public sector coming together in collaboration. Let me touch on six components of this FinTech ecosystem we are working on:

- First, people. Without people — their skills, their energy and their enterprise — there is no FinTech.
- Second, identity. Establishing who we are dealing with and authenticating information about that person is the first step in any digital transaction.
- Third, payments. Swift, secure and seamless payments are fundamental to a digital economy.
- Fourth, data governance. We must ensure the responsible use of data and seamless and secure flow of data.
- Fifth, applied research. We need to build strong capabilities in FinTech-related research directed at solving real-world problems.
- Sixth, platforms for innovation. We need mechanisms to foster collaboration and co-creation to translate ideas into products; bridge problems with solutions.

People

Let me start with the most critical part of the ecosystem — people. The shortage of tech skills and talent is a global phenomenon. For a small city-state like Singapore, it is almost existential — and that is why it is our top priority.

Singapore is taking a multi-pronged approach. Our institutes of higher learning are adapting their curriculum with industry input to develop students who are able to work with emerging technologies. Our financial institutions are putting in place programmes to help re-skill mid-career professionals to take on the jobs of the future; and we will continue to welcome and embrace top talents from across the world to augment our own talent pool and raise the game here.

Identity

Let me then move on to the pain of verifying identity — the KYC or "know-your-customer" problem. For personal KYC, the Singapore Government has taken the first step with the National Digital Identity (NDI) which every resident of Singapore can use to establish his legal identity in a secure manner — with two-factor authentication and a public-private key pair — when making online transactions.

A powerful component of NDI is MyInfo. This is a digital service that enables citizens to authorise third-parties to access their personal data sitting across many different government agencies. With consent, third parties can use MyInfo APIs to access government-verified data to authenticate their customers and make business decisions relating to those customers.

Last year, MAS and the Government Technology Agency of Singapore (GovTech) started a pilot with four banks to enable individuals to open a bank account online using MyInfo. Today, we can open a bank account or apply for a credit card — online and instantly — when we give consent to the bank to access our data through MyInfo. More than 20 financial institutions are now using MyInfo to provide more than 110 digital financial services.

We have substantially solved the personal KYC problem. But corporate KYC is far more complex. Last year, I shared with you that MAS is working with local and foreign banks to explore a shared services utility for doing corporate KYC. This is potentially a transformative project. And we made good progress in harmonising various banks' KYC systems and integrating the proposed KYC utility with the banks' infrastructure. This is no mean feat given the diversity of banks' KYC processes and internal IT systems. But the economics did not work out: our proposed solution was going to cost more than the savings that banks will get out of it. So we have decided to take a pause on the project.

The banks participating in the KYC project will publish a report this week on their learning experience. I hope this report will inspire new ideas to help solve corporate KYC problems in the most cost-efficient way. We tried, we failed, we will learn and we will do better next time.

Innovation is about experimenting and learning from setbacks. Just as we showcase our successes, let us also be open about our setbacks. This is the spirit of enterprise we need in the financial sector, and in Singapore. And we will continue to explore other ways to alleviate KYC pain for financial institutions and their customers.

MAS and GovTech are now working with the industry to facilitate financial institutions' credit assessment of SMEs using trusted government data. Today, young SMEs that wish to obtain bank financing may face difficulties due to the lack of credit history. We will help pool trusted data from government sources on the business and key individuals associated with the SMEs to facilitate a more informed credit assessment. We will run a pilot with three banks in the first half of next year.

Payments

Next, payments. We have substantially completed Singapore's national e-payment infrastructure.

- There is FAST, a 24x7 real-time funds transfer infrastructure.
- There is PayNow, which rides on FAST to enable instant money transfer to an individual or business, using their personal ID number, mobile phone number or unique entity number.
- There is UPOS, or unified point-of-sale terminal, that can accept all major credit card brands, whether using a smart chip, near-field communication (NFC) or QR code.
- And now we have SGQR, a single, standardised QR code that can represent multiple payment schemes; this is the first of its kind in the world.

The pain point that remains — for banks, businesses and individuals — is cross-border payments and settlement of assets. Cross-border payments involve multiple currencies and cross-border settlements involve multiple assets, and there is no single trusted central party. This is why we think distributed ledger technology holds promise in this area.

Many of you are familiar with Project Ubin. It involves MAS and the financial industry here working closely. It aims to make cross-border payments and settlements cheaper and faster at no compromise in security or privacy, using blockchain technology. In 2016, Project Ubin demonstrated that banks could pay one another without going through MAS, using a blockchain based digital representation of the Singapore Dollar. Last year, Project Ubin successfully achieved decentralised netting of payments while preserving transactional privacy. This year, we have made two more advances.

First, Project Ubin team has successfully harnessed blockchain technology for the settlement of tokenised assets. In the analogue world, payment and exchange of goods are done at the same time. In financial terms, we call this "delivery-vs-payment" or DvP. It eliminates settlement risk, i.e., sellers cannot abscond with money without delivering the goods. But how do we achieve DvP and eliminate settlement risk in the digital world?

MAS, Singapore Exchange and various industry partners worked together to tokenise digital currencies and securities assets so that they can be simultaneously exchanged, thus achieving final settlement and DvP. This has potentially powerful implications for not just the financial sector but also a broad spectrum of the economy. We have published a report from the experiment. Please take a look, consider the findings and work with us to advance this cause of real-time settlement. It is a holy grail in the world of finance that we must collectively solve.

Second, MAS is working with like-minded central banks to explore faster, cheaper and more efficient cross-border payments. MAS, together with the Bank of Canada, the Bank of England and various commercial banks, did an in-depth study of the inefficiencies of today's international payment systems. MAS and Bank of Canada have begun work on linking our respective blockchain platforms to explore the possibility of instant, 24x7 settlement of cross-border payments transactions. We are much looking forward to reporting our progress at next year's SFF.

Data Governance

The fourth element of FinTech ecosystem is data governance. The ability to aggregate, store, process and transmit data — especially across borders — is critical to the digital age. Yet, we all have deep-seated concerns about the privacy, confidentiality, security and ethical use of data. If we do not address these concerns, we will not have the consensus that is necessary to achieve the many benefits of technology.

What do we need to get right in data governance? Data must be protected — we must safeguard privacy, confidentiality and security. Data must be used in a responsible, transparent and ethical manner. We must be able to explain the results of data driven algorithms. We cannot hide behind the black box. Humans, not machines, are accountable for decisions driven by AI or data analytics. We must ensure that outcomes of data or AI driven processes are ethical, free of bias and socially acceptable. Only then, can we create an ecosystem where data flows seamlessly in a trusted manner.

MAS has been actively working with the industry to develop principles to guide the responsible use of data in financial services. We are pleased to release today a set of principles to promote Fairness, Ethics, Accountability & Transparency, or FEAT, in the use of AI and data analytics. I am told this is the first of its kind in the world — where the regulator and industry have come together to set guidance on the responsible use of AI and data analytics. This will be a living document that will be continually updated as we learn more.

Next, on the international front: we need more data connectivity, and less data localisation. Data localisation measures are on the rise around the world. This is a serious risk. If data cannot cross borders, the digital economy cannot cross borders and we will be poorer for it. Not all data localisation is bad: there may be some legitimate concerns about national security. But a good part of data localisation that is happening in the world today is due to misguided notions of cyber security or data privacy or, worse still, old-fashioned protectionism.

This is a key challenge for the technology community to solve together with policymakers — how to enhance data connectivity while taking into account the issues of data sovereignty. Many of the technologies do exist today: end-to-end encryption, anonymisation. Some experiments are already underway. For example, here in Singapore, UOB Bank is collaborating with Intel to test out an interesting solution. It will allow the bank's staff in Singapore to run a federated analysis of data residing in other countries and obtain an integrated output of that analysis, without seeing any actual data. MAS and Bank of Thailand are very keen on this project and are participating as observers.

We need common data standards across countries so that data can flow freely in an environment of trust and security. In the digital economy of the future, data connectivity agreements among countries will become as important as today's free trade agreements.

Applied Research

Another important element of FinTech ecosystem is applied research. Last year, MAS launched the $27 million grant scheme to support R&D in AI and data analytics for the financial sector. We have received more than 30 applications from financial and research institutions. We have now put out five calls for applied research proposals:

- in econometrics and data science,
- back-testing methodologies,
- quantum computing for the financial sector, and
- explainable AI.

Last year, MAS and the industry also began collaborating with MIT Media Lab to do serious FinTech R&D. MAS, industry professionals and MIT researchers have come together towards developing prototypes that look into applications of AI and distributed ledger technology in the financial sector. They include use cases in smart contracts, trade finance and central bank digital currencies.

And earlier this year, the Intellectual Property Office of Singapore established a FinTech Fast Track initiative for patents. Under the Fast Track, FinTech patents can be granted in as quickly as six months, compared to the industry convention which can be up to two years. Once patented in Singapore, applicants can leverage on our global patent highways to expedite the registration of their patents in more than 30 overseas markets.

Platforms for Innovation

The final piece in the FinTech ecosystem — platforms for innovation. Innovation does not occur in isolation. We need platforms to connect people and ideas, problems and solutions and foster collaboration.

One such platform we are excited about is AFIN — the ASEAN Financial Innovation Network. Let's begin with the problem statement. There are about 1.7 billion adults globally who are unbanked. One out of three of the unbanked come from just four countries in Asia — China, India, Pakistan, Indonesia. It is a shame that in this day and age, so many do not have access to a bank account, secure and efficient means of payment, or insurance protection.

The root of this problem is twofold:

- Banks face high costs in reaching out to customers in remote villages. And frankly, many of their mainstream financial services may not be suited to the needs of these customers.
- FinTech firms, on other hand, are able to create agile and mobile digital solutions to access and serve these underserved segments. But they lack the resources to scale and penetrate new markets.

This is where AFIN comes in, to bring banks and FinTech firms together to develop solutions to penetrate these hard-to-reach markets. AFIN is spearheaded by MAS, the ASEAN Bankers Association and the World Bank's International Finance Corporation.

This Wednesday, AFIN will launch API Exchange, or APIX. It is the world's first cross-border, open architecture platform to enhance financial inclusion. APIX is both an online FinTech Marketplace and FinTech Sandbox. As a marketplace, it will enable financial institutions to discover and connect with FinTech firms through APIs on a globally curated platform. As a sandbox, it provides a platform for financial institutions and FinTech firms to collaborate and experiment on solutions in a contained environment. Please step forward to participate in this exciting enterprise to deepen financial inclusion in ASEAN and the Asia-Pacific region.

Next, MAS and the InfoComm Media Development Authority (IMDA) are working together to create a cross-border innovation platform for SMEs called Business sans Borders. Business sans Borders will do two things:

- It will enable SMEs to connect in a global services marketplace, where they can explore synergies in digitalising their business processes and mutualise costs.
- It will allow solution providers to more effectively reach out to SMEs who tend to be highly dispersed and are sometimes hard to reach.

Business sans Borders will begin with a proof-of-concept next year, with three features:

- first, a sandbox where start-ups and established players come together to experiment and build relevant solutions;
- second, an "app store" where SMEs can access a wide range of services, from finance and logistics to human resources; and
- third, an AI engine to match SME suppliers with buyers for products and services, across ASEAN and beyond.

Conclusion

Let me end where I began. FinTech is not just about technology — though technology is very important in all that we do and will help to solve many real problems. FinTech is not just about finance — though we want to create a world where financial services are built around us, and we want to empower hundreds of millions of people to participate in the modern economy.

FinTech is about a spirit of enterprise that is infused with empathy and lifts us to be better people. It is about innovation, inclusion and inspiration.

Everything we do in FinTech must always have a larger purpose — to improve the lives of individuals, to build a more dynamic economy, to promote a more inclusive society.

This is the FinTech spirit. And over the next five days of this Festival, may you find that spirit and may you be inspired to break new ground, and seek a better, newer world.

Green Finance for a Sustainable World

Mr Ong Ye Kung
Minister for Education and Board Member, MAS
Singapore FinTech Festival 2019
11 November 2019

The Ultimate Global Commons Challenge

This year we are making green finance a major theme of the FinTech Festival. Finance, technology and innovation will be critical for our transition to a sustainable world.

Singapore will do its part, as a responsible global citizen, to reduce carbon emissions and help make the world greener. As Prime Minister Lee Hsien Loong put it recently, "climate change is the ultimate global commons challenge".

Singapore accounts for only 0.11% of carbon emissions in the world. By our actions alone, we cannot change the world. But through our actions, we hope we can inspire it, we can catalyse change.

We are developing our long-term low emission strategy. We are not building up from scratch, but from a strong foundation.

We are one of few countries in the world, and the only in Asia to have introduced a broad-based carbon tax to put a price on emissions. We are also one of few countries in the world that limit our car population, and price their usage. Today, growth of car population is 0%. As a principle of planning, we build greenery into our cityscape. We have a natural reserve in the middle of the city. We systematically create wetlands and mangrove swamps to absorb flood water and cushion storm surges. Today, we have a linear system of "take, make and dispose". Our Zero Waste Masterplan will transform Singapore to a Circular Economy, one that reuses resources in a continuous loop.

The Role of Green Finance

Our next ambition is to leverage green finance, to make the world greener. Finance fuels the economy and business. It determines investment decisions. It drives action. We must make finance green, to drive climate action — mitigate and adapt to climate change.

As a leading international financial centre, Singapore will do the right thing to help reduce carbon emissions and promote sustainable development in Asia and globally.

What does it mean to make finance green? It means what the Paris Agreement says: "making finance flows consistent with a pathway towards low greenhouse gas emissions and climate-resilient development". That in turn means mobilising global capital for the green economy. Channel them to new investments in green businesses, technology and infrastructure, reduce carbon emissions, while creating jobs and opportunities. It means a virtuous cycle that can bring about economic growth that is environmentally sustainable.

The last point is particularly important. Economic growth remains critical to the people of the world. It is inconceivable to tackle climate change and bring about a sustainable world, by telling the developing world to give up their dreams of economic development.

For many developing countries in Asia and other regions, they are still urbanising, populations are still aspiring to catch up from lower to middle-income living standards, and energy demand is still rising. The solution cannot be to curtail their growth and dampen their hopes.

That is why in 1992, the United Nations Framework Convention on Climate Change established the CBDR principle — Common But Differentiated Responsibilities, which forms the basis of the Paris Agreement.

We must dare to believe that we can bring about growth that is sustainable. It means making a quantum leap in improving energy efficiency, shifting the energy mix, including investing in renewable energy.

What is the extent of change needed? The International Energy Agency (IEA) developed a Sustainable Development Scenario up to 2040. Under this scenario, the world achieves universal energy access, yet reduces air pollution, and is on track to meet the goals of the Paris Agreement.

In this scenario, the use of fossil fuels falls by a quarter while hydro and other renewables increase fourfold. The ratio of fossil fuels versus hydro and renewables shifts from around 20:1 to 3:1 by 2040. This shift is accompanied by continuous improvements in energy efficiency.[1]

It is not a pipe dream. With technological advances, and widespread deployment of technology and green finance, we can have a good shot at achieving it.

IEA estimated that full utilisation of currently available and economically viable, energy-efficient technologies in industry, buildings and transport, will reduce global emissions by 11% from today's levels.[2] The technologies already exist. We need to deploy them.

From 2008 to 2017, coal's share in China energy supply fell from 70% to 64%, as renewables rose from about 3% to 6%.[3] Renewables costs have fallen due to technology, and at the frontier, renewables are more economical than fossil fuels.

In fact, solar and wind are highly competitive in the US.[4] And it can get cheaper in regions like ASEAN. ASEAN has set an aspirational target to increase renewables from 10% in 2015 to 23% of energy mix by 2025.[5] We are almost halfway there, at 15% today.[6]

In addition, we can use smarter grids, and battery storage systems to overcome the problem of intermittency of renewable energy.

---

1 World Energy Outlook 2018, IEA (2018).

2 Energy Efficiency 2018, Analysis and Outlook to 2040, IEA (2018).

3 World Energy Outlook 2018, IEA (2018).

4 Lazard's Levelized Cost of Energy Analysis Version 12.0, Lazard (2018).

5 ASEAN Plan of Action for Energy Cooperation (APAEC) 2016–2025 (2015).

6 Southeast Asia Energy Outlook 2019, IEA (2019).

These are significant changes, because Asia represents about half of global emissions and world population. If Asia shifts, I think the world shifts.

The shift in energy mix has to be determined but progressive, in tandem with technological advances, and not sudden, not disruptive. It is not realistic to replace fossil fuels with renewables overnight. But we have to make progressive and determined moves.

Singapore: A Leading Centre for Green Finance in Asia and Globally

There is a lot that we can do in green finance, to bring about the shift in the energy situation I just mentioned. Globally, finance is still well behind the curve.

Fossil fuel financing is still significant, totalling US$1.9 trillion over the three years following the Paris Agreement, with financing still rising each year.[7] Surely, the trend should start to reverse given that the energy mix has already started shifting?

Green bonds have started to take off, but still make up only a sliver of total bond issuance. Last year, global green bond issuance was US$168 billion[8] — just 2.5% of total bond issuance that year.[9]

Singapore's financial sector can play a decisive role in promoting sustainable development opportunities and powering the transition, especially in Asia.

We can spur investments in renewables technology, in grid infrastructure, in battery storage. We also need investments in green buildings, efficient cooling and industrial systems, to optimise energy consumption. In time, maybe even bring about investments in carbon sequestration.

With our experience in financing the region, and capabilities in technology, we can make a unique contribution. Our goal is to be a leading centre for Green Finance in Asia and globally. Today, let me outline some of the concrete steps that Singapore is going to take. There are three:

---

7 Banking on Climate Change, Fossil Fuel Finance Report Card, Rainforest Action Network (2019).

8 Green Bonds: The State of the Market 2018, Climate Bonds Initiative (2019).

9 Dealogic (2018).

- First, build financial system resilience to environmental risks.
- Second, develop green finance solutions and markets.
- Third, leverage innovation and technology.

Build Financial System Resilience to Environmental Risks

Let me start with building financial system resilience. Climate change poses two main risks to the financial system.

One, physical risks arising from climate change itself. Damage to assets and property caused by floods and rising sea levels. This can result in large insurance claims, and lower the collateral value of bank loans.

Over the last 30 years, the annual average worldwide costs of natural disasters is US$140 billion. In the last decade, seven out of 10 years exceeded this average. At a temperature rise of two degrees, US$1.7 trillion of global financial assets or about 2% of today's global GDP are estimated to be at risk.[10]

Two, transition risks arising from policy changes, technological advances, or changes in consumer preferences. Old fossil fuel assets can become stranded, and as a result, will devalue loans and investments in the energy sector.

The amount of stranded assets across the energy, industry and building sectors from now to 2050, could be up to US$20 trillion globally.[11]

These potential losses are large, can be compounded by other risks such as deforestation, land contamination, water and air pollution and threaten stability of the financial system.

Our financial institutions need to build up their resilience to climate change risks. This encompasses measuring, mitigating and disclosing these risks.

First, measuring risks. This is about risk assessments and forward-looking stress tests.

- What would asset values be when sea levels rise and carbon prices increase? Banks, insurers and asset managers will need to assess

---

[10] "Climate value at risk" of global financial assets, Dietz, Bowen, Dixon and Gradwell (2016).

[11] Perspectives for the Energy Transition, IEA and IRENA (2017).

the impact of climate change on balance sheets and their loan and investment portfolios.

- The industry is beginning to move, but it has to move more quickly. Global regulators, including MAS, are intensifying their supervisory focus in this area.
- MAS is working with our counterparts to enhance global practices in environmental risk management and disclosures. We do this through the Network for Greening the Financial System (NGFS), of which we are a founding member, and the Sustainable Insurance Forum.

Second, mitigating risks. This is about limiting and reducing exposures.

- The Association of Banks in Singapore (ABS) has issued Guidelines on Responsible Financing practices. Our three local banks — DBS, OCBC and UOB — have ceased financing new coal power plants, as they step up financing of renewable energy projects.
- Asset managers in Singapore have signed the UN Principles for Responsible Investment, and developed the Singapore Stewardship Principles for Responsible Investors.
- Financial institutions too, should make early strategic shifts in capital allocation from carbon-intensive to greener businesses, or risk being stuck with environmentally unfriendly "stranded assets".

Third, disclosing risks. This is about providing sustainability-related disclosures to better inform investors.

- Within Asia, India, Hong Kong and many exchanges in ASEAN,[12] including the Singapore Exchange, have implemented sustainability reporting on listed companies.
- It is a good start, but companies and financial institutions should enhance the quality, granularity and consistency of disclosures, for investors to make well-informed decisions.

To reinforce industry efforts and build financial system resilience, MAS

[12] Sustainable Stock Exchanges Initiative (2019).

will issue Environmental Risk Management (ENRM) guidelines across banking, insurance and asset management sectors. These guidelines will set standards on governance, risk management and disclosure. The guidelines will encourage the right-pricing of loans and investments, and thereby promote new opportunities for green investment. MAS will publish a consultation paper in Q1 2020.

Develop Green Finance Solutions and Markets

A second key thrust of our strategy is to develop green finance solutions and markets.

This will promote new economic opportunities in CleanTech and other growth areas, by financing the investments that these green sectors need to grow. Greening the financial system requires a range of instruments.

First, green bonds

MAS introduced a Green Bond Grant Scheme two years ago. To-date, more than $6 billion green bonds have been issued. The grant defrays the costs of external review against green bond standards.

We have expanded the scheme by reducing the minimum size, broadened its scope to include social and sustainability bonds and renamed it the Sustainable Bond Grant Scheme. We welcome more issuers to make use of our schemes and issue more of such bonds here.

For green bond markets to reach scale, we need common green bond standards. This is to avoid fragmenting capital pools across borders, and tackle greenwashing. This is the malpractice of making projects look green when they are not green.

Globally, there remains important work to harmonise green bond standards for better comparability. That said, there are already standards that are fit for use by issuers.

An example is the ASEAN Green Bond Standards, which provides a regional framework for cross-border issuance. We had worked with our ASEAN partners to develop and update the ASEAN Standards to be in line with international green bond principles.

Next, green loans

To make finance green in Asia, we need to make green lending not a niche activity, but mainstream.

Banks are the main source of financing, particularly in Asia where capital markets are still developing. But green lending in this region is more nascent than green bonds. This is therefore an area with significant potential for growth.

We are beginning to see early shoots in green lending. In the real estate sector, many developers have secured green loans from banks, to develop new green buildings, install solar panels and retrofit buildings with energy-efficient equipment.

In the broader market, sustainability-linked loans are gaining traction. Here, loan proceeds are not tied to specific green projects, and can be used for general corporate purposes so long as borrowers meet sustainability metrics.

Recently, Quadria Capital, a private equity fund in Singapore, became the world's first to tap on sustainability-linked loans for private equity. We wish to see more of such developments.

MAS will develop incentives to encourage growth in green and sustainability-linked loans. In order to access lending, firms will need to incur costs to develop sustainability frameworks, and engage external reviewers. MAS will develop grant schemes to help defray these costs for businesses.

Third, risk transfer solutions

In insurance, we need to develop new risk transfer solutions that will help meet disaster protection needs, while creating alternative investment opportunities.

We established the Southeast Asia Disaster Risk Insurance Facility (SEADRIF), with support from Japan and World Bank. SEADRIF provides flood risk pooling and strengthens the region's disaster resilience.

A good example of a risk transfer solution to promote green finance is insurance-linked securities (ILS), which enable the returns and risks to be distributed to investors via the capital markets.

To catalyse the growth of the ILS market in Singapore, MAS introduced an ILS Grant Scheme last year, to fund upfront issuance costs. Since then, we have seen the first catastrophe bond domiciled in Asia, and three catastrophe bonds issued.

ILS can be used to transfer other risks, not just catastrophe risk, and support the development of new climate risk insurance. MAS will study extending our ILS grant scheme beyond end-2020.

Fourth, green funds

MAS will launch a US$2 billion Green Investments Programme (GIP).

Under the Programme, MAS will place funds in public market investment strategies which have a strong green focus, with asset managers who are committed to deepening green finance activities and capabilities in Singapore.

This programme also supports MAS' efforts to generate sustainable long-term returns on its investment portfolio. It complements our broader range of initiatives to accelerate the growth of Singapore's green finance ecosystem.

As part of the GIP, MAS will also allocate US$100 million to the Bank for International Settlements' Green Bond Fund, in support of its global green finance initiatives.

Finally, green capabilities

As we develop solutions and markets, we need to build the requisite capabilities in green finance. We are collaborating with our universities, the Asia Sustainable Finance Initiative and the International Finance Corporation to build up capabilities amongst financial industry professionals.

MAS will develop a scheme to support external reviewers, and rating agencies who assess and certify green financing instruments, and encourage them to expand their operations here.

MAS will also work towards anchoring Centres of Excellence in Singapore, to contribute to Asia-focused climate research, which can be applied in the financial sector.

The Centres will support the development of innovative green finance solutions, deepen our understanding of climate risks and enhance climate risk management in Singapore. The Centres will also train and groom talent in green finance.

We have received keen interest from leading international research institutes and universities, to collaborate with our local universities to establish these Centres of Excellence.

Building such capabilities is extremely critical. This brings me to the third key thrust of our green finance strategy — leveraging on our strong FinTech ecosystem, and the capabilities and technologies it has to offer.

Leverage Innovation and Technology

Since we started our FinTech journey, we have built up a strong base of technological capabilities. We will build green finance on top of our technology stack.

We will harness the power of FinTech to spur green finance, by scaling up Reach, Innovation and Data. We are already beginning to see interesting FinTech solutions for green finance.

First, Reach.

- We will encourage the application of platform technologies for green finance to reach a wider pool of capital and market players.
- We can also use such technologies to connect supply chains. Bureau Vente Uganda develops digital platforms to monitor crops and financial transactions across supply chains, and to track data on crop yields and the sustainability of farming practices.

Second, Innovation.

- We will encourage the development of smart algorithms, smart contracts and distributed ledgers, to increase speed, ease and transparency of transactions.
- Solstroem developed a Blockchain system for generation and transaction of carbon offsets. The system auto-generates carbon

offsets, complete with time stamps and geo tags, using emissions data from smart meters. The records are secure, tamper-proof and transparent.

Third, Data.

- We will promote the application of Big Data and advanced modelling to measure climate and financial risks, and develop new climate risk insurance products.
- For example, Asia Risk Transfer Solutions developed a cloud-based risk analytics software for designing and pricing agriculture and natural catastrophe risk insurance products.

This is just the tip of the iceberg. Many more ideas and applications will emerge. Every year, as part of the SFF FinTech Hackcelerator, we gather and publish problem statements around key themes, for FinTechs to develop solutions.

This year, there were vertical themes for banking and insurance, and the horizontal theme of financial inclusion. Next year, we will introduce green finance as a key horizontal theme for the 2020 FinTech Hackcelerator. It will be exciting to see new Green FinTech solutions at SFF 2020.

Conclusion

Let me conclude by going back to our larger purpose, and why this is important.

Finance, innovation and technology are a force for good, to overcome challenges and improve lives. Climate change is the ultimate challenge for humankind. It cannot be that the two objectives of being green and pursuing growth are irreconcilable. With imagination, innovation, technology, determination, we can reconcile them.

Part of this solution is to make finance green because finance mobilises the resources of the world. I have therefore laid out our goal for Singapore to be a leading centre for green finance, promoting sustainable development in Asia and globally.

Harnessing the Power of Finance for a Sustainable Future

Mr Ravi Menon
Managing Director, MAS
Financial Times Investing for Good Asia Digital Conference
13 October 2020

What Has COVID-19 to Do With Sustainability?

The climate crisis is the existential challenge of our time. Never before have the effects of climate change been more keenly felt — soaring temperatures, extreme weather events, rising sea levels. Recent wildfires in Australia and the Western United States are the worst in history. Meteorologists tracking hurricanes across the Eastern United States have run out of names this season.

How we deal with climate change will define our future. The Paris Agreement calls for a concerted effort to limit global temperature rise by reducing emissions of greenhouse gases.

This call to action for a sustainable future has only grown stronger with the COVID-19 pandemic. COVID-19 has sensitised the world to how vulnerable we all are to the forces of nature. The pandemic has underscored the importance of taking timely and collective actions to mitigate global challenges.

As we look to building a more resilient world emerging from COVID-19, we have an opportunity to also make it more sustainable.

Resilience and sustainability are complementary. By improving environmental health and safeguarding biodiversity, we also strengthen public health. If resilience requires us to adopt a more decentralised way of living and working, there is opportunity to reduce the carbon footprint of daily commutes. Reducing waste and recycling resources not only enhances sustainability but also strengthens resilience.

Asia's Transition to Deeper Shades of Green

Asia accounts for about half of global greenhouse gas emissions. To move the needle on global emissions, Asia must move. But Asia's journey towards a low-carbon future will be different from that of Europe.

Asia is at a different stage of development — millions of people still do not have access to electricity, modern sanitation and drinking water. Demand for affordable energy will continue to grow strongly, especially with rapid urbanisation and modernisation. Most countries in Asia are still heavily dependent on fossil fuels for their energy needs. More than 80% of Southeast Asia's current and planned fossil fuel generation assets exceed the carbon budget under the Paris Agreement.[1] It is not realistic to suddenly replace fossil fuels with renewables. Asia cannot move quickly to a European standard of green without curtailing its economic and social development.

Asia's transition to sustainability has to be progressive yet determined — through ever deeper shades of green. There is considerable scope to make Asian cities greener and cleaner — by tapping on energy-efficient technologies and renewable energy solutions. Asia is also well-positioned to reap the vast potential of renewable energy. Large-scale solar farms have already become a common sight in Asia. According to the International Renewable Energy Agency, Asia is poised to become a world leader in wind energy by 2050.

A progressive transition to a low-carbon economy is consistent with inclusive economic growth. According to the Global Commission on the

1 Oxford Smith School Briefing Paper, October 2018, Carbon Lock-in Curves and Southeast Asia.

Economy and Climate, bold climate action could generate more than 65 million new low-carbon jobs globally in 2030.[2] Renewable energy projects, energy-efficient retrofits and green construction are labour intensive in the short run and a good means of creating jobs.[3]

Sustainable Singapore

Singapore has much at stake in global efforts to mitigate climate risk. We are a tropical island smaller in size than London, with most of the country lying just 15 metres above sea level. If temperatures were to soar or sea levels rise, our very existence could be in question.

Singapore has always been committed to the idea of sustainability. Right from the 1960s, as a newly independent developing country, we pursued sustainable development: economic growth with environmental protection and social inclusion. We embedded greenery in our urban landscape. We preserved a small tropical rainforest right in the middle of the city. We were one of the earliest countries in the world to limit our car population — through quotas and usage charges on roads leading into the city centre. Today, our car population is at 0% growth.

Now, with the threat of climate change and our commitments under the Paris Agreement, Singapore's sustainability agenda has taken on added urgency and broader dimensions. We are actively developing strategies to reduce our long-term carbon emissions. Singapore is one of few countries in the world, and the first in Southeast Asia to have introduced a broad-based carbon tax.

We are shifting towards cleaner energy sources and low-carbon technologies. Singapore is ramping up solar energy output, which is our most viable renewable energy source. We are looking to harness technologies such as hydrogen and carbon capture, utilisation and storage. We are exploring transmission lines to our neighbouring countries to tap on and trade in the renewable energy they produce.

---

2 New Climate Economy 2018 Report.

3 Oxford Smith School Working Paper, May 2020, Will COVID-19 fiscal recovery packages accelerate or retard progress on climate change?

We are re-designing our residential precincts through a Green Towns Programme. We are recycling rainwater and using cool paint to reduce ambient temperatures in our housing estates. In the upcoming Punggol Digital District, businesses will be connected to a network of sensors collecting real-time data on solar generation, building occupancy, rainfall and humidity; they can use this information to optimise their energy usage.

We are working towards a Circular Economy, where resource usage is reduced and resources are recycled. Singapore is the first country in the world to achieve circularity in the water sector. We collect every drop of used water, treat and purify it and turn much of it into clean water again.

Singapore is extending the circularity principle to other areas. We are experimenting with the use of treated incineration waste as construction materials for building roads. We are looking into transforming waste plastic into alternative fuels. We are recycling food waste into sustainable animal feed. Under the Zero Waste Masterplan, by 2030, Singapore aims to reduce by 30% the amount of waste per capita that we send to our landfills.

We are positioning Singapore as a carbon services hub to complement Asia's decarbonisation efforts. There is good potential in Southeast Asia to generate carbon credits. Singapore can play a role in facilitating the financing of projects that reduce or remove emissions through these credits.

A critical enabler for all these sustainability efforts — in Singapore and across Asia — is Green Finance. Finance fuels the economy, shapes investment decisions and drives action. The immense financing needed to build a greener world can only be met through a combination of public and private capital.

Singapore's Green Finance Action Plan

Last year, MAS launched a Green Finance Action Plan — to support a sustainable Singapore and to facilitate Asia's transition to a sustainable future. As a champion of sustainable development and as an international financial centre in the heart of Asia, Singapore is well-placed to support Asia's sustainability journey through green finance. Our vision is for Singapore to be the leading centre for Green Finance in Asia.

The Green Finance Action Plan comprises four key thrusts:

- strengthen the financial sector's resilience to environmental risks;
- develop green financial solutions and markets for a sustainable economy;
- harness technology to enable trusted and efficient sustainable finance flows; and
- build knowledge and capabilities in sustainable finance.

Let me elaborate on each of these.

Strengthening Resilience to Environmental Risks

First, strengthening the financial sector's resilience to environmental risks. Climate change poses two key risks to financial institutions. Physical risks arising from climate change — such as floods and rising sea levels damaging assets and properties, resulting in large insurance claims and reduced collateral values for bank loans. Transition risks arising from policy changes, technological advances or shifts in consumer preferences that reduce demand for fossil fuels, thereby devaluing loans and investments with a fossil fuel exposure.

These risks are not trivial and could well threaten the stability of the financial system. It is estimated that at a temperature rise of two degrees Celsius, US$1.7 trillion of global financial assets could be at risk of a write-down in value.[4] As for transition risks, it is estimated that up to US$20 trillion of assets across the energy, industry and building sectors globally could become stranded by 2050.[5] Financial institutions cannot afford to ignore these risks.

MAS has co-created with the financial industry a set of Guidelines on Environmental Risk Management. These Guidelines are distinct from those in other jurisdictions in two ways:

- First, they cover environmental risks beyond climate change — such as pollution, loss of biodiversity and changes in land use.

[4] "Climate value at risk" of global financial assets, Dietz, Bowen, Dixon and Gradwell (2016).

[5] Perspectives for the Energy Transition, IEA and IRENA (2017).

These risks can interact with climate effects to compound environmental degradation and depress asset values.

- Second, the Guidelines extend beyond banks to include insurers and asset managers, and are calibrated to each sector's business activities.

The Guidelines set out expectations for financial institutions to assess, monitor, mitigate and disclose environmental risks. Financial institutions should adopt sound methodologies and tools to identify and assess the environmental risks relevant to them. They should monitor their exposures to geographies and sectors with higher environmental risks, and the carbon intensity of customers and investee companies.

They should develop specific risk mitigation policies for sectors posing higher environmental risks and support the transition of riskier customers and investee companies towards sustainable business practices. They should disclose their approach to managing environmental risks and the impact of these risks on their financial performance. Disclosure should reference internationally accepted reporting frameworks, such as those by the FSB Taskforce on Climate-related Financial Disclosures (TCFD).

MAS will assess environmental risk in our supervision of financial institutions. This will include assessing how financial institutions integrate environmental risk management with their business operations. Within the next two years, MAS will incorporate climate-related scenarios in our annual stress tests for the financial industry.

Disclosure of environmental risk applies as much to non-financial corporates. Only then can investors price climate-related risks and opportunities and asset managers construct and manage sustainable portfolios for their clients. The Singapore Exchange (SGX) requires listed companies to produce annual sustainability reports on a comply-or-explain basis. SGX will soon include the TCFD recommendations within its existing guidance to assist listed companies with their climate-related financial disclosures.

As a central bank and financial regulator, MAS will practise what it preaches. MAS has begun to evaluate the resilience of its Official Foreign

Reserves under a range of short-term climate-related disruptions and longer-term climate scenarios.

MAS is also working on a roadmap to better integrate environmental risks across all our business functions. This will include measuring, reducing and disclosing our own carbon footprint. Next year, as we mark MAS' 50th anniversary, we will share in greater detail our strategies towards a more sustainable MAS.

Developing Green Financial Solutions and Markets

The second key thrust of our Action Plan is to develop green finance solutions and markets. We are:

- promoting sustainability bonds and loans;
- developing insurance solutions for climate risks;
- attracting green funds and asset managers with a sustainability focus;
- anchoring providers of sustainability rating and verification services;
- and collaborating with international partners to develop a common green taxonomy.

Sustainability bonds and loans provide corporates the incentive to embed sustainability considerations in their financing decisions.

MAS' Sustainable Bond Grant Scheme defrays the cost of external reviews to demonstrate the alignment of sustainability bonds with international standards. More than $8 billion in green, social and sustainability bonds have been issued in Singapore since the introduction of the Scheme in 2017.

They have supported a range of impactful outcomes:

- developing renewable energy projects;
- improving the energy efficiency of buildings;
- financing social enterprises aimed at helping lower income women; and so on.

MAS will launch by the end of the year a similar grant to support sustainability-linked loans. Corporates in Asia rely more on bank loans compared to bonds. MAS will therefore introduce a grant to fund the costs of conducting external reviews and ratings, for green and sustainability-linked loans. The grant will also promote the development of sustainable lending frameworks that provide simplified processes and standardised criteria for borrowers. This will reduce the cost of green borrowing and encourage more small and medium enterprises to tap on such loans.

Progress on the green bond and green loan fronts has been good. Singapore is now ASEAN's largest green finance market, accounting for close to 50% of cumulative ASEAN green bond and loan issuances.[6] Notably, sustainable financing and investment flows have held up well through the first half of this year, despite the pandemic and broad-based economic weakness.

Singapore is also steadily developing solutions such as Insurance-Linked Securities to address climate risks. MAS' Insurance-Linked Securities Grant Scheme has seen strong take-up since its launch in 2018. Within two years, we have seen nine catastrophe bond issuances in Singapore. This includes the first Asian sovereign and catastrophe bond covering earthquake and typhoon risks in the Philippines.

The strong expansion of wealth in Asia will provide a boost to sustainable investments. Personal wealth in Asia excluding Japan has seen an eightfold increase over the past two decades.[7]

Despite the economic disruption due to COVID-19, Asia is projected to have the strongest wealth growth in the world over the next five years. This wealth is increasingly being allocated to ESG causes and investments. A study by UBS estimates that close to 40% of family offices plan to allocate most of their portfolios sustainably in five years' time.[8]

This trend will be bolstered with the transfer of wealth to the millennial generation. An estimated US$15 trillion is expected to change hands to

6 ASEAN State of Market Report 2019 — Climate Bonds Initiative.

7 Boston Consulting Group Global Wealth Report 2020.

8 UBS Global Family Office Report 2020.

the next generation by 2030.[9] Several studies suggest that millennials desire to invest in companies with good ESG track records.[10] According to a survey by Morgan Stanley, 90% of millennial high net worth investors want to tailor their investments to their personal values.[11] As a leading wealth management hub in Asia, Singapore can play a strong role in wealth planning solutions that support sustainable development in Asia.

MAS launched last year a Green Investments Programme under which we will place US$2 billion of our funds with asset managers with a strong green focus. The aim is to grow the pool of asset managers that are committed to deepen green finance activities and capabilities in Singapore. We have shortlisted several asset managers with a view to appointing the successful applicants early next year.

Singapore has also begun anchoring providers of verification, review and rating services. These service providers are key in ensuring that sustainability targets being set by corporates are material, and to verify that financing proceeds will indeed be channelled to green and sustainable activities. Some of them have established Singapore as their regional hub to support corporates across Asia in building their sustainability capabilities.

Harnessing Technology to Enable Trusted Sustainable Finance Flows

The third key thrust of our Green Finance Action Plan is to harness technology to enable trusted and efficient sustainable finance flows.

FinTech has transformed the delivery of financial services; it can be a game-changer in sustainable finance too. We call it Green FinTech. We are beginning to see interesting examples. Temasek has partnered the University of Oxford on a project that uses satellite technologies to analyse climate risks for assets in the utilities sector. JP Morgan is applying artificial intelligence to trawl through non-financial data like patent filings to search

---

9 Wealth-X, June 2019, A Generational Shift Family Wealth Transfer Report 2019.

10 Royal Bank of Canada Wealth Management and The Economist Intelligence Unit, 2019, Motivated by more than money: Younger high-net-worth investors in Asia increasingly prioritise ethical investing; Ernst and Young, Sustainable Investing: The Millennial Investor.

11 Morgan Stanley Institute for Sustainable Investing, 2019, Sustainable Signals: Individual Investor Interest Driven by Impact, Conviction and Choice.

for keywords for potential sustainable investments.[12]

This year's Global FinTech Innovation Challenge organised by MAS is seeking solutions to specific challenges faced by financial institutions with respect to sustainability and climate risks.

The FinTech Innovation Challenge, organised as part of the Singapore FinTech Festival to be held this December, has received close to 600 submissions from more than 50 countries. Some of the shortlisted solutions are really interesting:

- an online do-it-yourself platform for small and medium enterprises to assess their environmental impact easily and affordably;
- an AI platform matching institutional investors with a range of social and environmental business opportunities; and
- an API-based modelling engine that utilises existing climate-related data (e.g., weather pattern predictions, sea level, etc.) to facilitate investment decisions.

Building Knowledge and Capabilities in Sustainable Finance

The fourth thrust of our Action Plan is to build knowledge and capabilities in sustainable finance.

We are encouraging financial institutions in Singapore to grow their sustainable finance teams here. Global banks and asset managers like ING, Standard Chartered and Aberdeen Standard Investments have dedicated Asia-Pacific sustainable finance teams based in Singapore. Deutsche Bank has recently located its Asia-Pacific ESG Head in Singapore; Fidelity's Global Head of Stewardship and Sustainable Investing is also based here.

We are seeking to anchor centres of excellence, think tanks and research networks. MAS is bringing together experts in our universities and financial institutions to undertake sustainability research tailored for Asia's needs.

Today, I am pleased to announce the launch of the Singapore Green Finance Centre — a collaboration between Singapore Management

12 Financial Times, November 2019, "Artificial intelligence promises to enhance sustainable investing".

University (SMU) and Imperial College Business School (Imperial).

The Centre will conduct rigorous research tailored to the Asian context, synergising SMU's strength in financial economics and Imperial's forte in climate finance. The Centre will also groom a pipeline of talent in green finance across the career spectrum — from the undergraduate to the executive education levels. The Centre has strong support from our financial industry, which will play a key role in steering the Centre's focus towards market-oriented outputs. I would like to thank the founding partners — Bank of China Limited, BNP Paribas, Fullerton Fund Management, Goldman Sachs, HSBC, Schroders, Standard Chartered Bank, Sumitomo Mitsui Banking Corporation and UBS AG.

MAS will continue to promote a vibrant green finance research and talent development ecosystem. We will look to anchor more centres of excellence with different strengths and focus areas — to provide a diversified pool of research and talent in green finance.

Conclusion

People across the world — and in Singapore — are increasingly concerned about climate change and environmental degradation. And they want to do something about it. Climate change is becoming a rallying cry to inspire people to step up to a higher cause, to take collective action for the common good of our planet.

The looming climate crisis poses not just an existential challenge to be overcome but also an economic opportunity to be seized. The coming revolution in sustainability has the potential to remake the world, cleaner and greener, creating new value and new jobs.

Let us harness the power of finance to help create such a world, and a sustainable future.